READINGS IN INVESTMENTS

READINGS IN
INVESTMENTS

✿ ✿ ✿

EDITED BY

Richard E. Ball

UNIVERSITY OF CINCINNATI

Allyn and Bacon, Inc.   Boston, 1965

Library of Congress Catalog Card Number: 64-8947

Printed in the United States of America

To my family

Preface

COMPILING A SELECTION OF READINGS from the varied literature on investments and investment management is a lesson in humility and frustration, for the scope of the problem is large and the range of writing is broad. Both academicians and practitioners have helped analyze the many facets of the security markets and the related problems of investment management. Learned and scientific journals have joined profession and practice-oriented publications in treating the dynamic and ever-changing problems of our investment areas. No final answers have been uncovered, but the resultant search and analysis have increased sophistication among the members of the investment industry and knowledge and interest among the investors who participate in the investment decisions vital to our capital-conscious economy.

This volume is intended to serve several purposes. The readings should be helpful to undergraduate and graduate students who are studying investments and investment management from case materials or from basic texts. Exposure to these readings should broaden concepts, tighten analytical talents necessary for sounder judgment, and offer in a convenient form some of the wisdom of the many experts on investment problems.

But this book is not directed to college students alone. Rather, it should provide a serious learning experience for individual investors, as well as for investment managers in their professional roles as decision-makers and monitors of the securities markets and the broader fields of corporation finance and capital management.

I am indebted to several persons who provided both leadership and material resources for the completion of this task. My thanks are due to Dr. Campbell Crockett, Dean of the Graduate School, University of Cincinnati, for his generous provision of research assistance, and to Dr. Kenneth Wilson, Dean of the College of Business Administration, University of Cincinnati, who has been a continuous and enthusiastic supporter of my aims while also facilitating their accomplishment. Mr. Larry V. Shingleton, Graduate Assistant in Finance, has been invaluable as a research colleague.

Grateful acknowledgment is given the publishers and authors of these compiled readings for their kind permission to use their materials. Author and publication source are identified at the beginning of each article.

Richard E. Ball
Cincinnati, Ohio

Contents

READINGS IN INVESTMENTS

GROWTH STOCKS—
RISKS AND REWARDS

I ·

INTRODUCTION

HIGH FASHION IS NOT LIMITED to female apparel, for its counterpart in the investment world is the enthusiasm which professionals and amateurs alike demonstrate for the "growth stock." Rarely has a concept been more overworked than this generally-accepted paragon of investment virtue; the romance and excitement which surround high-flying market leaders breed headlines and envy. Stocks commonly accepted as "growth stocks" become status symbols, and by their popularity subject professional managers and neophytes to crises of analysis and conscience seldom experienced in other economic fields.

What are the characteristics of growth stocks, where are they found, and when should one find them? These are problems of varying sizes to which almost everyone with investment capital has devoted some thought at some time. Professional literature is filled with a variety of views concerning the proper techniques of analysing and managing these popular issues, regardless of market movements and eras. Growth stocks have come to symbolize capital maximization drives, and their attraction for portfolio management use has increased as investment objectives have grown to stress capital appreciation within the broad framework of our current investment period.

The first essay in this section, by Robert W. Anderson, is a pioneering study in sharpening the theory of growth stocks, along with benchmarks for the identification needed to produce the proper rewards from this favored form of investment. A second essay by a prominent investment counselor, Peter L. Bernstein, takes issue with many of the popular notions regarding the characteristics of growth stocks and growth companies, and introduces unorthodox standards for more precise identification, with a subsequent reduction of risks.

  David Durand has used mathematical techniques to penetrate the common casual and often over-emotional appraisal of the future earnings and dividend returns from growth stocks. He warns the reader about the particular risks of exaggerated valuation of growing companies, using the unusual analogy of mathematical underpinnings for games of chance.

  This section closes with a tightly-reasoned, tightly-researched article by Norman O. Miller identifying the risks involved in loosely-appraised securities whose immediate record seems to promise substantial future capital and income growth. But, suffice it to say, the case is not closed, and tomorrow's literature will undoubtedly still emphasize the growth stock model, for it is the perennial lodestar for all types of investors.

I. UNREALIZED POTENTIALS IN GROWTH STOCKS*

❋ Robert W. Anderson

Why don't investors concentrate on growth stocks more consistently? This pioneering study of performance records shows what they are missing.

DURING THE YEARS SINCE 1936 an extraordinarily interesting story has been written about growth stocks—written in the records of private and institutional investors, the growth companies themselves, the stock market. With the cooperation of some expert analysts, professional counselors, and two prominent trust companies, my staff and I have been able to pull some parts of this story together. Different people will draw different conclusions from it, but I hope that most readers will agree that the story—

Puts a different light on the relative disadvantages and advantages of growth stocks—Examination of the records confirms the notorious reputation of growth stocks as a class for their low current yields, but makes them look superior in the long run to the income stocks, both in terms of principal and of income.

Has a pertinent moral for the professional investor—Looking back, we can see that many skillful investors—investment trust managements, for example—could have taken greater advantage of growth

* From *Harvard Business Review*, (March-April, 1955), Vol. 33, No. 2, pp. 51–67. Reprinted by permission of *Harvard Business Review*.
Author's Note: I wish to acknowledge the invaluable help of my staff, particularly Mr. Kenneth J. Thornhill, who did most of the primary research.

stocks than they did. (Of course, they did not have the advantage of whatever degree of hindsight it was impossible to keep out of this article.) In searching for the best relative values, professional investors should guard against past tendencies to become impatient with growth stocks and to buy and sell them too frequently.

May help the investor to utilize growth stocks more effectively in the future—Examination of the characteristics of growth companies and industries should be helpful in a constructive way, while analysis of the serious risk factors may help to avoid some of the pitfalls in growth-stock investing.

Focuses the investor's attention on investment value rather than growth at any price—This is a problem of choosing not only between investing in growth stocks and investing in income stocks but also between paying a high multiple of earnings for a rapidly growing company and paying a low multiple for a company with slower growth.

In this article I shall report the whole story as we found it, winding up with a summary of the most important conclusions. For the reader who wants the highlights in figure form, I call particular attention to the summary exhibits in the text. . . .

BENCH MARKS

For the purposes of this study "growth stocks" and "growth companies" have been defined conservatively:

> 1. There must exist a current and/or prospective increase in unit demand for the company's products or services; and the demand must be of such basic nature as to indicate that it will be relatively long sustained. Thus, we exclude companies whose growth is based primarily on a rise in the prices of its goods or services.
> 2. Growth in sales is not enough; there must also be a growth in net earnings, cash flow, or asset values.
> 3. There must have been an actual historical growth over a period of years—say, three to five years for an older rejuvenated company, or seven to ten years for a new company under untried management. This excludes companies with little or no past but a potentially brilliant future (for example, Great Plains Development Company).

Furthermore, since we shall be considering various types of investors, it may be well to classify them specifically:

1. The investor in growth, strictly for the long pull—characterized by:

    a. The adoption of an extremely long view.

    b. A willingness to disregard even major fluctuations in market prices, provided the outlook for the company in question indicates sufficient growth to support eventually a substantial appreciation in the price of its shares.

2. The buyer of "value"—characterized by:

    a. The adoption of an investment view of variable length, that is, the determination to hold an investment just long enough to achieve his targets (or full retreat from the investment as a mistake in judgment) but no longer.

    b. A willingness to buy only stocks which are "undervalued," in the sense of being currently available in the market at a price significantly below what it seems likely buyers will be willing to pay at some subsequent time. (The opinion that buyers will later be willing to pay a higher price may be based on one or a combination of such factors as current or prospective earnings, assets, unrecognized developments, a new management, and so forth.)

    c. A willingness to search for "undervaluation" in any company or industry, regardless of popular investment reputation. (Although this type of investor would prefer to find his undervalued securities in growth companies, he does not insist on growth. In other words, for such an investor almost any security would become attractive at some price.)

3. The investor for stable income—characterized by:

    a. The attachment of great importance to the regularity of dividend income.

    b. A preference for the moderate but dependable income obtainable from stocks like the public utilities to the potentially larger but less dependable income from, say, the steel stocks.

MEASUREMENT OF RESULTS

One aim of our study was to set forth on a comparative basis what could have been accomplished by an investor who bought and held a number of growth stocks over a long period of time. Here two problems were involved:

1. It was necessary, of course, to select that period of time for the analysis which would produce the most realistic and significant results. To avoid the distortions which can creep into any such study based on a few years, it was felt that the time period should not be less than 10 years, while 15 to 20 would be preferable.

Moreover, the period selected should bridge completely over the distorted years of World War II and should span at least one complete cycle in business activity and the stock market. Since our time period ends September 30, 1954, a time when business activity and the stock market were at comparatively high levels, it seemed desirable that the starting date should also be at a point relatively high in an earlier business cycle.

For these reasons, December 31, 1936, was selected as the starting point; and the study covers the subsequent 18 (more precisely 17¾) years.

2. It was also necessary to select a list of growth stocks for our imaginary investor without endowing him by hindsight with an unrealistic degree of investment skill and foresight. For this purpose we asked two large and active trust companies, a prominent firm of stockbrokers, and a leading investment counsel firm to examine their records of actual recommendations made to their clients during or about the second half of 1936. From these recommendations each firm selected a list of industrial companies (public utilities and rails were arbitrarily excluded) meeting approximately these qualifications:

> a. Each company must have had a history of continuous or nearly continuous growth over the whole 18-year period with due allowance for cyclical fluctuations, the impact of the war, and other factors beyond the control of the company's management. In other words, the stock of each company might well have been retained throughout the period by an investor having long-term growth as one of his primary objectives.

> b. Each company must have been well enough established on December 31, 1936, so that an intelligent and industrious investor would have had a reasonable chance of recognizing its stock as a potentially attractive investment. Our cooperating firms were asked to avoid the obscure and exceptional, sticking to fairly prominent and well-known companies.

From these sources we made a composite list of 25 stocks. . . . In measuring what would have been achieved by investing in such a list, it was assumed that $100,000 was invested in each of the stocks at the closing price on December 31, 1936. For the first stage of the study, it was further assumed that the resulting portfolio of $2,500,000 was held through September 30, 1954, unchanged except for receipt of stock dividends and splits. No assumptions were made regarding possible reinvestment of income from cash dividends.

BASIS FOR COMPARISON

To make the results of the analysis more interesting and instructive, they have been compared with what would have been achieved by investing an equal principal in various other media. For this comparison we chose four groups:

1. Twenty-five "income" stocks;
2. The Dow-Jones Industrials;
3. The Standard Statistics Average of 50 Industrials;
4. Ten investment trusts.

The portfolio of income stocks was obtained from the same professional sources and compiled by the same methods used in setting up the growth-stock portfolio. The aim here was to select those stocks which might have been owned throughout the period by an intelligent investor primarily concerned with obtaining the maximum current income consistent with substantial stability of income and safety of principal. . . .

In selecting the investment trusts we chose prominent trusts having good reputations for sound management. We confined ourselves to trusts of medium size in order to avoid the possibility that the massive size of some trusts might have hampered their mobility and therefore the free exercise of their management's best judgment. We avoided also all trusts which specialize in any particular segment of common stocks, such as chemicals. We tried to obtain a cross section of both conservative and aggressive managements, as well as the open-end and closed-end types of trusts. Our list is:

Fundamental Investors
General American Investors
Incorporated Investors
Lehman Corporation
Loomis Sayles Mutual Fund
Massachusetts Investors Growth Stock Fund
   (with two predecessors: Supervised Shares, Inc., to August 1940, and
   Massachusetts Investors Second Fund to May 1952)
National Investors
Scudder, Stevens & Clark Fund
State Street Investment and Research Corporation
Wellington Fund

Our calculations on the ten trusts were based on the assumption that $250,000 was invested in each trust as of December 31, 1936, and maintained through December 31, 1953 (data for September 30, 1954, were not available when this article was written), unchanged except for stock splits and for adjustment for dividends paid out of capital gains. . . .

INVESTMENT PERFORMANCE

Turning now to the results of our study, how does the investment performance of growth stocks compare with that of other stocks?

APPRECIATION OF PRINCIPAL

Our study revealed striking differentials in principal appreciation. Exhibit I-A . . . shows that during the 18-year period the investment in growth stocks more than tripled, while both of the market averages approximately doubled and the income stocks rose by 64%. Over the 17 years to December 31, 1953, eight of the ten investment trusts outran the market averages and the income stocks; in fact,

Exhibit I. *How Does Investment Performance of Growth Stocks Compare With That of Other Stocks?*

(Initial investment of $2,500,000; selected years; dollar figures in thousands; values at year-end)

YEAR	GROWTH STOCKS	INCOME STOCKS	STANDARD 50 INDUSTRIALS	DOW-JONES INDUSTRIALS	TEN INVEST-MENT TRUSTS
A. The Principal Grows Much Faster When Cash Income Is Not Reinvested					
1936	$2,500	$2,500	$2,500	$2,500	$2,500
1937	1,707	1,774	1,554	1,679	1,632
Change					
1936–1937	−31.8%	−29.0%	−37.8%	−32.9%	−34.7%
1945	$2,949	$2,995	$2,546	$2,681	$3,498
1948	3,141	2,582	2,290	2,464	3,058
Change					
1945–1948	+6.3%	−13.7%	−10.0%	−8.2%	−12.6%
1953	$6,160	$3,683	$3,768	$3,904	$5,020
Change					
1936–1953	+146%	+47%	+51%	+56%	+101%
1954 †	$7,879	$4,107	$5,043	$5,009	*
Change					
1936–1954	+215%	+64%	+102%	+100%	*

Exhibit I. *Continued*

YEAR	GROWTH STOCKS	INCOME STOCKS	STANDARD 50 INDUSTRIALS	DOW-JONES INDUSTRIALS	TEN INVEST-MENT TRUSTS

B. *The Principal Also Grows Faster, in the Long Run,* *When Cash Income Is Reinvested*

YEAR	GROWTH STOCKS	INCOME STOCKS	STANDARD 50 INDUSTRIALS	DOW-JONES INDUSTRIALS	TEN INVEST-MENT TRUSTS
1936	$ 2,500	$ 2,500	$ 2,500	$ 2,500	$2,500
1941	2,051	2,347	1,785	2,000	1,774
1947	4,766	4,713	4,065	4,259	4,573
1953	11,755	8,779	9,579	9,442	9,133
1954 †	15,353	10,109	13,232	12,509	*
Change 1936–1954	+514%	+304%	+429%	+400%	*

C. *Current Yields Are Distinctly Inferior*

YEAR	GROWTH STOCKS	INCOME STOCKS	STANDARD 50 INDUSTRIALS	DOW-JONES INDUSTRIALS	TEN INVEST-MENT TRUSTS
1937	5.4%	6.7%	8.7%	7.3%	4.2%
1938	2.7	5.3	3.2	3.2	2.1
1940	4.4	5.7	6.3	5.4	3.7
1947	3.7	5.2	5.5	5.1	3.8
1954 ‡	2.9	4.6	4.5	4.6	*
Average of 18 annual yields	3.8%	5.2%	5.6%	5.3%	3.5% §

D. *Annual Dollar Income Lags at First But Soon Catches Up —* *Cumulative Income Catches Up More Slowly*

YEAR	GROWTH STOCKS	INCOME STOCKS	STANDARD 50 INDUSTRIALS	DOW-JONES INDUSTRIALS	TEN INVEST-MENT TRUSTS
1937	$ 93	$ 119	$ 133	$ 122	$ 68
1938	59	112	64	69	42
1940	80	119	98	98	62
1947	118	142	124	128	119
1954 ¶	229	188	227 ‖	230	*
Total for 17¾ years	$2,255	$2,418	$2,412 #	$2,464	*

* Not available.
† As of 9/30.
‡ Income for 12 months ended 9/30/54 as percentage of principal as of 9/30/54.
§ Average of 17 annual yields.
¶ For 12 months ending 9/30/54.
‖ Estimated.
Last 9 months estimated.

two of the ten trusts outstripped even our growth stocks. Hence, the trusts were not merely drifting, and they did exhibit real professional skill. Nevertheless, as a group they trailed well behind the growth stocks. This is true even if we adjust their "permanent reserves" to a basis of investment in equities.

The indication that growth stocks may be about as resistant to broad declines in the stock market as the income stocks, which are usually considered to be "defensive," is one of the interesting by-products of the research summarized in Exhibit I-A. During the 1936–1937 period—which included the market slump of 1937—both the growth and the income stocks declined somewhat less than the market averages and the investment trusts, and the income stocks did only a bit better than the growth stocks. During 1945–1948—which covered the sharp market slump of the second half of 1946 and then a period of drifting without much net change up into the early part of 1949—the growth stocks actually rose more than 6% while all other groups declined moderately, with the "defensive" income stocks down most of all. While these findings are far from conclusive, we think they should provide food for thought for investors interested in "stability" and "defense."

Up to this point we have made no allowance for possible reinvestment of part or all of the cash income received on our hypothetical investments. However, for an investor in a low bracket, particularly an institution such as a life insurance company or an accumulating charitable fund, this factor of compounding the cash income can be very important. Hence, we extended our research to test the comparative results, assuming reinvestment of all cash income by that rara avis, the investor in a zero tax bracket.

The results are presented in Exhibit I-B. . . . As might be expected, during the first five years the income stocks, benefiting both from the compounding of a higher yield and from a moderately superior performance of principal during a period when the general market was off 20% on the Dow-Jones averages, outstripped the growth stocks. It was not until the end of 1947 that the growth stocks, having earlier surpassed both of the market averages and also the trusts, overtook the income group. From 1947 to September 30, 1954, the growth stocks increased their lead over the other media, with the income stocks ending up in last place.

YIELDS AND INCOME

While there are frequent exceptions, growth stocks are notorious as a class for their low current yields; our study confirms this general impression. Exhibit I-C . . . sets forth yield data expressing the annual income from each of our five investment media as a percentage of the principal in each respective fund at year-end values. While this method of expressing current yield is subject to distortion in any year of major change in the level of the stock market, over a period as long as 18 years it seems sufficiently accurate for our purposes here.

Throughout the period our growth stocks afforded distinctly inferior yields, which ranged from a low of 2.7% to a high of 5.4% and averaged only 3.8% as compared with averages of better than 5% for our income stocks and the market averages. Yields on the growth stocks are still low, amounting to 2.9% on principal as of September 30, 1954, as compared to about 4.6% on the income stocks and market averages. However, if we think of actual incomes as yields on our starting principal of $2,500,000 in each group, we find that yield on the growth stocks has mounted up to a generous 9.2% as compared with 7.5% on the income stocks. The market averages are also yielding about 9.2% on starting principal.

What about actual dollar income, as opposed to yields? Exhibit I-D . . . shows that, reflecting the low current yield, actual dollar income from the growth stocks in 1937 was 22% below that from the income stocks and 30% below that from the Standard Industrials. However, as the years went by, dollar income on our growth stocks roughly kept pace with the growth in principal, thus rising much more rapidly than income on any of our other media. By 1949 annual income on the growth stocks had overtaken and passed that on the income stocks; and in 1953 and 1954 the growth-stock income was about equal to that for the market averages.

However, on a cumulative basis, income from the growth stocks, because of the lag during the earlier years of the period, has not yet overtaken income from the income stocks and market averages. The cumulative income on the growth stocks of $2,255,000 is roughly 10% below the totals for the income stocks and market averages. But with income on the growth stocks running about $40,000 annually above that on the income stocks, it seems clear that within a few years cumulative income on the growth stocks will overtake that on the income group.

It happens not infrequently that an investor finds himself the owner of stock in what was formerly a growth company, acquired years ago at costs which are extremely low in relation to existing market value. If it now appears, after the most careful analysis the investor can make, that this company has lost the major part of its momentum and its stock has become a mere income producer, this investor faces a difficult problem. If he sells his stock, capital gains taxes will leach away a significant portion of his principal. If he then reinvests his shrunken principal in a low-yielding growth stock, will his investment results over the long run be as good as if he had kept a larger principal at work producing a larger current income?

If we assume the most extreme case—i.e., that sale will reduce principal by 25%—we can deduce from Exhibit I-A that an investment of $2,500,000 in stock of this type, shrunk down by taxes in 1936 to $1,875,000, would have mounted up to approximately $5,900,-000 at September 30, 1954, and would still be substantially greater than our income stocks and market averages. Similarly, we can deduce from Exhibit I-B that such a shrunken fund would have mounted up to about $11,500,000 (assuming reinvestment of all cash dividends) which would still be larger than our income stocks on the same basis.

WITHDRAWING PRINCIPAL

One of the obvious conclusions to be drawn from the preceding material is that, in the very long run, the investor in growth stocks obtains greater current income than the investor in income stocks. Hence the investor who can sacrifice something in immediate income for the sake of a larger income some years in the future would be well advised to buy growth stocks in preference to the stable income stocks. Even those investors who cannot afford to sacrifice immediate income would do well to avoid the stable income stocks, provided they are willing to spend a modest amount of principal during the early years to supplement the meager income from growth stocks in that period. This conclusion is supported by the figures in Exhibit II.

Annual dipping into principal for current spending does, of course, slow down the cumulative appreciation of our growth stocks;

Exhibit II. *Principal and Income of Growth Stocks Show Up Favorably Even With Modest Withdrawals from Principal*
(Same conditions as Exhibit I)

YEAR	PRINCI-PAL OF GROWTH STOCKS	INCOME RECEIVED	SPEND-ABLE FUNDS REQUIRED	DRAWN DOWN FROM PRINCI-PAL FOR SPEND-ING*	PRINCI-PAL OF INCOME PORTFOLIO (FOR COM-PARISON)
1936	$2,500				$2,500
1947	2,472	$ 90	$142	$52	2,673
1953	4,621	171	175	4	3,683
1954 †	5,900	124	135	10	4,107

* Considered as difference between income from income stocks and income from growth stocks.
† For 9 months ended 9/30/54.

the principal comes to only $5,900,000 as of September 30, 1954, compared with $7,879,000 when no principal has been spent. . . . Even so, however, our growth stocks are substantially ahead of the income stocks in terms of principal, while the current income on the reduced portfolio of growth stocks has almost overtaken that on the income stocks.

Thus far, the evidence seems to show that on several different bases the investment performance of growth stocks since the end of 1936 has been superior to that of income stocks, market averages, or a group of prominent investment trusts. Suppose we had selected a different starting point? How would this have affected the comparison? In the course of our study we did start one analysis at the end of 1933 with a somewhat different group of growth stocks and traced the comparative results for 20 years to the end of 1953. We found a much greater differential in favor of the growth stocks.

PROFESSIONAL INVESTORS

If growth stocks offer an easy and direct road to successful investing, we might logically expect that skillful and experienced investors would concentrate on growth stocks almost to the exclusion of everything else. To what extent have professional investors thus concentrated their efforts and how successful have they been? To uncover evidence bearing on these questions we examined the year-end portfolios of each of our ten investment trusts. Some of the information thus gleaned is shown in Exhibit III. In thinking about this information, the reader should bear in mind two facts:

1. Only two of these ten trusts have shown a rate of capital appreciation equal to the percentage rise in our growth stocks, while the average for the ten trusts lagged significantly behind our growth stocks. By hindsight, therefore, we can say that these trusts would have achieved better results had they concentrated their investments in our growth stocks or equally good ones not on our list.

2. These trusts during most of the years under review owned lists of industrial stocks amply broad enough to have contained all of our growth stocks, with plenty of room left over to satisfy any reasonable desire for additional diversification.

FAILURE TO OWN

The extent to which our growth stocks were owned by these trusts can be gauged in comparison with maximum ownership. (If each of our trusts had held a given stock in its year-end portfolio during the entire 18-year period of 1936–1953, the maximum number of times it would have appeared is 180, *i.e.* 18 times in the portfolios of each of ten trusts.) Column 3 of Exhibit III shows for each of our growth stocks the "incidence of ownership" as a percentage of this maximum.

Not unexpectedly, Standard Oil of New Jersey was the most consistently owned, scoring 54.4% of maximum, followed by Continental Oil with 53.8%, Amerada with 51.7%, and du Pont with 51.1%. The average incidence for all of our growth stocks was only 34.1%. In other words, the skillful and experienced trust managements preferred not to own our growth stocks almost two-thirds of the time during a period when hindsight tells us that they would generally have profited by doing so.

It is interesting to note also that stocks with such fine records as International Business Machines, Humble Oil, Dow Chemical, Minneapolis-Honeywell, Hartford Fire, and Insurance Company of North America were owned less than 25% of maximum, with the latter two companies being almost completely ignored. In fact, some of these stocks were not owned at any time by certain trusts.

FAILURE TO HOLD

As indicated by Column 5 of Exhibit III, the managements of the trusts displayed a marked unwillingness, once having bought any of our growth stocks, to retain them throughout the entire period. Behind their change of mind may have been such factors as loss of confidence in the individual growth company, a belief that they had found a still better investment, or simply the belief that they could buy the growth stock back again later at a lower price.

This tendency to move into and out of the stocks is brought out still more strikingly by Columns 6, 7, and 8. Here we see, for example, that, out of the eight trusts which at some point owned International Business Machines, five of them sold it and never repurchased. By hindsight, again, this must be a matter of regret, since IBM on September 30, 1954, had an adjusted value of 8.6 times its value on December 31, 1936. Similarly, stocks as fine as Standard Oil of New Jersey, Humble Oil, and Union Carbide were sold out and never repurchased by more than half of those trusts which at one point owned them.

Sometimes also, as shown by Column 8, the trusts sold out and then repurchased the same stocks. For example, du Pont was sold completely out and later repurchased six times, Union Carbide six times, Westinghouse nine times, and American Can ten times.

Of course our 25 stocks would, at most, comprise only a small fraction of all the industrial stocks held in the portfolios of the various trusts. So, to see what further we could learn, we studied in detail the complete list of industrials owned by three of the ten trusts at each year-end for 1936 to 1953. The following tabulation sets forth some of the results:

	TRUST A	TRUST B	TRUST C
Total number of individual stocks appearing at least once during the period	351	191	180
Maximum number held in any year-end portfolio	149	65	63
Minimum number held in any year-end portfolio	99	36	29

Note the breadth of these portfolios. Note the high rate of turnover, which is even more significant. Each of the trusts bought and sold a number of stocks equivalent to a complete turnover of its

Exhibit III. *The Ten Investment Trusts Fail to Hold Our Twenty-Five Selected Growth Stocks Consistently*

GROWTH STOCK	(1) MAXIMUM NUMBER OF TIMES THIS STOCK COULD HAVE APPEARED AT YEAR-END IN THE PORTFOLIOS OF ALL TEN TRUSTS COMBINED	(2) ACTUAL APPEARANCES IN YEAR-END PORTFOLIOS OF ALL TEN TRUSTS COMBINED	(3) INCIDENCE OF OWNERSHIP (COL. 2 ÷ COL. 1)	(4) NUMBER OF TRUSTS NOT OWNING THIS STOCK AT ANY YEAR-END	(5) NUMBER OF TRUSTS OWNING THIS STOCK THROUGH-OUT ENTIRE PERIOD	(6) NUMBER OF TRUSTS OWNING THIS STOCK ON AT LEAST ONE YEAR-END DURING THE PERIOD	(7) NUMBER OF TRUSTS WHICH ELIMI-NATED THIS STOCK AND DID NOT REPUR-CHASE	(8) NUMBER OF TIMES THIS STOCK WAS ELIM-INATED AND REPURCHASED BY ALL TRUSTS THAT OWNED IT ON AT LEAST ONE YEAR-END
Du Pont	180	92	51.1%	1	2	9	1	6
Hercules Powder	180	37	20.5	4	0	6	5	0
Monsanto	180	80	44.4	0	1	10	4	4
Union Carbide	180	82	45.6	1	0	9	5	6
Dow Chemical	180	39	21.7	3	0	7	2	5
General Electric	180	91	50.6	0	0	10	4	6
Westinghouse Electric	180	90	50.0	1	0	9	6	9
Libbey-Owens-Ford	180	43	23.9	4	0	6	5	3
Owens-Illinois	180	43	23.9	2	0	8	7	1
Johns-Manville	180	85	47.2	0	1	10	5	6
U. S. Gypsum	180	63	35.0	5	0	10	9	6
Minneapolis-Honeywell	180	40	22.2	2	0	5	2	3
Amerada	180	93	51.7	2	3	8	1	3
Continental Oil	180	97	53.8	2	2	8	2	4

Humble Oil	180	40	22.2	5	1	5	3	1
Standard Oil of California	180	79	43.8	1	0	9	3	8
Standard Oil of New Jersey	180	98	54.4	0	0	10	6	6
J. C. Penney	180	47	26.1	1	0	9	7	2
Sears Roebuck	180	91	50.6	0	0	10	5	6
Eastman Kodak	180	43	23.9	4	0	6	5	4
International Business Machines	180	37	20.5	2	0	8	5	2
American Can	180	57	31.7	2	0	8	4	10
National Steel	180	55	30.5	3	2	7	3	3
Hartford Fire	180	9	5.0	7	0	3	1	0
Insurance Company of North America	180	5	2.8	8	0	2	1	0

whole industrial portfolio about once every five years. This does not mean that there was a literal turnover (some stocks were held; some turned even faster), or even a shifting of dollar amounts equivalent to such a turnover. But one thing is clear: there was plenty of room for holding more growth stocks in the portfolios without risks to the managements' diversification policies.

Furthermore, one phenomenon already noted in connection with the ten trusts showed up even more strongly on this closer analysis. Either because of what was judged to be a deterioration in the stocks or because some other potential asset seemed still more attractive, during the period under study the three trusts eliminated from their portfolios not only a majority of our growth stocks but also such other fine companies as Alcoa, Goodrich, International Paper, and Crown Zellerbach.

In sum, our ten trusts showed, not poor judgment, but something less than perfect judgment. Remember that as a group they did produce significantly better results as to principal than both income stocks and the market averages. Further, they did this without the benefit of any hindsight.

OTHER PROFESSIONALS

Investment trust managements represent only one group of professional investors. What about other professionals' attitudes toward growth stocks? Unfortunately, data for such groups as the insurance companies, trust companies, the trust departments of commercial banks, and private professional trustees are very difficult to obtain. However, through the cooperation of a prominent trust company we got a complete listing of the industrial stocks held in its common trust fund at the end of each year for a considerable period in the past. (While it is impossible to say just how typical this fund is, my guess would be that it is somewhat more "growth stock minded" than most trust company funds.) Very briefly, the following significant points stand out:

1. The complete list shows many of the stocks which might now be considered as among the leading growth stocks, including 21 out of our 25.

2. However, we could discern no tendency to concentrate on growth at the expense of such other considerations as current earnings, current yield, stability, and diversification.

3. The list is very broad, comprising 78 industrials; and at one point or another during comparatively recent years the fund has owned 118 different stocks.

4. During these years the fund has sold out 40 different stocks, thus revealing again some tendency toward turnover, although to a much smaller degree than we found in our investment trusts.

PROBLEMS AND RISKS

Why is it that many competent professional investors do not, apparently, concentrate on growth stocks or at least hold on longer to the ones they do buy—in spite of the potential profit in doing so? Obviously, there must be enough problems and pitfalls to investing in growth stocks to make this quite difficult to do consistently and successfully. Let us examine some of these problems; they are very real.

YOUNG INDUSTRIES

As would-be investors in growth stocks, we would naturally expect important new economic forces to create investment opportunities for us. For example, no one questions that atomic energy will create somewhere the kind of long-range growth companies we are looking for. However, partly because of its quasi-governmental character and partly because it has already become so complex and ramified, it is extremely difficult for us to decide which of all the many companies affected in some degree by atomic energy is likely to provide the best investment vehicle. Should we buy into a uranium mine, a rare metal company like Foote Mineral, an engineering firm like Consolidated, a maker of equipment like General Electric, or some other one?

Even where the new development takes the form of a clearly defined young industry with brilliant prospects for growth of volume, pitfalls still exist because competitive conditions may develop in such a way as to prevent earnings of the constituent companies from growing satisfactorily over an extended period. For example, during the 1920's the rapidly developing business of manufacturing radio receiving sets must have enticed many growth investors, but it has been something of a disappointment in terms of earnings. Many financial students are now asking whether the rapidly growing ammonia business may not be laying the foundation for similar disappointments in the years to come.

Assuming, however, that we succeed in finding and analyzing an industry which offers the strongest assurances of future growth of both volume and profits, we are still far from our goal of successful investing. If the industry is substantial in scope, there will be at least several and possibly many companies therein. Which of these companies is most likely to win the competitive struggle and therefore participate most fully in the profits of the industry? Look at the automobile industry: it has expanded enormously since 1905 and, on the whole, has been highly profitable; but the vast majority of the companies which entered the business are now defunct.

Again, take the current trend toward automatic factory operations, which has been greatly stimulated by developments in electronics. Ten or fifteen years hence, which companies will be the surviving leaders in this field of automation? Will they be makers of machine tools like Cincinnati Milling Machine; a small company like Cross, which buys the factory equipment of others and then ties it into complex "teams" with its own electronic directional equipment; or a designer and manufacturer of factory-wide instrument systems like Minneapolis-Honeywell with its Brown Instrument Division?

OLDER INDUSTRIES

Difficult problems also face anyone trying to invest in older growth industries. One such problem is posed by technological change. Fundamentally, the growth process is deeply rooted in technological developments; but these changes, which are always creating our future investment opportunities, can also blight our present investments. For instance, the rise in the per-capita use of copper, while irregular and not really brilliant, has been substantial over the years. But how will it be affected in the future by the development of polyethylene tubing, weldable aluminum, irradiated plastics, and printed circuits? The answers to such questions are not necessarily adverse, but they do arise to plague the investor and shake his confidence.

Both whole industries and individual companies frequently pass through discernible life cycles: they are young, they mature, and sometimes they die. However, in some cases they only seem temporarily to have matured, and this type of development can be peculiarly baffling. Here are two examples, with some interesting variation:

About 1945–1949 some intelligent investment people concluded that General Electric had an uninspiring future. Holding the stock at that time required courage and patience. But we now know that sale in 1949 was unwise, unless the investor happened to be skillful and lucky in choosing his reinvestment.

A good many years ago Allied Chemical began to exhibit signs of lethargy. Should the investor of those days have concluded that Allied was experiencing a mere pause in what was still a youthful and vigorous growth trend? If so, he would have owned a laggard stock for an uncomfortably long time. Now, years later, after the infusion of new blood into the management, the company once more seems to be moving ahead vigorously. Should the growth investor have sold out; and, if so, when? And when should he have bought back?

QUESTION OF "VALUE"

In many respects, the most difficult problem faced by the investor is that of deciding which stocks, out of the many which are available for purchase and on which the investor has sufficient information to base an intelligent decision, offer the greatest "value." (. . . we use that term to mean the extent to which any given stock may be currently selling below what it seems likely buyers will be willing to pay at some subsequent time. Under this broad concept, both the growth stocks and the shares of the great number of more slowly expanding companies would have value at the right price.)

Assuming that the investor is not committed, as a matter of policy, to buying for the extremely long range, will he obtain better investment results by paying a high multiple of earnings for a rapidly growing company or a low multiple of earnings for a company having slower growth? If he chooses the former, he faces the risk that the growth may cease or greatly slow down before earnings have risen sufficiently to sustain a higher price for the stock; once the investing public decides that the company is no longer dynamic, reduced price-earnings ratios will prevail. For example:

During the middle 1930's investors still regarded Coca-Cola as being a great growth stock; and in 1937 the stock sold as high as 170, equivalent to 30 times the company's earnings for that year and 36 times the earnings for the previous year. Since that time, the investing public's hopes for the company have diminished irregularly, with the result that this stock was recently selling 35% below what some growth investor paid for it in 1937, notwithstanding the fact that earnings per share in 1953 were 15% above those in 1937.

If, on the contrary, the investor pays a low multiple of earnings for a stock of slower growth, he has two chances to obtain appreciation: (a) from continued moderate growth in earnings; and (b) from the possibility of an improvement in the investment standing or reputation of the stock—in other words, from a willingness of the investing public to pay a higher price-earnings ratio for the same earnings. This latter type of development can be an extremely potent force. Witness, for example, the tremendous increase in the prices of the leading shares of the paper and rubber industries, a development which has been based in part on an improvement in the investment standing of the industries. At the present time, there is some reason to believe that the steel stocks are going through the same cycle.

The high price-earnings ratios which prevail for the recognized growth stocks are founded in part upon psychological and emotional attitudes which surround certain industries and stocks with "halos." To illustrate:

The investor may buy or retain du Pont on a 4.3% yield basis (average on mean prices, 1939–1953) while ignoring Beatrice Foods, an old established company which has grown earningswise nearly as fast as du Pont and has been on a 6.7% yield basis. The explanation must lie in the fact that most investors think of chemicals as a most dynamic growth industry, whereas the food industry is thought of as growing only slightly faster than population. What is overlooked is that both foods and chemicals are broad fields, each consisting of a whole complex of component "industries" which are growing or retrogressing at varying rates; and that a capable and energetic management will search out those products and processes which result in growth of earnings.

What I have been trying to convey in this section can be summed up by pointing out that it is possible to pay too much for growth, both in an absolute sense (as for Coca-Cola) and in terms of comparative investment value. It is this search for the best relative value which probably explains most of the tendencies on the part of the investment trusts to buy and sell frequently—the only criticism being that apparently they failed to exercise sufficient patience.

GROWTH CHARACTERISTICS

The fact that there are inherent problems and risks does not mean that the investor should stay away from growth stocks, or indeed that he should not try to concentrate on them more than most professional investors have in the past. Rather, with the rewards to be won as revealed by hindsight, it means that more knowledge is needed of just what kind of stocks are going to turn out to be growth stocks, as a basis for greater confidence and patience in holding them.

(The following comments refer to industrial companies only. Although some of the same growth characteristics apply in the case of banking, insurance, public utilities, railroads, and so on, these fields do involve special circumstances of their own and warrant a separate, fresh approach.)

INDUSTRY AND PRODUCT

Theoretically it may be possible for a growth company to exist in a stagnant industry, simply because it possesses an exceptionally capable management. At best, however, such instances are rare. As a practical matter, the investor should look for growth companies in growth industries. Such an industry should be a basic element of the country's standard of living, and it should have existing products or services which have met with such increasing public acceptance that unit demand is rising at an average rate significantly greater than the average rate of unit growth of the economy as a whole, although not necessarily dramatic.

More specifically, we would expect to find good candidates among companies which produce goods or services which are high in economic utility in relation to price. This insures a favorable competitive position and enables any increase in costs of production to be passed on to the consumer. Generally, we will find such a

company selling a product or service which shows one of the following characteristics:

    1. Long-range cost on a unit volume basis below that of competing
products. For example, a cubic foot of aluminum is cheaper than a cubic
foot of copper; and a dollar's worth of high-price nylon will outlast a
dollar's worth of a cheaper material like cotton.)
    2. An indispensable part of another growing product or process,
with cost small relative to the value of the finished product. (An example
is the service performed by the Halliburton Oil Well Cementing Company.)

RESEARCH PROGRAM

Of all the characteristics of growth companies, perhaps the most
commonly emphasized is research. The research program should be
formal, organized, and staffed in the upper echelons with people
having good reputations among those in a position to judge their
competence. The top guidance for the program should be practical
rather than theoretical, with profit potentialities as a prime guid-
ing factor. The research and product development program of the
Minnesota Mining and Manufacturing Company is an excellent example of this type of work. Furthermore, the research program
should, in nearly all cases, cover the search for new and more efficient
processes as well as new products.

    How large should such research expenditures be? Beyond the
fact that they should increase as the company grows, it is impossible
to say. Obviously, the cost of research work varies with the nature
of the products and processes which are under study, as well as with
the stage in their economic cycle. Hence, we would expect research
expenditures as a percentage of sales to run higher in a complex,
"young," and rapidly changing industry like chemicals than in a
business like oil-well cementing where the technique changes little
and where the process is adaptable to few, if any, other lines of
business. The investor should simply try to satisfy himself that research expenditures are large enough, of sufficiently good quality,
and well enough directed to keep the company in the forefront of
developments in its particular industry.

    Over a period of years (any shorter period of time may be sub-
ject to serious distortions), one test of the practical results of research expenditures is that there should be a significant upward

trend in the proportion of total sales derived from comparatively new products and processes. As Keith Powlison has pointed out, the development of new products and processes has an important counterpart in the elimination of obsolete or unprofitable products and techniques, the retention of which tends to absorb a part of the time and skills of management which should be concentrated on more profitable lines.[1] The importance of this apparently negative aspect of growth is illustrated by the accomplishments of the American Home Products Company during recent years. In brief, we would expect the more mature and complex growth companies to be characterized by a substantial sloughing off of unprofitable activities.

CAPITAL EXPENDITURES

Ordinarily the development of new and successful products requires additional plant and equipment for their manufacture. Likewise, new processes and methods normally require new equipment. Consequently, we would expect growth companies (with some exceptions) to be characterized by relatively large expenditures for new plant and equipment. However, new equipment will make an effective contribution to new growth only where the new products are in sufficient demand to keep the equipment running at a satisfactory rate or where the increase in the efficiency of operations on older products will so reduce unit cost of production as to earn a satisfactory return on the capital invested.

Obviously, it is also possible to spend too much on new plant and equipment. If that condition prevails for any considerable period, the effects should show up in a declining return on total capital invested in the entire business. Consequently, where the test of increasing capital expenditures is applied, it should always be accompanied by a thoughtful analysis of the return on invested capital.

MERCHANDISING

While there may be certain exceptions, normally one of the traits of a true growth company is a pronounced stress on the development of efficient and effective methods of merchandising. Here let me make a distinction between selling and merchandising. By the former,

[1] Keith Powlison, "Obstacles to Business Growth," *Harvard Business Review*, Vol. 31, No. 2, March-April 1953, p. 48.

I mean simply the struggle to sell more goods, which is frequently accomplished by direct or indirect price cutting, with consequent downward pressure on profit margins and earnings on capital invested. In contrast, by the term merchandising, I mean a carefully planned program encompassing:

1. The development of new ideas for conveying to the buyer the merits of the company's products or services in the light of the buyer's problems and needs.

2. Where necessary, the modification of the product to meet trends in the market which seem basic and relatively permanent. (For example, the most successful companies in textile weaving have been those that studied carefully the problems and needs of the cutters and then made whatever changes in raw materials and weaving processes were necessary to produce the desired fabrics.)

PRODUCT AND PROCESS PLANNING

One of the foundation stones of the successful growth company is the ability of its management to choose products (a) which will command a sufficiently large market to insure a significant contribution to total sales, and (b) whose costs of output and distribution, relative to economic value, are such as to afford a generous margin of profit. The leading chemical companies are exemplary in this respect because they refuse to enter upon the production of proposed new products which do not meet these qualifications.

Accordingly, we should expect growth companies to carry on careful market research to evaluate the probable demand for proposed new products at varying price levels. Likewise, growth companies should carry out thorough testing of proposed new processes of manufacture, if possible on a semi-work basis, to determine accurately the practical feasibility of the process and to develop the best possible estimates of manufacturing costs before plunging into costly construction of a full-scale plant. The importance of thorough and careful work in both these areas of planning is illustrated by the recent unfortunate experiences of certain companies in the fertilizer and artificial fiber industries.

PERSONNEL POLICY

In the very long run a company cannot grow without an adequate supply of thoroughly competent executives at all levels of management. Nor can it grow while its plants are on strike. Consequently, we should expect growth companies to lay considerable stress on carefully thought-out programs to maintain good employee relations. They should develop an adequate supply of younger executives both for the staffing of new departments or divisions necessitated by the development of new products and also for replacement of older executives as they reach retirement age. One practical test of the success of a company's personnel program is its relative freedom from strikes and slowdowns, as well as its ability to attract and hold young men.

FINANCIAL CHARACTERISTICS

Growth companies normally possess certain traits readily measurable by financial analysis:

1. There should be an upward trend in sales which, on a basis of units sold per share of common stock outstanding (adjusted for splits and stock dividends), should be growing more rapidly than the national economy, and also than other companies in the same industry.

2. Since growth companies are characterized by the development of new products and processes which normally carry profit margins above average within their respective industries, we would expect growth companies (with occasional exceptions) to report relatively wide margins.

3. A somewhat more effective financial test is the return on total capital employed in the business, which for the successful growth company should be relatively generous. As to the trend of return on capital, we should expect a healthy growth company to show a well-maintained ratio or at least no significant decline. When the prospective investor is studying the data on return on capital for any particular company or industry, he should bear in mind that the ratio tends to rise during periods of national expansion accompanied by rising cost levels.

4. An increase in the unit volume of business obviously requires increasing amounts of capital both to finance inventories and sales (particularly during a period of rising prices) and to construct new plant and equipment. To raise this new capital management has, broadly speaking, two main alternatives: it can finance its growth internally by retaining earnings, or externally by selling additional common stock or floating senior capital. Normally we find growth companies adopting some combination of these alternatives; but a very prominent characteristic of nearly all growth companies is the payment of cash dividends which are low in relation to reported net earnings—a sign of internal financing.

The important point about capital structure is that the investor should not find himself owning the stock of a company whose research department is turning out excellent ideas for new products which it is financially too weak to exploit.

MANAGEMENT'S PHILOSOPHY

While the top executives' thinking is an intangible factor and may be difficult to appraise, nevertheless it is important. One clue is the management's reputation among both suppliers and customers for alert and vigorous intelligence as well as fair dealings. For our purposes here we are interested in two main aspects of management's attitude toward future growth:

1. Does the management have a well-defined and carefully reasoned policy as to branching out into new fields? If the company is not growing in a definite and logical direction, the addition of new and unrelated products should eventually result in complicating the problems of production, selling, and research to the point where management's functions begin to break down and the whole company loses efficiency, with a consequent decline in profit margins and return on invested capital.

Just where the addition of new products ceases to be sound growth and becomes merely undue complexity is impossible to say. General Motors, General Electric, and du Pont make a long and diversified list of products and operate successfully. However, the principal divisions of these companies have one thread of homogeneity running through them; that is, their processes are based on a fundamentally similar type of engineering, either mechanical or chemical. Without being able to prove the point, I believe that companies (or divisions of companies) which have lost this "thread of homogeneity" have, at the same time, lowered their over-all efficiency. It will be very interesting to watch the degree of success attained in the future by such companies as Food Machinery and Olin-Mathieson.

2. Is management focusing primarily on expansion of volume or on the building up of net earnings for the owners of the business? If the former, it is likely to lead to the addition (either by internal development or externally through mergers) of products carrying inadequate profit margins. Ultimately such a policy should lead to a decline in over-all operating efficiency and in the return on invested capital.

Such characteristics as these may be more significant than a record of past or current sales expansion. Naturally a company that is in the process of growing, or just beginning to grow, will show increases in sales volume. But the fact of rising sales, just by itself, does not necessarily indicate growth. A company may already be at the top of its cycle; the "halo" some stocks have as a result of growth to date—often in the form of an already high price-earnings ratio—may even be a danger signal of approaching maturity and stagnation. Or the new volume may simply represent a one-time surge caused by merger or purchase of outside products for resale.

Growth, in the sense in which we use it here, means more than mere expansion in dollar sales, and it depends on a whole complex of characteristics such as will be likely to bring about greater earnings over the years ahead.

CONCLUSIONS

1. The record seems to show that a portfolio of established, recognized growth stocks (even at relatively high price-earnings ratios) retained on a long-range basis will give investment results superior to those of the stable income stocks and the market averages. Over a long period of time this should be true in terms of both principal and income.

2. Hence all those who invest for income, except those who must have maximum current income and cannot invade principal, would be well advised to buy growth stocks in preference to stable income stocks.

3. Growth stocks seem indicated also for investors who are committed, as a matter of policy, to extremely long-range buying or who for their own particular reasons wish to buy into a company with the firm intention of never selling until it shows clear signs of deterioration.

4. However, growth stocks are by no means foolproof; and frequently they sell too high either in an absolute sense or in terms of comparative investment value. An intelligent and industrious analyst, or an investor who has access to such, should be able to find better investment value and to achieve better investment results over the long range by avoiding the "haloed" growth stocks, and by trying instead to find stocks now having substantial (though perhaps no better than average) growth prospects yet still selling at a sufficiently low price-earnings ratio to provide very clear evidence of strongly attractive investment value.

5. The search for such "value" stocks should be conducted imaginatively and with an open mind because they are frequently to be found in unexpected places. The most fruitful areas for this search are industries which enjoy an underlying growth trend, but which have been held in low esteem for any one of such reasons as overcapacity, unstable prices for raw materials or finished product, threat of technological change, and so forth. Any fundamental clearing up of the basis for investors' fears should result in (a) a rise in price-earnings ratio, and (b) a rise in earnings per share based on the underlying growth trend.

6. In his appraisal of growth prospects, whether for an established growth company or for a company which merely promises investment

value, the would-be investor ought to conduct a most thorough and careful study, first of the industry and then of the company in question. While such work is time-consuming and will necessarily limit the number of stocks in the investor's portfolio, better results will be obtained from a few well-understood investments than from a larger number superficially known. Diversification is probably an over-rated concept, anyhow.

7. In his appraisal of the company the investor should give by far the greatest weight to management. Management's policies and philosophy should be examined from every practical aspect which the analyst's imagination can conceive, including: aggressiveness and direction of growth, research, merchandising, personnel (especially the development of younger executives), competitive efficiency, focus on the need for adequate margins and net return on capital invested, and financial management.

8. Having made his choice and invested his funds, the investor should be patient, since the working out of an investment in an undervalued stock depends partly upon public recogition of its investment merit—something which may be very slow to come. Similarly, he must be courageous, willing to stick with his convictions and his investment as long as recurrent careful reviews uncover no flaws in his original thinking and no fundamental deterioration in the company's position.

2. GROWTH COMPANIES VS. GROWTH STOCKS*

❁ Peter L. Bernstein

Without presuming to select individual stocks for investment, but concerned that current thinking may mislead managements as well as stockholders, this article points up a distinction between two inconsistent concepts.

GROWTH COMPANIES HAVE RECEIVED so much attention in recent years that the term threatens to become our leading economic cliché. Whether it is management leadership, national importance, or simply prudent investment that one seeks to find, the method is always the same: look to the growth company.

But what is a growth company? Is it a company characterized by unusual technological activity and innovation? Is it merely a company whose sales and earnings have risen more rapidly than most? And what is a growth stock? Are all securities of "growth companies" *ipso facto* growth stocks?

The questions are deceptively simple—but tremendously important. If the phrase "growth company" is to blanket every company which does research or is doing more business this year than it did five or ten years ago, the term will be so broad as to be utterly useless. Only if we can pin it down to a practical, workable definition can we hope to distinguish it in a useful way from the concept of "growth stock."

* From *Harvard Business Review*, (Sept.-Oct., 1956), Vol. 34, No. 5, pp. 87–98. Reprinted by permission of *Harvard Business Review*.

The object of this article is not only to try to provide answers to these questions but also to demonstrate two rather heretical—but, I believe, constructive—points of view: (1) that growth companies constitute a very small and select rather than a broad and important roster of corporate enterprises; and (2) that growth stocks are a happy or haphazard category of investments which, curiously enough, have little or nothing to do with growth companies.

A Step Forward

By getting away from our present muddled belief that growth companies and growth stocks are identical, we can take a long step toward a clearer understanding of the characteristics that set the creative, imaginative management groups in industry apart from other managements. By what signs shall we know them? We have often tended, it seems to me, to confuse leaders and followers. We have been inclined to use the label of "pioneer" indiscriminately, putting it on many a management that merely responds or reacts to its environment as well as on the true "growth company" that actually goes out and shapes economic trends and business conditions.

Better criteria for distinguishing between the two types of companies—and I am thinking here not only of qualitative standards but also of statistical measures of company performance—should be of practical interest to many business leaders, who are by and large a self-critical group of men, proud of the contribution which they make through their companies to the economy, and always eager to draw any valid comparisons between their firms and competitors.

Better criteria should also be of interest to the investor who seeks some way of comparing publicly owned corporations on the basis of the dynamism, the imagination, and the trail-blazing potentials of their managements—qualities which, needless to say, are significant in the investment picture.

It should be emphasized, however, that stocks of some companies which do not meet the criteria of growth used here may appreciate in value just as much as stocks of companies which do, and the stocks of some companies which do fulfill the criteria may turn out to do less well. There are many accidental factors that can influence the results, not the least of which is concerted misjudgment by investors. But the point is that, by and large and over a period of time, the factors of true growth, being more fundamental, are more likely to be a reliable guide for the future than are past increases in market price or current evaluation by the market—or, at least, than either of these without the addition of the particular growth concept set forth here.

Later in this article I shall outline a new statistical method of analysis which demonstrates the soundness of this proposition and implements it for action.

True Growth

Economic development or growth occurs in three different processes: in the increase of population, in the accumulation of capital, and in the technological progress which enables us to produce more things, better things, different things, or the same things more cheaply.

Each of these growth processes affects a business differently. As a businessman, the individual executive or owner can have no direct influence on the first of these three factors; his business may be affected by it, but he cannot have any effect on it. Not so with the other possibilities for growth, however; these are internally generated by business firms on their own initiative. This point is basic to the whole matter: true growth is organic and comes from within.

Since this is the crux of the argument, perhaps it will be helpful to use a homely metaphor to make it clear:

A man wears a larger suit of clothes than a boy, and a boy's clothes are larger than a baby's. Obviously, however, the increase in the size of the clothing is not growth but only a symptom or result of growth. The independent, dynamic force is the development of the child into the boy and then into the man. This is internally generated and is an active, not a passive, process.

CHARACTERISTICS ILLUSTRATED

A good way to pinpoint the distinguishing characteristics of a growth company is to look at some cases which show what a growth company is not. Bear in mind that the crucial question is whether the firm's expansion is the result of internally determined conditions or simply a response to external events over which it has no control.

A company which expands by acquiring other outfits is not a growth company. The acquisitions, once absorbed, may so change its character that it later becomes a growth company, but the process of expansion by acquisition as such is not growth in our terms here.

Firms whose business increases simply because they serve growing markets are not growth companies, for they are not causing the market to grow but are only responding passively to outside events. Of course we must also resist being dazzled by an impressive earnings progression resulting largely from a company's ability to raise its prices in a sellers' market faster than its costs go up.

For example, it is fashionable to consider the oil companies in the growth class. Certainly their sales and earnings have expanded impressively. However, the growth in their operations has resulted primarily from a rising demand for oil which the oil companies themselves have capitalized on but did very little to create. Without the rising automobile population, the high volume of construction (which created the demand for space heating), and the growth of other industries (like electric power) which use oil for fuel, there would have been very much less expansion in the oil industry.

Most of the paper companies should probably be excluded from the growth company group, although they usually are included. The lines of demarcation are admittedly a little fuzzy here, for some of these companies have developed new products or found new uses for paper which did not exist in the past. Essentially, however, they have benefited from the burgeoning demand for paper for packaging, for newspapers and magazines, for paper towels, tissues, napkins, and so forth. This rising demand was a function of higher industrial production, higher incomes, and increased population; the paper companies took advantage of these developments but had little to do with causing them to come about.

Some observers have even gone so far as to call the steel industry a growth industry in recent years. It is true that the financial results of the big steel companies have been outstanding even when compared with the most successful growth companies, and it is also a fact that the per capita consumption of steel is rising persistently. However, with modest exceptions, the steel companies are still selling to the same old markets (73% of steel consumption in 1955 was accounted for by automobiles, construction, machinery, and containers), and it is the growth of those markets which explains the rising demand for steel.

To be sure, new uses for steel have been developed, but either they have been worked out in response to a need first expressed by the customers, as in the case of certain stainless steels, or they do not make a significant contribution to the earnings of the big producers. Furthermore, the steel industry's earnings are unusually dependent on the maintenance of a highly inflated price structure, which has gone up more than twice as fast as the average of all non-agricultural commodities since the period 1947–1949 (as compared, for instance, with only a nominal increase in the price of chemicals). If steel prices were pushed back to 1947–1949 levels, all the steel companies would operate at substantial losses. This would not be the case with most true growth companies.

As a general rule, it would seem that most raw material producers have to be excluded from the growth company category, partly because their growth is dependent on the demand for final products which they can have little influence on, and partly because substantial increases in earnings are basically the result of inflated prices. An obvious and significant exception to this statement is the aluminum industry. The demand for aluminum has grown and is growing phenomenally, not simply because the major consumers of aluminum are doing more business than they used to do but, perhaps more important, because the aluminum companies themselves have found so many new uses for the metal, and therefore so many new consumers of it. The aluminum industry is carving out its own market.

"INNER-DIRECTED"

The ability to create its own market is the strategic, the dominating, and the single most distinguishing characteristic of a true growth company.

The reason for this is not simply that the development of new products, new processes, and new uses for old products leads to higher sales and bigger profits. More important is the fact that the quality of a growth company's sales and earnings is fundamentally different from that of other companies.

A new product or a highly differentiated one is, for a brief period of time at least, unique; it has a virtual monopoly. There is only one Terramycin, one Dacron, one Univac, one Centravac; but the identical steel can be bought from Bethlehem or United States

Steel, and the same copper from Kennecott or from Anaconda. Thus, growth company products tend to provide larger-than-average profit margins and to postpone or possibly even eliminate the danger of price competition. At the same time, the continuous development of new products and new markets offsets declining sales in old products and, perhaps most important of all, tends to insulate the company from many of the hazards of general economic trends.

In short, the real growth company is, to borrow sociologist David Riesman's phrase, "inner-directed" rather than "other-directed." [1] It is a nonconformist in economic society. It adapts the outside world to itself by creating something or a demand for something which did not exist before, instead of adapting itself to changes in the outside world. It does not necessarily grow faster than the economy as a whole, but it does grow faster than the markets in which its products are sold.

This is why so many (but by no means all) of the chemical, electrical equipment, and electronic companies fall into the true growth company class. These companies are at the dynamic and technological frontiers of our society and are continuously developing new uses for old products, new products to replace old products, new products with new functions, and new processes for turning out goods and services of all types.

CREATIVE MERCHANDISING

But the creation of a market does not depend solely on the introduction of a new product or a new use for an old product. A market can be created in less glamorous industries, where dynamic merchandising creates such strong brand loyalty that consumers are convinced the product is unique and hence abandon other products in its favor. Growth, in other words, need not be the result of creating new demand; it can occur when a company wins a larger share of existing markets. For example:

Scott Paper Company has a fundamentally different character from most of the other paper companies and a far more successful earnings record. Of course, Scott Paper has developed new products or tangibly improved versions of old products, but in reality its

---

[1] For a critique of Riesman's views, see Theodore Levitt, "The Changing Character of Capitalism," *Harvard Business Review*, July-August 1956, p. 37. — The Editors

merchandise is part of the stuff of everyday life. Yet Scott's merchandising methods to both the general public and to its important market among manufacturers and institutions have brought it unusually close to its customers and have created the feeling of assurance that its products are of superior quality.

As a result, Scott has more influence over its market than most other paper companies. Its success as an active rather than passive agent in the economy is dramatically illustrated by the way it persistently increased its earnings during the Great Depression and by the degree to which the growth in its earnings has markedly outpaced the rest of the industry in recent years.

Growth potentials can emerge where one least expects to find them, particularly where new markets are developed for old products. An intriguing development in this connection is the effort of the chewing gum manufacturers to take advantage of the salesmanship of the American GI in developing a taste for chewing gum in foreign countries during the war.

Perhaps my point can best be brought out by asking whether the successful automobile companies are growth companies. A good case can be made for the argument that they do not meet the criteria. The automobile is no longer a new product. A major share of the cars sold today are replacements rather than first purchases of a car. The expansion in the automobile market has largely been the result of a rising population and a higher level of personal incomes, and in this sense the automobile companies have been adapting to outside conditions rather than creating their own market.

Yet, when one studies what has happened in this industry in recent years, one wonders whether there is not another side to the question. Through dramatic and persistent changes in style and engineering, the automobile companies have created a new product and made old ones obsolete. Who can say whether the $3,000 car of 1956 with all its new gadgets is or is not more expensive than the same $2,000 brand in 1946? If the creation of new products has not been achieved, how else can we explain the fabulous success of the 1955 models, introduced during a recession and when most statistical tests indicated that the automobile market was well saturated? Does not the effort to sell a second car to every family open up a potentially enormous market? Thus, at least the leading companies in the industry would seem to come close to qualifying as growth companies.

SHARPER FOCUS

As I am sure most readers are aware, there are many definitions of a growth company, and I do not claim that the one just outlined is the "last word." But it is, to my mind, a useful concept for the specific purpose of distinguishing the selected group of really dynamic, pioneering firms from the general run of well-managed firms. In particular, it should aid us in refining, building upon, and carrying a step further Robert W. Anderson's provocative analysis in the March-April 1955 issue of HBR [*Harvard Business Review*], "Unrealized Potentials in Growth Stocks."

It will be remembered that Anderson would include as a growth company any firm which shows expansion, whether or not the impulse comes from within the organization itself. For example, in connection with his belief that growth companies are likely to turn up only in growth industries, he has this to say:

> Such an industry should be a basic element in the country's standard of living, and it should have existing products or services which have met with such increasing public acceptance that unit demand is rising at an average rate significantly greater than the average rate of unit growth of the economy as a whole, although not necessarily dramatic.

But within these terms—and this is the significant point—we would include the major elements of industries such as construction, food, fertilizer, and printing, where growth has been to a major extent a response to expanding demand rather than the creator of it, and where, furthermore, the financial results of the vast majority of companies have been mediocre to say the least and have been far from immune to the business cycle.

The remainder of Anderson's analysis establishes certain criteria, such as research programs, product and process planning, attitudes of management, and so on, which no growth company can be without. But are not these the characteristics which, by and large, one should seek in any well-managed company? Standard Oil of New Jersey, as a case in point, would probably meet Anderson's criteria every bit as well as, say, Scott Paper or Minnesota Mining and Manufacturing. However, if the emphasis is on the difference between active and passive growth, there can be no question that Scott and "3M" are growth companies, while there would be a substantial measure of doubt about Standard Oil of New Jersey in that regard.

FINANCIAL TEST

Now let us turn from the qualitative criteria of growth companies to the expression of those criteria in financial performance. A growth company's sales and earnings should be expected to show a rising trend, and the trend should climb more steeply than the average. "Results are what count."

For instance, the sheer size of appropriations for research and merchandising—sometimes used as a criterion—by itself means nothing. In fact, such expenses are "down the drain," since (a) they cannot justifiably be capitalized, (b) they cannot be turned off without running the risk that the company will lose its position, and (c) a large proportion of selling and research expense can only lay a foundation for future growth and does not bring in any immediate return. Activities of this sort can pay off only if they ultimately bring in substantial returns which will both recapture the money "down the drain" and provide a high return on capital; and the more expensive they are, the truer this is.

Actually, even a better-than-average uptrend in sales and earnings is not enough. A true growth company's financial results should meet the following test criteria as well:

1. The uptrend in earnings should be relatively smooth. Earnings need not rise every single year, but they should increase in more years than they decrease, and they should show an increase in at least as many years as the "average" company's earnings increase.

2. What is true of earnings should also be true, in most cases, of dividends. There is little point in buying a stock yielding 2% or 3% unless over a reasonable period it pays out more than a fixed-income security or less "dynamic" stock.

3. Certainly, return on net worth should be maintained; and if the dividend payout is abnormally low, then return on net worth should actually be rising. In other words, the stockholder's money which is reinvested instead of paid out should earn at least as much as the old capital which produced these earnings. This ratio is indeed the most significant indicator of management's over-all ability and agressiveness.

4. Increases in earnings and/or net worth should of course reflect an increase in the physical volume of output or at least a beneficial shift in product mix—rather than merely larger dollar results reflecting a rising price level.

33 FIRMS ANALYZED

Now, financial performance has the added advantage of being readily subject to statistical measurement.

Exhibit I. *Statistical Measures of Growth of 33 Corporations*

COMPANY	NUMBER OF YEARS IN WHICH INCREASE OCCURRED, 1947–1955		PERCENTAGE INCREASE, 1947–1949 TO 1953–1955		PERCENTAGE INCREASE IN PRICE, 12/31/47 TO 12/31/55	RETURN ON BOOK VALUE		RATIO OF PRICE TO EARNINGS* 12/31/55	RATIO OF PRICE TO INCREASE-INEARNINGS† 12/31/55
	EARN.	DIV.	EARN.	DIV.		1947–49	1953–55		
American Cyanamid	5	5	67%	142%	234%	14.2%	11.6%	20×	50×
Bethlehem Steel	5	4	85	149	382	12.4	13.9	11	24
Corning Glass	7	4	300	333	760	15.5	23.0	28	38
General Motors	7	6	86	100	395	30.9	26.8	15	31
International Paper	5	6	24	77	528	20.4	14.5	18	92
National Lead	7	7	174	269	664	13.9	20.7	26	41
Scott Paper	6	8	106	176	535	18.2	14.8	30	59
U. S. Steel	5	4	103	74	346	7.6	11.0	13	25
Johns-Manville	4	4	39	116	120	13.5	12.4	14	51
Minneapolis Honeywell	5	4	80	99	363	28.0	18.4	28	63
U. S. Gypsum	5	6	47	47	195	17.1	16.9	16	51
Du Pont	7	6	109	108	402	20.2	21.0	32	61
Dow Chemical	5	8	50	239	427	16.9	11.4	39	116
Hercules Powder	4	4	32	41	160	20.1	17.2	25	104
Monsanto Chemical	4	2	36	27	142	18.8	11.6	28	124
Union Carbide & Carbon	4	5	22	56	244	20.4	16.2	29	159
American Can	5	6	18	70	146	13.2	10.8	17	116
General Electric	7	6	68	139	382	19.5	18.1	26	65

Westinghouse Electric	6	3	0	67	106	13.7	9.1	15	—
Libbey-Owens-Ford	6	6	71	31	244	22.6	22.8	17	40
Owens Illinois	5	3	64	36	86	11.3	13.3	19	49
Hartford Fire Insurance	5	3	3	96	213	11.9	6.7	17	640
Insurance Company of North America	5	5	30	101	240	10.6	6.0	18	77
Eastman Kodak	5	7	37	78	190	17.3	15.0	23	84
IBM	7	8	59	53	404	26.2	18.2	37	99
Amerada	6	3	22	55	279	31.0	20.5	28	161
Continental Oil	5	5	4	61	284	20.0	13.8	23	550
Humble Oil	5	4	13	19	186	22.0	15.0	24	210
Standard Oil of California	7	7	55	78	246	16.4	15.0	14	39
Standard Oil of New Jersey	5	7	60	200	325	15.9	15.0	16	42
J. C. Penney	5	3	6	46	136	26.5	18.5	19	382
Sears, Roebuck	5	3	15	39	176	21.4	14.7	19	144
National Steel	4	6	20	109	166	16.6	11.1	12	75
Dow-Jones Industrial Average	6	7	40	65	160	13.6	12.4	15	53
Moody's Industrial Average	5	6	43	70	210	16.4	14.5	16	54

* Average annual earnings per share 1953–1955, calculated on the number of shares outstanding on December 31, 1955.
† Increase in average annual earnings per share from 1947–1949 to 1953–1955, calculated on the number of shares outstanding on December 31, 1955.
NOTE: All data calculated on a per-share basis and on the number of shares outstanding on December 31, 1955.

Exhibit I shows how a number of companies have met the foregoing test of financial performance. The sample includes Anderson's list of 25 "growth companies," plus 8 additional companies, chosen to give deeper perspective to the yawning gap between the qualitative and quantitative characteristics of leading American corporations. (The additions are American Cyanamid, Bethlehem Steel, Corning Glass, General Motors, International Paper, National Lead, Scott Paper, and United States Steel.)

This is by no means an all-inclusive list of growth companies. Conversely, quite a few of the companies in the sample are not growth companies at all, at least in terms of our qualitative criteria. But this very make-up should help to sharpen the distinction between our concept of growth companies and the usual idea of growth stocks. The rationale for the table is as follows:

For the 33 companies, 1947–1949 average data are compared with 1953–1955 average data. The two periods are sufficiently separated in time to be revealing. Also, each includes a recession year, a reasonably good year, and a boom year.

Of course, it would be desirable to make the comparison over a longer period of time to avoid the effect of short-run influences. However, as we all recognize, the economy as a whole and many individual companies are basically different today from what they were in prewar days, so it would be more of a distortion to start with an earlier date. In any event, the comparison here is intended for purposes of general demonstration rather than for anything like selecting specific investment opportunities, so the effect of a few variations is not important.

All figures are expressed on a per-share basis, adjusted for stock splits and stock dividends—that is, they are expressed in terms of the number of shares outstanding at the end of 1955. (This applies to companies that pay regular as well as irregular stock dividends, which explains why the IBM and Dow Chemical figures may look a little unfamiliar to some readers.)

The figures in Exhibit I bear careful study. On the one hand, they largely confirm the ability of companies which do fulfill the qualitative criteria to meet the financial test as well. For instance, the five companies whose earnings show the greatest percentage increase between 1947–1949 and 1953–1955 include four clear examples of true growth companies (marked with asterisks), all but one of which, Scott Paper, increased the return on net worth:

Corning Glass*	up 300%
National Lead*	up 174%
Du Pont*	up 109%
Scott Paper*	up 106%
U. S. Steel	up 103%

On the other hand, the five companies whose earnings show the least increase over the period include only one which seems to fufill our qualitative criteria of a growth company (marked with asterisk):

Westinghouse Electric*	up 0%
Hartford Fire Insurance	up 3%
Continental Oil	up 4%
J. C. Penney	up 6%
Humble Oil	up 13%

The same correspondence between increased earnings and growth criteria shows up throughout the whole list, though not quite to the same degree. With special or temporary circumstances always in the picture to alter or mask the financial results, there are bound to be some companies which have the qualitative requirements of a growth company but fail to meet the financial test (at least for the short run), and at the same time some companies which do not fulfill the qualitative criteria but show superior financial results (although it is a good question whether this superiority would persist through all economic vicissitudes).

SCREENING TOOL

Of course, it must also be borne in mind that whether a company meets qualitative criteria or not is a matter of judgment. In the case of an oil company, for example, one might be justified in calling it a growth company because it was energetically increasing its holdings of oil lands for the future; or one might decide just the opposite. I also hesitate to single out company names for another reason; I do not wish to appear to be touting individual companies, and I certainly want to avoid damning other companies with faint praise. However, as a guide to the reader in following my train of thought, I do think that I can and should say this much:

1. There would probably be general agreement that Corning Glass, National Lead, Scott Paper, Du Pont, Dow Chemical, General Electric,

and IBM come as close as any to meeting all the qualitative criteria and the items in the financial test.

    2. In my opinion American Cyanamid, Minneapolis Honeywell, Libbey-Owens-Ford, and Eastman Kodak also belong relatively high up on any list of true growth companies.

    3. Beyond this there are certain other companies which undoubtedly qualify as growth companies too, but which neither I nor others could demonstrate to be such with the same degree of finality or faith.

I am afraid, in short, that readers will have to make their judgment of my judgment as I have just described it. But to the extent that they do accept it, then true growth characteristics as envisaged in this article are in fact usually expressed in superior financial results.

Accordingly, the items comprising our financial test do make an effective tool for screening out companies which fulfill the qualitative criteria we have established for true growth. If it works four times out of five, or anywhere near that much, that is a high rate of reliability, particularly when compared with the statistical basis of increased market value as used by Anderson. Indeed, the following facts raise the fundamental question whether any list selected like Anderson's 25 companies is representative of growth situations either in terms of company or of stock:

    1. Only 10 of the 25 companies showed an increase in earnings over the 1947–1949 base which was better than the increase in earnings of the Dow-Jones Industrial Average. (Although the 30 companies in the Dow-Jones Industrial Average are used to represent the "average" company in this discussion, the Moody's Industrial Average of 125 companies would have resulted in only minor and insignificant differences in results.)

    2. Only 13 of them raised their dividends by more than the increase in the dividend on the Dow-Jones Industrial Average.

    3. Only 2 increased the rate of return on book value between 1947–1949 and 1953–1955. As a matter of fact, only 7 of the 33 companies in the table achieved this result. If we seek the number of companies which more or less maintained their rate of return, say, within two percentage points, then we can still add only 5 companies to this list.

    4. The earnings of the Dow-Jones Industrial Average rose in three out of the five years 1947–1952 and in six out of the eight years 1947–1955. But 9 of the 25 companies failed to equal this result in the shorter period, and 14 of them failed to do so in the longer period.

    5. The dividend on the Dow-Jones Industrial Average was increased four times during 1947–1952 and seven times during 1947–1955. But 15

of the 25 companies increased their dividends less than four times in the
shorter period (9 of them increased their dividends less than three times)
and 20 failed to do as well as the Dow-Jones Industrial Average in the
longer period (11 failed to increase their dividends even five times).

COMPANY VS. INDUSTRY

Exhibit I is revealing in another sense. It suggests that superior
financial results are apparently not the fortuitous outcome of being
a member of a growth industry. Instead, such results seem to reflect
significant differences in management concepts, policies, and techniques. Wide variations in performance appear among companies
in the same industry; for example, compare General Electric with
Westinghouse, Bethlehem with National Steel, Du Pont with Union
Carbide or Monsanto, Standard Oil of New Jersey with Continental
Oil. Again, General Motors has an outstanding statistical record,
but perhaps only one of its competitors would show up as well as
does the average of the 33 companies in Exhibit I; and the same is
substantially the case with IBM and its competitors.

This is not to say that the stocks of all the companies which our
table singles out as leaders are necessarily good buys for the future
or, on the other hand, that the stocks of all the others can be expected
to perform poorly in the years ahead. For instance, Hercules Powder
appears lackluster in Exhibit I, but actually it may have a growth
potential today which few of the companies in the table can match.

The point here is simply that any broad generalizations drawn
from statistical comparisons can be misleading when it comes to
the selection of individual stocks for future appreciation. Qualitative analysis must also be brought to bear—to explore for special
circumstances and, in particular, to determine to what extent the
company exhibits the characteristics we have been discussing, i.e.,
whether it dynamically creates its own markets, has quasi-monopolis-
tic features reflected in higher profit margins, is sufficiently inner-
directed to be relatively immune to business fluctuations, and has
turned in a consistent record of growth in earning power, dividends,
and return on net worth.

Furthermore, one other dimension must be added—i.e., market
price—before we have anything that can serve as a guide to investment opportunity. As a matter of fact, as I shall point out in the
next section, the statistical method itself must be more refined before
it can be really useful for the purposes under consideration.

The Investor's Problem

Now let us tackle the specific problem of what this all means to the investor who is looking for appreciation in value. The factors we have been discussing—particularly higher-than-average profit margins and superior growth in earning power, dividend payments, and return on net worth—obviously affect market values and are therefore of considerable interest to the investor. And, needless to say, the market effect is also of considerable importance to the growth company's management, for the investor's decisions influence the supply of equity capital. But do these factors dominate market value, or at least influence it to such an extent that growth companies are likely to be synonymous with growth stocks, and growth stocks with superior buys? That is the question.

POWER OF GLAMOR

One of the quickest and most forceful ways to answer this question is to turn again to Anderson's list of 25 corporations. This list, as we have already seen, includes a substantial group of companies that do not qualify as growth companies according to our criteria and which indeed have not returned as impressive financial results as the average of the 30 Dow-Jones Industrials. Now comparison of market prices in relation to earnings reveals that financial return such as would be consistent with true growth was not the main thing investors were interested in anyway. In fact, it shows that they were apparently more interested in glamor than in growth.

Keeping in mind that the Dow-Jones Industrial Average at the end of 1955 was selling for 15.3 times the average earnings in the 1953–1955 period, note that:

1. Only 3 of Anderson's 25 companies (National Steel, Johns-Manville, and Standard Oil of California) were selling at a price-earnings ratio lower than the Dow-Jones Average—proof of the upward pressure on prices exerted by investors. At the same time, while for a variety of reasons the three companies mentioned may have been low on glamor, as a group they showed average or better-than-average financial results.

2. General Motors, United States Steel, and Bethlehem Steel were also selling at less than 15 times 1953–1955 earnings at the end of 1955, although there is no question that the financial results of these 3 companies were outstandingly impressive.

3. Of Anderson's 25 companies, 12 were selling for more than 20 times 1953–1955 earnings, even though this group included companies with clearly subaverage financial results, such as Union Carbide & Carbon, Hercules Powder, and Continental Oil.

To be sure, there are cases where the market price of the stock in relation to earnings is in line with its true growth characteristics. Thus, Scott Paper, Du Pont, IBM, and Dow Chemical, which happen to be the most expensive companies of our list of 33, do appear well qualified for their exalted price-earnings ratio of more than 30 times 1953–1955 average earnings; they clearly meet our qualitative criteria, and their financial results are well above average by any standard of measurement. But in many other cases investors have pushed the price far above what is justified not only in terms of current earnings but in terms of growth potential as well.

From the mass of contradictory evidence available, is it possible for the investor to find some guide or bench mark in his search for "value"? How can he make a choice among a group of such outstanding companies with such widely dispersed price-earnings ratios? How can he decide whether General Motors at 14 times 1953–1955 earnings is a better buy than Dow Chemical at nearly 40 times, or whether it is worth paying nearly twice as much for a dollar's worth of General Electric's earnings as for a dollar's worth of Westinghouse's?

VALUING EARNINGS GROWTH

There is a possible basis for answering these questions, but it involves a rejection of the conventional ratio of price to earnings as a measure of value. While the method to be proposed, even if accepted by the investing public, would hardly go so far as to shift the main focus of market interest from growth stocks to growth companies, it might well be used by the managements of undervalued growth companies as an effective tool in gaining more recognition from investors.

There are two parts to this task of selecting stocks for future appreciation. The investor must satisfy himself (1) that the company is likely to continue to grow in earning power, and (2) that the stock is priced relatively low enough at time of purchase so the increase in earning power has a good chance to be reflected in greater value to the holder.

The first part we have of course already discussed in terms of qualitative analysis of the company (not the stock); a consistent upward trend in earnings and dividends, with the greatest possible potential based on dynamic management and supported by relative immunity to business fluctuations, should certainly indicate the prospects for continued growth in earning power.

The second part, which is our concern at this point, involves statistical analysis of the market price of the stock to determine whether it is a good buy in the sense of not being valued so high that in effect the results of future growth are already discounted (as so often happens when stocks become glamorized, particularly so-called growth stocks which do not have the characteristics of true growth to back them up).

But if the investor simply looks to see whether the stock is cheap or expensive on the basis of how many times earnings it is selling for, he ignores the primary consideration in his search—the discovery of growth. Earnings in any given period of time are a static concept. They are therefore only partly relevant to the valuation of growth companies. What the investor should look at is the change in earning power between two periods of time.

Accordingly, my suggestion is that the ratio of price to increase-in-earnings may be more significant than the conventional ratio of price to earnings. Investment requires a look into the future; intelligent appraisal of the future must be based on developing trends already in action and ascertainable; and this is one way of doing it. For example:

Let us take two fictional stocks, the Deadhead Company selling for $20, and the Zoomar Company selling for $30. If they are both currently earning $2 a share, Deadhead is selling for 10 times earnings and certainly looks cheaper than Zoomar, which is selling for 15 times. But if five years ago Deadhead's earnings were $1.60 while Zoomar was earning only $1.00, Deadhead's price is 50 times its $0.40-a-share increase-in-earnings, while Zoomar's price is only 30 times its $1.00-a-share increase-in-earnings. Now Zoomar clearly seems like the better value.

If the investor believes that the two companies will continue to grow in the future at about the same rates they showed in the past, there is no question that Zoomar is cheaper. Five years hence Zoomar will again have doubled its earnings and will be making $4 a share; thus its present price of $30 is only 7.5 times its future earnings. Deadhead, on the other hand, will be earning only $2.50 five years from now, so its present price of $20 is 8 times its future earnings.

The ratio of price to increase-in-earnings makes some stocks look cheaper and some more expensive than the values indicated by the more conventional price/earnings measurement, as Exhibit II shows. (The figures are presented for illustrative purposes only. In any serious application of the method, it would naturally be wise to examine the increase-in-earnings records for any "windfalls"—large one-shot government contracts, and so forth—and make any adjustments deemed necessary.)

Exhibit II. *Price/Earnings-Increase Ratios of 10 Stocks*

	END-OF-1955 PRICE AS A MULTIPLE OF	
	1953–1955 EARNINGS	INCREASE-IN-EARNINGS 1947–1949 TO 1953–1955
IBM	36.5×	99×
Du Pont	32.3	61
Scott Paper	30.4	59
National Lead	26.4	41
Corning Glass	28.4	38
Hartford Fire Insurance	17.3	640
Continental Oil	22.6	550
J. C. Penney	18.7	382
Humble Oil	24.2	210
Union Carbide	28.6	159
Dow-Jones Industrial Average	15.3	53

Indeed, Exhibit II shows clearly that the investor gets a wholly different "slant" on matters if he uses the ratio of price to increase-in-earnings rather than the more conventional ratio; the companies with superior financial results almost always appear to be more attractively priced on the new basis—notably, for instance, National Lead and Corning Glass. But it is also worth noting that, as Exhibit III illustrates, some stocks were cheap at the end of 1955 by both standards of measurement—the explanation probably being that these are stocks where the glamor factor is relatively low, and thus the refinement of our method makes less difference.

Exhibit III. *Stocks Undervalued on the Basis of Both
Price/Earnings and Price/Earnings-Increase Ratios*

	12/31/55 PRICE AS A MULTIPLE OF	
	1953–1955 EARNINGS	INCREASE-IN-EARNINGS 1947–1949 TO 1953–1955
Bethlehem Steel	11.0×	24×
U. S. Steel	12.9	25
General Motors	14.5	31
Standard Oil of California	13.5	39
Standard Oil of New Jersey	15.8	42
Johns-Manville	14.3	51
U. S. Gypsum	16.3	51

In short, the price to increase-in-earnings ratio does serve to produce a different and presumably a truer, or at least more helpful,
picture when the market is running ahead of growth in earning
power, yet at the same time it causes no distortion when the opposite
is the case.

UNDERVALUED STOCKS

Now, how effective in actual practice is the increase-in-earnings ratio
as the second part of our method for selecting stocks for future
appreciation—in other words, for determining whether the stock of
a growth company is also a good buy for this purpose in terms of
current market price?

A test based on data for our sample of 33 companies at the end
of 1952 reveals rather impressive results. To give expression to the
first part of our method, the sample was combed out to select those
companies with the most consistent records of rising earnings and
dividends and with the best record of maintaining or increasing return on net worth. From this group, the 5 companies with the lowest
and the 5 companies with the highest ratios of price to increase-in-
earnings—in other words, the 5 cheapest and 5 most expensive stocks
—were chosen as if for purchase. What the results would have been
as of the end of 1955 are compared in Exhibit IV (the companies are
listed in ascending order of their price to increase-in-earnings ratios
at the end of 1952).

Exhibit IV. *Price to Increase-in-Earnings Ratio Applied*

	PERCENTAGE INCREASE IN PRICE 12/31/52 TO 12/31/55
Five cheapest companies in 1952	
Bethlehem Steel	221%
U. S. Steel	183
General Motors	108
Libbey-Owens-Ford	114
Standard Oil of New Jersey	96
Average	114
Five most expensive companies in 1952	
National Lead	160%
Westinghouse	25
Dow Chemical	45
Amerada	0
IBM	116
Average	69
Dow-Jones Industrial Average	65

Although this test is based on a relatively short time period with plenty of peculiarities, the results are highly consistent. It may be seen that as a group the cheapest companies in terms of the ratio of price to increase-in-earnings far outperformed the most expensive ones. It is also significant that all five of the cheapest companies went up by more than the Dow-Jones Industrials, while three of the expensive companies turned in very poor results.

Of course there also are a few stocks of companies on the list which fail to meet the qualitative criteria of growth and yet show appreciation like the stocks of the best growth companies. This simply emphasizes the fact that no statistical analysis is perfect or self-sufficient, and that inspection of the individual situation must always be brought into the decision to buy a stock. But at least this approach is far more fruitful than simply purchasing so-called growth stocks. Indeed, Anderson's own data prove this point. His 25 income stocks outperformed his 25 growth stocks from 1936 through 1945. For the entire period he reviews—1936 through 1954—his growth stocks were outperformed as a group by such "nongrowth" stocks as Goodyear, Bethlehem Steel, Beatrice Foods, and Truax-Traer Coal.

Here is one moral. In investing, nothing beats the discovery of an undervalued stock, no matter what the nature of its business or the past trend of its earnings. But simply purchasing so-called growth stocks tends to lead to the selection of overvalued stocks.

Furthermore, investors cannot wholly ignore the very low income return on most growth stocks—particularly institutional investors with little or no income tax to pay. The annual income on Anderson's 25 growth stocks did not catch up to that on his income stocks for 12 years or to the Dow-Jones Industrials for 14 years. By the end of 1954, the entire amount of income received on the growth stocks from the beginning of 1936 was still less than on the income stocks or the Dow-Jones Industrials.

Or look at it this way. In 1955, the dividend on the Dow-Jones Industrials was equal to 10.2% of the price at the end of 1947. On General Motors it was 23%, on Bethlehem Steel 24%, and on National Lead 26%. But on 17 of Anderson's 25 growth companies it was less than 10%, and 3 were actually yielding less than 6% on the 1947 price.

Thus, for those investors who can reinvest and compound income and for those who require a relatively high income, the very high premiums which some supposed growth stocks command may turn out to be less than worthwhile, even if satistfactory price appreciation results. For analysis proves that both appreciation and a large income can be realized with proper selection—i.e., selection of true growth companies with a relatively low ratio of price to increase-in-earnings.

Conclusion

The magic words "growth company" are high praise in the business world today. It is perfectly proper for the spotlight to focus on those companies which are either making a significant contribution to, or benefiting greatly from, the vigorous growth patterns of our modern economy. But in order to avoid dangerous over-simplifications and in order to apply the term "growth company" only where it has some useful meaning, the following considerations should be borne in mind:

1. Growth is a dynamic concept. The growth company can never be a passive beneficiary of economic change. Rather it must be an active

agent at the technological or geographical frontiers of our society. Thus, it is not enough to be in, say, the chemical or electronic industries; a firm cannot become a growth company "by association." There may be more elements of growth—i.e., market creation—in a company like General Motors than in many chemical or electronic companies.

2. It is a mistake to believe that superior earning power is to be found only among growth companies, but it is a very decisive test for all such firms. Creativity and ambition in product development and merchandising alone are not enough; the ability to make money out of creativity is certainly at least as important.

3. The enchantment which some growth companies convey to the stock market lends a premium to their common stocks which is not always justified by the statistical background. An investor may do well with such stocks, but there is good reason to believe that he can do even better by giving the financial results—such as those shown by measures of increase-in-earnings power—a completely cold-blooded and objective analysis. No amount of study in this area can minimize the importance of trying to buy at a fair price; buying at any price and hoping that the future will take care of itself is a good short cut to disappointing results.

Indeed, perhaps the most important conclusion of this analysis is that the term "growth stock" is meaningless; a growth stock can be identified only with hindsight—it is simply a stock which went way up. But the concept of "growth company" can be used to identify the most creative, most imaginative management groups; and if, in addition, their stocks are valued at a reasonable ratio to their increase-in-earnings power over a period of time, the odds are favorable for appreciation in the future.

3. GROWTH STOCKS AND THE PETERSBURG PARADOX*

❁ David Durand

AT A TIME LIKE THE PRESENT, when investors are avidly seeking opportunities for appreciation, it is appropriate to consider the difficulties of appraising growth stocks. There is little doubt that when other things are equal the forward-looking investor will prefer stocks with growth potential to those without. But other things rarely are equal—particularly in a sophisticated market that is extremely sensitive to growth. When the growth potential of a stock becomes widely recognized, its price is expected to react favorably and to advance far ahead of stocks lacking growth appeal, so that its price-earnings ratio and dividend yield fall out of line according to conventional standards. Then the choice between growth and lack of growth is no longer obvious, and the astute investor must ask whether the market price correctly discounts the growth potential. Is it possible that the market may, at times, pay too much for growth?

Most problems encountered in appraising growth stocks seem to fall into two categories. First there are the practical difficulties of forecasting sales, earnings, and dividends. Then come the theoretical difficulties of reducing these forecasts to present values. For a long time it seems to have been assumed, altogether too casually, that the present value of a forecasted dividend stream could be represented simply as the sum of all expected future payments discounted at a

* From *The Journal of Finance*, Vol. XII, No. 3 (September, 1957), pp. 348–363. Reprinted by permission of *The Journal of Finance*.

uniform rate. Doubts, however, are beginning to manifest themselves. As early as 1938, J. B. Williams suggested non-uniform discount rates, varying from payment to payment.[1] More recently, Clendenin and Van Cleave have shown that discounting forecasted dividends at a uniform rate in perpetuity may lead to absurdities or paradoxes, since implied present values of infinity sometimes result. "We have not yet seen any growth stocks marketed at the price of infinity dollars per share," they remark, "but we shall hereafter be watching. Of course, many investors are skeptical and would probably wish to discount the very large and remote dividends in this perpetually growing series at a high discount rate, thus reducing our computed value per share to a figure somewhat below the intriguing value of infinity."[2] Clendenin and Van Cleave might have made a good point even better had they noticed a remarkable analogy between the appraisal of growth stocks and the famous Petersburg Paradox, which commanded the attention of most of the important writers on probability during the eighteenth and nineteenth centuries.

THE PETERSBURG PARADOX

In 1738 Daniel Bernoulli presented before the Imperial Academy of Sciences in Petersburg a classic paper on probability, in which he discussed the following problem, attributed to his cousin Nicholas: "Peter tosses a coin and continues to do so until it should land 'heads' when it comes to the ground. He agrees to give Paul one ducat if he gets 'heads' on the very first throw, two ducats if he gets it on the second, four if on the third, eight if on the fourth, and so on, so that with each additional throw the number of ducats he must pay is doubled. Suppose we seek to determine the value of Paul's expectation."[3]

One may easily obtain a solution according to the principles of mathematical expectation by noting the sequence of payments

[1] John B. Williams, *The Theory of Investment Value* (Cambridge, Mass.: Harvard University Press, 1938), pp. 50–60.
[2] John C. Clendenin and Maurice Van Cleave, "Growth and Common Stock Values," *Journal of Finance*, IX (1954), pp. 365–76. Quotation appears on p. 369.
[3] Daniel Bernoulli, "Exposition of a New Theory on the Measurement of Risk," *Econometrica*, XXII (1954), pp. 23–36, which is a translation by Dr. Louis Sommer of Bernoulli's paper "Specimen Theoriae Novae de Mensura Sortis," *Commentarii Academiae Scientiarum Imperialis Petropolitanae*, V (1738), pp. 175–92.

Table 1

SEQUENCE OF TOSSES	PROBABILITY	PAYMENT
H	1/2	1
TH	1/4	2
TTH	1/8	4
TTTH	1/16	8
TTTTH	1/32	16

and probabilities in Table 1: Paul's expectation is the sum of the products of probability by payment or

$$\frac{1}{2} + \frac{2}{4} + \frac{4}{8} + \frac{8}{16} + \frac{16}{32} + \ldots$$

If the players agree to terminate the game after n tosses, whether a head shows or not, the series will contain n terms and its sum will be $n/2$; but if they agree to continue without fail until a head shows, as the rules of the game stipulate, then n is infinite and the sum $n/2$ is infinite as well. Thus the principles of mathematical expectation imply that Paul should pay an infinite price to enter this game, but this is a conclusion that virtually no one will accept. A variety of explanations have been given to show that the value of the game to Paul is, in fact, only a finite amount—usually a small finite amount; and all of these explanations are relevant to growth stock appraisal. But before considering them, we shall do well to examine an important modification of the original Petersburg problem.

One modification, which is obvious enough, consists in stipulating some figure other than $\frac{1}{2}$, say $1/(1 + i)$, for the probability of tossing a tail and some figure other than 2, say $1 + g$, for the rate of growth; but this has no particular interest for security appraisal. A more extensive modification, which is of interest, provides for a series of increasing payments, instead of a single lump sum. In effect, Peter agrees to pay D ducats if the first toss is a tail, $D(1 + g)$ if the second is a tail, $D(1 + g)^2$ if the third is a tail, $D(1 + g)^3$ if the fourth is a tail, and so on until a head shows—at which point the game ceases. Then, if the probability of a tail is $1/(1 + i)$, the mathematical expectation is (see Appendix)

$$\frac{D}{1 + i} + \frac{D(1 + g)}{(1 + i)^2} + \frac{D(1 + g)^2}{(1 + i)^3} + \ldots \tag{1}$$

This series is arithmetically equivalent to a discounted series of dividend payments, starting at D ducats, growing at a constant rate g, and discounted at rate i.[4] The summation of the series is a simple exercise in actuarial mathematics. The sum of the first n terms is[5]

$$D \frac{1 - (1 + g)^n/(1 + i)^n}{i - g} , \tag{2}$$

provided i is different from g; and the sum of an infinite or very large number of terms approaches the very simply formulated quantity

$$\frac{D}{(i - g)} \tag{3}$$

provided that i exceeds g. If, however, $g \geqq i$, the sum of an infinite number of terms would again be infinite—as in the original Petersburg Problem—and a reasonable Paul might again object to paying the price.

The applicability of formulas (2) and (3) to growth stock appraisal is not new. In 1938, for example, J. B. Williams[6] derived (3), or its equivalent, in order to appraise the retained portion of common-stock earnings He made the derivation, using quite different notation, on essentially the following assumptions: first, that in any year j, earnings per share E_j bear a constant ratio, r, to book value, B_j; second, that dividends, D_j, bear a constant ratio, p, to E_j. Then,

$$B_j + 1 = B_j + E_j(1 - p) = B_j[1 + r(1 - p)].$$

Hence, book value, dividends, and earnings are all growing at the same constant rate $g = r(1 - p)$ and formula (3) can be rewritten

$$\frac{D_1}{i - g} = \frac{E_1 p}{i - g} = \frac{B_1 p r}{i - g} . \tag{3a}$$

[4] Possibly the objection may be raised that series (1) is conceptually quite different from a discounted series of dividends on the grounds that the discount rate ordinarily represents the price paid for waiting in addition to the price paid for assuming risk. To meet this objection, it suffices to discount the dividend series twice, first, by an amount just sufficient to cover the price of waiting, and second, by the amount required to cover the risk of dividend termination when Peter finally tosses a head. Then, the growth rate g in (1) would represent the real growth rate less an adjustment for waiting, and i would represent only the risk of termination.

[5] See, for example, Ralph Todhunter, *The Institute of Actuaries' Text-Book on Compound Interest and Annuities-Certain*, 4th ed., revised by R. C. Simmonds and T. P. Thompson (Cambridge, England: University Press, 1937) pp. 48–49.

[6] Williams, *op. cit.*, pp. 87–89, 128–135.

Williams realized, of course, that these formulas are valid only when i exceeds g, and he mentioned certain other limitations that are best discussed with some of the proposed solutions for the Petersburg Paradox.

ATTEMPTS TO RESOLVE THE PETERSBURG PARADOX[7]

The many attempts to resolve the paradox, summarized very briefly below, fall mostly into two broad groups: those denying the basic assumptions of the game as unrealistic, and those arguing from additional assumptions that the value of the game to Paul is less than its mathematical expectation.

The basic assumptions of the game are open to all sorts of objections from the practically minded. How, in real life, can the game continue indefinitely? For example. Peter and Paul are mortal; so, after a misspent youth, a dissipated middle age, and a dissolute dotage, one of them will die, and the game will cease—heads or no heads. Or again, Peter's solvency is open to question, for the stakes advance at an alarming rate. With an initial payment of one dollar, Peter's liability after only 35 tails exceeds the gold reserve in Fort Knox, and after only three more, it exceeds the volume of bank deposits in the United States and approximately equals the national debt. With this progression, the sky is, quite literally, the limit. Even if Peter and Paul agree to cease after 100 tosses, the stakes, though finite, stagger the imagination.

Despite these serious practical objections, a number of writers chose to accept the assumption of an indefinitely prolonged game at face value, and to direct their attention toward ascertaining the value of such a game to Paul. First among these was the Swiss mathematician Gabriel Cramer, who early in the eighteenth century proposed two arbitrary devices for resolving the Petersburg Paradox by assuming that the utility of money is less than proportional to the amount held.[8] First, if the utility of money is proportional to the amount up to $2^{24} = 166,777,216$ ducats and constant for

---

[7] For a general history of the paradox, see Isaac Todhunter, *A History of the Mathematical Theory of Probability from the Time of Pascal to that of Laplace* (reprint, New York: G. E. Stechert & Co., 1931) pp. 134, 220–222, 259–262, 275, 280, 286–289, 332, 345, 393, 470. For a briefer treatment, see John Maynard Keynes, *A Treatise on Probability* (London: Macmillan and Co., 1921), pp. 316 ff.
[8] Cf. Bernoulli, *op. cit.*, pp. 33 ff.

amounts exceeding 2^{24}, so that the utility of the payments ceases to increase after the 24th toss, Paul's so-called moral expectation is about 13 ducats. Second, if the utility of money is assumed equal to the square root of the amount held, Paul's moral expectation is only about 2.9 ducats. Cramer believed that 2.9 was a more reasonable entrance fee than 13.

A little later and apparently independently, Daniel Bernoulli devised a solution only slightly different from Cramer's. Assuming that the marginal utility of money is inversely proportional to the amount held, he derived a formula that evaluates Paul's expectation in terms of his resources at the beginning of the game. From this formula, which does not lend itself to lightning computation, Bernoulli estimated roughly that the expectation is worth about 3 ducats to Paul when his resources are 10 ducats, about 4 ducats when his resources are 100, and about 6 when his resources are 1000.[9] At this rate, Paul must have infinite resources before he can value his expectation at infinity; but then, even his infinite valuation will constitute only an infinitesimally small fraction of his resources.

An interesting variant of Bernoulli's approach was proposed about a century later by W. A. Whitworth[10]—at least some of us would consider it a variant, though its author considered it an entirely different argument. Whitworth was, in fact, seeking a solution to the Petersburg Problem that would be free of arbitrary assumptions concerning the utility of money; and he derived a solution by considering the risk of gamblers' ruin, which is always present when players have limited resources. Thus, for example, if A with one dollar matches pennies indefinitely against B with $10, it is virtually certain that one of them will eventually be cleaned out; furthermore, A has 10 chances out of 11 of being the victim. Accordingly, a prudent A might demand some concession in the odds as the price of playing against B. But how much concession? Whitworth attacked this and other problems by assuming a prudent gambler will risk a constant proportion of his resources, rather than a constant amount, on each venture; and he devised a system for evaluating ventures that entail risk of ruin. Applied to the Petersburg Game, this system indicates that Paul's entrance fee

[9] *Ibid.*, pp. 32 ff.
[10] W. A. Whitworth, *Choice and Chance* (Cambridge, England: Deighton, Bell & Co., 4th edition, enlarged, 1886), chap. 9.

should depend upon his resources. Thus Whitworth's solution is reminiscent of Bernoulli's—particularly when one realizes that Whitworth's basic assumption implies an equivalence between a dime bet for A with $1 and a dollar bet for B with $10. Bernoulli, of course, would have argued that the utility of a dime to A was equal to the utility of a dollar to B. Finally, the notion of a prudent gambler seeking to avoid ruin has strong utilitarian undertones, for it implies that marginal utility of money is high when resources are running out.

But Whitworth's approach—regardless of its utilitarian subtleties—is interesting because it emphasizes the need for diversification. The evaluation of a hazardous venture—be it dice game, business promotion, or risky security—depends not only on the inherent odds, but also on the proportion of the risk-taker's resources that must be committed. And just as the prudent gambler may demand odds stacked in his favor as the price for betting more than an infinitesimal proportion of his resources, so may the prudent portfolio manager demand a greater than normal rate of return (after allowing for the inherent probability of default) as the price of investing more than an infinitesimal proportion of his assets in a risky issue.[11]

Although the preceding historical account of the Petersburg Paradox has been of the sketchiest, it should serve to illustrate an important point. The various proposed solutions, of which there are many, all involve changing the problem in one way or another. Thus some proposals evaluate the cash value of a finite game, even when the problem specifies an infinite game; others evaluate the utility receipts, instead of the cash receipts, of an infinite game; and still others foresake evaluation for gamesmanship and consider what Paul as a prudent man should pay to enter. But although none of these proposals satisfy the theoretical requirements of the problem, they all help to explain why a real live Paul might be loath to pay highly for his infinite mathematical expectation. As Keynes aptly summed it up, "We are unwilling to be Paul, partly because we do not believe Peter will pay us if we have good fortune

---

[11] Section 87 of the New York Insurance Law states: "Except as more specifically provided in this chapter, no domestic insurer shall have more than ten per cent of its total admitted assets invested in, or loaned upon, the securities of any one institution; . . ." Section 81, subsection 13, places additional restrictions on common stock investment.

in the tossing, partly because we do not know what we should do with so much money . . . if we won it, partly because we do not believe we should ever win it, and partly because we do not think it would be a rational act to risk an infinite sum or even a very large sum for an infinitely large one, whose attainment is infinitely unlikely."[12]

IMPLICATIONS OF PETERSBURG SOLUTIONS FOR GROWTH-STOCK APPRAISAL

If instead of tossing coins, Peter organizes a corporation in a growth industry and offers Paul stock, the latter might be deterred from paying the full discounted value by any of the considerations that would deter him from paying the full mathematical expectation to enter the Petersburg game. And again, these considerations fall into two categories: first, those denying the basic assumptions concerning the rate of indefinitely prolonged growth; and, second, those arguing that the value of the stock to Paul is less than its theoretical discounted value.

Underlying J. B. Williams' derivation of formula (3) is the assumption that Peter, Inc., will pay dividends at an increasing rate g for the rest of time. Underlying the derivation in the Appendix is a slightly different assumption: namely, that Peter will pay steadily increasing dividends until the game terminates with the toss of a head, and that the probability of a head will remain forever constant at $i/(1 + i)$. Under neither assumption is there any provision for the rate of growth ever to cease or even decline. But astronomers now predict the end of the world within a finite number of years—somewhere in the order of 10,000,000,000—and realistic security analysts may question Peter, Inc.'s ability to maintain a steadily increasing dividend rate for anywhere near that long. Williams, in fact, regarded indefinitely increasing dividends as strictly hypothetical, and he worked up formulas for evaluating growth stocks on the assumption that dividends will follow a growth curve (called a logistic by Williams) that increases exponentially for a time and then levels off to an asymptote.[13] This device guarantees

---

[12] Keynes, *op. cit.,* p. 318.
[13] Williams, *op. cit.,* pp. 89–94.

that the present value of any dividend stream will be finite, no matter how high the current, and temporary, rate of growth. Clendenin and Van Cleave, though not insisting on a definite ceiling, argued that continued rapid growth is possible only under long-run price inflation.

The assumption of indefinitely increasing dividends is most obviously objectionable when the growth rate equals or exceeds the discount rate ($g \gtreqless i$) and the growth series (1) sums to infinity; then formula (3) does not even apply. If Peter, Inc., is to pay a dividend that increases at a constant rate $g \gtreqless i$ per year, it is absolutely necessary, though not sufficient, that he earn a rate on capital, $r = E/B$, that is greater than the rate of discount—more exactly, $r \gtreqless i / (1 - p)$. But this situation poses an anomaly, at least for the equilibrium theorist, who argues that the marginal rate of return on capital must equal the rate of interest in the long run. How, then, can Peter, Inc., continually pour increasing quantities of capital into his business and continue to earn on these accretions a rate higher than the standard rate of discount? This argument points toward the conclusion that growth stocks characterize business situations in which limited, meaning finite though not necessarily small, amounts of capital can be invested at rates higher than the equilibrium rate. If this is so, then the primary problem of the growth-stock appraiser is to estimate how long the departure from equilibrium will continue, perhaps by some device like Williams' growth curve.

If, for the sake of argument, Paul wishes to assume that dividend growth will continue indefinitely at a constant rate, he can still find reasons for evaluating Peter's stock at somewhat less than its theoretical value just as he found reasons for evaluating his chances in the Petersburg Game at less than the mathematical expectation. The decreasing-marginal-utility approach of Cramer and Bernoulli implies that the present utility value of a growing dividend stream is less than the discounted monetary value, because the monetary value of the large dividends expected in the remote future must be substantially scaled down in making a utility appraisal. Or again, Whitworth's diversification approach implies that a prudent Paul with finite resources can invest only a fraction of his portfolio in Peter's stock; otherwise he risks ruinous loss. And either argument is sufficient to deter Paul from offering an infinite price, unless, of course, his resources should be infinite.

THE PROBLEM OF REMOTE DIVIDENDS

There is, moreover, another important limitation on Paul's evaluation of a growth stock that has not arisen in the discussion of the Petersburg Paradox, namely, the remoteness of the large dividend payments. Conventional theory argues that dividend n years hence is adequately evaluated by the discount factor $1/(1 + i)^n$, but this is open to question when n is very large. The question is, of course, academic for ordinary instruments like long-term bonds or preferred stock, since discounted coupons or preferred dividends many years hence are negligible when discounted in the conventional manner. Thus, for example, if $5.00 a year in perpetuity is worth exactly $100.00 (assuming 5 per cent compounded annually), then $99.24 is attributable to the first 100 payments. But for a stock growing according to series (1) and with $g \geqq i$, the discounted value of remote dividends, say 10,000 years hence, is anything but negligible; in fact, it may be astronomic. But how should Paul evaluate such remote growth dividends?

If Paul is a real live person without heirs or other incentives for founding an estate, his problem is fairly clearcut. Dividends payable beyond his reasonable life span are useless to him as income, although claims on them may be convertible into useful income through the medium of the market place. At retirement, for example, he might easily be able to increase his income for the remainder of his life by selling long-term securities and buying an annuity. If, however, Paul has heirs, he may look forward several generations and place a very real value on dividends that will be payable to his grandchildren and great-grandchildren. But even here his investment horizon may be limited by the uncertainty of planning for offspring not yet born.

If Paul is a life insurance company, he has a special interest in evaluating remote dividends; for the shades of obligations currently contracted may extend far into the future as the following fanciful though not impossible sketch will indicate. In 1956 John Doe, aged 21, buys for his own benefit a whole life policy containing the customary guaranty of a rate of interest if the insured elects to settle the proceeds in installments. In 2025, aged 90, John Doe decides to settle this policy on his newborn great-grandson Baby Doe and directs the insurance company to accumulate the proceeds at the guaranteed rate of interest until Baby Doe shall reach the age of 21 and thereupon pay them out to him as a life income, according to the table of guaranteed rates in the policy. Encouraged by his monthly checks, Baby Doe now lives to the ripe old age of 105, so that only in 2130 does the insurance company finally succeed in discharging its obligation of 1956, based on the then current forecasts of long-term interest rates.

Even though the case of John Doe may be a bit out of the ordinary, it illustrates forcefully why life insurance companies must concern themselves with dividend income up to perhaps 200 years hence and how a future decline in the earning rate on assets may threaten the solvency of an insurance fund. Although the purchase of long-term bonds is an obvious form of protection against falling interest rates, it is not entirely effective when the liabilities extend too far into the future. To illustrate the difficulty of long-term protection, it will be convenient at this point to introduce a concept called "duration" by Macaulay,[14] which may apply to an individual security, a portfolio of securities, or even to a block of liabilities. Duration, incidentally, must not be confused with a related concept known as "equated time."

The duration of an individual security or a portfolio is the arithmetic mean of the several coupon or maturity dates, each date weighted by the present value at the valuation rate of interest of the expected income on that date. The duration of an E bond or non-interest-bearing note is simply the term to maturity; and the duration of a portfolio consisting, for example, of two $100 E bonds due two years hence and a $500 E bond due five years hence would be

$$\left[\frac{2 \times 200}{(1.03)^2} + \frac{5 \times 500}{(1.03)^5} \right] \div \left[\frac{200}{(1.03)^2} + \frac{500}{(1.03)^5} \right],$$

if evaluated at 3 per cent compounded annually. The duration of an interest-bearing bond is less than the term to maturity, because the long term of the principal payment at maturity must be averaged against the shorter terms of the various coupons. Macaulay's formula for the duration of interest-paying bonds is somewhat complex; but for perpetuities, such as Canadian Pacific

---

[14] F. R. Macaulay, *Some Theoretical Problems Suggested by the Movement of Interest Rates, Bond Yields and Stock Prices in the United States since 1856* (New York: National Bureau of Economic Research, 1938), pp. 44–51.

debenture 4's, it simplifies to $(1 + i)/i$.[15] At $i = .03$, the duration of a perpetuity is therefore about 34 years.

In seeking suitable methods for matching the assets of a fund to its liabilities so as to minimize risk of loss from fluctuations in the interest rate, British actuaries have shown that the possible loss is very small when both present value and duration of the assets equal present value and duration of the liabilities; and, indeed, they have given examples where the "loss" is a small gain for fluctuations either up or down.[16] But although the portfolio manager can ordinarily achieve satisfactory matching by merely selecting long- and short-term bonds in such proportions that their average duration equals that of the liabilities, he runs into difficulty when the duration of the liabilities is exceptionally long. Thus, for example, the duration of the liability of a pension fund with many young workers and only a few pensioners can easily exceed 40 years: and this is too long to be matched by a portfolio consisting wholly of perpetuities, whose duration at current interest rates is only about 30 years. In such a difficulty, however, growth stocks offer a possible solution; for when dividends are growing according to series (1), the duration is longer than a perpetuity. In fact, if we define

$$1 + b = \frac{1 + i}{1 + g} \cdot$$

then $(1 + b)b$ is the duration of the series.[17] Thus growth stocks provide a possible means of increasing the average duration of

---

[15] Macaulay, *op. cit.*, pp. 49–50. In Macaulay's formula for perpetuities (p. 50) let $R = 1 + i$.

[16] See, for example, J. B. H. Pegler, "The Actuarial Principles of Investment," *Journal of the Institute of Actuaries* (England), Vol. 74 (1948), pp. 179–211; F. M. Redington, "Review of the Principles of Life Office Valuations," *ibid.*, Vol. 78 (1952), pp. 286–340; G. V. Bayley and W. Perks, "A Consistent System of Investment and Bonus Distribution for a Life Office," *ibid.*, Vol. 79 (1953), pp. 14–73; A. T. Haynes and R. J. Kirton, "The Financial Structure of a Life Office," *Transactions of the Faculty of Actuaries* (Scotland), Vol. 21 (1953), pp. 141–218; D. J. Robertson and I. L. B. Sturrock, "Active Investment Policy Related to the Holding of Matched Assets," *ibid.*, Vol. 22 (1954), pp. 36–96. Also see Paul A. Samuelson, "The Effect of Interest Rate Increases on the Banking System," *American Economic Review*, XXXV (1945), 16–27, especially p. 19.

Interest of the British in this subject, which seems to be greater than that of the Americans, may be due in part to their relative freedom from liability for policy loans. Although the British companies are prepared to make such loans, they are not forced to do so.

[17] This can be proved by using Macaulay's method of finding the duration of a perpetuity and making the substitution $b = i$.

a portfolio when the composition of the liabilities requires this. W. Perks has, in fact, hinted as much.[18]

There is, in fact, no theoretical limit to the duration of a stock with dividends growing as in (1). When $g = .05$ and $i = .06$, say, the duration is approximately 100 years; and as the difference between g and i decreases, durations of 1,000 years, 10,000 years, or even 1,000,000 years might result. Moreover, when $g \geqq i,\ b \leqq 0$ and formula $(1 + b)/b$ is no longer valid; then the duration is infinite as well as the present value. But although securities with a duration of 100 years might be useful to British life companies for increasing average duration of pension fund assets, or for providing protection against contingencies illustrated by the case of John Doe above, securities with much greater duration would begin to lose appeal. The essential characteristic of a very long duration is that the security holder or his legatees must expect to wait a long time before the security begins to pay a substantial return; and with those hypothetical securities having infinite duration, the legatees must literally expect to wait forever. Even the most forward looking of investors, who are probably those who leave bequests to such institutions as universities and religious organizations, cannot afford to look that far into the future; for, to paraphase Keynes, it would not be a rational act to risk an infinite sum or even a very large sum for an infinitely larger one, whose attainment is infinitely remote. In effect, the very remote dividends in series (1) cannot be worth their actuarially discounted value when g is large; whether they are worth it when g is small is probably academic, for then the discounted value will be negligible.

To allow for various uncertainties in evaluating dividends in the very remote future, Clendenin and Van Cleave made a significant suggestion, namely, to increase the discount rate applicable to the more remote dividends. The difficulty, of course, is to find some reasonable, objective basis for setting up an appropriate schedule of rates. To illustrate their suggestion, Clendenin and Van Cleave worked out valuations for hypothetical securities by discounting the first twenty years of dividends at 4 per cent, the second twenty at 6 per cent, the third twenty at 8 per cent, and considering all subsequent dividends as worthless. But although such a schedule,

[18] See his remarks following the paper by Redington, *op. cit.*, p. 327.

3. *Growth Stocks and the Petersburg Paradox* 69

totally disregarding all dividends after 60 years, might appeal to
a man aged 40 without heirs, it would not appeal to insurance
companies and pension managers, who have to look forward 150
to 200 years; and it would certainly not appeal to the loyal alumnus,
who wishes to leave a bequest to alma mater. But the essential point
is that by setting up a schedule of discount rates that increase fast
enough to render very remote dividends negligible, one can assure
himself that the present value of any increasing stream of dividends
will be finite. An although many investors would object to neglecting
dividends after 60 years, few would object to neglecting them after
600.

SUMMARY AND IMPLICATIONS FOR SECURITY
APPRAISAL IN GENERAL

There are, to sum up, a number of potent reasons any one of
which suffices to dissuade Paul from paying an infinite price for a
growth stock under even the most favorable circumstances, namely
when $g \geqq i$ and the sum of series (1) is infinite. Moreover, these
reasons do not lose all their force when $g \leqq i$ and the sum of (1) is
finite. In appraising any growing stream of dividends, Paul might
wish to make provision for eventual decline and perhaps cessation
of the growth rate, as suggested by J. B. Williams; he might adjust
large dividends to allow for the decreasing marginal utility of
money, somewhat in the manner of Cramer and Bernoulli; or again
he might apply Whitworth's reasoning and scale down his valuation
to a sum he can afford to risk, given his resources; or finally he
might, following Clendenin and Van Cleave, apply a very high
discount rate to remote dividends that have no significance to him.
And he might, of course, apply a combination of such approaches.

But, oddly enough, the very fact that Paul has so·many good
reasons for scaling down the sum of series (1) when g is high, and
so many ways to accomplish this end, leaves him with no clear
basis for arriving at any precise valuation. Thus, the possible
adjustments for the decreasing marginal utility of money are many
and varied. Cramer's two proposals yielded very different appraisals
if applied to rapidly growing growth stocks; and Daniel Bernoulli's
proposal would yield yet another result. Or again, there are many

ways by which Paul can allow for an eventual decline in the current rate of growth, all of which entail major forecasting problems. Williams' formula, for example, which is stated here in the form[19]

$$V = D \left[\frac{(1 + g)^n - (1 + i)^n}{(g - i)(1 + i)^n} + \frac{(2g + i + 2gi)(1 + g)^n}{i(g + i + gi)(1 + i)^n} \right]$$

after the substitution $D = \Pi_0 (1 + g)$ and some rearrangement, rests on the somewhat restrictive assumption that dividends grow annually at a constant rate g for n years and then taper off exponentially to a level equal to exactly twice the dividend in the nth year. Even when the assumptions are acceptable in principle, practical application of the formula may require more accurate information on g, i, and n than one could possibly expect to obtain. This is particularly true when n is large and g is only slightly larger than i; then $g - i$ in the denominator of the first fraction is small and tremendously sensitive to errors in either g or i. Nor is this difficulty peculiar to Williams' formula. Table 2, abridged from Clendenin

Table 2

GROWTH PERIOD	RATE OF GROWTH	
	5 PER CENT	4 PER CENT
0	$18.93	$18.93
10	28¼	26
20	37	32½
30	45¼	37½
40	52¼	41½
50	57¾	44¼
60	60	45½

and Van Cleave,[20] gives the present value of 60 dividend payments discounted at 5 per cent. It is assumed that the initial dividend rate of $1.00 grows at either 4 per cent or 5 per cent for a period of years and then remains constant for the remainder of the 60-year period, after which dividends either cease or are considered worthless. This table again illustrates the difficulty of making appraisals

[19] Williams, *op. cit.*, formula (27a), p. 94.
[20] *Op. cit.*, Table 4, p. 371.

without an accurate forecast of the growth rate and the length of the growth period.

More conventional securities such as bonds and preferred stocks, though much less troublesome than growth stocks, still present some of the same difficulties of evaluation, and a single example should make this clear. In evaluating bonds—even bonds of supposedly uniform quality—one must make some adjustment for term to maturity. Ordinarily one does this by summing a discounted series of coupons and principal

$$\frac{C}{1+i_n} + \frac{C}{(1+i_n)^2} + \cdots + \frac{C}{(1+i_n)^n} + \frac{P}{(1+i_n)^n}$$

in which the uniform discount factor depends on the number of years to maturity. Alternatively, however, one could follow the suggestion of Clendenin and Van Cleave, which would entail summing the series

$$\frac{C}{1+i_1} + \frac{C}{(1+i_2)^2} + \frac{C}{(1+i_3)^3} + \cdots + \frac{C}{(1+i_n)^n} + \frac{P}{(1+i_n)^n}$$

in which each discount factor i_1, i_2, i_3, etc., depends on the date of the coupon or principal payment discounted. But whether one prefers the conventional method or the alternative, the issue is clear: one cannot apply a standard discount factor i uniformly to all bonds; some adjustment for the length, or duration, of the payment stream is essential.

The moral of all this is that conventional discount formulas do not provide completely reliable evaluation. Presumably they provide very satisfactory approximations for high-grade, short-term bonds and notes. But as quality deteriorates or duration lengthens, the approximations become rougher and rougher. With growth stocks, the uncritical use of conventional discount formulas is particularly likely to be hazardous; for, as we have seen, growth stocks represent the ultimate in investments of long duration. Likewise, they seem to represent the ultimate in difficulty of evaluation. The very fact that the Petersburg Problem has not yielded a unique and generally acceptable solution to more than 200 years of attack by some of the world's great intellects suggests, indeed, that the growth-stock problem offers no great hope of a satisfactory solution.

APPENDIX

Proof of Formula (1) for Paul's Expectation in the Modified Petersburg Game

The table below lists a few possible outcomes, with associated probabilities, for the modified Petersburg Game, in which Peter pays Paul a series of dividends according to the number of tails that occur before a head finally shows. There is, of course, an infinite number of such possible outcomes, because every finite

SEQUENCE OF TOSSES	PROBABILITY	DIVIDEND	TOTAL PAY (CUMULATED DIVIDENDS)
H	$i/(1+i)$	O	O
TH	$i/(1+i)^2$	D	D
TTH	$i/(1+i)^3$	$D(1+g)$	$D+D(1+g)$
TTTH	$i/(1+i)^4$	$D(1+g)^2$	$D+D(1+g)+D(1+g)^2$

sequence of tails, no matter how long, has a finite, though possibly very small, probability of occurring. It is assumed, moreover, that throughout even the longest sequence, the probability of a tail remains constant at $1/(1+i)$, leaving $i/(1+i)$ as the probability of a head.

Paul's mathematical expectation is obtained by summing the products of probability in the second column by payout in the fourth. Thus, the sequence TTH, for example, has probability $i/(1+i)^3$ and results in the payout of two dividends, D and $D(1+g)$. The product appears in the table below along with similar products for the sequences H, TH, and TTTH.

SEQUENCE	PRODUCT
H	0
TH	$Di/(1+i)^2$
TTH	$[D+D(1+g)]i/(1+i)^3$
TTTH	$[D+D(1+g)+D(1+g)^2]i/(1+i)^4$

To sum these products, it is convenient to break them up and to rearrange the parts in powers of $1 + g$. Thus, for example, all elements containing $(1 + g)^2$ form an infinite series

$$\frac{Di(1 + g)^2}{(1 + i)^4} \left[1 + \frac{1}{1 + i} + \frac{1}{(1 + i)^2} + \ldots \right],$$

where the factor in the bracket is a well-known actuarial form having the sum to infinity $(1 + i)/i$. Thus, the sum of all elements in $(1 + g)^2$ is $D (1 + g)^2/(1 + i)^3$, which is one of the terms in series (1). The other terms are obtained in an analogous manner.

4. ARE GROWTH STOCKS REALLY PROFITABLE?*

❀ Norman O. Miller

Research has shown very little basis for the "growth industry = good stocks" theory of selection

F OR SOME YEARS NOW the fashion in Wall Street has been to invest in "growth stocks." Amateur investors with relatively small sums to commit in securities have been seeking industriously to pick those particular common stocks that will experience unusual growth in market value and in size of dividend payments over a period of years. Professional security analysts have struggled valiantly with the problem of identifying and selecting stocks with unusual appreciation prospects.

One of the most popular rules for selection of growth stocks is that they are usually to be found in growth industries. Concepts of growth industries vary somewhat, but they are commonly defined as those increasing their sales at a greater rate than the rate of growth of the total economy. The theory is that a company in a growth industry is likely to experience a greater-than-average increase in sales, which is likely to result in a pronounced improvement in profitability, an increase in earnings and dividends per share, and appreciation in market price for common stock.

* From *Business Horizons,* Vol. 1, No. 5 (Winter, 1958–59), pp. 45–50. Reprinted by permission of *Business Horizon.*

Research recently completed at Indiana University shows there is very little basis in the experience of the past 20 years for the growth industry idea and that, in fact, industry growth is a poor basis for selection of growth stocks. A survey of nine leading industries revealed that the greatest improvement in profitability in the period 1935–54 occurred in an industry that has expanded at about the same rate as the national economy, namely, the steel industry. The third greatest improvement in profitability was found in copper metals and mining, an industry that has been declining relative to the national economy. One of the industries with the strongest growth trends, the chemical industry, ranked seventh among the nine industries in rate of increase in profitability. This study shows that, even if one had been able to forecast accurately in the 1930's the future growth of our major industries, the forecast would not have provided a reliable basis for selection of common stocks.

Growth and Profitability

One of the difficulties of the "growth industry" idea is the loose use of the term. Many people who use it do not define it, and many others seem to regard any industry that shows an increase in sales over a period of years as a growth industry. In the expanding economy of the United States, growth is a relative term. An industry is a growth industry only if it is growing relative to the total economy. An industry that is increasing its sales in absolute dollar amounts, but at a lesser rate than the expansion of the total economy, is actually a relatively declining industry.

In this statistical study we have measured the absolute growth in nine major manufacturing and mining industries by constructing for each industry an annual index of sales (average annual sales for 1935–39 = 100). To measure the growth of the economy in terms of sales of the manufacturing and mining companies we took the aggregate annual sales of 143 companies in 18 different industries and made an index for aggregate sales (1935–39 = 100). The sales index for each of the nine industries was then divided by the aggregate sales index for the 18 industries to obtain a relative sales index for each industry, which shows the growth of an industry in relation to the growth of industrial companies in general. An industry experiencing a more rapid expansion of sales than industrial companies generally has a sales index rising above 100, while one experiencing a less rapid expansion of sales than industrial companies generally declines below 100.

By this method three of the nine industries studied were identified as growth industries, four as neutral industries, and two as declining industries (Table 1).

Table 1. *Classification of Industries by Relative Growth in Sales*

	RELATIVE SALES INDEX, 1952–54*
Growth Industries	
Paper and paper products	149
Chemical	130
Tire and rubber	127
Neutral Industries	
Oil	104
Steel	103
Cotton textile	97
Food products	93
Declining Industries	
Copper metals and mining	79
Cigarette tobacco	76

* Growth over the 20-year period is measured by averaging the annual relative indexes for the last three years of the period.
Source: All of the data used in this study are derived from an investment service published by Studley, Shupert, & Company, Inc., of Boston, Mass. The industry classifications used are those established by this service. The companies included in each industry are the principal companies in which there is a public investment interest.

Relative growth in sales for an industry, according to the growth industry thesis, is supposed to cause an increase in the profitability of companies engaged in that industry. The term "profitability" is often loosely used, but we have defined it for the purpose of this study as the relationship between amount of profit and amount of total capital. Profit is the annual amount remaining after all income and expenses except fixed charges, income taxes, and preferred dividends. Total capital is the sum of noncurrent debt, preferred stock, common stock, and surplus. Thus, profitability is measured as a rate of profit on total capital, and changes in profitability appear as changes in this rate.

We have measured changes in relative profitability of the nine industries over the 20-year period by the same statistical technique as was used to measure relative growth of sales. The annual rate of profit for each industry was converted to an index with the average of 1935–39 = 100. The same kind of index was computed for the aggregate of 18 industries. Thus, an industry that has had an improvement in profitability greater that that of industrial companies generally has a relative profitability index above 100, while an industry whose profitability has improved less shows a relative profitability index below 100.

Comparison of the relative sales indexes for the several industries with the relative profitability indexes shows very little correlation (Table 2).

Table 2. *Relative Indexes* of Industry Growth and Profitability*

	SALES INDEX	PROFIT-ABILITY INDEX	ORDER OF SALES INDEX	ORDER OF PROFIT-ABILITY INDEX
Growth Industries				
Paper and paper products	149	143	1	2
Chemical	130	82	2	7
Tire and rubber	127	118	3	4
Neutral Industries				
Oil	104	101	4	6
Steel	103	179	5	1
Cotton textile	97	104	6	5
Food products	93	67	7	8
Declining Industries				
Copper metals and mining	79	121	8	3
Cigarette tobacco	76	46	9	9

* *Source*: Derived from data published by Studley, Shupert & Co., Boston, Mass.

There is some support for the growth industry approach to common stock selection in the fact that two of the three growth industries experienced relative growth in profitability and, in a negative way, by the fact that the industry with least growth in sales shows the lowest relative index of profitability. Other facts, however, are quite inconsistent with the growth industry idea. The steel industry, which has expanded only at about the same rate as the total economy, had considerably greater improvement in relative profitability than any of the growth industries. The chemical indus- try, with the second greatest rate of growth, had the seventh greatest rate of improvement in relative profitability; and the copper industry, which has experienced a marked relative decline in sales, had a better improvement in relative profitability than two of the three growth industries.

Theory and Experience

There are some good reasons for thinking that a particularly favorable growth trend in an industry should result in a better-than- average improvement in profitability. A marked improvement in sales ought to permit a spreading of fixed costs over a constantly increasing volume of production and thus exert a favorable in- fluence upon profit margins. A relatively rapidly growing industry also has the best opportunity for rapid upgrading of fixed assets, that is, of adding new plant and equipment of the latest design and efficiency. Upgrading of assets should result in cost reduction and improvement of profit margins to the extent that economies can be retained. It might be expected, too, that in the more rapidly growing industries the competitive pressures would be somewhat less because of the favorable development of markets.

Probably all of these influences upon profitability tend to operate to some extent in growth industries, but in any particular period of time their effect often tends to be diluted or offset by other influences. Thus, the effect of spreading fixed costs over greater volume may be offset over a period of time by an increase in fixed costs due to price inflation. The greater efficiency of new plant and equipment may be counterbalanced by increases in labor costs per unit of product. Even in the more rapidly growing indus- tries, price competition may press very severely upon profit margins.

In any such statistical study as this, an important influence upon the results is the general prosperity of the economy at the beginning and the end of the period of observation. Some industries are much more sensitive profitwise to the business cycle than others, and any historical record of changes in profitability is bound to be distorted to some extent by cyclical fluctuations. We have endeavored to measure trends over a relatively long period of time—a score of years—and we have tried to minimize cyclical fluctuations by averaging annual data for the five years 1935–39 as the base period and for the three years 1952–54 as the terminal period. The fact remains that the economy was more prosperous in 1952–54 than it was in 1935–39.

The difference in prosperity of the country during the two periods certainly had an influence upon the relative trend of profitability for the several industries in this study. In general, the more stable industries through the business cycle experienced less benefit profitwise from the higher level of business activity in 1952–54, and the more unstable industries experienced the greater profit. The steel industry led all the rest in increase in relative profitability because it was experiencing a very low rate of profit on total capital during the relatively depressed period of the late 1930's. Its profitability was greatly improved by the much more favorable business conditions of the early 1950's. The paper and paper products industry, too, was relatively depressed in the latter 1930's and booming in the early 1950's. In both industries the difference in general business conditions in the two periods probably had more to do with change in their relative profitability than did influences attributable particularly to long-term growth.

On the other hand, the cigarette tobacco industry, which makes the poorest showing of the nine industries in terms of relative profitability, is a notably stable industry. It was earning an excellent rate of profit on capital in the 1935–39 period and about the same rate in the 1952–54 period. Because the already high rate of profit did not increase, as did the rates for other industries that were depressed in the latter 1930's, the relative profitability of the tobacco industry declined. The showing of the chemical industry was also affected by its comparatively favorable profit experience in 1935–39. In spite of its distinct growth trend, the industry was not able to increase its good rate of profit as much as some other industries with less favorable profit experience in the earlier period.

It may be that differences in the general prosperity of the economy from one period to another, combined with differences in the sensitivity of profits in different industries to the condition of the economy, largely invalidate any conclusions that may be drawn from a statistical study of the growth and profit experience of

industries over two decades of time. If this is so, it supports the
conclusion that the long-term growth trends of industries are by
no means a controlling influence upon changes in the relative
profitability of industries. It suggests, instead, that even over comparatively long time periods, changes in the relative prosperity of
the total economy are a major influence.

EQUITY CAPITAL PROFITABILITY

The rate of profit on total capital measures most accurately the
profitability of an industry or a company. It does not, however,
measure exactly changes in the profitability of common equity
capital, and common stock investors are particularly interested in
the returns on common stock and surplus. Between profit on total
capital and profit on equity capital lie income taxes and, for many
companies, interest on noncurrent debt or preferred dividends, or
both. Changes in these expenses may cause changes in the profitability of equity capital different from changes in the profitability
of total capital. Table 3 shows that, in fact, there have been considerable differences between the relative indexes of rate of profit on
total capital and rate of profit on equity capital for the industries in
this study.

The correlation between industry growth and rate of profit
on equity capital is even less than that of industry growth and
profitability of total capital. Of the three growth industries in this
study, only the paper and paper products industry experienced a
greater than average increase in rate of profit on equity capital.
Its improvement ranked third among the nine industries in size
of relative increase. The first and second industries in order of size
of improvement were neutral industries—the oil and the steel
industries. A declining industry, copper metals and mining, was
the fourth industry that showed a relative increase in rate of profit
on equity capital. It is worth noting that two of the growth industries ranked sixth and seventh among the nine industries in relative
improvement in profitability of use of equity capital.

One cause of difference between rate of profit on total capital
and rate of profit on equity capital is income taxes. During the
period of this study, the rates of the federal income tax increased
markedly with corresponding increases in the proportion of sales

Table 3.   *Profitability of Total Capital and of Equity Capital*

	SALES	TOTAL PROFIT	EQUITY PROFIT †	TOTAL PROFIT INDEX	EQUITY PROFIT INDEX
	RELATIVE INDEX NUMBERS*			ORDER OF MAGNITUDE	
Growth Industries					
Paper and paper products	149	143	124	2	3
Chemical	130	82	70	7	6
Tire and rubber	127	118	66	4	7
Neutral Industries					
Oil	104	101	125	6	2
Steel	103	179	261	1	1
Cotton textile	97	104	94	5	5
Food products	93	67	55	8	8
Declining Industries					
Copper metals and mining	79	121	106	3	4
Cigarette tobacco	76	46	39	9	9

* For 1952–54 based on 1935–39 as 100.
† The relative indexes of rate of profit on equity capital have been computed by the same method as the relative indexes of rate of profit on total capital.
Source: Derived from data published by Studley, Shupert & Company, Inc.

absorbed by federal income tax payments. However, the increase in tax rates had no general effect on our relative indexes of rate of profit on equity capital, since the indexes for each industry were computed on an after-tax basis, as was the index for 18 industries.

The relative indexes of profit on equity capital for the different industries varied from their relative indexes of profit on total capital because of change in "leverage." (The term "leverage" is generally used to mean the proportion of the total capital structure of a company represented by senior securities, that is, bonds and pre-ferred stock.) A successful company with senior securities in its capitalization normally "makes money" for its common stockholders by the use of this senior capital because the rate of interest on bonds, or of dividends on preferred stock, is less than the rate of profit earned by such a company on its senior capital. The excess of earnings on senior capital over its cost reverts to the equity owners of a business. Thus, for a successful company, an increase in the proportion of senior securities over a period of time causes the rate of earnings on equity capital to improve more than the improvement in rate of earnings on total capital.

Only three of the nine industries in our study increased the proportional use of senior capital from 1935–39 to 1952–54. One was a growth industry, one a neutral industry, and one a declining industry. Apparently the increase in leverage in these industries— chemical, food products, and cigarette tobacco—was influenced more by the relative cyclical stability of their earnings than by long-term growth.

Two of the three growth industries, paper and paper products and tire and rubber, greatly reduced the proportion of senior securities in their capital structures, and this development in financial policy caused a decline in their relative indexes of rate of profit on equity capital.

Among the growth industries, the chemical industry was the only one that increased the proportion of senior securities in its capitalization. This change tended to benefit the rate of earnings on equity capital even though the rate declined relative to that for the 143-company aggregate. The benefit is evidenced by the fact that chemical industry's relative index of equity profit in 1952–54 was sixth in size among the nine industries, while its relative index of profit on total capital was seventh.

Both the paper and products industry and the tire and rubber industry had a very large proportion of senior capital in the base period 1935–39, and both industries substantially reduced the percentage of bonds and preferred stock in the period to 1952–54. The reduction in leverage had an adverse influence upon the rate of profit on equity capital. During this period, the tire and rubber industry, which ranked fourth in rate of profit on total capital, ranked seventh in the rate of profit on equity capital.

EVALUATION

This survey shows little relationship between the rate of growth of industries (as measured by their annual sales and improvement) and the rate of profit earned on common equity capital. There may be a basic tendency for the more rapidly growing industries to improve their earnings on total capital to a greater extent than industries growing less rapidly, but the tendency is only one of a number of variables affecting earnings and dividends per share of common stock and the value of stock in the market.

We have observed that the business cycle is an influence, even upon experience over a considerable period of years. In our study the more cyclical industries tended to show better experience profitwise because the initial period of observation was one of relative economic depression and the terminal period was one of relative economic prosperity. Price inflation, the rate of technological development of products, the rate of improvement in production processes, and change in the intensity of competition also tend to affect the profitability of different industries.

The policies of industries and companies in the use of senior capital is a second major variable. Change in degree of senior capital leverage may cause the rate of profit on equity capital to change in a considerably different manner than change in the rate of profit on total capital.

Common stock investors also have to take into account the fact that the profit experience of different companies in the same industry often varies widely, with some succeeding amazingly while others fail. They must remember that growth of earnings per share of common stock is affected not only by the rate of profit on equity capital but also by the increase from year to year in amount of equity capital per share caused by retention of earnings. And, finally, there is the well-known emotionalism of investors that causes them at one time to pay one price for a dollar of earnings and at another time to pay twice as much for the same dollar of earnings.

Andrew Carnegie is said to have paraphrased a patriarchal maxim to read, "Put all your eggs in one basket and watch the basket." This remark has been seized upon by some observers and applied, in a rather indiscriminate way, to the investment of money. . . . Mr. Carnegie's epigram may be intelligently applied to any line of enterprise in which a man's talents, knowledge, and capital are involved, but not to the investment of his surplus wealth.

—Thomas Gibson
Simple Principles of Investment

COMMON STOCK
ANALYSIS AND
VALUATION

II ❈

INTRODUCTION

WITH THE INCREASING POPULARITY of common stocks as a medium for investment since World War II, individuals and institutions now have a greater stake in the ownership of industry. This has also created responsibilities for increasing knowledge of this medium. The current attitude towards equities reflects strongly the long-term favorable experience investors have had since 1949 during a period marked by general confidence in the long-run virtue of owning common stocks.

The attractiveness of common stock investment today seems to depend on a number of favorable factors, which grow stronger as our economy moves through the 1960's. These factors include the assured growth of population and gross national product, elimination of major business depressions because of the federal government's commitment by law and philosophy to prevent or quickly counteract declining business activity, perennial high federal government expenditures for domestic and foreign programs, and the strong influence of increasing numbers of financial institutions interested in owning these stocks.

The readings chosen for this section analyze the main problems of common stocks. Emphasis is placed on the major determinants of their value, the benchmarks and criteria needed for the fruitful choice of equity holdings.

The courageous and difficult task of projecting common stock values to 1970 is the burden of the first essay by Professor Harry C. Sauvain. This task is also accepted by Benjamin Graham in his essay, which emphasizes traditional value analysis as a defense of accumulating common stocks for investment. While he is optimistic, Graham assesses historical patterns for clues to future performance, and advocates respect for businessman valuation yardsticks when viewing the problems of common stock ownership.

James E. Walter's article is a scholarly review of the relationship between dividend policies and common stock prices, suggesting that over the long term stock prices reflect the present values of expected future dividends. John C. Clendenin reinforces this valuation technique, aiming in his analysis at some easy rule-of-thumb methods for comparing the values of non-growth, slow-growth, and fast-growth equities. O. K. Burrell is interested in refining the problem of investor attitudes toward growth stocks; in this area there is too often a seemingly irrational approach by investors to dividend policy as related to earnings. The final essay is somewhat specialized, with a strong case being made by Frederick W. Page for long-term commitment in public utility common stocks. The complex factors for valuation in this specialized area are identified and weighed against the peculiar characteristics of public utility operation and social regulation.

5. COMMON STOCK PRICES IN THE SIXTIES*

❀ Harry C. Sauvain

DURING THE PAST DECADE OR SO, common stocks have become more popular than ever before in the history of the country. Literally millions of people throughout the land and in all walks of life have become owners of common stocks, and most types of investing institutions have expanded their common stock holdings. Stock ownership by business managers has become the rule rather than the exception. And a great many corporate officers confidently expect to receive an important part of their compensation in the future by the exercise of options to buy common stock in their company.

Present-day attitudes toward common stocks, particularly industrial stocks, reflect to a considerable extent the very favorable experience of investors with this type of investment since 1949. From that year to the end of 1959, the market value of a broad group of leading industrial stocks approximately quadrupled.[1] The average annual rate of price appreciation over the ten-year period was about 15 per cent. Dividends on this group of stocks in 1949 provided a return of about 7.5 per cent on average 1949 prices; in 1959 they amounted to about 12.6 per cent on 1949 prices. This has been one of the greatest and longest bull markets in history, and more people have profited financially than ever before.

* From *Business Horizons*, Vol. 3, No. 3 (Fall, 1960), pp. 33–38. Reprinted by permission of *Business Horizons*.
[1] Standard & Poor's price index for 425 industrial stocks has been used to measure the general rise in market prices.

Table 1. *Earnings, Dividends, and Prices . . . Standard & Poor's 425 Industrial Stocks*

THE PAST RECORD

YEAR	EARNINGS PER SHARE	DIVIDENDS PER SHARE	PRICE * PER SHARE (1941–43 = 100)
1949	$2.40	$1.14	$15.13
1950	2.93	1.53	18.70
1951	2.54	1.45	22.72
1952	2.46	1.44	25.41
1953	2.60	1.47	24.49
1954	2.89	1.57	31.84
1955	3.78	1.68	43.87
1956	3.53	1.78	50.13
1957	3.50	1.84	46.71
1958	2.95	1.79	51.42
1959	3.53	1.90	61.83

THE PROJECTION

YEAR	EARNINGS PER SHARE	DIVIDENDS PER SHARE †	PRICE INDEX MULTIPLE OF 1959 PRICES 12	15	18
1960	$3.71	$2.23	$44.52	$55.65	$66.78
1961	3.90	2.34	46.80	58.50	70.20
1962	4.10	2.46	49.20	61.50	73.80
1963	4.31	2.59	51.72	64.65	77.58
1964	4.53	2.72	54.36	67.95	81.54
1965	4.76	2.86	57.12	71.40	85.68
1966	5.00	3.00	60.00	75.00	90.00
1967	5.25	3.15	63.00	78.75	94.50
1968	5.51	3.31	66.12	82.65	99.18
1969	5.79	3.47	69.48	86.85	104.22
1970	6.08	3.65	72.96	91.20	109.44

* Annual average of price index at end of each quarter.
† At 60 per cent of earnings.
Source: Standard & Poor's Trade and Securities Service and author's calculations.

Thus, investors' attitudes toward common stocks have completed the full swing from deep disillusionment and mistrust in the 1930's to great confidence and optimism as we begin the seventh decade of the century. The sharp decline in the stock market early in 1960 and the subsequent irregular movement of prices may have dimmed slightly the glamour of common stocks, but there seems to have been little change in the general level of confidence during the last several years. Is this continued optimism about the future of common stock investments justified by prospects for the 1960's? The question can be put and an answer developed only on the basis of long-term trends in the economy and in financial markets. The question is difficult enough in terms of trends; it is impossible in terms of cyclical fluctuations in business and in the stock market.

The left-hand part of the figure shows the strong rise in prices for industrial stocks in the 1950's and the much more modest upward movement in average earnings and dividends per share for Standard & Poor's 425 industrial stocks. The right-hand part of the figure shows a projection of these series for the period to 1970. The data from which the figure was drawn are presented above in tabular form.

The projection of trend lines for industrial stock prices, average earnings, and average dividends per share for the next decade is an exercise in statistical model-building. We have made some assumptions about developments in the economy in the 1960's, some more assumptions about how investors will think about common stocks, introduced some value judgments, and then quantified conclusions into a projection of data for Standard & Poor's industrial stocks.

The model for the 1960's is based largely on the experience of the fifties. Looking backward, we observe a distinct but moderate upward trend in average annual earnings and dividends per share for industrial stocks. For Standard & Poor's 425 industrial stocks, average annual earnings per share increased irregularly from $2.40 in 1949 to $3.53 in 1959. This is an increase at an average annual rate of about 4 per cent.

The upward movement in earnings per share was not due to an increase in the profitability of industrial companies in the 1950's. Actually the industrial enterprises in this group experienced a marked decrease in average rate of profit earned on common equity capital. In 1950, average average earnings per share amounted to 19.7 per cent of average book value per share. This ratio declined

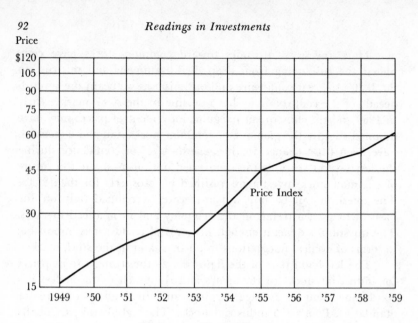

Figure 1. *The Past Record.*

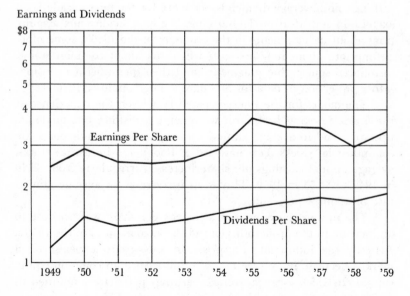

Figure 2. *Earnings and Dividends.*

to 13.9 in 1953, rose to 17.2 in 1955, and stood at about 12 per cent in 1959. The trend for the period was downward.

The rise in average earnings per share in the face of lower rates of profit was a result of the policy of retaining a large part of earnings and adding these funds to the capital represented by common stock. The percentage of average earnings per share paid out in cash dividends varied from about 52 to 60 per cent during the 1950's, with a slightly rising trend in the proportion of earnings distributed. As a result, the average book value per share increased from $13.74 at the end of 1949 to an estimated $29.80 at the end of 1959. Thus the amount of capital represented by an average share of stock more than doubled. The increase in amount of capital per share more than compensated for the decline in rate of profit per dollar of equity capital and produced the up-trend in earnings per share.

How will these relationships work out in the next ten years? The figures that seem most reasonable are: (a) an annual rate of profit on common equity capital averaging about 12 per cent and (b) an average pay-out of 60 per cent of earnings.

These two conclusions are based on a number of assumptions that ought to be expressly recognized, that are debatable as to validity, and that may have to be changed as we go along. First, it is assumed that the economy will continue to grow in volume of production of goods and services at an average annual rate of about 4 per cent. This seems to be the consensus of gross national product projectors at the present time. If it should develop that the growth rate is higher, the assumed rate of earnings might have to be revised upward because more rapid growth would probably reduce competitive pressures on profits. The assumed pay-out ratio might have to be lowered because more rapid growth would increase the need for additional capital. If the growth rate is lower, there would be the opposite implication for these two figures.

In the construction of this statistical model, a rise in the general price level at an average annual rate of about 2 per cent has been assumed. This is the rate at which the price level has been rising in the past decade and seems to be the consensus of economists' estimates for the future. A more virulent price inflation would probably increase the rate of earnings and reduce the pay-out ratio.

A third assumption is that the amplitude of cyclical fluctuations in general business activity will be about the same as during the

1950's. We project past experience because there seems no very good reason for doing anything else. However, a more severe and prolonged recession than those of recent experience would reduce greatly the rate of earnings on equity capital for the period of depression and would probably result in an average annual rate for the decade below the projected rate of 12 per cent.

Competitive conditions in business generally are assumed to be about the same in the 1960's as in the later 1950's. During the last few years rising costs, continued expansion in productive capacity, and somewhat restrictive federal credit policies have increased the pressure of competition upon profit margins and brought about lower rates of earnings than during the earlier years of the 1950's. Looking ahead, there is little on the horizon to suggest less competitive pressure on profits.

The broadest assumption of all, and possibly the most dubious, is that American industry will continue to operate in a political climate favorable for private business. This assumes that industry will not operate under wartime conditions or conditions of major preparations for war. It also assumes no major change in the relationship of government to private business. If this assumption proves seriously invalid, the whole statistical model will be wrecked.

If the average annual rate of profit on equity capital runs at about 12 per cent, and if about 60 per cent of earnings are paid out in cash dividends, average earnings per share will increase at a compound annual rate of 5 per cent.[2]

This is a somewhat higher growth rate for earnings per share than we actually experienced in the 1950's. In that period, the rate of earnings on common equity capital had a downward trend; for the next decade, we have projected the rate at a constant level. The rate of increase in dividends would also be at 5 per cent since they

---

[2] Rate of earnings growth is the rate of earnings on equity capital multiplied by 1 minus the percentage of earnings paid out, divided by 1 minus the rate of earnings, multiplied by 1 minus the percentage of earnings paid out. That is:

$$Rg = \frac{Re(1 - Po)}{1 - Re(1 - Po)}$$

By substitution:

$$Rg = \frac{.12(1 - .60)}{1 - .12(1 - .60)} = \frac{.048}{.952} = 5\%$$

The author is indebted to Robert T. Flaherty for the development of this formula.

have been projected at a constant 60 per cent of earning. The higher rate of earnings and dividend growth in the 1960's would provide a better base for market price appreciation than we had in the 1950's.

However, there is another very important statistical quantity in the projection of market prices. This is the price-earnings ratio, or market price divided by current annual earnings per share. In purely quantitative terms, the principal explanation for the bull market of the fifties is the remarkable increase in price-earnings ratios. The data for Standard & Poor's industrial stocks show that price-earnings ratios rose from 6.3 in 1949 to 17.5 in 1959. What this means is that investors were paying almost three times as much for a dollar of current earnings per share in 1959 as in 1949. When this tripling of the price-earnings ratio is compared with the quadrupling of stock prices in the same period, it becomes apparent that about three-fourths of the rise in stock prices in the past decade was caused by the bidding up of prices relative to earnings.

There was a similar development in the relationship of market prices to current annual dividends. In 1949, average prices were 13.3 times cash dividends; in 1959, prices were 32.5 times dividends.

If the tripling of the price-earnings ratio in the past decade could be projected into the next decade, the model would show an even greater rise in market prices than that of the fifties. But such a projection does not seem at all reasonable, given the assumptions about developments in our economic and social system set forth above. It would mean that in 1970 average industrial stocks would sell at 53 times earnings and provide a dividend yield of only a little more than 1 per cent.

The historical record of marked variation in the relationship of prices to earnings suggests that during the next decade changes in this ratio will be the most important influence upon the level of stock prices. Recognizing the wide range of possible variation, we have projected stock prices at 12, at 15, and at 18 times projected earnings per share. The projected price trend lines in the figure indicate the area within which prices will probably fluctuate if our assumptions are approximately correct.

These three price-earnings ratios represent extrapolation of past experience modified by some subjective conclusions. There have been few times in history when the price-earnings ratio for a broad group of stocks has exceeded 18, and these periods have

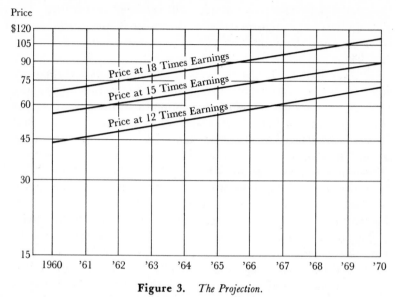

Figure 3.   *The Projection.*

been of relatively short duration. When the price-earnings ratio gets up around this level, stocks come to be regarded as high-priced, market observers talk of overvaluation, and investors become more cautious. Also, at such a high ratio of prices to earnings, dividend yields fall to such low levels that stocks become less attractive than bonds to investors interested in income. At 18 times earnings and with a 60 per cent dividend payout ratio, stocks would yield 3⅓ per cent.

Common stocks have often sold at less than 12 times earnings in the past, and lower ratios have prevailed for periods of years. But the assumptions we have made about the growth of the economy, continued creeping inflation, moderate cyclical fluctuations in business, and a political climate generally favorable to the private enterprise system imply that the 12-times-earnings level will be approximately the minimum for the next decade. Lower ratios will develop only if investors experience a substantial loss of confidence in the future profitability of American business. At 12 times earnings, stocks would yield 5 per cent. In the economy we visualize, this rate would be attractive to investors seeking income relative to yields on other kinds of investments.

The projection of stock prices at 15 times earnings is simply a splitting of the difference between the figures taken to represent the approximate upper and lower limits of the price-earnings ratio. It is the median around which this ratio is expected to fluctuate. At 15 times earnings, stocks would yield 4 per cent.

The stock price trends for the sixties developed from our earlier calculation of average earnings per share and these three levels of price-earnings ratios show a continued upward movement. If the ratio of 12 times earnings predominates, the Standard & Poor's industrial stock average will increase very modestly in the next decade from the 1959 average of $61.83 to about $72.96 in 1970. That is an increase of only about 18 per cent for the period, and is tiny relative to the 400 percent increase of the fifties. Our most optimistic projection at the level of 18 times earnings shows a 77 per cent increase in the value of stocks in the sixties. This is a healthy rate of growth, but it falls considerably short of the strong bull market of recent years.

The picture of stock price trends in the 1960's that finally emerges from this process of reasoning and arithmetic may fall short of the current expectations of optimistic investors, but it amply supports the proposition that diversified investments in common stocks of leading industrial companies are likely to provide good returns over the longer term. The rise in market prices in the 1960's will be much less steep than in the 1950's because the

Earnings and Dividends

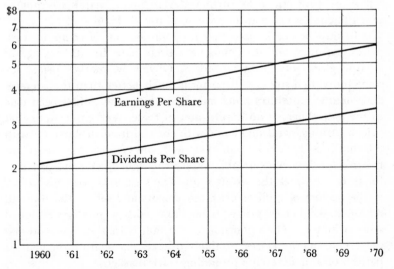

Figure 4. *Earnings and Dividends.*

inflation of stock prices in relation to earnings has about run its course. But the prospect for growth in earnings per share at an average annual rate of 5 per cent provides the basis for continued appreciation in market prices for common stocks. At a constant price-earnings ratio, the growth of earnings per share would result in price appreciation at the average annual rate of 5 per cent.

The rate of dividend income would be between $3\frac{1}{4}$ and 5 per cent at time of purchase, depending upon the level of stock prices at the time. If we take the median yield of 4 per cent and add average annual price appreciation at about 5 per cent, the combined return is 9 per cent a year. This rate certainly compares favorably with conventional rates of return on investment. Moreover, dividend income should increase over the long term, and capital gains are not subject to income tax until realized (and then only at a maximum rate of 25 per cent).

Any statistical model of prospective future developments such as the one we have developed is subject to error because no one can foresee the future. But the process of building a model is probably the best way we have of trying to estimate the future. It requires one to think in an orderly fashion, to set forth explicitly his assumptions and judgments, and to translate his conclusions from general terms to quantitative terms. When the model has been built, it can easily be re-examined from time to time, and, if need be, altered. To revise projections as further developments require is not so much to confess error as to make good use of the model.

It must be emphasized that these projections of common stock prices, earnings, and dividends have been made for the average of a large group of industrial stocks. Obviously, market prices for some individual stocks will perform much better than the average, and some will perform much more poorly, as has always been true in the past. There is no implication in these trend projections that prices, earnings, and dividends will not continue to fluctuate with the business cycle. The market will always provide abundant rewards for those who are able to pick the right stocks, and penalties for those who pick the wrong ones. The sagacious people who buy at the bottom of cyclical price movements and sell at the top will realize much better profits than those with a poorly developed sense of timing. The important conclusion is that all these normal vagaries of market prices are likely to take place within the general pattern of a moderately uptrending stock market.

6. SOME INVESTMENT ASPECTS
OF ACCUMULATION
THROUGH EQUITIES*

❋ Benjamin Graham

I

THE TERMS OF REFERENCE for this paper relate to systematic plans
for saving or accumulation through common stocks. Such plans
might include (a) a pension plan concentrating on equities, such
as the CREF arrangement for college professors; (b) the very similar
mechanics of the newly developing variable annuities; (c) systematic
purchases of mutual-fund or closed-end investment company shares;
and (d) an individual dollar-averaging plan, such as the monthly-
purchase program of the New York Stock Exchange.

The chairman has asked me to consider investment aspects of
such plans in longer perspective and to give my views on the following questions: What results can be expected from them in the future
as compared with the results either of the shorter-term past—i.e.,
since 1949—or of the longer-term past, going back into the last
century and farther? How good will common stocks be as an
inflation hedge in the future? Can dollar-averaging be counted on
infallibly to produce satisfactory results? More specifically, can the
much better performance of common stocks as against bonds be
counted on to repeat itself in the next fifteen years?

* From *The Journal of Finance*, Vol. XVII, No. 2 (May, 1962), pp. 203–214. Reprinted by permission of *The Journal of Finance*.

I shall leave the chances and the effects of atomic war out of the following discussion, except for some observations regarding the indefinite continuance of the Cold War. Which of the two past periods will the future stock market resemble more closely—that of 1949–61 or that of, say, 1871–1961?

The latter comprises the 90 years for which we have common-stock indexes of earnings, dividends, and prices, as compiled first by the Cowles Commission and then continued by Standard & Poor's. In discussing equity experience in terms of the future behavior of these indexes, we are assuming that the various equity-accumulation plans within our purview are likely to show results, in the aggregate, approximating those of the S-P Composite or 500-Stock Index. It would seem easy enough to equal these average results; all that is needed is a representative diversification "across the board" and without that selectivity which is a watchword of today. But, paradoxically, if it is easy to equal the averages, it seems almost impossible for the average skilled investor to beat them.

We have very full information regarding the operations and achievements of the investment funds. For the 1949–60 period, as in the earlier years, they have not managed as a group to outperform the S-P 500 Stock Composite. It may be that professionally managed funds are too large a part of the total picture to be able to outperform the market as a whole; it may also be true, as I suspect, that certain weaknesses in their basic principles of stock selection tend to offset the superior training, intelligence, and effort that they bring to this task. But our main point is to establish that what happens to the stock market in general is going to happen to the typical or average accumulator of equities by any plan or under any auspices.

Let us attempt to summarize briefly the chief characteristics of the two market periods to which we are turning for clues to the future and among which we may have to choose. Table 1 gives some data covering the three salient factors of earnings, dividends, and price behavior. We bring down the 1949–61 period into two 6-year halves. The longer span can be handled in a variety of ways; we have decided to supply average computations for each of the nine decades between 1871 and 1961.

A cursory study of our table shows a number of striking differences between the exhibits of the two periods. Molodovsky has demonstrated that the over-all gain to investors for the 88 years,

Table 1.* A Picture of Stock-Market Performance, 1871–1960 and 1947–61

PERIOD	AVERAGE PRICE	AVERAGE EARNINGS	AVERAGE P/E RATIO	AVERAGE DIVIDEND	AVERAGE YIELD (PER CENT)	AVERAGE PAYOUT (PER CENT)	ANNUAL GROWTH RATE † EARNINGS (PER CENT)	DIVIDENDS (PER CENT)
1871–80	3.58	0.32	11.3×	0.21	6.0	67	—	—
1881–90	5.00	0.32	15.6	0.24	4.7	75	−0.64	−0.66
1891–1900	4.65	0.30	15.5	0.19	4.0	64	−1.04	−2.23
1901–10	8.32	0.63	13.1	0.35	4.2	58	+6.91	+5.33
1911–20	8.62	0.86	10.0	0.50	5.8	58	+3.85	+3.94
1921–30	13.89	1.05	13.3	0.71	5.1	68	+2.84	+2.29
1931–40	11.55	0.68	17.0	0.78	5.1	85	−2.15	−0.23
1941–50	13.90	1.46	9.5	0.87	6.3	60	+10.60	+3.25
1951–60	39.20	3.00	13.1	1.63	4.2	54	+6.74	+5.90
1951	22.34	2.45	9.1	1.41	6.3	58	—	—
1961 (H)	72.20	3.10	23.2	1.97	2.7	64	+2.5	+3.5
1947–49	15.71	2.18	7.1	0.97	6.4	45	—	—
1953–55	31.64	3.02	10.1	1.51	4.8	50	+5.7	+7.8
1959–61	59.70	3.24	18.3	1.91	3.2	58	+3.5	+5.9

* The above data are based largely on figures appearing in N. Molodovsky's article "Stock Values and Stock Prices," *Financial Analysts Journal*, May, 1960. These, in turn, are taken from the Cowles Commission book *Common Stock Indexes* for years before 1926 and from the spliced-on Standard-Poor's 500-Stock Composite Index for 1926 to date.

† The annual growth-rate figures are Molodovsky compilations covering successive 21-year periods ending in 1890, 1900, etc. The 1961 price is the high to December 7.

1871–1959, has averaged about 5 per cent per annum in dividend return and $2\frac{1}{2}$ per cent per annum in price appreciation—both taken against annual market prices. The $2\frac{1}{2}$ per cent annual increase, compounded, in market price was closely paralleled by the annual rate of growth in both earnings and dividends.[1]

But between 1947–49 and 1959–61 the growth rates for the various components have been quite diverse, and they have also varied sharply between the first and the second halves of the period. Thus we get very different indications of recent performance if we consider earnings rather than market price and if we consider the last 6 years rather than the last 12.

The behavior of the stock market itself has been significantly different in the last 12 years from any previous period of equal length covered by our records. We have experienced what appears to be a single bull market, beginning at 13.55 for the composite index and rising to a current high of 72. The advance has been interrupted by three recessions, each on the order of some 20 per cent. Under the usual terminology, these would be characterized as corrections or setbacks within a bull market.

As is well known, the long-term history of the stock market has been completely different. The picture, shown in Table 2, is one of a succession of bull and bear markets of varying duration and amplitude. Between 1899 and 1949 there were ten such well-defined cycles, thus averaging 5 years in length. (The longest period between peaks was 10 years, from 1919 to 1929, and the shortest was 2 years, from 1899 to 1901 and from 1937 to 1937.) Most of the declines in the industrial averages were in the range of 40–50 per cent; in the earlier years the composite average had somewhat smaller losses. The largest, of course, was the shocking fall of the Composite Index from 31.92 in 1929 to a low of only 4.40 in 1932, a loss of 86 per cent. About the same proportionate decline was shown by the Dow-Jones Industrial Average.

It should be pointed out also that the gyrations of past stock markets may not properly be viewed as taking place around a well-defined and persistent upward trend line, sloped at $2\frac{1}{2}$ per cent per annum. Both the price record and the earnings record disclose an irregular, rather than a regular, trend line. This should be evident

---

[1] See N. Molodovsky, "Stock Values and Stock Prices," *Financial Analysts Journal*, March, 1960.

Table 2. *Major Stock-Market Swings Between 1871 and 1949*

	Cowles-Standard 500-Composite			Dow-Jones Industrial Average		
YEAR	HIGH	LOW	PER CENT DECLINE	HIGH	LOW	PER CENT DECLINE
1871	—	4.74	—	—	—	—
1881	6.58	—	—	—	—	—
1885	—	4.24	28	—	—	—
1887	5.90	—	—	—	—	—
1893	—	4.08	31	—	—	—
1897	—	—	—	—	38.85	—
1899	—	—	—	77.6	—	—
1900	—	—	—	—	53.5	31
1901	8.50	—	—	78.3	—	—
1903	—	6.26	26	—	43.2	45
1906	10.03	—	—	103	—	—
1907	—	6.25	38	—	53	48
1909	10.30	—	—	100.5	—	—
1914	—	7.35	29	—	53.2	47
1916	10.21	—	—	110.2	—	—
1917/8	—	6.80	33	—	73.4	33
1919	9.51	—	—	119.6	—	—
1921	—	6.45	32	—	63.9	47
1929	31.92	—	—	381	—	—
1932	—	4.40	86	—	41.2	89
1937	18.68	—	—	197.4	—	—
1938	—	8.50	55	—	99	50
1939	13.23	—	—	158	—	—
1942	—	7.47	44	—	92.9	41
1946	19.25	—	—	212.5	—	—
1949	—	13.55	30	—	161.2	24

from an inspection of our successive 10-year average figures between 1871 and 1950 and the Molodovsky growth rates appended thereto.

The price-earnings ratio has also shown wide fluctuations. Since earnings have been even more unstable than prices—because of the recurrent business cycles—there has been a clear-cut tendency for the highest earnings multipliers to be established in years of depression, when profits tended toward the vanishing point. Our average figures by decades smooth out this type of variation; but they do not show the upward trend in price-earnings ratios that we might have expected to accompany improvement in the underlying strength of our corporations and in the dependability of published earnings pictures. Actually, the ratio of 6.2 times for 1949–50, at the beginning of the present bull market, was the lowest for any 2-year period in our 90-year history of stock prices and earnings. A devotee of the pendulum-swing theory of economic phenomena might well explain the current record-high multiplier as a reaction to the opposite extreme from the 1949–50 depreciation of the earnings dollar.

II

With these two quite diverse stock-market pictures before us, let us now inquire what are the respective arguments for considering the 1949–61 period as an integral continuation of the 1871–1949 span or for recognizing it as a new dispensation which will determine the character of the markets of the future. It is not too difficult for the student to fit the pattern of the recent market into that of the longer past. True, both the duration and the extent of its rise are already greater than those of any other.[2] But that a pattern of many decades should establish new records of various kinds from time to time is only to be expected. A new record does not create a new pattern or character.

Is it possible, then, that we are living through a modified, but not necessarily different, version of the experience of the 1920's? That there must be impressive differences goes without saying; for otherwise all of us would have been so struck by the incipient similarity as to make its continuation impossible. What may be more likely—speaking in abstract terms—is that the original differences have convinced us that the 1929 experience is irrelevant but that the similarities have been developing later, gradually, and so insidiously as to find us psychologically incapable of recognizing them. Let us attempt an enumeration of the major differences and resemblances between the current market and that of the 1920's, as they appear to this observer.

The two major internal differences relate to financial manipulation of various sorts and to excessive borrowing for speculation. The bull-market heights of 1929 were made possible

[2] These statements refer to the S-P Composite Index. The percentage rise in the industrials was somewhat larger from 1921 to 1929 than from 1949 to date, because it started from a relatively lower level.

by a huge wave of buying on thinner margins than are now permitted. Brokers' loans rose from $2.769 million in 1926 to $8.549 million in 1929, at which time they constituted about half of total member-bank loans. By contrast, the corresponding rise to date has been relatively much smaller. (Borrowings on smaller margins through other sources are no doubt significant at present but not sufficiently so to change the broad picture.) In the field of financial practices, the major abuses of the 1920's consisted of crass manipulation of stock prices by speculative pools and of corporate pyramiding through successive tiers of holding companies of various types. Both stock-market manipulation and corporate-structure manipulation have been greatly restricted by the SEC legislation and by tighter stock-exchange supervision. The amount that escapes detection is comparatively small, in my view. Although the various investigations now under way produce some startling exposés, whatever abuses now exist will not be found to have permeated the whole fabric of finance as was the case 30 years ago.

An exception to the above reassuring statement may have to be made in the field of new offerings of common stocks. Here I think a set of at least semi-manipulative practices has developed in handling so-called "hot issues." The number of such offerings has been increasing steadily in the last 2 years, and their quality has been retrogressing at an equal rate. It is in this speculative area that I sense the closest parallel between the internal market conditions of the late 1920's (and particularly of 1919) and those of today. Whether the new-issue financing of dubious merit will prove to be so heavy in aggregate dollars as ultimately to turn the market scales definitely downward, I shall not venture to guess. It is not impossible.

The widespread belief that we are in a new stock-market era, differing in its essential character from the bull-and-bear sequences of the past, rests on a number of claimed differences between then and now. These go well beyond the reforms in stock trading and in corporate financial practices. The case to justify the present unprecedented level of stock prices and earnings multipliers is essentially that which would justify the concept of a permanently changed character and future for the stock market. The safety and attractiveness of common-stock investment today is thought to be solidly grounded on a complex of favorable factors. Among them are (a) assured growth of population and GNP; (b) a rate of expansion more rapid than formerly, created by technological progress and the rivalry with Russia; (c) an assurance against major depressions provided by the government's new responsibility to prevent or quickly terminate them; (d) the public's recognition that common-stock investment is a necessary protection against continued inflation; and (e) the emergence of mutual funds, pension trusts, and other institutional investors as the chief source of demand and continuous support for common stocks.

Those who study the record of the 1920's will find that reasons similar to most, but not all, of the above were advanced to justify the ill-fated market rise of those years. The doctrine of "Common Stocks as (the Best) Long-Term Investments" emerged in 1924 and was made the cornerstone of the market's philosophy and its excesses. There was the same optimism about the future growth of the country and perhaps a better-founded confidence in the share of common-stock earnings in that growth. (The rate of return on invested capital was better maintained between 1922 and 1929 than between 1950 and 1961.) Old standards of value—particularly the once normal relationship between bond yields and common-stock yields—were thrown aside then as now, on the grounds that they had no relevance to the new economic climate. There was great confidence, also, in the future stability of business and its immunity from severe depressions. This was founded on the idea that scientific management, careful control of inventories, the absence of inflation, and other factors would help our business leaders avoid the costly mistakes of the past.

In my view, there are three major differences between the economic realities of the 1920's and the present. The first relates to the inflation factor, the second to the Cold War, and the third to the role of government in business. The bull market of the 1920's ran its course without the aid of commodity-price inflation; the market rise since 1949 has been accompanied by an irregular, but virtually continuous, advance in wholesale and consumer prices. It is difficult to say whether the investor's current emphasis on future inflation possibilities should be considered primarily as a recognition on his part of objective fact or rather as a strong subjective reaction to an element that is by no means new to the financial scene. We had more inflation in wholesale prices from 1900 to 1910 than from 1950 to 1960; the rise from 1900 to 1920 also exceeded that from 1940 to 1960 (the equivalent of from 36 to 100 versus from 51 to 120). Most of us believe that inflation is the path of least resistance for governments, labor leaders, and business heads and that hence it will be followed. But the record of the past will not help us much to determine what the amount of inflation will be over future decades, whether its course will be regular or interspersed with sharp deflations, as in 1921 and 1932, and whether investors will remain as inflation-conscious in the future as they are today. The reaction to inflation, like almost every other investment and speculative attitude, seems to be more the result of the stock market's behavior than the cause of it.

My view of the effects of the Cold War on common-stock values is quite a personal one, not shared by many, I am sure. In the first place, I think that it has contributed a good deal to the business expansion and relative stability of the past decade. But, in a contrary sense, I cannot see how the kind of Cold War we are now living through can continue throughout "our lifetime and that of our children." Sometime within the present decade, a way will have to be found to terminate the Cold War, or it will be transformed into large-scale hostilities, with all their nuclear implications. If our prosperity since 1949 has, in fact, rested rather heavily on our defense expenditures and if, in truth, we must fairly soon have either no war or nuclear war in place of Cold War, then today's international situation cannot be termed more favorable for common stocks than the cloudless one of 1929.

The government's commitment to prevent large-scale unemployment and serious depressions is both a new factor and one of major importance. The most logical reason for expecting a different kind of stock-market cycle in the future than in the long-term past would appear to be by analogy with the business cycle. The record since 1949 strongly supports this thesis. The new material on "Business Cycle Developments," now available monthly, shows four periods of business contraction since 1948—in 1949, 1953–54, 1957–58, and 1960. All these were very moderate, as compared with the sharp recession of 1937–38 and the major depressions after 1919 and 1929. The three declines of about 20 per cent each in the stock averages since 1950 appear to correspond fairly well to the three setbacks of about 10 per cent in the index of industrial production. If we have now entered a new era that excludes old-time business depressions, it seems reasonable to deduce that we are also in a new era that precludes old-fashioned bear markets.

III

Both my analysis and my instinct warn me that there may be a catch in this plausible and reassuring parallel. If the recent picture had been one of the stock market's advancing in step with the national product and in close proportion with it also, then the observer might conclude—somewhat to his amazement—that not only has the economy been reformed but human nature as well. But here the facts part company with the hypothesis. The stock-market level has not been governed primarily by the level of business but rather by the development of new investment theories and attitudes and by a typical growth of speculative interest and activity. Some of the old financial abuses that characterized former bull markets have, indeed, been virtually eliminated. But some have again raised their heads, and some new ones have appeared and are spreading apace. These are in the areas of corporate reporting, corporate financing, the quality of the enterprises offered for public sale, and the ways in which new issues of common stocks are offered and subsequently traded.

Equally important and dangerous, in my eyes, is the ready acceptance by security analysts of the going market levels and earnings-multipliers as the proper standard of value and of comparison for any issue under study. The new analytical concepts of growth-stock valuation, of "cash flow," of the desirability of tax-free dividends from companies which are triumphantly able to report earnings deficits—all have enough plausibility and lack of inner discipline to lead both investors and speculators far astray. In sum, the new investment theories and techniques remind me very much of 1928–29, and the outpouring of common-stock issues of secondary and lower-degree enterprises reminds me equally of 1919. If the relative stability of general business and corporate profits produces an unlimited enthusiasm and demand for common stocks, then it must eventually produce instability in stock prices. We have already seen the working of this paradox in the area of growth stocks. The price of a successful and promising concern such as Texas Instruments can be driven up so high by speculative emphasis on its prospects that the ensuing reaction has cut the price in half—with no change in the underlying worth of the business. Examples of this sort are now numerous. Conceivably, this behavior of issues in the growth-stock class may give us a preview of the ultimate behavior of the general market—as represented by comprehensive averages—if common-stock investment becomes essentially identical with common-stock speculation. In that case the stock market will have a life-cycle of its own, quite independent of the business cycle. The market cycle will once more prove to be the human-nature cycle; its economic background will have changed but not its basic character or the consequences of its character.

These arguments against a new character for the stock market are not necessarily arguments that the present levels are too high, although they certainly would be adjudged so by older standards. Conceivably and even probably, new factors in the economic figure have moved upward the central value of the average dollar of corporate earnings and justify a more favorable relationship than heretofore between stock yields and bond yields. This would certainly be true if the general business picture can be counted on to continue indefinitely the relative immunity to depression it has shown since as far back as 1941. What we are concerned with here is not the future central value of the stock market but rather the amplitude and the consequences of possible future variations around this value.

To soften a possible charge of old-fogyism and prejudice against new standards of value, may I take this paragraph to show how the recent record level of stock prices may be justified by some not implausible calculations. Let us assume that the investor wants an over-all return of $7\frac{1}{2}$ per cent annually, as a composite of dividend income and average market appreciation. (This $7\frac{1}{2}$ per cent target is itself taken from the long-term record of dividend yields and price advances; it seems reasonable as a guide to the future.) Assume, next, that earnings and dividends will grow in the indefinite future at the annual rate of $4\frac{1}{2}$ per cent, which appears to be the projection for this decade. Then the investor should be satisfied with a 3 per cent dividend return. This would justify a current level of 65 for the S-P Composite, only 10 per cent below the recent high. A small adjustment here or there would put us over the top.

It is by no means impossible to assume a permanent growth rate of $4\frac{1}{2}$ per cent; we have been told that we must increase our GNP faster than this or lose out in the race with Russia. The basic objection is that it is only an assumption, that the experience of the longer past puts the figure rather at $2\frac{1}{2}$ per cent and that the difference between $4\frac{1}{2}$ and $2\frac{1}{2}$ per cent in this calculation means the difference between 65 and 39 for the value of the S-P Composite. My experience leads me to predict that the action of the market will govern the investor's choice as to probable future growth rates rather than vice versa.

This completes my case for and against a new era and character for the stock market. If the market since 1949 foreshadows the stock markets of the future, the investment aspects of equity accumulation are unbelievably favorable. All that will be needed will be the funds to buy a representative assortment of common stocks and a little patience to sit through periods of mild reaction. The annually compounded rate of over-all return from the 500-Stock Composite has been about 13 per cent—curiously enough, this has been about the same as the average from a selected list of growth stocks.[3] A much lower annual rate, without severe interruptions, will prove amply rewarding.

IV

But if, as I deem more likely, the fundamental character of the stock market must be as unchanging as that of human nature, then the accumulator of equities who starts today is faced with quite a different prospect. The new appearance of the variable annuity suggests a broad analogy with the 1920's. It was during that bull market that investment trusts had their first important development in this country. Most of the arguments in their favor were the same as those now used for the sale of mutual-fund shares and for equity accumulation in general. The collapse of 1929 resulted in a severe and protracted setback for the investment-trust movement, as part of a widespread loss of faith in common stocks generally. It is true that many—although perhaps less than half—managed to survive the bitter subsequent experience and to re-establish themselves more firmly than before in public esteem. Furthermore, the principle of dollar-cost averaging—which is the most systematic of the equity-accumulation techniques—was able to vindicate itself in the end, after perhaps 20 years of unsatisfactory-to-mediocre results.[4]

[3] See, for example, J. F. Bohmfalk, Jr., "The Growth Stock Philosophy" *Financial Analysts Journal*, November, 1960, Table A.
[4] For calculated results of dollar-cost-averaging results for 10-year periods ending from 1929 through 1952, see Lucile Tomlinson, *Practical Formulas for Successful Investing* (New York: Wilfred Funk, 1953), Table 3, p. 62.

The computations made of theoretical dollar-averaging experience in the past embolden us to predict that such a policy will pay off ultimately, regardless of when it is begun, provided that it is adhered to conscientiously and courageously under all intervening conditions. This is by no means a minor proviso. It presupposes that the dollar-cost-averager will be a different sort of person from the rest of us, that he will not be subject to the alternations of exhilaration and deep gloom that have accompanied the gyrations of the stock market for generations past. This, I greatly doubt—particularly because most of the dollar-cost-averagers we are speaking of will be typical members of the public who have been persuaded to embark on an equity-accumulation program by the arts of salesmanship now so highly developed in the mutual-fund field.

Let me return once again to the problem of the proper perspective for viewing the character of the stock market and the investment aspects of equity accumulation. At the outset I presented a statistical comparison of the market's behavior over the last 12 years and over the last 90 years. But our knowledge of stock-market behavior goes back a good deal more than 90 years—a full two centuries and a half, in fact, to the inception of the South Sea Company in 1711. In our first edition of *Security Analysis,* published in 1934, we characterized the stock-market madness of the 1920's as a repetition or rerun of the famous South Sea Bubble. By comparison, the behavior of our present market appears more rational, dignified, and reassuring. No one today, not even ingrained conservatives (like this speaker), expects consequences to this market and the economy even faintly resembling the catastrophe of 1929–32. Yet I have a feeling that the financial world has become too complacent about the future, too confident of the invulnerability of common stocks as a whole to a drastic change in their fortunes.

A great corporation can withstand great vicissitudes; the same is true of great institutions, among which not the least important is common-stock investment and equity accumulation over a span of time. But a bull market has never become a financial institution, and I have great doubts whether this attractive development is an admissible possibility, when the frailty of human nature is taken into account.

My own inward picture of the present stock market is that of an institution cut adrift from old standards of value without having found dependable new standards. (In this respect present-day investment may be in somewhat the same position as present-day painting.) The market may either return to the old measures of central value or—as is perhaps more probable—eventually establish a new and more liberal basis for evaluating equities. If the first happens, common stocks will prove highly disappointing over a long period for many accumulators of equities. If the newer and higher value levels are to be established on a sound basis, I envisage this working out by a process of trial and error, covering an unpredictable period of time and a number of pendulum swings of unforeseeable magnitude. I do not know whether bonds will do better than stocks over the next 15 years, but I do know that the people behind College Retirement Equity Fund (CREF) are eminently wise in insisting that its beneficiaries have at least an equal dollar stake in bond as in stock investment.

7. DIVIDEND POLICIES AND COMMON STOCK PRICES[*]

❀ James E. Walter

I

IN A RECENT ISSUE OF THIS JOURNAL, Professor Harkavy presented a statistical analysis of the relationship between retained earnings and common stock prices.[1] His principal conclusion is that, while common stock prices vary directly with dividend payout ratios at any given time, their degree of appreciation over a period of time is associated with the proportion of earnings which are retained. Only brief reference is made to the fact that the crucial consideration is the profitable utilization of investors' funds. Empirical studies of this type should be encouraged and are of definite value provided careful consideration is given, both before and after their preparation, to the underlying theoretical propositions.

Based upon the belief that stock-market behavior is susceptible of rationalization, an attempt is made in this paper to fabricate a theoretical model which depicts the relationship between dividend policies and common stock prices. Attention is of necessity restricted to the common stocks of large public corporations because of the imperfect market for the securities of small companies and of the

[*] From *The Journal of Finance*, Vol. XI, No. 1 (March, 1956), pp. 29–41. Reprinted by permission of *The Journal of Finance*.
[1] Oscar Harkavy, "The Relation between Retained Earnings and Common Stock Prices for Large, Listed Corporation," *Journal of Finance*, Vol. VIII, No. 3 (Sept., 1953), pp. 283–97.

close identification of small firms with their principal shareholders. The fundamental premise upon which the formulation rests is that, over longer periods, stock prices reflect the present values of expected dividends.[2] The phrase "over long periods" is inserted to permit abstraction from the distortions caused by short-run speculative considerations.

Granted this premise, retained earnings influence stock prices principally through their effect upon future dividends. The fact that some stocks may have substantial market value even though little or no dividends are anticipated in the foreseeable future need not contradict this proposition. Undistributed earnings are immediately realizable to the shareholder, at least in part, provided prospective investors can be found who are willing to wait and to assume the required risk.

In analyzing the present worth of future dividends, the concept of capitalization rate is utilized in preference to that of multiplier, which is customarily employed by security analysts. The capitalization rate for any stock is simply the reciprocal of the multiplier. Since capitalization rates are expressed in percentage terms, their use simplifies the presentation and facilitates direct comparisons with rates of return on additional investment.

Capitalization rates are determined by the underlying yield on safe securities and by the required risk premiums. The yield on safe securities is conditioned by such factors as monetary and debt policy, income distribution, the intensity of present as opposed to future wants, and productivity. The basic risk premium, as measured by the difference between the yield on safe securities and the capitalization rate on high-grade common stocks, is dependent upon the economic climate and government policy. Interindustry differences in size, capital structure, efficiency, and diversification occasion substantial variations in capitalization rates among corporations.

The level and diversity of capitalization rates influence the succeeding analysis in at least two respects. The higher the level of capitalization rates, both individually and generally, the fewer are the companies whose stocks qualify as growth stocks. The greater the diversity of capitalization rates and the more numerouus their determinants, the less feasible it becomes to talk in terms

[2] See J. B. Williams, *The Theory of Investment Value* (Cambridge: Harvard University Press, 1938), p. 6, for a similar position.

of average or normal capitalization rates. The concept of market capitalization rate must therefore be defined arbitrarily in order to exclude irrelevant heterogenity.

The proposition that all common stocks behave in a reasonably uniform manner does not appear to be warranted by the observed variations in stock prices. As a result, three groups, referred to respectively as growth stock, intermediate and creditor stock categories, are isolated for consideration. A fourth possibility, the declining stock category, is ignored because of its presumed unimportance in a growing economy.

Diversity of dividend policy is often regarded as one of the principal features which differentiate among these groups. Growth stocks are customarily characterized by low dividend payout ratios; intermediate stocks, by medium to high ratios; and creditor stocks, by fixed dividend rates irrespective of short-run earnings. With the possible exception of creditor stock, however, the dividend-earnings relationship is neither a necessary nor a sufficient condition for assigning stocks to any given category. The crucial consideration is the rate of return on additional investment. The greater the profitability, the more likely is management—in the interests of rapid expansion—to retain a substantial percentage of earnings.

II

The concept "growth stock" is familiar to investors and is understood to refer, in general terms, to common stocks which possess superior prospects for long-term appreciation. Surface characteristics of growth stocks include low dividend payout ratios, high market multipliers (i.e., low capitalization rates), and prices which increase through time with relative rapidity. Low dividend payout ratios constitute an accepted feature of growth stocks, since shareholders are presumed to benefit more from the retention of earnings than from their employment elsewhere at the going rates.

In qualifying for membership in the growth stock category, marginal profitability is the basic criterion. The rate of return on additional investment determines the magnitude of future dividends obtainable from given amounts of retained earnings or external financing. The anticipated level of future dividends, when discounted at the appropriate capitalization rate, in turn yields the present value for a given stock. If the rate of return on added investment is sufficiently great, it follows that low dividend payout ratios may add to, rather than subtract from, stock values.

For the purpose of demonstrating the potential influence of retained earnings upon stock prices, let us assume that earnings retention is the sole source of additional funds; that both the rate of return on added investment and the market capitalization rate are constants; and that all increments to earnings are immediately distributed to shareholders. The market capitalization rate for any given corporation is defined as the reciprocal of the multiplier which would prevail in the market if the dividend payout ratio were 100 per cent.[3] Treating the stream of future earnings as perpetual (or at least of indefinite duration), the present value of any common stock can then be expressed in mathematical terms as

$$V_c = \frac{D + \dfrac{R_a}{R_c}(E - D)}{R_c} = \frac{E}{R_c} + \frac{R_a - R_c}{R_c{}^2}(E - D), \qquad (1)$$

where D is cash dividends, E is earnings, R_a is the rate of return on additional investment, and R_c is the marked capitalization rate.[4]

Equation (1) reveals the importance of both the dividend payout ratio and the relationship between R_a and R_c. Whenever R_a exceeds R_c, the present worth of future dividends resulting from

[3] This definition is introduced simply to preclude the possibility that capitalization rates will be interpreted to reflect the effect of varying dividend policies. To illustrate, let us assume that companies A and B have identical earnings per share ($10), R_a (20 per cent), and R_c (10 per cent), but have payout ratios of 75 per cent and 50 percent respectively. Substituting in equation (1), we find that A has a V_c *of* $125 and B, of $150. The ratio of E to V_c, which might be called the unadjusted or composite capitalization rate, is thus 8 per cent for A and 6-2/3 per cent for B. The difference is attributable to divergent dividend policies.

[4] The second version of equation (1) is presented to show the extent to which V_c will exceed (or fall short of) the ratio of E to R_c. As in the case of most gross simplifications, equation (1) presents difficulties if used without modification. To illustrate the point and to indicate the type of modification which might be made, let us consider time as an endless succession of periods. Based upon equation (1) and its underlying assumptions, the value of the stock in question will rise in each period (without cessation) by an amount equal to $R_a (E - D)/R_c$. Since diminishing returns are an almost inevitable consequence, R_a must be viewed — for practical purposes — as a weighted average of $r_1, r_2, \ldots, r_{n-1}$, where r represents the rate of return on added investment at any given point (period) in time and $r_n = 0$. By weighted is simply meant that r_1, r_2, etc., must, because of the proximity to the present, be assigned greater importance than r_{n-1}, r_{n-2}, etc.

the retention of earnings is greater than the dollar magnitude of retained earnings. The lower the dividend payout ratio, under such circumstances, the higher is the value of the growth stock.

A currently high rate of return on additional investment for a given corporation need not automatically transform its stock into a growth stock. In the first place, the high rate must persist over a reasonable period of time. The market's judgment of a common stock is of necessity based primarily upon past experience. The corporation's willingness to invest is also influenced by the anticipated permanence of R_a to the extent that increments to earnings lag behind the retention of earnings. In the second place, high rates of return on added investment must not be offset by correspondingly high market capitalization rates. In so far as new industries are characterized by small, insufficiently capitalized firms and mature industries by large, conservatively financed companies, R_a and R_c may well be directly associated.

As observed in footnote 4, modifications in equation (1), which provide added realism at the expense of simplicity, do not alter the results in any fundamental respect. Anticipated declines in the return on additional investment (R_a) affect stock values and raise serious doubts as to the propriety of permanently low dividend payout ratios. As long as R_a continues to exceed R_c, however, the substantial retention of earnings appears beneficial to shareholders.

The recognition of external sources of new financing enables growth stocks to possess low "composite" capitalization rates even in the presence of high dividend payout ratios.[5] The market in effect endeavors to forecast the willingness and ability to use external sources and discounts future dividends attributable thereto. Despite this consideration, stock prices can still be expected to vary inversely with dividend payout ratios, provided R_a exceeds R_c.

Even without reference to capital gains taxation, the market appears justified in according special treatment to growth stocks in the sense of low "composite" capitalization rates. The all-pervasiveness of uncertainty may of course occasion conservative interpretations of future earnings and may restrict recognized membership

---

[5] The prevailing ratio of earnings to stock prices for a given company at any time can be thought of as a composite rate. The basic component is the market capitalization rate (R_c), as interpreted above. From R_c is deducted (if a growth stock) a percentage equivalent to the relative increase in the present worth of future dividends which is attributable to earnings retention or, as the case may be, to external financing.

in the growth stock category to a relatively few outstanding corporations. For doubtful cases, retained earnings and dividends may simply be regarded as equivalents. Alternatively, the prices of marginal growth stocks may be adversely affected, provided dividend payout ratios are below what the market believes to be a reasonable compromise.

At least one further factor functions to lessen the present worth of retained earnings relative to current dividends. This consideration concerns the emphasis placed upon balanced portfolios, i.e., diversification by investors. To the extent that the market values of growth stocks appreciate through time more rapidly than those of their asset holdings, investors may be induced to redistribute the increment among all components of their portfolios.[6]

Whenever portfolio readjustment must be achieved through the sale of shares, as opposed to the utilization of cash dividends, certain costs and risks are incurred.[7] Transfer costs, comprising commissions and taxes, have to be met. Market prices are conditioned by short-run influences and need not reflect longer-run capitalized values at any given time. In addition, the augmented supply of growth shares on the market—resulting from efforts to diversify—may depress their prices below what they otherwise would have been.

The consequence is that the appropriate test for growth stocks from the viewpoint of shareholders may not be simply R_a exceeds R_c, but rather R_a exceeds R_c by an amount sufficient to cover the cost of added diversification. That is to say,

$$V_c = \frac{D + \dfrac{R_a}{R_c + p}\,(E - D)}{R_c}, \tag{1a}$$

where p is the premium associated with the cost of diversification.

Except for outstanding cases, the isolation of growth stocks for empirical study does not appear to be a simple task. As suggested previously, changes in earnings from period to period are likely to

[6] The line of reasoning is quite similar to that underlying the "substitution effect" in the theory of consumer choice. For the sake of simplicity, however, it is assumed that the problem of present versus future consumption does not arise.
[7] As indicated subsequently, these considerations may be partially offset by the preferential tax treatment of capital gains.

be discontinuous and to be associated with past, rather than current, sources of funds. The reason is simply that the expansion of both facilities and markets takes time. The reported levels of historical earnings, which is the principal basis for estimating future earnings, are dependent upon arbitrary accounting techniques. In addition, price-level changes often provide a misleading illusion of growth. In some instances, these and other factors lead the market astray; in other cases, they lead the analyst to believe that the market's evaluation is incorrect when in actual fact it is not.

III

Preferential tax treatment of capital gains, as opposed to dividend income, affects growth stocks in at least two respects. It augments the value of retained earnings and hence increases growth stock prices, provided personal income taxes levied upon marginal shareholders exceed zero. It also gives certain superior non-growth stocks the status of growth stocks.

Wherever rates of return on additional investment are positive, the retention of earnings by corporations raises both the anticipated level and the present worth of future dividends. As the present values of future dividends change through time and are reflected in stock prices, shareholders are able to realize these gains by selling portions of their holdings. Shareholders benefit from this form of income realization to the extent that the preferential tax treatment of capital gains reduces their total tax. In addition, the realization criterion for the capital gains tax enables shareholders to time security sales so as to minimize further their total tax burden.

The presence of organized security exchanges limits rather substantially the observed impact of capital gains taxation. The more perfect the market in which common stocks are traded, the less is the ability to distinguish among buyers or sellers unless legal or institutional barriers are erected. In the absence of discrimination and of individual bargaining, only the tax savings derived by marginal shareholders from capital gains taxation will be reflected in security prices.

Equation (1) indicates that, given certain simplifying assumptions which do not distort the underlying relationships, a dollar of retained earnings is the equivalent of a dollar of dividends multiplied by the ratio of R_a to R_c. If this equivalence is adjusted for the special tax treatment of capital gains, the equation becomes

$$s = \frac{R_a}{R_c}; \quad \text{or} \quad R_a = \frac{t}{s}R_c, \tag{2}$$

where s is one minus the tax rate on capital gains and t is one minus the marginal tax rate on personal income, both as related to marginal shareholders. If allowance is also made for the existence of dividend tax credits, as provided in the recently passed technical tax relief bill (1954), form (2) is transformed into

$$R_a = \frac{t + c}{s}R_c, \tag{2a}$$

where c is the dividend tax credit, expressed in percentage terms.

Equations (2) and (2a) demonstrate that superior non-growth stocks may be raised to the status of growth stocks as a result of preferred tax treatment for capital gains. That is to say, the retention of earnings need not be disadvantageous to shareholders even though R_a is somewhat less than R_c.

For illustrative purposes, let us assume that the marginal tax rate on the personal income of marginal shareholders is 50 per cent; that the tax rate on capital gain is 25 per cent; that the dividend tax credit is 4 per cent; and that the market capitalization rate (R_c) is 10 per cent. Substituting these figures into equation (2a), R_a is found to be 7.2 per cent. At this point it is immaterial to marginal shareholders whether earnings are retained or distributed. In the event that R_c exceeds 7.2 per cent, under these conditions the stock in question takes on the characteristics of a growth stock.

Alternative assumptions may produce significantly different results. If, for example, the marginal tax rate on personal income is 20 per cent and the rate on capital gains is 10 per cent, R_a becomes 9.3 per cent. The basic propositions nonetheless continue to hold.

IV

A substantial majority of all "listed" industrial common stocks undoubtedly belong to the intermediate stock group. Surface characteristics of this category are dividend payout ratios in excess of

50 per cent, multipliers which range in the neighborhood of the average multiplier for all "listed" corporations, and prices which increase slowly through time. Shareholder pressure is exerted for substantial payout ratios, since stock prices tend to vary directly with the level of dividend payout ratios. Although the retention of earnings leads to appreciation in stock values, shareholders benefit from the receipt of dividends and their investment elsewhere at the going market rate.

In assigning stocks to this category, the underlying consideration is whether the present value of future dividends attributable to retained earnings at the margin is greater or less than the corresponding dollar amount of earnings retention. This question is essentially the same as that raised in connection with growth stocks. Its resolution hinges, in similar fashion, upon the relationship between R_a adjusted for the preferred tax treatment of capital gains, and R_c. As shown by equation (1) and as modified by equation (2), if "adjusted" R_a exceeds R_c, the common stock in question is a growth stock; if "adjusted" R_a is less than R_c but greater than zero, it is an intermediate stock.

The preponderance of the intermediate stock group, particularly where large and mature public corporations are concerned, apparently leads many investment analysts to recommend high dividend payout ratios as a general rule. The best-known advocates, Graham and Dodd, state that the investment value of any industrial common stock equals

$$M(D + \tfrac{1}{3} E), \tag{3}$$

where M, the multiplier, is the reciprocal of the "assumed" appropriate capitalization rate, D is expected dividends, and E is expected earnings.[8] Essentially theirs must be regarded as a conservative approach which presumably emphasizes both the uncertainness of future earnings and the inevitable decline, at some point in time, in the rate of return on additional investment even for expanding enterprises.

Since equation (3) stresses the dividend factor, it is reasonably well adapted to the intermediate stock category. In the equation proper, a dollar of dividends is presumed to be the equivalent of

[8] B. Graham and D. L. Dodd, *Security Analysis* (New York: McGraw-Hill Book Co., 1951; 3d ed.), p. 410.

four dollars of retained earnings. In terms of equation (1), the ratio of "adjusted" R_a to R_c is thus fixed at one-fourth. Inasmuch as the numerous other possible relationships between R_a and R_c are ignored, the multiplier must be adjusted for differences between the assumed normal relationship and the actual relationship in any given circumstance. For growth stocks, the magnitudes of the adjustments required in M assume such significance that the general application of equation (3) does not appear to be feasible.

Whatever the approach employed to evaluate intermediate stocks, the presumed level of current dividends is important, but not all important. Expansion may still be beneficial to shareholders even though R_a is less than R_c, provided the added investment is financed at least in part by borrowed funds.[9] The essential requirements are that the corporation in question be conservatively financed and that the excess of R_a over the interest rate be sufficient to offset the excess of R_c over R_a. If conservatively financed, the augmented use of borrowed funds need not appreciably affect either the multiplier or its reciprocal.

For illustrative purposes, let us assume that the conventional debt-equity ratio is one-half; that the market capitalization rate is unaffected as long as this relationship holds; and that added investment is financed by the same proportions of debt and retained earnings as the conventional ratio. If, under such conditions, R_a is 6 per cent and the interest rate is 3 per cent, the rate of return on retained earnings becomes 7.5 per cent. The retention of earnings is thus beneficial to shareholders, provided R_c is less than 7.5 per cent.

Even if the use of borrowed funds is ignored, the maximum feasible dividend payout ratio is likely to be something less than 100 per cent for intermediate stocks. In some instances, maintenance of relative position within the industry may be essential for profit maintenance. Whatever the relation of R_a to R_c, the affected corporation must then keep pace with the industry and with other firms. Otherwise, the company loses out, and its over-all profit rate declines. In other instances, a substantial portion of reported

---

[9] Unlike the case of capital gains taxation, benefits derived from the use of borrowed funds do not accrue automatically to shareholders. Their existence depends upon management policy. For this reason, the possibility of utilizing borrowed funds is introduced simply as a qualification to the intermediate stock category.

earnings may be attributable to price-level changes. If the real position of a given company is to be maintained, a portion of reported earnings will then have to be retained. In still other instances, cash may simply be unavailable for dividends.

V

A third group, the creditor stock category, may now be isolated for examination. Creditor stocks are so named because they possess many of the attributes of debt instruments. The most important of similarities is that, in determining the present worth of creditor stocks, almost exclusive emphasis is placed upon the prevailing level of dividends. Average yields on creditor stocks are somewhat higher than those on bonds, for shareholders lack protection and have no equity cushion upon which to rest. The limited ability of institutional investors to hold any type of equity share, due principally to legislative restrictions and to the nature of their obligations, also contributes to the yield differential between bonds and creditor stocks.[10]

As contrasted with the growth and intermediate stock categories, the retention of earnings occasions little or no appreciation in creditor stock prices over time. The low present value of retained earnings may be attributable to the fact that the rate of return on additional investment approximates zero. It may be attributable to management which elects to retain earnings during prosperous periods and to hold them in liquid form for distribution during depressed periods. It may be attributable to public regulatory commissions which pass the benefits derived from earnings retention on to the public.

In a relevant sense the inclusion of this category modifies, as well as extends beyond, the preceding analysis. Stocks can no longer be said to qualify automatically for membership in the growth and intermediate stock groups depending upon whether "adjusted" R_a is greater or less than R_c. The ultimate distribution of additional earnings is not a foregone conclusion; retained earnings need not be employed in most profitable fashion; and economic considerations are not the sole criterion.

[10] As the pressure to obtain satisfactory yields on investments increases, however, the gradual relaxation of legislative restrictions is likely to occur.

The ability of shareholders to influence the policies of either management or regulatory commissions is frequently circumscribed. As a result, stock prices are of necessity conditioned by the expected behavior of management and government in the light of their past actions. If management and/or regulatory commissions regard shareholders as creditors and if the underlying economic conditions permit their treatment as such, it follows that the stocks which are thus affected will assume many of the characteristics of credit instruments.

Common stocks of large, well-established public utilities offer excellent possibilities for inclusion in the creditor stock category.[11] Public utilities in general are characterized by an underlying element of stability and by close regulation. Rates tend to be adjusted so as to provide reasonable and stable returns to shareholders. Dividend payout ratios normally range in the neighborhood of 75 per cent, and sources of additional funds are largely external.[12]

The acceptance of the idea that shareholders are creditors is reflected in the dividend policy of the largest of all public utilities. For more than three decades American Telephone and Telegraph has annually declared a nine-dollar dividend.

Common stocks of large, mature industrial corporations whose earnings possess a reasonable degree of stability are likely to exhibit at least some features of creditor stocks. Management often elects to stabilize the dollar amount of dividends declared annually, thereby reducing dividend payout ratios during prosperous periods and raising them during depressed periods. To the extent that retained earnings are then held in liquid form, "cash" cushions are created which bear marked similarities to the equity or earning-power cushions provided for senior securities.

Needless to say, the point of delineation between intermediate stocks and creditor stocks is difficult to ascertain.[13] Given the separation of ownership from control for large, public corporations, it

[11] It is not meant to imply that all, or even the great majority, of utility stocks are creditor stocks. Some may actually be growth stocks. The crucial considerations appear to be whether regulatory commissions permit retained earnings to augment the invested capital base and whether the allowable rate of return exceeds or falls short of R_c.

[12] Postwar payout ratios are noticeably below those for the immediate prewar period, perhaps reflecting the impact of substantial price-level changes.

[13] In other words, R_a—in the sense of most profitable uses of funds—may be less than R_c, but greater than zero, for creditor stocks as well as intermediate stocks.

may well be that shareholders are generally viewed by the managements of these companies as a form of creditor. In numerous instances, however, the nature of the corporation may be such that this attitude cannot readily be translated into policy.

A further consideration relates to the willingness of the market to recognize and accept creditor stocks. Unless the corporation in question is extremely well known and has a long and stable dividend record, it is doubtful whether the market will accord its stock special treatment. Special treatment, in this instance, refers to lower capitalization rates and to more stable stock prices than would otherwise be the case. If market acceptance is not forthcoming, the stock remains simply an inferior member of the intermediate stock category.

As a final point, the behavior of creditor stock prices can still be expected to resemble in many respects that of common stock prices in general. First, even where common stocks are creditor oriented, dividends ordinarily exhibit some relation to earnings and vary accordingly. This proposition follows from the absence of contractual agreements between management and shareholders. Second, since common stocks have no maturity dates, creditor stock prices are not conditioned by maturity values. This situation is, however, little different from that of bonds possessing remote maturities and no different from that of Consols.

Third, wherever regulatory commissions exist, rate revisions customarily operate with a lag. During the interim, higher earnings attributable to the retention of earnings may permit higher dividends. The converse is, of course, also true. Finally, the possibility is always present that, as management and commissions change, policies may also change.

VI

The basic premise that stock prices, over longer periods, reflect the present values of anticipated future dividends permits derivation of a model which possesses substantial plausibility. In distinguishing between growth and intermediate stocks, the crucial question becomes whether or not the capitalized values of future dividends attributable to the retention of earnings are greater than the dollar magnitudes of retained earnings. Wherever greater, i.e., wherever

rates of return on additional investment exceed market capitalization rates, the common stocks in question belong to the growth
stock category. In the case of growth stocks, low dividend payout
ratios can be expected to enhance stock values.

In certain instances, common stocks may assume the characteristics of growth stocks despite the fact that rates of return on added
investment are less than market capitalization rates. The preferred
tax treatment of capital gains augments the worth of retained
earnings and enables more stocks to qualify as growth stocks. In
addition, the combined use of borrowed funds and retained earnings
makes it beneficial to retain earnings under special circumstances.

For most large industrials, rates of return on additional investment are presumed to exceed zero, but to be less than the corresponding market capitalization rates. This condition leads to the
commonly observed, direct relationship between dividend payout
ratios and common stock prices. Although earnings retention
occasions appreciation in stock prices over time, shareholders benefit
from the distribution of the maximum feasible amount of earnings.

Acceptance of the fact that the control over large public
corporations is often vested in management and regulatory commissions gives rise to the creditor stock category. For this group, the
principal determinant of common stock prices is the prevailing level
of dividends, capitalized at appropriate rates. Although retained
earnings may augment dividend stability and thereby reduce
capitalization rates, they contribute little to the prospects for higher
dividends for the future.

Granted the inadequacies and diversity of statistical data, a
model of this style has considerable utility as a foundation for
empirical analysis. Most important of all, it provides a tentative
basis for classifying common stocks. Even in the event that the
model is not entirely valid, the heterogeneity of the statistical
sample may still be reduced. Secondly, it specifies the necessary
information and establishes interesting relationships for empirical
verification. Finally, if—as is more than likely—the statistical data
are inadequate for thorough-going analyses, they may nonetheless be
sufficient to confirm or deny the model.

8. DIVIDEND GROWTH AS DETERMINANT OF COMMON STOCK VALUES*

❀ John C. Clendenin

ALTHOUGH THE SELECTION OF STOCKS for long-term holding must always involve a number of criteria, the heart of the problem is usually productivity—how much over a period of time can be expected from Stock A, and how does this compare with Stock B or other available alternatives? Some high-quality stocks are stable dividend producers, promising immediate and continuing good yields. Others are "growth stocks" promising small yields now but better ones later. If the portfolio can use either, which will be the more productive over the longer term, a stable producer priced to yield 5½ per cent or a growth stock yielding 3 per cent? As of now there is no standard approach to an answer. The securities business has neither an accepted theory of growth stock values nor a device for measuring them.

It is the purpose of this article to advance a simple and familiar theory of stock values—a theory based entirely on future dividend productivity—and to suggest some easy rule-of-thumb methods for comparing the values of non-growth, slow-growth, and fast-growth stocks. We shall show, for example, that a non-growth stock at 17 times dividends, a medium-growth stock at 26 times dividends, and

* From *Trusts and Estates,* Vol. 96, No. 2 (February, 1957), pp. 104–106. Reprinted by permission of *Trusts and Estates.*

a fast-growth stock at 36 times dividends may all be equally attractive in price—and we shall show how to find out if they are.

Our methods are not intended to predict the course of the stock market or even to predict the prices which a trading market will assign to individual stocks. Rather, they are intended to indicate, for the stocks and groups of stocks to which they are applicable, the long-term average yield to be expected on stock investments made at existing prices, or, conversely, the stock prices upon which desired average yields may be expected.

We shall not neglect the capital gains aspect of earnings and dividend growth. Our stock value theory will indicate the causes of the great gains of the past decade and provide a basis upon which future possibilities may be judged.

THEORY OF STOCK VALUE

The most satisfactory theory for our purpose is the old and familiar concept upon which bond tables are based—namely, that the investment value of any security is the total of the mathematical present values of all future distributions to be obtained from it, with present values computed at interest rates (yields) commensurate with the risk and other features of the security.[1] This theory implies that in the last analysis stockholders will obtain nothing from a stock investment except such cash dividends (plus possibly a few rights, spinoffs, and other fringe benefits) as the corporation may pay before its ultimate oblivion. The dividends represent value of the probable future dividends as foreseen at that time. Since a future sale of a share will merely transfer subsequent dividends to the purchaser, a share held for sale has the same value as one for permanent investment.

It is sometimes urged that a theory of stock value based upon the dividends of future years is impractical because long-term dividend forecasts cannot be exact. It is true that long-term dividend

---

[1] This approach is not confined to securities. It is also basic to the valuation of installment notes, mortgages, buildings, farms, and most other property. Nor is its application to stocks a new idea. It was utilized 20 years ago by J. B. Williams in his *Theory of Investment Value,* and has recently been discussed by Parker in the *Analysts Journal,* by Bing in the *Commercial and Financial Chronicle,* and by Clendenin and Van Cleave in the *Journal of Finance.*

projections are not likely to be perfect, but it is also essential to remember that future dividends are in the long run the sole source of value, and the long-term investor who fails to anticipate them is ignoring the basic reason for his investment—the payments which will return his principal and the earned income. Investors who arrive at stock appraisals by multiplying past or current earnings and dividends by capitalization factors, or who rely on book values or market price histories, are simply obtaining substitutes for the dividend values which they need to evaluate. Whether these vaguely related substitute figures come any closer to sensible appraisals than an "inexact" estimate of the essential future dividends is somewhat doubtful.

Table 1 illustrates the ideas involved in this present-value-of-dividends approach. The table is purely mathematical; the figures in it are the current price-dividend ratios applicable to any stocks which fit into the table. For example, the stock of a company whose business, earnings record, balance sheet, and other factors imply an indefinite continuation of the existing dividend rate is worth 17.01 times dividends, assuming a stock quality to which the table's 4–5–6–7 per cent yield schedule properly applies. However, the existence of an average 3 per cent per year dividend growth trend which gave promise of continuing for the next 30 years would permit a current price-dividend ratio of 26.08, and still (under the conditions of the table) afford the investor the yields contemplated by the table. Similarly, a 5 per cent growth trend expected to

Table 1. *Approximate present values of all future dividends on a stock now paying $1.00 per annum, if the dividend is expected to increase at the indicated compound rate for the indicated period of years and then remain stable until 100 years from today, and if the dividends of the first decade are discounted at 4%, those of the second at 5%, those of the third at 6%, and those of the remaining 70 years at 7%.*

GROWTH PERIOD	ANNUAL GROWTH RATES				
	5%	4%	3%	1%	0%
None	$17.01	$17.01	$17.01	$17.01	$17.01
10 years	24.85	23.04	21.37	18.37	17.01
20 years	31.21	27.51	24.27	19.12	17.01
30 years	35.97	30.55	26.08	19.51	17.01
40 years	39.65	32.67	27.22	19.69	17.01
50 years	42.63	34.23	27.99	19.80	17.01

continue for 20 years would justify a current price-dividend ratio of 31.21, and one expected to continue for 30 years would justify a ratio of 35.97.

Table 1 can also be used to check the rationality of quoted prices. For example, a $200 price for du Pont would be 30.8 times the 1956 dividend of $6.50; a projection of du Pont's long-term growth rate plus an allowance for future inflation suggests a possible dividend growth approximating 5 per cent per year. The table indicates that a price of 30.8 times current dividends would meet its yield standards (4–5–6–7 per cent) if a 5 per cent dividend growth rate continued for about 20 more years, or 4 per cent rate for 30 years.

Table 2 is included in our presentation to console the skeptics who hesitate to base stock valuations upon uncertain estimates of the dividends of far distant years. (These skeptics base their valuations upon past earnings and dividends which have no bearing at all on value recoveries in the future.) Table 2 shows the present values of dividends under assumed conditions for each of the next three decades and for the ensuing 70 years, and a total which in each case is the theoretical proper current price-dividend ratio for the stock.

It will be observed that on a non-growth stock the theoretical value is 70 per cent recovered in the first two decades, and only

Table 2. *Approximate present values of the future dividends on a stock now paying $1.00 per annum, if the dividends are expected to grow at the indicated rates for 20 years and then remain stable for the next 80 years, and if the dividends of the first decade are discounted at 4%, those of the second at 5%, those of the third at 6%, and those of the remaining 70 years at 7%.*

GROWTH RATE PER YEAR	FIRST DECADE	SECOND DECADE	THIRD DECADE	NEXT 70 YEARS	TOTAL
			PRESENT VALUES		
6%	$10.85	$11.36	$7.36	$5.96	$35.53
5%	10.35	9.84	6.09	4.93	31.21
4%	9.87	8.53	5.03	4.08	27.51
3%	9.40	7.37	4.14	3.36	24.27
2%	8.96	6.39	3.41	2.76	21.52
1%	8.53	5.52	2.80	2.27	19.12
0%	8.11	4.74	2.30	1.86	17.01

about 11 per cent of the value arises in periods more than 30 years hence. On a stock promising a rapid 5 per cent growth the first two decades account for about 65 per cent of the value, and the period beyond the third decade about 16 per cent. These figures clearly indicate that the bulk of the value attaching to any stock tends to originate in the dividends of the first two decades, which are not beyond the scope of reasonable estimate.

DIVIDEND GROWTH TRENDS

In the process of studying dividend growth we have examined the long-term per-share earnings and dividend records of many stocks and a number of market averages. Three salient facts emerge. First, it appears that most major stocks other than the rate-regulated utilities have ultimately earned and paid more—perhaps about proportionately more—as a result of the 1940–1953 price-level inflation. Inflationary tendencies still persist, and therefore must be allowed for both in judging the past and in estimating future earnings and dividends. Second, when we remove the effects of price-level change from the historical figures, average dividend growth rates on major stocks during the past 30 years have not been very fast—for example, about 4 per cent per year for du Pont, 3 per cent for General Electric, an average of 3 per cent for 8 major growth stocks, 2 per cent for Standard and Poor's index of 50 industrials, 0 for a group of 10 good quality non-growth industrials which we compiled ourselves. Third, the growth rates and growth patterns are diverse, and except for the very large companies, are more predictable when combined into groups.

Despite stout resistance by the Federal Reserve System and an anti-inflationary attitude by the administration, the general price level in the United States has risen nearly 5 per cent in the past four years. These have been good years, it is true, but it is also evident that public policy is basically inflationary, and for the long pull it seems reasonable to count on an average of one per cent per year of price-level inflation. The one per cent per year figure is only a guess, and it will accrue intermittently rather than steadily, but almost certainly something of the sort can be expected to influence future earnings and dividends, and must therefore be included as a factor in any estimates.

Thus far we have repeatedly referred to a need for estimates on future earnings and dividends, without suggesting any methods. There are many statistical approaches to this type of estimation, including projections based on GNP, on industry growth trends, and on product and resource development. We have been charting past earnings and dividend trends deflated for prices to obtain an idea of current and historic growth rates, and projecting these into the future with arbitrary allowances for industry and company outlook and our ideas of future price levels. Admittedly we are guessing, but we are guessing at indispensable data, and we feel that our guesses are good enough to be worth while on the stocks of large established concerns and on groups of stocks combined.

A word of caution is in order on the subject of earnings and dividend growth trends. We think that the rapid growth rate in the years 1946–1956 is in many cases abnormal, since the period is one of recovery from wartime price controls and excess profits taxes, of unusual technological progress and of almost uninterrupted prosperity. A long-term "trend" continuing the profits progress of 1946–1956 would be almost too good to be true.

YIELDS ON STOCKS

Although "yields" of 4 to 5 per cent are commonplace on the market averages and considerably lower ones are accepted on leading growth stocks, these are not generally regarded as the measure of long-range performance on stock investment. Most dividends are expected to grow and long-range performance thus will exceed the current yield.

An inspection of the yields (based on cash dividends plus non-diluting rights if any) on high-grade non-growth or slow-growth stocks since 1950 leaves the impression that the market has usually offered between 5 and 6 per cent on good quality non-growth industrial equities. Since it seemed only reasonable that near-term dividends of fairly certain amounts should be evaluated at lower rates of yield than were applied to the rather conjectural dividend estimates of distant years, we decided that our evaluation tables (Tables 1 and 2, previously discussed) should evaluate the dividends of the first decade at 4 per cent yield, the second decade at 5 per cent, the third decade at 6 per cent, and the balance of significant time at 7 per cent. Other tables of various sorts were constructed, but this one seems to fit market experience and common sense better than most. In our opinion, the table is applicable only to quality stocks with established dividend and earnings records.

It would be possible, using Table 1 and a few others based on different growth and yield assumptions, to make very practical comparisons of the prices of stocks being considered for long-term investment. However, Table 1 calls for certain specific estimates which may be bypassed if one of two rule-of-thumb methods is used.

Two Practical Rules of Thumb

A rule of thumb is a convenient calculation process which obtains approximate results by short-cut methods. Because of the compensating tendencies of certain mathematical factors, two such short cuts seem feasible. These short cuts are specifically designed to give results consistent with the 20-year growth values presented in Table 1.

Method No. 1. Estimate the probable annual payment rate (dividends plus rights) twelve years hence, and divide by current prices. This process will provide comparable estimates of weighted average future yields on the current prices of fast-growth, slow-growth, and non-growth stocks. Its chief weakness, if it be a weakness, is its inherent assumption that the growth trend embodied in the 12-year dividend estimate will continue for a total of about 20 years and then level out. For a strong growth stock this is probably conservative—but, on the other hand, it may not be conservative to pay cash money for any growth trend beyond its 20th year.

An illustration of Method No. 1 may be in order. The 1956 du Pont dividend was $6.50 per share, a figure which seems quite in line with the company's earning power and policies. Rights do not appear to be a significant factor. Next, a study of the company's long-term past growth on a constant-dollar basis indicates a growth rate of about 4 per cent per annum compounded. If this growth rate is accepted as continuing (and here we are illustrating, not predicting), our expectation of a future average annual price-level inflation of 1 per cent will lead us to place our dividend growth estimate at 5 per cent compounded. It therefore appears reasonable to estimate du Pont's dividend 12 years hence at $6.50 $\times$ 1.05^{12}, or $11.65 per share. On du Pont's recent price of 190 this would "yield" 6.13 per cent—and we think that this yield provides an arithmetic comparison with yields similarly calculated on other stocks and by conventional methods on preferred stocks or bonds. Quality factors other than growth tendencies could obviously justify differences in yields, and optimism regarding the duration of a growth trend would lead to a belief that the computed yield was understated or overstated.

Method No. 2. Estimate the annual distribution rate twelve years hence, and appraise the stock by multiplying by 15 to 19 depending on stock quality. In this context the word quality does not include growth capacity, but does include capital structure, trade position, management and other strength aspects of the firm. Most of the inherent assumptions of Method No. 1 and its conservative handling of strong growth trends are inherent in Method No. 2 also.

Obviously, stock appraisals made by this method will be out of line with both high and low markets. They are chiefly useful as devices for comparing the values of different stocks, and to a lesser degree in establishing intrinsic values for comparison with market quotations.

CAPITAL GAINS

Thus far our discussion has stressed dividends and prospective dividends and has largely disregarded future stock prices. Two observations on the subject of capital gains are now in order.

First, a growth stock which is correctly appraised at the present time will show a higher appraisal a decade or two hence, for when the predicted larger dividends have become current or imminent their present values (hence, presumably, the market value of the stock) become substantially greater. This is not an advantage over non-growth stocks; the non-growth stocks pay more in the earlier years, and the value gains in the growth issues merely represent the compensating deferred income as it becomes more imminent. If taken by sale as a low-taxed capital gain, this is of course an advantageous form of income.

Second, a growth stock which is bought at a price which contemplates 15 to 20 years' growth, but which retains its growth tendencies for a longer period, will obviously show a great profit. There would be an equal or greater profit in a non-growth stock which began to grow or in a growth stock which grew faster than anticipated—and disappointments could occur too. But we make a particular point of years of growth because conservative appraisals must needs estimate strong growth trends at 15 to 20 years' duration, whereas history shows the clear possibility of longer periods. These longer periods may be recognized by the market in higher prices almost year by year, if time passes without any evidence of slackening growth capacity.

A Word of Caution

Before concluding this article it seems desirable to emphasize the need for common sense in the appraisal of growth stocks. As our tables indicate, it is easy to "prove" that a fast-growth stock is worth 40 to 50 times current dividends, simply by assuming as impending 40 or 50 years of rapid growth and a 6 per cent or less yield basis. But we feel that growth rates projected beyond 20 or 30 years should be evaluated at rather high yield rates—at least 7 per cent—and if this is done, our tables indicate that 30 or 35 times current dividends (and this would usually mean 20 to 27 times current earning power) is high enough for all but the most promising stocks and too high for most.

It is perhaps necessary to defend any counsel of conservatism in growth stocks, for since the war almost any indiscriminate purchase of a growth issue has seemed to result in a large profit. There have been a number of factors behind this, and in our opinion most of them are nonrecurring. Among these factors are the following:

1. *General Market Rise.* The post-1950 popularity of stock investments has resulted in increased price-earnings and price-dividend ratios for all high-grade stocks, including growth stocks.
2. *The General Price-Level Inflation.* Corporate earnings and dividends since 1945 have been "catching up" to the general inflation of 1940–1953. During this period many growth stocks doubled their earnings and dividends in real terms and the price-level inflation doubled them again, resulting in multiplication by four.

3. *Commencement of Growth.* When a stock enters a promising long-term growth phase its value may rise rapidly from 15 or 20 times dividends to 30 or 35 times dividends. Thereafter, even as the expected growth takes place, the present value of future dividends (and presumably the price of the stock) may rise relatively slowly.

4. *Irregular Growth.* Long-range earnings and dividend progress is often made in irregular spurts and market recognition occurs similarly. In consequence, short-term gains of sizable amounts give an impression of high-average speed.

5. *Improved Quality.* Many spectacular stock price gains since the war have reflected the "growing up" of a company or its industry, with a consequent shift from a speculative 7 per cent yield basis to an investment-grade low-yield rating for the stock. This gain will of course occur but once.

When all of the nonrecurring elements in these five factors are given due weight, the postwar record can hardly be held to prove that any growth stock at any indiscriminate price is certain to provide capital gains in the future.

9. RELATIVE VALUE OF EARNINGS: RETAINED AND DISTRIBUTED*

❂ O. K. Burrell

THE LAST DECADE HAS WITNESSED the beginning of attempts to measure with as much precision as possible some of the value making factors in common stocks. It is entirely evident that these studies can never be truly scientific because value exists in the minds of men and precise measurement of all of the variables that might conceivably influence human attitudes and behavior is simply not possible. Nevertheless, significant advances have been made in more precise measurement of some of the forces that relate to common stock valuation.

The role of the payout ratio in common stock valuation has been the subject of a significant number of inquiries. How much more in market value is generated by a dollar earned but retained in the business? Until about a decade ago it was perhaps understood that earnings distributed made a greater impact on valuation than earnings retained but it seems doubtful if very many analysts really understood how much greater is the impact upon valuation of distributed earnings as compared with retained earnings.

* From *The Commercial and Financial Chronicle*, Vol. 186, No. 5656 (Thursday, July 18, 1957), p. 1. Reprinted by permission of *The Commercial and Financial Chronicle*, 25 Park Place, New York 7, New York.

Two pioneer studies in 1945 and 1946[1] appeared to suggest that distributed earnings were worth as much as four times as much as retained earnings in utility common stock valuation. Graham and Dodd in the third revision of their classic "Security Analysis"[2] in 1951 offered a specific formula to express the relative importance of earnings retained and distributed. This formula was suggested in the belief that the dividend factor should have a coordinate position with earnings in the valuation process. This formula was:

$$V = M (D + \tfrac{1}{3}E)$$

Where V = value, D = expected dividend, M = multiplier, and E = expected earnings.

It will be observed that this formula yields the same results as the traditional approach only when the dividend payout is $\tfrac{3}{4}$. If the payout is more than $\tfrac{3}{4}$, V will exceed $M (E)$ and where the payout is less than $\tfrac{3}{4}$, V will be less than $M (E)$.

If a stock is expected to earn $3 and if the multiplier is 10 with a normal payout of $\tfrac{3}{4}$, then with a full payout the value according to the formula would be 40, or $10(3 + 1)$, but with a zero payout the value would be 10, or $10(0 + 1)$. The formula suggests, then, that $1 of earnings paid out in dividends exerts an influence on market price four times as great as $1 of earnings not distributed.

This conclusion was subsequently verified in a study by the present author based on a small sample of paired stocks.[3] In a more comprehensive study based on the Cowles All-Stock Index for the period 1871–1937 and several Standard and Poor Indexes, Harkavy[4] demonstrated, (1) that at any given time, there is a tendency for stock prices to vary directly with the proportion of earnings distributed, and (2) over a period of years, the stocks of those corporations retaining the greater proportion of earnings tend to exhibit the greater price appreciation. But his studies of individual

[1] *Valuing Utility Earnings Distributed and Retained*, Hugh Pastoriza, *Analysts Journal*, July, 1945. *Factors Influencing Utility Price Earnings Ratios*, Harold H. Young, *Analysts Journal*, Spring, 1946.
[2] Benjamin Graham and David Dodd, *Security Analysis* (New York: McGraw-Hill, 1951).
[3] O. K. Burrell, "Dividends Versus Retained Earnings as Market Force," *Commercial and Financial Chronicle*, Aug. 21, 1952.
[4] Oscar Harkavy, "Retained Earnings and Common Prices," *The Journal of Finance*, September, 1953.

companies indicated that retention of income was not the cause of outstanding price appreciation; the crucial factor was considered to be the profitable utilization of investor's funds since in many cases there was little appreciation even where payout ratios were low. In other words, the payout ratio was low because of opportunity for profitable expansion but the growth in share price was not caused by low payouts.

GROWTH STOCKS

There is no real contradiction in asserting that at any given time the price-earnings ratios of common stocks vary directly with their payout ratios while over a period of time greater price appreciation will be associated with lower payouts. Nevertheless it had been rather generally taken for granted that the payout ratio played a less important role in the valuation of growth stocks than in the valuation of non-growth stock. Graham and Dodd[2] expressed the view that while a low payout ratio is not considered by investors to be an advantage even in the case of growth stocks that it is largely ignored "when a company is considered to be highly dynamic."

Apparently the first attempt to measure the impact of the payout ratio on market price was made by Harkavy in the study previously mentioned.[4] For the Cowles Chemical Stock Index, 1908–1937 he found a high correlation (0.78) between price-earnings ratios and dividend earning ratios. This is to say that for chemical stocks which have had a strong growth trend it appears that at any given time investors prefer dividends over reinvested earnings.

Notwithstanding this evidence, Walter[5] has proposed a formula for common stock valuation in which the impact of the dividend ratio is closely related to the relationships between the rate of return on additional investment (for the particular corporation) and the market capitalization rate. The formula follows:

$$V = \frac{D + \dfrac{R_a}{R_c}(E - D)}{R_c}$$

[5] James E. Walter, "Dividend Policies and Common Stock Prices," *Journal of Finance*, March, 1956.

Where D is cash dividends, E is earnings, R_a is the rate of return on additional investment and R_c is the market capitalization rate. It should be noted, however, that R_c is the market capitalization rate adjusted to a 100% payout ratio.

It will be observed that whenever R_a is greater than R_c the lower the dividend payout ratio the higher will be the valuation. Under these circumstances a dividend reduction or omission would serve to increase the value of the stock. The following illustration would appear to be reasonably typical of growth stock:

Earned per share	$4.00
Rate of return on new capital investment (R_a)	16.0%
Capitalization rate assuming full dividend payout	8.0%

The suggested formula would produce the following values at varying dividend rates:

Dividend	Valuation
4	50.00
3	62.50
2	75.00
1	87.50
0	100.00

It was assumed apparently that owners of corporate stock regard the corporation as a sort of bank and that undistributed earnings are in effect "deposited" to the credit of the stockholders. If this assumption is valid it is clear that in the case of growth companies the lower the dividend payout ratio the higher the valuation. The premium on such low payout growth stocks could be regarded as the price of the privilege of "depositing" undistributed earnings at the high marginal rate of return earned by the corporation.

Whether this assumed investor attitude is rational is not the subject of this inquiry. The purpose of this study is to determine, if possible, whether in the case of growth stocks investors do in fact place a value on the dividend that is independent of the earnings factor. General observation indicates that prices of growth stocks are positively related to dividend payout ratios. This was Harkavy's conclusion in the case of chemical stocks in the 1908–1937 period. This appears to be the only study of the relationships of price-earnings ratios and payout ratios of a group of stocks that may be reasonably described as growth stocks. But the sample was limited to a single industry and, in addition, it is not impossible that investor attitudes have changed since 1937. Indeed there is some reason to suppose that investor attitudes may have changed during the test period 1908–1937. The concept of the growth stock cannot be dated with any precision but it was certainly many years after 1908.

The present study will be concerned, then, with investor attitudes toward earnings retained and distributed at a given moment of time. It will not attempt to determine whether earnings retention is or is not a cause of growth. Indeed, Harkavy has demonstrated that it is growth that causes earnings retention and not vice versa. This study will not attempt to determine what investor attitude ought to be. It will be concerned solely with the relative impact upon valuation of growth stocks of earnings retained and earnings distributed.

WHAT IS A GROWTH STOCK?

The definition of a growth stock is not easy. It is not simply a stock whose price has risen greatly. Neither can a growth stock be defined as the stock of a company able to earn a high return on new capital investment. The railroad industry is certainly not considered to have growth characteristics even though the rate of return earned on new capital investment has been quite high. The return on total investment has been low and the opportunity for continued investment at high marginal rates is considered to be limited. Perhaps a growth stock is the stock of a company that is considered to have an excellent prospect to earn a high return on repeated increments of new capital over an extended or indefinite period of time.

But the precise definition of a growth stock is not at all essential. We are concerned with investor's attitude toward the dividend factor in stocks that the investor regards as growth stocks. This simplifies the problem. A growth stock is one that is widely regarded by investors as having growth characteristics. It is probably true that generally such stocks are characterized by low yields and high price-earnings ratios. But clearly not all stocks with low yields and high price-earnings ratios are considered to be growth stocks by investors. Low yield may be merely a consequence of an expectation of near term increase in dividend rate. A high price-earnings ratio may reflect temporarily low earnings or a high degree of stability in earning power.

The stocks included in the sample were simply the stocks included in the portfolios of two open-end investment companies whose announced investment objective is long-term appreciation through holdings of common stocks considered to have growth characteristics. In both cases the term "growth stock" was included in the name of the fund. Presumably these stocks were selected by fund managers because they were considered (correctly or incorrectly) to be growth stocks. Moreover, buyers of open-end funds at least are given an opportunity to scrutinize the portfolio of such funds and it is not unreasonable to suppose that buyers of these funds generally accepted the idea that these portfolio stocks had growth characteristics. The hardened cynic may consider that the stocks were selected by the fund managers not on the basis of a belief that they were in fact growth stocks but rather that they were stocks that buyers of investment fund shares would consider to be growth stocks. Even if this view were correct it would only support the conclusion that these portfolio stocks are accepted quite generally as having growth characteristics.

METHOD OF STUDY

The following outline more precisely describes the data and methods of analysis used:

1. The sample of growth stocks was the stocks in the June 30, 1956 portfolio of Growth Industry Shares Inc. and the Aug. 31, 1956 portfolio of Massachusetts Investors Growth Stock Fund. The gross number of items in these two portfolios was 122. From this list were eliminated (1) stocks of companies for which no 1956 earnings estimate was available in the November 1956 S & P Stock Guide, and (2) stocks of companies whose annual dividend rate was not clearly indicated or included a regular dividend payable in stock rather than cash. After these eliminations and after allowing for duplications there remained a sample of 80 stocks.

2. Dividend payout ratios and price-earnings ratios were then computed for these 80 stocks. The earnings used was the weighted average per share earnings (adjusted to present capitalization) for the years 1954, 1955 and the S & P estimate for 1956. Since recent earnings were considered to be more significant than more remote earnings, the weights assigned were one for 1954, two for 1955 and three for 1956. The dividend payout ratio was computed by dividing the annual dividend rate by the weighted average earnings for the three-year period. The price-earnings ratio was computed by dividing the Oct. 31, 1956 closing price (or bid price in the case of unlisted stocks) by the weighted average earnings.

3. Paired stocks were then selected from the sample. The basis of pairing was essential similarity in all respects except payout ratio and dissimilarity in payout ratio. Perfect pairing is, of course, impossible but an attempt was made to pair only stocks of companies in the same industry and with closely similar previous growth records. Perhaps the most valid criticism of the selections is that in some cases the pairing did not involve a really high payout against a really low payout stock but rather a low payout paired with a much lower payout company. In the extreme case, American Airlines with a payout ratio of about 40% was paired with Eastern Airlines with a payout ratio of 21%. Mean and median price-earnings ratios, payout ratios, and dividend yields were then computed for the high payout group and for the low payout group.

4. The entire sample of 80 stocks was then arranged in quartiles, according to payout ratios. Mean and median yields, and price earnings ratios were then computed for each quartile.

5. The entire sample of 80 stocks was then arranged in quartiles, according to price-earnings ratios. Mean and median payout ratios and yields were then computed for each quartile.

The pairs selected were:

HIGH PAYOUT—	LOW PAYOUT—
Searle (G. D.) Company	Smith, Kline and French
American Home Products	Pfizer (Charles) Co.
American Cyanamid	Merck Co.
Du Pont	Union Carbide
American Airlines	Eastern Airlines
Aluminium Ltd.	Reynolds Metal
Corning Glass	Gustin Bacon Mfg.
Republic Natural Gas	Shamrock Oil & Gas
Amerada	Skelly
Scott Paper	Sutherland Paper
National Lead	Caterpillar
General Electric	Radio Corporation of America
General Motors	Ford Motor of Canada A
Ex-Cell-O Corporation	Chicago Phenumatic Tool

Results of Statistical Analysis

The high payout group rather consistently sold higher in relation to earnings than did the low payout group. Details are shown in the table below:

	HIGH PAYOUT	LOW PAYOUT
Mean payout ratio	63.8%	43.8%
Median payout ratio	70.5%	49.8%
Mean price earnings ratio	20.9%	15.2%
Median price earnings ratio	23.5%	14.4%
Mean yield	3.2%	3.2%
Median yield	3.2%	3.2%

The evidence here seems to be rather clear. The payout ratio is positively rather than negatively related to valuation of stocks of companies that are believed to have growth characteristics. Indeed, the identical dividend yields on the two groups might suggest that investors pay little attention to anything other than dividends. But this would be an oversimplification. That there are many variables other than the payout ratio is indicated by the variations in payout ratio within each group.

The relationship of higher price-earnings ratios with higher payout ratios was consistent. In only four cases out of the 14 pairs was the higher price earnings ratio associated with the lower payout stock. In these instances the differences were not great and are probably due to imperfect pairing or to differences in investor appraisal of the quality of earnings.

When the entire sample was arranged in quartiles according to payout ratio, the mean and median yields and price earnings ratios were as shown in the table below:

	QUARTILE 1 LOW PAYOUT	QUARTILE 2	QUARTILE 3	QUARTILE 4 HIGH PAYOUT
Mean payout ratio	36.0%	48.7%	54.8%	73.3%
Median payout ratio	38.5	49.5	54.4	71.1
Mean yield	2.8	3.4	4.0	3.7
Median yield	3.0	2.9	3.9	3.7
Mean price earnings ratio	13.9	17.8	14.5	21.3
Median price earnings ratio	12.8	16.8	13.8	18.1

It is evident that payout ratios tended to cluster in the 40%–50% range. It seems clear that really high payout rates are associated with high price earnings ratios and really low payout ratios with low price earnings ratios. But it is equally clear that the relationship between payout and price earnings ratio is not linear. Stocks in the third quartile on payout ratio had price earnings ratios only a little higher than stocks with the lowest payout ratios.

Finally, the 80 stocks were arranged in quartiles, according to price-earnings ratios, and median and mean payout ratios and yields computed. The results are shown in the table following:

	1ST QUARTILE	2ND QUARTILE	3RD QUARTILE	4TH QUARTILE
Mean price earnings ratio	10.0%	13.7%	16.8%	26.5%
Median price earnings ratio	10.1	13.8	16.9	24.3
Mean payout ratio	45.1	50.0	56.3	60.7
Median payout ratio	48.2	50.6	58.1	53.9
Mean yield	4.6	3.7	3.4	2.3

There appears to be a somewhat greater measure of internal consistency indicated in this arrangement of the data. Price earnings ratios and payout ratios are positively correlated. The higher the payout the higher the price relative to earnings.

CAUSE AND EFFECT

When two factors are closely related it is never possible to be scientifically positive as to which is cause and which is effect, or indeed whether both have a common cause. Nevertheless, it seems evident that the payout ratio is the cause and the price-earnings ratio is the effect. The only conceivable basis for suggesting that the price-earnings ratio is a causal factor would be to assume that only corporations with high price-earnings ratios can sell additional stock to stockholders or the public and are therefore in a position to have a high payout during expansion. This does not appear to be a valid assumption since the period examined was one of high stock prices. Examination of companies in both high and low payout quartiles show no apparent difference in ability to sell additional

common stock. Stocks in each category have done new common
stock financing in recent years.

You may conclude then that payout ratio is a positive causal
factor in the valuation of stocks considered to have growth characteristics. Investors do not regard retained earnings as equivalent
to money deposited at a high earning rate. Investors want cash
dividends even when it can be demonstrated that the rate of
return on new corporate investment is high.

10. INVESTMENT MERITS OF UTILITY COMMON STOCKS*

❂ Frederick W. Page

THERE IS NOT MUCH DOUBT that the utility industry is going to be relatively more dependent on the capital markets over the foreseeable future than any other single industry in America. If one projects trends in demand for the next ten years, the amount of capital required to build the capacity to meet this demand becomes staggering. This is true for all segments of the industry—electric, gas, telephone and water. Technological developments requiring proportionately heavy capital expenditures will also have an effect on overall capital requirements. Consequently it appears that the problem of raising new capital will be with utilities for many years to come, and it will be one of their major problems.

Obviously, to be successful in meeting this problem, securities must be made attractive to investors who have many areas in which they can invest their savings. To make them attractive and to keep them attractive is not a one-shot operation requiring only occasional thought and attention. As I hope to develop a little later, it takes years of efforts to compile a record which will give securities investment appeal.

Although there are many types of securities which utilities can sell to raise their capital, I would like to limit my remarks to common stock financing. Not only is this highest cost capital, but

* From *The Commercial and Financial Chronicle,* Vol. 191, No. 5956 (Thursday, June 2, 1960), p. 7. Reprinted by permission of *The Commercial and Financial Chronicle,* 25 Park Place, New York 7, New York.

the cost will vary considerably, both from year to year and between companies, and if utilities can make these securities attractive, they will find that they have added to the investor appeal of their prior securities. Moreover, my knowledge of bonds and preferred stocks leaves much to be desired, but having spent 27 years as a student of the industry, and being largely responsible for one of the largest portfolios of utility common stocks in the country, I feel that I can speak with some authority about common stocks and what gives them investor appeal.

Our four investment companies—Tri-Continental, Broad Street Investing, National Investors, and Whitehall Fund—have been particularly partial to utility common stocks, and these holdings have served us well over many years. As of March 31, 1960, we held approximately $155,000,000 of these stocks, and they constituted the largest single industry investment in each of the companies.

BASIC INVESTMENT PHILOSOPHY

What attracts investors to common stocks generally and causes them to select particular stocks from the supply of thousands of issues? Some invest to obtain income, some invest to obtain capital appreciation, others emphasize safety, or there can be a combination of objectives with varying weights given to these objectives. But over a period of time it is possible to detect in the market an investment philosophy that predominates.

Recently I read in a brokerage letter a statement expressing the belief that basic investment philosophy changes only about four times in a generation. The more I thought about this, the more I was inclined to agree. By "basic investment philosophy" I do not mean fads such the popularity of the uranium stocks which quickly come and go. Rather I mean the main investment theory that greatly affects the flow of a substantial segment of the country's savings. This basic investment philosophy is slow to change, and changes are usually brought about only by some substantial shock.

Following World War I and continuing throughout the 1920's, the basic investment philosophy was to make a quick fortune by borrowing funds and taking other undue risks. In the utility field this was reflected in the highly pyramided holding companies. In the stock market it was reflected in substantial purchases of common stocks on high margins by individuals who knew little about stocks and relied largely on market tips. You were crazy not to take the opportunity of making a fortune by borrowing money to buy stocks recommended by your barber.

This era was brought to an end by the stock market crash of 1929 and the subsequent deep and lengthy depression. Fortunes were lost and people were badly in debt. The public decided almost to the man that it would never touch the stock market again. Savings mostly went into life insurance, savings accounts, or bonds. When common stocks were bought, they were purchased almost solely on the basis of safety and yield. Retained earnings were deeply discounted because a dollar in the corporation's treasury was not worth as much as a dollar in the stockholder's hand. There was to be no growth, for the economy had matured and the prospects were for recurring depressions. This philosophy prevailed throughout World War II and the early post-war period. The expected post-war depression was always just around the corner, and corporate earnings were appraised at very low values. The popular form of investment continued to be life insurance, savings accounts, war bonds, and other fixed income securities.

The shock that brought this era to an end was the outbreak of the Korean War. This event convinced the public that the United States would have to maintain a large military establishment on practically a permanent basis. This meant continued high tax rates, and with the political philosophy of full employment, it meant continuing inflation. At about this time, war bonds in large volume matured and the investing public was dramatically shown how poorly bonds treated holders in terms of purchasing power during an inflationary period. The continuance of high tax rates detracted from the appeal of current income, and capital gains with their limited tax rate became more desirable. With inflation detracting from the appeal of bonds, and with capital gains becoming more attractive than current income, the public in increasing numbers turned to stocks as a haven for their savings.

Upon studying long term charts of the stock market, the public discovered that the market was in a strong long term upward trend. Of course, there were periods of decline, but generally these were minor relative to the long term results and they usually were of short duration. If stocks were properly selected and the holder was not in the position of being forced to sell, he was sure to realize a gain eventually. Two lessons of the 1920s were kept in mind. Buying on margin was held to a minimum, and instead of relying on tips, the public sought professional advice and management. This resulted in the extraordinary popularity and growth of the mutual funds and pension funds, with the latter investing an increasing proportion of their assets in common stocks.

There is not much doubt that the popularity of common stocks increased enormously during the 1950s. It is evident that the public both directly and indirectly through legislation puts its stamp of approval on common stocks. Legislation in many states permitted life insurance companies and savings banks to invest in common stocks, and New Jersey is to have variable annuities. All of this would have been unthinkable in the 1930s. This change was the result of loss of favor on the part of fixed income securities, even though interest rates rose from 3% to 5%, and the premium placed on capital gains. With the surge in population and the great technological developments, the economy was sure to grow. To capitalize on this, one should buy common stocks and avoid fixed income securities.

A refinement of this basic investment philosophy crept into the picture to an important degree in 1957, and it has become more pronounced in the last two years. This refinement does not change the basic philosophy but affects selectivity. The public is now seeking stocks in companies that show the fastest growth in per share earnings. With confidence in the future, they are willing to pay many times current earnings in order to obtain higher earnings in the future. It is through this growth that they hope to get their capital appreciation and eventually higher income.

INVESTORS' RECOGNITION OF FUTURE EARNINGS

To illustrate why growth in per share earnings has become so important in the investor's mind, and to show the results he expects to obtain, I will give the example of two utility stocks we hold in our portfolio. If measured by capital structure, Company A is sounder financially than Company B since it has only 41% debt and 49% common equity, as contrasted to Company B's 50% debt and 33% common equity. In spite of its capital strength, Company A sold at only 14.6 times earnings and yielded 4.9%, whereas

Company B sold at 18.4 times earnings and yielded 3.7%. Was the market wrong in its appraisal of these two stocks? I do not believe so, and a projection of the earnings of the two companies will show why.

Throughout the 1950s, the earnings of Company A had grown at the compound rate of 1% a year which permitted only an occasional slight increase in the dividend. Company B, however, had shown a growth rate of 9% compounded annually, and had increased its dividend somewhat every year. Assuming that Company A could expand its growth rate to 3% and determining that there was no reason to expect a decline in Company B's growth rate, we projected earnings for the former to rise 3% per year, and for the latter to continue its trend of 9% per year. Using the resulting projection of earnings for 1963, we found that Company A's price-earnings ratio had declined from 14.6 to 13.3, and that these earnings with a normal payout would permit a dividend that yielded 5.2% on the present price. Company B's projected 1963 earnings resulted in a price-earnings ratio of 14.4 as compared to the current ratio of 18.4, and the estimated dividend for that year produced a yield of 5.2%. Projecting just a little further to 1965, we found that on these earnings, Company A was selling at a ratio of 12.5 as compared to Company B's 12.2, and Company A's stock yielded 5.2% compared to 5.9% for Company B's stock. Thus, for anyone able and willing to look three to five years ahead, Company B's stock represents a better investment than that of Company A even though it is higher priced relative to current earnings and dividends.

This points up the fact that the investing public is looking ahead to what earnings will be and not what they are. It is for this reason that they are willing to buy Company B's stock on a 3.7% yield basis even though Company B's mortgage bonds yield 5%. They expect the yield on the stock to rise above the bond yield in the next three years. This emphasis on future earnings is why many electronic and other growth stocks sell at more than 40 times current earnings and yield less than 1%. It is obvious the buyers are looking to the future, and are seeking growth in per share earnings. Current yields are more or less ignored and a dollar of earnings is no longer considered to be worth less than a dollar in the stockholder's hands. As a matter of fact, a premium is placed on the reinvested earnings because they will earn additional dollars, undiminished by a tax bite.

As earlier stated, basic investment philosophies are slow to change, and changes are normally brought about only by some substantial shock. The current philosophy can be summarized as follows. With a continuing high tax rate and an inflationary economy, common stocks are better investments than fixed income securities. From a long range point of view, properly selected common stocks are almost sure to show appreciation in the absence of a forced sale during a low market. A key factor in proper selection is the rate of growth in per share earnings and the faster the rate of growth, the higher will be the price-earnings ratio. Obviously this philosophy is predicated on confidence in the future of the economy. I believe this philosophy will continue to dominate the market until some shock occurs to undermine this confidence. Shock by its very definition is unpredictable, so no one can say how long the current philosophy will dominate the market. However, with our population surge, an ever increasing standard of living, and great technological developments, it is difficult to see the economy failing to expand over the foreseeable future. Therefore, companies should strive for growth in per share earnings in order to make their securities attractive to investors. If they succeed, their stocks are almost sure to sell at an expanded price-earnings ratio.

How can utilities obtain a growth in earnings when their rate of return is restricted by regulation, and why should they be interested in a high price-earnings ratio for their stock, are natural questions to be asked at this point.

GROWTH IN PER SHARE EARNINGS

Reputation of earnings growth is neither easily earned nor quickly lost in the stock market. Such reputation is based either on a long-term earnings record or on factors which lead the investor to believe that there will be future earnings growth. As examples, reason indicated that utilities even though they had strong growth in terms of physical units could not have strong growth in earnings because earnings were limited by regulation. It took actual earnings results for many years to convince the market that there were utilities such as Florida Power & Light, Texas Utilities, Houston Lighting & Power, Florida Power, Atlantic City Electric, and Virginia Electric

& Power, which had an earnings growth comparable to that of the faster growing industrials. In determining the growth rate, the investor usually determines the rate at which earnings grew over the past five or 10 years, and then reasons whether or not there is likely to be any change in this rate. This is why a reputation of growth is not easily earned but requires continuing efforts over a long period of years. And once acquired, the reputation is not quickly lost as is indicated by Houston Lighting & Power's record. From 1950 through 1956 its earnings expanded at the compound rate of about 16% annually, but for 1957 through 1959, the growth rate was a very mediocre 2%. Still Houston has the reputation of being a growth company and its stock sells at a healthy 25 times earnings.

The market place will also put a growth reputation on stocks that have very little earnings record if reasoning indicates prospective future growth. This is the present situation for many electronic companies whose stocks sell at very high price-earnings ratios even though they have a very limited earnings record. In the case of utilities though, reasoning will not give these results. The market has to be shown by actual results extending over a period of years.

Return limited by regulation narrows opportunities for producing earnings growth. However, although the rate of return is very important, it is not the only factor affecting earnings. For example, Company B, previously cited as having a growth rate of 9% compounded annually for the decade of the 1950s actually showed a decline on its return on invested capital between 1950 and 1959. In 1950 its operating income amounted to 6.7% of its invested capital, whereas in 1959 it was only 5.9%. Still its per share earnings more than doubled from 1950 to 1959. This is cited to indicate the importance of "below the line" financial factors.

In addition to rate of return, other "below the line" factors affecting per share results are reinvested earnings, capital structure, cost of prior capital, and the price obtained from sale of common stock relative to book value. This latter factor can have a most important bearing on earnings as will be shown a little later.

Reinvested earnings can have an important, even though relatively slow, effect on the growth of earnings of a utility. Not only do you have the earning power on this added capital, but the increase in equity permits a firm to sell a proportionate amount of prior securities. If the cost of these prior securities is less than the allowable return, the company can obtain additional earnings for the common stock. The resulting compounding of earnings can be quite attractive depending on the allowable return and the cost of prior money. Actually, if many stockholders did not need the income, it would be best from their long term point of view to reinvest all earnings. I can think of no other industry where a compounding of earnings could be so effective with the same amount of certainty over a period of years. However, since many stockholders do require income on their investments, dividends must be paid. There has been much discussion in financial and academic circles about dividend payout, and it has often been said that a payout of about 75% is proper for utilities. My own feeling is that such a generalization is meaningless. The payout should vary by companies and should be geared to the risk involved or stockholders' requirements if they can be determined. I would consider 75% pretty much of a maximum unless there was no likelihood of growth in earnings. If earnings do show a good growth trend, some small annual increment in dividends is an effective way of proving to the market that you do have growth. With a five to ten year record of a constant growth in dividends, even though it is not substantial, investors will calculate yields on future expectations depending on their state of confidence rather than on the basis of current dividends. Once again, it is anticipation that really counts in the market value of a stock.

Under certain market conditions, changes in capital structure can have an important effect on the trend of earnings. Back in the early 1950s when bonds could be sold on a 3% basis and preferred stocks could be sold on a 4% basis, the industry had a most unusual opportunity to build a record of growth which would have added to the market appraisal of its earning power. Capital added at this low cost contributed enormously to future earning power. But many utilities missed this opportunity and built up equity positions instead. The proportionately large sales of common stock at that time not only were made at low prices relative to earnings, dividends and book value, but they tended to dilute the per share earnings, thus obscuring the trend in net income. While this extraordinary opportunity no longer exists, still it is possible to add to the common stock's earning power if prior securities can be sold at a lower cost than what utilities are allowed to earn on their overall investment.

TAILORING CAPITAL STRUCTURES

Whether or not utilities should take this route to increased earnings depends on a number of factors. Can they reasonably expect to earn the full allowable rate of return over a period of time? What is their present capital structure, and will it permit the addition of prior securities without taking away all flexibility on future financing? How costly is the alternative of common stock financing? What is the likely trend in the cost of prior securities? There are no general answers to these questions, for they depend on a company's specific situation and requirements. However, I would like to make a few comments on capital structure. As in the case of dividend payout, there has been much discussion of standards for capital structures. I feel here, too, there is danger in generalization. Capital structures should be tailored to the inherent risks which means that they will vary not only by industry but by companies within the industry. Certainly a company with a very stable earnings experience does not require as large an equity position as a company with volatile or uncertain earnings. In addition, capital structures should vary from year to year depending upon markets for various classes of securities. During periods of low interest rates and preferred stock costs, they should rely relatively heavily on this type of financing and not be influenced to any important degree by the resulting effect on their capital ratios. Conversely, when interest rates are high, common stocks are likely to be in favor. Under such conditions they should rely more heavily than normally on common stock financing, especially if their stock is selling at a good premium over its book value. However, offerings of common stock should not be so large or so frequently made that per share earnings are completely diluted. The ideal time to offer common stock is during a year when they foresee a large enough gain in earnings to more than offset the added number of outstanding shares so that per share results will show a gain. This type of flexibility, which can mean so much to the earnings record and, therefore, the cost of financing, becomes valueless if management or regulatory bodies prescribe capitalization ratios without a great deal of give in them. A federal agency setting capital structure standards for an entire industry would add unnecessarily to the cost of financing for many companies.

The rising cost of prior capital is almost sure to have a negative effect on the growth record under current market conditions. If prior securities can be sold at a lower cost than the average cost of existing outstanding prior securities, a company will increase earnings on the common stock through this type of financing. Conversely, if the cost of new prior capital exceeds the average cost of outstanding issues, per share earnings will be diluted, everything else being equal. To illustrate how this works, we will take a hypothetical utility with $100,000,000 of invested capital which requires $50,000,000 of new capital for expansion purposes. In order to show the effect of the cost of prior capital, we will keep all other factors affecting earnings constant. Thus we assume that there is no change in the rate of return, there are no reinvested earnings, capital structure ratios are kept constant, and all sales of common stock are made at book value. The only factor to show a variation is the cost of prior capital, with the new capital costing $5\frac{1}{2}\%$ as compared to a 4% average cost on existing issues. The allowable rate of return is 6%, the capitalization is 70% prior capital, and 30% common stock surplus. It has outstanding 1,000,000 shares of common stock with a book value of $30 a share.

The 6% return on the present $100,000,000 of capital produces operating income of $6,000,000. From this is deducted the 4% charges on its $70,000,000 of prior capital or $2,800,000. This leaves $3,200,000 for the common stock or $3.20 a share. The $50,000,000 of new capital is raised through the sale of $35,000,000 of prior securities and $15,000,000 of common stock to preserve the 70–30 capital ratios. The common stock being sold at the book value of $30 requires the issuance of 500,000 shares and the sale of prior capital at a $5\frac{1}{2}\%$ cost increases fixed charges by $1,925,000. Under these conditions, the per share earnings work out as follows: The 6% return on the $150,000,000 of invested capital would produce operating income of $93,000,000. Deducting the new fixed charges of $4,725,00 leaves $4,725,000 available for the common stock. This on 1,500,000 shares gives earnings of $2.85 a share—an 11% decline from earnings prior to the expansion. If there were no escape from these results, management would soon be under pressure to hold capital expenditures to a bare minimum, and service would then deteriorate. If this continued over an extended period of time, utilities would have financial problems similar to those of the railroads.

OFFSETTING FACTORS

However, there are some other offsetting factors. First of all, there would be some retained earnings. Assuming that the 50% expansion was spread over a five year period, and the company paid out 75% of earnings, retained earnings would amount to $4,000,000, making it necessary to raise only $11,000,000 instead of $15,000,000 of new common stock money. The sale of this amount at the book value of $30 a share would require the issuance of 366,667 shares, so that there would be 1,366,667 shares outstanding after the expansion. The net income available for common on this number of shares would give earnings of $3.13 a share, which would still be slightly less than earned before the expansion. Under these conditions, stockholders still would not be happy. Instead of the growth that they are seeking, they would see some deterioration in spite of having reinvested $4,000,000 of their earnings. With the stock out of favor, new shares would difficult to sell except at sacrifice prices, and the tendency would be to curtail capital expenditures.

There would remain only two factors that could give the common stock investor appeal. One would be a higher rate of return which commissions are reluctant to give, and the other would be selling the new common stock at a premium over book value. This latter factor is not fully appreciated by many investors, utility managers, or regulators. To show its effect, we will carry our calculations on the hypothetical utility a step further.

First, we will assume that in raising the $11,000,000 of new common money the company is able to sell the stock at a 50% premium over book value, or at $45 a share. This would require the issuance of only 244,444 shares, so that at the end of the expansion there would be 1,244,444 shares outstanding. On this basis, earnings would work out to $3.43 a share. The stock is now becoming somewhat more attractive, but still leaves something to be desired.

Now we will assume that the new stock can be sold at a 150% premium over book value, which is very possible in the present market. At a price of $75, only 146,667 shares would have to be sold. Pro forma earnings would then be $3.73 a share as compared to the $3.20 earned before the expansion. This illustrates how important the premium over book value can be. The premiums are largely the result of a high price-earnings ratio, and this is why the utility and the commission should be interested in the price-earnings ratio of the stock.

PRICE-EARNINGS RATIOS

With high price-earnings ratios contributing to the premium at which stock sells over its book value, and this premium being such a strong stimulant to earnings growth, the utility should continuously do whatever it can to attain a maximum ratio for its stock. This will give lowest cost common stock financing which helps to offset higher cost prior security financing, and even in connection with the latter it will have a beneficial effect.

As has been stressed earlier in this paper, growth in per share earnings is the greatest single contributor to high price-earnings ratios. And as was stated, the rate of growth for a particular stock is determined by its past record, particularly in the case of a utility stock. This is one strong reason why I feel that stock dividends are by and large undesirable. Statistical services, security analysts, and most stockholders do not adjust the earnings record for stock dividends unless they are substantial. If a company has a growth rate of 6%, which is slightly above average, and pays an annual 3% stock dividend, the historical growth record will show a 3% trend which is somewhat below average. Because of the apparent difference in growth rates, the price-earnings ratio will be adversely affected. The initial market response to a stock dividend may be favorable, but over the long run the better earnings record that will be shown where there are no stock dividends, will have a more favorable effect on the market price of the stock.

FROWNS ON STOCK DIVIDENDS AND RIGHTS

It is true that there are many investors who like to receive the additional shares that go with a stock dividend. They feel that they are receiving something for nothing and that the proceeds from the sale of the new shares are the equivalent of an extra dividend. Actually it does not work out this way. Although they have received additional pieces of paper that are impressively engraved, their proportionate interest in the company is actually unchanged. If they sell these shares, their interest is actually reduced. Thus, such a sale really results in a reduction in capital, and in no way does it produce income as an "extra dividend." If this extra "income" is essential to the stockholder, the very same results can be obtained by the sale of a proportionate number of shares of his present holdings. The issuance of shares through a stock dividend is expensive, creates considerable bookkeeping for all concerned, actually gives the stockholder nothing, and obscures the growth in earnings with a resulting adverse effect on the price-earnings ratio. By and large, stockholders are hurt rather than benefited by stock dividends over the long run.

The effect of preemptive rights in the sale of common stocks is quite similar to that of stock dividends. Although many stockholders, not understanding the long term implications, are in favor of rights, actually they are hurt by such an offering. The sale of stock through a rights offering, by its very nature, requires that the stock be sold well below the market price in order to give a value to the rights. When this is done, the premium over book value which the company receives and which is so important to low cost financing is greatly reduced.

Moreover, more shares must be sold to produce the same number of dollars than would have to be sold if the stock were priced at its full market value. This unnecessary dilution, if repeated often, can slow down the rate of growth in earnings. With the slower growth, the price-earnings ratio is likely to suffer so that even the stockholder who subscribes does not realize the full potential of a better price-earnings ratio. But experience indicates that most stockholders either are unable financially or are unwilling to increase their investment in the company, so sell their rights in the market. The market price of the rights is based on the market price of the stock which is normally under pressure during the rights period. As a result, most stockholders sell their rights in a poor market and are happy to receive a few extra dollars because they do not understand the longer-term implications. Actually, they would be better off if the company sold stock at the maximum premium over book value and avoided the unnecessary dilution that is implicit in a rights offering. The added earnings and the probable improvement in the price-earnings ratio resulting from the better growth would far outweigh the few extra dollars obtained from the sale of rights.

IMPORTANCE OF MANAGEMENT

Although growth in earnings is the largest single factor in price-earnings ratios under present market conditions, there are other factors. Management is a very important factor. The investor wants to feel that the officers are working in the interest of the owners of the enterprise. It is amazing how many managements give the impression that their first concern is maintaining themselves in office. Still others give the impression that they are working for the consumers or the employees. Indications of this are often portrayed in annual reports, conversations, speeches, and most importantly in the earnings record and the financial policy pursued. Another important factor is the political risk. Is the utility vulnerable to subsidized government competition? What about the regulatory climate? Many commissions either through attrition of the rate base, regulatory lag, unrealistic rates of return, or the usurping of managerial prerogatives on financial matters, have made it impossible for a company to compile a record of growth. Stocks of utilities operating under this type of regulation usually sell at relatively low price-earnings ratios. There are a number of states in which we refuse to invest funds because of a regulatory climate that makes earnings growth next to impossible.

There are other factors which have a bearing on the price-earnings ratio but are not as important as growth, management, and regulation. Does the stock have a broad market? This is important to large investors who not only may want to buy large quantities of the stock, but also want to know that they can dispose of the stock if circumstances change. A company's efforts in keeping investors and the financial community informed about its operations is another factor with some bearing on the price-earnings ratio of its stock. Full information not only gives an investor confidence, but it often clears up preconceived, erroneous opinions. When Atlantic City Electric first became independent of its holding company, it was amazing how many sophisticated investors thought that it was nothing but a boardwalk company. It takes a continuous effort to keep the financial community educated, but the effort is usually worthwhile in its contribution to lower financing costs.

The economy of the firm's territory and the population growth are given weight in the market price of its stock, as is its capital structure. In my opinion the importance of the latter has been greatly exaggerated by many financial people in the past. An overly strong capital structure often indicates to me that the management is more interested in maintaining the prestige of its office than it is in obtaining maximum earnings for its common stockholders. The conditions that make me interested in a utility with a high common stock equity ratio are (1) the stock is selling at a tremendous premium over its book value, or (2) there are indications that financial policy has changed and that the equity ratio will be allowed to decline, thus adding earnings to the common stock if the cost of prior money is less than the return on investment.

COST OF CAPITAL

There is one final subject on which I would like to offer a few comments. This has to do with the cost of capital theory in determining the allowable rate of return in regulatory proceedings. This poses the greatest danger which the utility industry faces from both the consumers and the stockholder's point of view. If not very carefully applied, it could prove chaotic for the entire privately financed industry. The strict adherence to the cost of capital theory in which the cost of common stock capital is calculated on the basis of current earnings would definitely result in a higher cost of overall capital. Utility securities and particularly the common stock would become unattractive and a company would have difficulty in obtaining sufficient capital to meet its increasing demands, not to mention new capital required for improvement in service.

The cost of capital theory is difficult to apply, and there is great risk that the rate will be incorrectly calculated. The cost of prior capital can be determined within a slight degree of accuracy, but even here there is room for some argument. However, when it comes to calculating the cost of common stock money, I do not see how it can be done with any degree of accuracy. As has been pointed out throughout this paper, the market price of stock is determined not by its present earnings but by what the investing public believes its earnings will be some time in the future. How far into the future they are willing to look depends upon their degree of confidence. Consequently to accurately measure the cost of common stock money, one would have to know what level of earnings was being estimated and how far into the future these earnings were being projected. With these two unknowns being subject to dispute, the tendency is to use current earnings which is definitely inaccurate. Thus calculated, a stock selling at 20 times earnings would be considered to have a capital cost of 5%, but actually the stock is selling at 20 times earnings only because investors looking at past history believe it will have higher earnings in the future. It is very unlikely that a stock with a record of no growth would sell at this high a ratio, but more likely would sell at about 10 times earnings.

The use of current earnings in this calculation by its very nature would eventually contribute to a low price-earnings ratio, for as the price-earnings ratio rose, the cost of common stock money thus calculated would decline and result in a lower allowable rate of return. This lower rate of return would minimize earnings growth if not eliminate it, and without growth the stock would lose favor. It would sell at a much lower premium over book value and, as was shown earlier, either this premium or a higher rate of return is required to offset the higher cost of prior capital. This ability to sell common at or above book value is essential to a financially healthy industry with a growing demand. To sell stock below book value would have an opposite diluting effect on existing stockholders who would become reluctant to authorize the sale of new shares. The railroad industry seldom raises new capital through the sale of common stock.

If cost of capital must be used in rate proceedings, the cost of the common stock component should be based on some estimate of future earnings and then the overall results should be used merely as a rough guide rather than an accurate measure of the cost to the company. In my opinion a much more satisfactory way for all concerned would be to allow some spread ranging from 1% to 2% above the cost of prior capital. To stay financially healthy the utility industry must be able to raise this type of money profitably and show a growth in per share earnings on the common stock.

PORTFOLIO MANAGEMENT— THEORY AND PRACTICE

III ☼

INTRODUCTION

I F INVESTING WELL IS AN ART rather than a science, as is generally accepted, then the highest form of this art is the management of security portfolios. A delicate balance is demanded to maintain principal and generate income from investable funds. Analysis precedes selection, but that is only a part of the total problem of tailoring security portfolios to both individual and institutional needs. The tenets of security selection must be combined with an appraisal of the many economic and personal factors which enter into decision-making for the optimal portfolio. Traditionally, most of the focus has been on the techniques of security selection, with only modest attention paid by analysts and writers to the portfolio selection process. The authors of the essays in this section hope to redress this imbalance, while exposing the still disturbing problems surrounding the selection of investment media for money management.

Geoffrey P. Clarkson and Allan H. Meltzer have combined to produce a paper which challenges the thesis that a positive theory of portfolio selection does not yet exist. Computer assistance afforded the opportunity of testing a model against a wide variety of observed behavior, with exciting results. That we are embarking on new adventures in portfolio management seems assured from the results of this recent research.

The second essay in this group, by Frederick N. Goodrich, follows the traditional approach to portfolio selection, ranging from prudent philosophical considerations to the mechanical yardsticks which professionals have found reliable. Several essays follow which assess the challenges to portfolio management of long-term economic factors and the investment media necessary to offset these ravages. John C. Clendenin's research emphasizes the suitability of common stocks as high-grade investment holdings during periods of price level instability. Harry C. Sauvain shows the impact of changing interest rates on the traditionally conservative bond medium, and the resultant pressures on portfolio management. The excellent research of Harold G. Fraine and Robert H. Mills quantifies the problem of reserves for anticipated portfolio losses using medium and high-grade corporate bonds. They point out the real risk which can be absorbed when contractual forms of investment media are overemphasized in portfolio construction.

Mechanical aids to portfolio management, and the resultant attempts to time market movements, are scathingly denounced by A. Wilfred May with a credo that honors the traditional value approach to investing. The essay by Rodger W. Bridwell cautions against indiscriminate use of single mechanical formulas with an evaluation of the risk factors in the popular program known as "dollar averaging".

11. PORTFOLIO SELECTION: A HEURISTIC APPROACH[*]

❀ Geoffrey P. Clarkson
Allan H. Meltzer

INTRODUCTION

THE PROBLEM OF SELECTING a portfolio can be divided into two components: (1) the analysis of individual securities and (2) the selection of a portfolio or group of securities based on the previous analysis. Up to now, the majority of writers have focused on the first part of the problem and have developed several, well-accepted methods of analysis.[1] Little attention has been paid to the second phase of the problem. It is to this second part of the portfolio selection process that this paper is principally devoted.

Recently a normative approach to portfolio selection for a particular kind of investor has been proposed by Markowitz.[2] He defines a decision problem (in this case the selection of a set of securities), assumes a decision function, and observes the behavior which the system generates when inputs are varied. In his analysis, Markowitz shows that, for given securities, a rational investor can

[*] From *The Journal of Finance,* Vol. XV, No. 4 (December, 1960), pp. 465–480. Reprinted by permission of *The Journal of Finance.*
[1] B. Graham and D. Dodd, *Security Analysis* (3d ed.; New York: McGraw-Hill Book Co., Inc., 1951), is an example of one of the more comprehensive works in this area.
[2] H. Markowitz, *Portfolio Selection* (New York: John Wiley & Sons, 1959).

determine the "efficient" set.[3] To obtain an optimal portfolio from the efficient set, additional assumptions are required: namely, a Markowitz investor must choose that combination of mean and variance which provides maximum utility. But, whatever form the decision function takes, it must be such as to make its mathematical representation tractable and soluble.

A positive theory of portfolio selection does not yet exist. Such a theory must describe and predict the investment behavior of individuals under uncertainty. Whether one constructs a positive theory or compares the results of a normative theory with existing procedures, knowledge of actual behavior is a prerequisite. Since neither a theory nor an adequate description of the selection process is available, the aim of this paper is partially to fill both gaps.

The focus of our study is the investment of trust funds held by banks. We view this process as a problem in decision-making. A heuristic[4] model, written as a computer program, simulates the procedures used to assign accounts to a common trust fund or to select particular portfolios. The analysis is based on the operations at a medium-sized national bank (with trust assets approximately equal to the average for all national banks). The decision-maker of our problem is the trust investment officer;[5] our simulation asks the computer program to select a portfolio based on information available to the investment officer at the time his decision is made.

This approach is related to the traditional literature of financial analysis and portfolio selection. Like the traditional approach, it is based on rules of thumb (heuristics) which guide the decision-maker from the original input of information about the client, the securities markets, and the economy to the choice of particular portfolios. But, unlike that approach, the rules must be completely specified, unambiguous, and capable of being refuted by empirical tests. When the rules for processing information (or heuristics) yield results consistent with those obtained by human

---

[3] *Ibid.* Portfolios which provide the maximum return for a given variance are "efficient."

[4] Heuristics are important, as they often lead us quickly to solutions which we would otherwise reach much more expensively by analytic techniques. For a more extensive discussion of heuristic programs see H. A. Simon and A. Newell, "What Have Computers To Do with Management?" (RAND Publication P-1708, May 21, 1959).

[5] It should be noted carefully that our results reflect the behavior of one investor and hence may not describe the general case.

subjects, the model is said to have "simulated" the decision process; the set of heuristics (or simulation model) has "predicted" the behavior of the subject.[6]

Even if the model fails to predict, simulation provides valuable information about the decision process in the form of a step-by-step record of the procedures used. Sources of error can frequently be identified and eliminated. In this way, the model, through a series of successive tests, can be designed to approximate the behavior of the subject or subjects.

Simulation accommodates both the inductive and the deductive approach. One may simulate the processes used by a number of individuals and attempt to generalize the results. Alternatively, one can construct a model and test it against a wide variety of observed behavior. The latter approach has been used in this paper.

Simulation need not involve a computer, just as addition does not require an adding machine. The advantage of the computer is its ability to solve complex problems more accurately. Moreover, the computer permits the addition to the simulation program of as many mechanisms as are interesting and important, subject only to the speed and storage capacity of the computer. Thus, by using the computer, one can move farther away from an assumed decision function and focus on the actual operations performed by a decision-maker.

The next section briefly describes some recent developments in the theory of human problem-solving. Section III discusses the application of problem-solving to the trust investment decision. We then describe the computer model which selects the assets to be held in particular accounts. The results of some of the tests of the model are shown in the appendix.

COMPUTERS AND THE THEORY OF HUMAN PROBLEM-SOLVING

Recent interest in the theory of human problem-solving[7] has focused on the computer programing of mental processes. Most of this work

---

[6] For a more complete discussion of the theory and technique of simulation see the . . . symposium on simulation in the December, 1960, *American Economic Review*.

[7] This section is largely based on A. Newell and H. A. Simon, *The Simulation of Human Thought* (RAND Corporation, June, 1959).

has been directed toward developing an understanding of the operations performed in thinking; some recent work has focused on the application of these techniques to industrial or business problems.[8]

Basic to these studies is the assumption that thinking processes can be isolated as well as identified and that they can be represented by a series of straightforward mechanical operations. This is not to say that thought processes are simple and easy to represent but rather that they can be broken down in their elemental parts, which, in turn, consist of collections of simple mechanisms. These operations are written as a set of statements and rules which, when coded in computer language, become a computer program. The program is tested by running it on a digital computer, and, as in the more familiar case of mathematical theory, the logical consequences of the initial conditions are derived by performing the operations according to the specified rules.

In an actual simulation the derived computer statements are compared with the output of human subjects who have verbally reported (in detail) their thought processes and decisions. If the humans and the computer use similar processes, the computer is said to have successfully simulated the behavior of the humans. Moreover, if this occurs, the computer program is sufficient to account for the "observed" behavior.

It must be remembered, however, that computers are neither necessary nor sufficient devices for building heuristic models. A human can replace the computer and perform each operation as directed by the program. But humans are inefficient at this task and are usually replaced by digital computers.

One particular characteristic of computers, called "transfer" or "branching," is essential to the study of problem-solving and infor-

[8] For examples, see the following: L. A. Hiller, Jr., and L. M. Isaacson, *Experimental Music* (New York: McGraw-Hill Book Co., Inc., 1959); A. Newell, J. C. Shaw, and H. A. Simon, "Empirical Explorations of the Logic Theory Machine," *Proceedings of the Western Joint Computer Conference*, February 26–28, 1957, pp. 218–30; A. Newell, J. C. Shaw, and H. A. Simon, "Chessplaying Programs and the Problem of Complexity," *IBM Journal of Research and Development*, No. 2 (October, 1958), pp. 320–35; E. A. Feigenbaum, "An Information Processing Theory of Verbal Learning" (unpublished Ph.D. thesis, Carnegie Institute of Technology, 1959); J. Feldman, "An Analysis of Predictive Behavior in a Two-Choice Situation" (unpublished Ph.D. thesis, Carnegie Institute of Technology, 1959); and F. M. Tonge, "A Heuristic Program for Assembly Line Balancing" (unpublished Ph. D. thesis, Carnegie Institute of Technology, 1959).

mation-processing. Conditional transfer operations permit a program to choose between alternatives and/or fellow strategies.

As a hypothetical example, in a problem-solving context, consider the following translation problem:[9] The computer is supplied with a Russian-language dictionary, a program, and a Russian story. The program specifies that symbols representing Russian words be read and that the corresponding English words be printed out. The program finds a word in the Russian story. It is instructed to search through a list of commonly used words (or dictionary), until it finds symbols identical with the symbols it is using to represent the Russian word. The conditional transfer operation specifies that (1) if the symbols are identical, replace the Russian symbols with the corresponding English symbols and transfer to the next word (set of symbols) in the story, then repeat the process for the next Russian word in the story, but (2) if the symbols are not identical, transfer to the next Russian word in the dictionary.

Three points are worth emphasizing. First, the program is iterative, i.e., it uses its operations repetitively to process different pieces of information or to solve quite separate problems. During the processing, it sorts information, retaining those parts which are useful, discarding the irrelevant. Second, the program is capable of modifying the "dictionary" or lists. Frequently used "words" may be separated, to narrow future search activity in the interests of economizing time. Third, the hypothetical program described above is general. Any type of list could replace the Russian dictionary as an input without necessitating modification of the search-compare-transfer operations.

While the general processes which the computer follows remain unchanged, each successful simulation must recognize the constraints which arise within the context of the particular problem. These constraints restrict the program to those processes that are consistent with the operations performed by humans engaged in similar tasks. In the translation example, a constraint might call for initiating search by looking at the first letter of the word; in searching a list of Treasury notes, the computer might first consider their yields or maturities.

In our work, a list of common stocks becomes the basic list of the problem—i.e., the dictionary. The goals of the client and the

[9] While this is not the process followed by most translation programs, it is illustrative of the economics inherent in conditional transfer operations.

amount of money to be invested represent the Russian story of our example. And conditional transfer operations allow the program to follow the strategies of portfolio selection.

When the constraints which arise in the choice of portfolios are imposed on the general theory of human problem-solving, a theory of portfolio selection emerges. The following section describes the constraints and the resulting theory.

SIMULATION OF THE TRUST INVESTMENT PROCESS

An investor is confronted with a large assortment of information which he may use in making decisions. There is a wide variety of data, past and current, on the operation of firms and the market valuation of their stocks. There are many published predictions about the present and future state of the general economy, the stock market, and particular industries and firms. There are legal restrictions and the desires of clients to be considered when an investor acts in an agency of fiduciary capacity. These factors, when evaluated and combined with an investment policy, ultimately result in a decision to buy specific quantities of particular stocks and bonds.

An investor choosing a portfolio is processing information: he sorts the useful from the irrelevant and decides which parts of the total information flow are most important. As we have seen, the theory of human problem-solving was built to handle problems of this type. The postulates of the theory particularly relevant for our purposes are that the following exist:

   1. A control system consisting of a number of memories, which contain symbolized information and are interconnected by various ordering relations. . . .
   2. A number of primitive information processes, which operate on the information in the memories. . . .
   3. A perfectly definite set of rules for combining these processes into whole programs of processing. From a program it is possible to deduce unequivocally what externally observable behavior will be generated.[10]

[10] A. Newell, J. C. Shaw, and H. A. Simon, "Elements of a Theory of Human Problem Solving," *Psychological Review*, LXV (1958), pp. 151 ff.

In the portfolio selection problem, these postulates consist of (1) The memory, i.e., lists of industries each of which has associated a sublist of companies. The memory also contains lists of information associated with the individual companies.[11] (2) Search procedures for selecting a portfolio from the information stored in the memory. These function in a manner similar to the traditional clerk who prepares lists of stocks suitable for current investment by scanning a master list. (3) A set of rules or criteria which guide the decision-making processes by stipulating when and how each primitive process is to be used. The set of rules constitutes the processing program for an individual investor. It might be compared with the heuristics of the traditional "expert," but, as noted, there is an important difference—the program must be unambiguous.

Like any problem-solving program, the simulation of the portfolio selection process relies principally on this set of basic operating rules. The rules are specified in advance and may be modified by the outcome of specific decisions. In particular, the record of past successes, failures, and the processes involved in each are stored in memory. The program modifies its behavior by eliminating such unsuccessful procedures. In this sense it learns from its past experience.[12]

In common with other heuristic programs, the process is iterative. Lists of industries and companies are searched for particular attributes; sublists are created, searched, and again divided. For example, to obtain a high-growth portfolio, the list of companies stored in memory is searched to obtain shares with the desired characteristics. Additional criteria are employed to narrow (or expand) this list. Further search and matching against desired criteria yield the specific selection of stocks to buy.

Like the investor it simulates, the computer stores the final result (list) for future use. When the same problem recurs, the entire search process need not be repeated. The list may be judged

---

[11] Investors categorize companies by industry. Not all investors may associate identical companies with a given industry, but the process of classification by industry remains invariant as the primary basis for listing companies in the memory. The information associated with each company also varies among investors, but each has a list of attributes and values stored in memory (e.g., growth rate, dividend rate, price/earnings ratio, expected earnings, expected yields, etc.).

[12] For a complete discussion see G. P. E. Clarkson and H. A. Simon, "Micro-Simulation: The Simulation of Individual and Group Behavior," *American Economic Review*, December, 1960.

by present criteria, accepted, adapted to new conditions, or completely rejected. In the latter event, the computer would use a
conditional transfer operation to renew search activity until a new
list had been formed.

Within this general framework, the problem of constructing
a model of investment behavior becomes a problem of uncovering
the basic rules (operations) which lead to a decision to purchase
particular securities. The following procedure was used to obtain
these data: First, the trust department of a local bank was observed
by attending committee meetings called to review past and future
decisions. Interviews were then conducted with departmental officers
to obtain a better understanding of the lines of authority. From
these procedures it became apparent that the investment officer
was the primary locus of all decisions relevant to the choice of
portfolios.

Interviewing as a technique provided helpful background
information. However, as portfolio selection has a well-developed
lore, this technique failed to separate the relevant from the irrelevant
criteria.

Second, the history of several accounts was examined. Naive
behavioral models were constructed to approximate the recorded
behavior and to help uncover those processes which appeared to
be invariant between accounts.

Third, and most important, the investment officer was asked
to permit "protocols" to be made of his decision processes.[13] To
accustom the subject to verbalizing his procedures, the first case
was based on an account with which he had dealt before. Artifici-
ality was introduced into the description of the beneficiary and the
past history of the account. Successive protocols recorded the
investment officer's decision processes for accounts which arose in
the course of his work. The decisions made during these problem
sessions determined the particular securities which were purchased
for these accounts.

---

[13] A "protocol" is a transport of the verbalized thought and actions of a subject
when the subject has been instructed to think or problem-solve aloud. Thus the
transcript is a record of the subject's thought processes while engaged in making
a decision. Since a protocol is a detailed description of what a person does, it
avoids some of the problems inherent in interview and questionnaire techniques,
which ask the subject to state his reasons for behaving as he does. For further
discussion see Newell, Shaw, and Simon, "Elements of a Theory of Human
Problem Solving," *op. cit.*

From these protocols a program of the investment decision process was built. As yet, the number of protocols is insufficient to answer all the problems that are raised in writing such a program. But our experience has shown that programming focuses our attention on precisely those details for which our specific knowledge is weakest. To date, there are still large gaps in our understanding of the decision-making process, especially in the areas of goal formation[14] and the association of particular industries with particular goals. Also the selection process which determines the particular company and the number of shares to be purchased has not been completely determined. However, an adequate amount of information has been gathered to program a substantial part of the portfolio selection process.

THE PORTFOLIO SELECTION PROCESS

This section describes the step-by-step simulation of the trust investment process in a medium-sized bank. At present we are directly concerned with the way in which common stocks are chosen for individual portfolios. The selection of bonds and preferred stocks has not yet been explicitly considered.

The investment officer's behavior can be described by a flow chart (Fig. 1) detailing the sequential pattern followed in the decision-making process. Each of the elements in the flow chart requires a specific decision by the investment officer. Although the model operated with a basic list of eighty stocks, specification of the goal of the account (step 2) eliminates securities inconsistent with the goal and reduces the list to approximately thirty stocks.

The model was required to predict the portfolios for two accounts with different goals. That is, operations 6–9 were performed as directed by the program. The output was compared with the investment officer's recorded decisions. The results are shown in the appendix.

The descriptions which follow detail the processes used. Translated into symbolic form, they become the computer program.[15]

---

[14] E.g., the precise way in which a "growth account" differs from an "income account."

[15] The program was written in an information-processing language IPL-V (Newell and Simon).

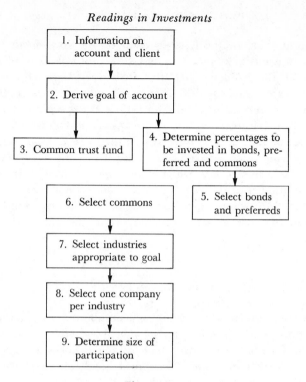

Figure 1.

Information on account and client.   There are two basic
sources of information on each account: the administrative officer's
interviews with the client and the written record, containing a copy
of the legal instrument (often a will) setting up the trust.[16] From
the accumulated data and the subjective impressions of the administrative officer, the investment officer proceeds to step 2: formulating
a concept of what the client wants the trust to do, i.e., the goal of
the account. Before transforming this concept into a goal (or
investment policy) for the account, the investment officer must
choose between two courses of action. Conditional transfer operations direct the program to (1) invest the assets in the common

---

[16] In most cases, this contains information about the beneficiaries, the investment
powers of the bank, what is to happen to the principal, what should be done
with the income, etc. From these sources he also gets information on the
beneficiaries' age, marital status, number and age of dependents, place of legal
residence, income tax bracket, and status and age of future beneficiaries, if any.

trust fund (C.T.F.),[17] (2) set up an individual portfolio for the account.

The bank prides itself on the "individual" investment service which it offers to its customers. Thus there are clear preferences for setting up individual accounts whenever the size of the account permits. The following rules (or procedures) guide the decision to invest the assets in the common trust fund:

> a. All "legal" [18] trusts are eligible for investment in C.T.F. The funds of beneficiaries who have waived legal requirements are not so invested.
> b. All legal trusts which have less than $K[19] in assets are automatically placed in the C.T.F.
> c. Legal trusts greater than $K may or may not be placed in C.T.F., depending on the goals of the beneficiary. However, as noted, no account may participate for more than $100,000. Thus, in the range between $K and $100,000 the decision will be determined by the goal of the account.

If the client has goals consistent with expected C.T.F. results and does not have assets which permit the purchase of five common stocks in round lots, C.T.F. is indicated, and the process ends.[20]

The investment of assets in the C.T.F. is an all-or-none

[17] The common trust fund was established to provide a medium for the collective investment of trust funds held by the bank in a fiduciary capacity. Investments are restricted to those considered legal for investment in Pennsylvania. Under Federal Reserve Board regulations, no account may participate for more than $100,000. Under Orphan's Court rulings, not more than 10 per cent of the fund may be invested in securities of any one corporation, with the exception of direct and guaranteed obligations of the United States government. In addition, the fund may not own more than 5 per cent of any one class of stock of any corporation or have the amount invested in common stocks exceed one-third of the total investment in the fund.

[18] " 'Legal investment' statutes fall into two general categories: (1) those that restrict all or part of the investments to specific investments or specific classes of investments, and (2) those that limit investment in non-legal securities to a given percentage of the account or fund. The statutory limitations on investment in non-legal securities range from 30 per cent to 50 per cent of the market value (in one state, inventory value) of the fund" ("Survey of Common Trust Funds, 1958" *Federal Reserve Bulletin,* May, 1959, p. 477). Many people, when setting up the trust relation, specifically waive these investment restrictions. Thus "legal" refers to situations in which the investment officer must comply with these investment restrictions.

[19] To protect the bank's anonymity, the precise dollar values are not revealed. Nationally, the average C.T.F. participation is approximately $22,000 (*Federal Reserve Bulletin,* May, 1958, p. 537).

[20] This problem and many of those which follow clearly lend themselves to "conditional transfer" operations in computer terminology.

decision. But all legal accounts greater than $100,000[21] and all which are not of a fiduciary nature have their own portfolios. The minimum size for these accounts depends on the asset composition. For accounts with participation in bonds, as well as common stocks, a minimum of $\frac{1}{2}$K is required; if the account participates only in common stocks, a minimum of $0.4K is required. Smaller accounts are refused or placed in C.T.F. The funds of very small accounts are deposited in a savings bank.

Derive the goal. For all portfolios not invested in C.T.F., the investment officer must formulate a goal. Data previously collected are transformed into an investment policy that approximates his perception of what the client wants. The number of possible combinations is very large. But the goal he decides on must lie somewhere along a continuum between the extremes of growth and income. The bank's records indicate that accounts are categorized into four or five classes: pure growth, growth with some income, income with some growth, and income alone.[22]

Determine percentages to be invested in bonds, preferreds and commons. The main function of the program is to select the particular common stocks to be held in any given account.

In legal trusts, the maximum amount that can be invested in common stocks is 33$\frac{1}{3}$ per cent.[23] In trusts where the legal require-

---

[21] As yet, we have not programed the heuristics underlying the choice of the C.T.F. portfolio. As noted above, we are concerned here only with explaining the mechanisms underlying the decisions on common stocks for individual accounts.

[22] A growth account is roughly defined as one in which the monetary value of the assets appreciates at an average rate of 10 per cent per year for a five-year period. In an account seeking current dividend and interest income, a minimum yield of 4–4$\frac{1}{2}$ per cent is expected. In a mixed growth and income account, a capital appreciation of 5 per cent combined with a dividend of 3–4 per cent is customary.

The goal of an account is determined from the initial data in the following manner. Data on the client: lawyer, high current income, high tax bracket, no pension on retirement, married with no children, desires security after retirement, earnings to be reinvested. The goal of growth with current income as a secondary goal is indicated for the present. Income will be emphasized after the client has retired and is in a lower income tax bracket.

[23] This figure is determined by Pennsylvania state law (Act. No. 340 of 1951) and is the amount designated by the state as constituting a "prudent investment." The prudent-investment criterion limits banks, in practice, to choosing securities which, if preferred stocks, have paid dividends for 16 years and which, if commons, have had positive earnings and have paid dividends in 12 out of 16 years. A list of securities meeting these requirements is prepared by the Pennsylvania Bankers Association.

ments are waived or do not exist, this decision is left to the investment officer. Except under unusual circumstances, such as a
statement that the entire fund be placed in commons, the amount
invested in commons ranges between 40 and 65 per cent.[24]

Select industries appropriate to goal. Despite the large overlap
between industries, the investment officer associates a set of industries
with each goal. These are chosen from a previously selected "preference list."[25] A one-to-one correspondence between goal and industry
does not exist. But each goal invokes a search of the preference
list (memory), which leads to the selection of a particular list of
industries. The length of the list depends on the size of the account,
since each industry is represented only once in any given account.
Thus the association of industries with goals narrows the search for
appropriate securities to a much shorter list.[26]

Select companies. Once an industry has been selected, the
company to be chosen for participation is picked by the
following series of conditional transfer operations. Companies are
examined on the following criteria: (i) subject to tax in Pennsylvania, (ii) legal in Pennsylvania, (iii) current uncertainty, (iv)
growth, (v) yield, (vi) expected earnings, (vii) past earnings, (viii)
expected dividends, (ix) expected price-earnings ratio, (x) past
price-earnings ratio, (xi) amount spent on expansion and/or re-

---

[24] It is abundantly clear from the protocols that the process involved in choosing
government bonds is similar to the ones described for common stocks. Under
present market conditions, it appears to consist of selecting the highest yield
from a table listing short-term governments. Hence it is a search procedure
using established processes within a given memory.

[25] The preference list is the investment officer's working list of stocks. This list
of approximately 80 stocks is categorized by industry. The investment officer
refers to it on every selection that he makes. The preference list is designed to
cover various economic situations. Although it is re-examined every three months,
few changes are made. We take the list as given.

[26] The investment officer's rule of thumb seeks to spread risk by diversification.
But, as Markowitz (*op. cit.*, p. 109) has shown, when the returns on securities
are correlated, this may not be accomplished if the amount which the client
deposited is relatively small.

Further recording of protocols is expected to specify the selection process that
associates particular industries and particular goals. However, it is clear that this
association depends on the characteristics of the goal and the general characteristics
of the companies within each industry. Some industries contain companies which
vary only slightly in their individual characteristics, e.g., banks or utilities. Others,
like oils, are more heterogeneous, i.e., appear on several lists.

search and development.[27] The first three criteria are used in an absolute manner to reduce the lists further:

> *Rule a:*   If the beneficiary is a resident of Pennsylvania, reject all stocks which are subject to personal property tax in Pennsylvania.
> *Rule b:*   If the trust is a legal trust, reject all stocks which do not have legal status in Pennsylvania.
> *Rule c:*   Reject further purchases of stocks in which there are "current uncertainties." The investment officer would not buy du Pont stock pending the court's decision on what they are to do with their holdings in General Motors. During the Middle East crisis of 1958, international oil companies were labeled "current uncertainties."

The next two criteria (iv and v) are used in a somewhat similar manner. If the goal is growth, all stocks which do not meet minimum growth criteria are rejected. Similarly, if income is desired, low-yielding stocks are rejected.

The rest of the criteria are used in a relative manner. A rough simulation has been achieved by matching the remaining companies on these criteria and seeing which has the most points in its favor. To do this, the program sets up a three-valued scale for each criterion (low = 1, medium = 2, high = 3) and makes binary choices by subtracting the value of a particular criterion of one company from the value of the same criterion for the other company. The result of any one comparison will be a positive, negative, or zero number. All the remaining criteria are matched in this manner, and the resulting scores are added algebraically to yield a unique value for the particular comparison. Since one company's criteria are always subtracted from the other's, a positive sign on the summation will denote that the first company is chosen; a negative sign, the second company. In the case where the sum is zero, no choice has been indicated.[28]

[27] Large current expenditures for plant expansion and/or research and development will lower current dividends while raising expectations of future earning power. For companies heavily dependent on the discovery of new products, e.g., chemicals, drugs, and office equipment, the amount spent on research and development is used as an indicator of the company's intention to continue developing new and profitable products.
[28] More recent protocols suggest an alternative selection routine, which lists all the companies in a preference order on the two basic criteria of growth and income. For the goal of growth or income the program would take the first company on the growth or income list and check through each of the remaining

An example will clarify this process. Assume that a portfolio of high-yield stocks is required and that the selection process has reached the point where it is starting to select stocks on the basis of attributes vi through xi. At this point the choice lies between Company A and Company B. Since we are considering only attributes vi through xi, let their values for Company A be given by the vector (3, 3, 1, 3, 3, 2) and for Company B by the vector (2, 3, 1, 3, 2, 2). As mentioned above, the selection process consists of subtracting the values of the attributes of Company B from the values of the similar attributes of Company A. In this case the result of this subtraction yields a vector whose values are given by the following six numbers: 1, 0, 0, 0, 1, 0. Since the algebraic sum of these numbers is positive, Company A is selected. If more alternatives are available, a transfer operation directs the program to match Company A against the next alternative.

Determine the size of participation. The investment officer divides the accounts into two classes. For accounts with less than $5/8K to invest in commons, his rules are as follows:

> a. Given the amount to be invested and the number of participations, determine the average amount which can be invested in each company.
> b. Divide this average amount by the current price of the stock to obtain the number of shares which can be purchased.[29]
> c. Since each purchase may be slightly over or under the average dollar amount to be spent, maintain a continuous count of "funds remaining" figure and not the average number.

In accounts with more than $5/8K to invest in commons, a different procedure is used. Once the amount to be invested and the number of participations are determined as above, the minimum

---

criteria to see whether it met a specified standard or not. If it did, the company would be interchanged with the second company on the list, and the test would be repeated. Changes in suitability occur because the stored data on price, income, earnings, dividends, etc., are kept up to date.

[29] If this number of shares is 90 or greater, 100 shares (a round lot) are purchased; if less than 90, but greater than 10, the number is reduced to its nearest multiple of 5, and that number of shares is purchased; if less than 10 but greater than 5, 10 shares are purchased; if less than 5, 5 shares are purchased. Note, however, that in general, this process will not lead to selection of a portfolio which is "Markowitz-efficient."

round lot is purchased for each company that is selected. Again a "funds remaining" account is kept to determine the size of the last participation.

CONCLUSIONS

In recent years new techniques for the study of human problem-solving have been developed. Of these, the simulation of individual behavior is most apposite to the study of problems of choice under uncertainty. Application of this technique has been facilitated by the use of digital computers capable of storing and processing large blocks of information.

This paper proposes the use of simulation as a basis for studying portfolio selection. Clearly, the choice of securities by individuals or their agents is an application of the theory of decision-making under uncertainty. We contend that focusing on the decision-making process per se is a more appropriate technique for dealing with this problem than those which, though mathematically more elegant, either (1) lead to non-testable implications or (2) rest on probabilistic assumptions.

Building computer programs focuses attention on areas of least knowledge. Moreover, since computer statements must be operational, hypotheses advanced most clearly specify assumptions about the mechanisms at work.

Using information recorded from "protocols," we programmed portions of the decision rules employed by a trust investment officer. The program was tested by two simulations, and, although such small samples are never conclusive, we believe that the results strongly indicate the potential power of the theory as a predictor. (A crude test for "goodness of fit" is shown in the appendix.)

Future work will be directed at discovering the rules that are used in the formation of goals, in the association of industries with goals, and on parts of the present program that are not yet fully defined. As programs are added, we expect to generate more of the recorded behavior. We suggest that in this way a descriptive theory of portfolio selection can be developed to serve either (1) as a predictor of investor behavior or (2) as the basis for a theory of optimal portfolio selection.

APPENDIX

RESULTS OF SIMULATION OF ABC ACCOUNT, 7/7/58

Description of Account:

1. Agency account
2. Revocable
3. Goal of account: high growth with little or no concern for income; fluctuations in principal not a problem
4. Investment restrictions: not a legal trust, hence not restricted to legal list; donor stated that all assets were to be invested in common stocks
5. Amount available for investment in common stocks: assumed to be given

The program selected the following portfolio for the ABC Account:

The portfolio selected by the investment officer on 7/7/8 was:

85 shs. Monsanto Chem. comm.	80 shs. Monsanto Chem. comm.
10 shs. I.B.M. comm.	10 shs. I.B.M. comm.
50 shs. Continental Oil comm.	45 shs. Continental Oil comm.
45 shs. Owens Corning comm.	50 shs. Owens Corning comm.

The funds-remaining figure was too small to generate new activity.

RESULTS OF SIMULATION OF XYZ ACCOUNT, 3/28/58

Description of Account:

1. Agency account
2. Revocable
3. Goal of account: high income and stability of income
4. Investment restrictions: not a legal trust, hence not restricted to legals

5. Amount available for investment in common stocks: assumed to be given

The program selected the following portfolio for the XYZ Account:	The portfolio selected by the investment officer on 3/28/58 was:
100 shs. Philadelphia Elec. comm. 100 shs. Equitable Gas comm. 60 shs. Socony Mobil Oil comm.	100 shs. Philadelphia Elec. comm. 100 shs. Equitable Gas comm. 50 shs. Socony Mobil Oil comm.

12. A PROFESSIONAL BLUEPRINT FOR INDIVIDUAL PORTFOLIO MANAGEMENT*

❂ Frederick N. Goodrich

In my comments, I want to touch on four topics: (1) Distinctive features of investing for individuals; (2) Principal versus income; (3) Choosing a stock portfolio; and (4) Determining bond proportions; types and maturities.

Distinctive Features of Investing for Individuals

Income taxes accentuate the differences between aggressive and conservative investors. The aggressive investor is encouraged to emphasize growth by the limitations on income after taxes. The conservative investor is encouraged by the same limitations to seek safety and tax exempt income. Low tax brackets diminish these differences. Taxes encourage a large portion of individual investors to seek capital gains yet discourage many from cashing these gains.

Income taxes and the changing tastes of investors have encouraged a trend toward smaller cash payouts by many corporations and larger plowbacks for growth. In our thinking about the resulting capital gains types of income, confusion has arisen be-

* From *The Commercial and Financial Chronicle*, Vol. 192, No. 5972 (Thursday, July 28, 1960), p. 1. Reprinted by permission of *The Commercial and Financial Chronicle*, 25 Park Place, New York 7, New York.

tween plowed back earnings—certainly a form of income if one
has confidence in the corporation—growth of earnings for other
reasons, and the growth in the price of the stock.

The use of trusts by individuals—particularly where there is
no provision for paying out principal—frequently forces us back to
emphasizing income. On the other hand, trusts are frequently created by estate planning for the avowed purpose of investing for
growth.

Long life expectancy and high earned income generally encourage the seeking of growth. Short expectancy generally discourages seeking growth yet also discourages cashing any large gains
on existing holdings.

A charitable nature—coupled with the tax laws—makes it easier
to cash capital gains through gifts. A charitable nature also makes
a larger dividend income seem more worthwhile.

Other personal characteristics also profoundly affect the investor's investment actions; courage to assume necessary risks and
ignore fluctuations; patience to wait for long term results; broad-
mindedness to pay capital gains taxes when desirable; the good sense
to accept professional advice; and vision to look at the long term
prospects.

Principal and Income

The prudent and the far-sighted have always understood that attention must be given to principal first, income second: attention
to principal both to conserve it by resisting the temptation of higher
current income and to make it grow by focusing on the future
potential. The long bull market—and the tax laws—have encouraged
an increasing number to concentrate on growth. After all, purchases
in mid-1949—11 years ago—of a portfolio of General Electric, Eastman Kodak, American Home Products, International Business
Machines, Minnesota Mining and Minneapolis Honeywell—all
pretty high grade situations—would have resulted in average gains
of about 1400%, taxable at most at 25%, or over 1000% after taxes.
This is in excess of a 25% compounded annual return. Even if these
stocks were selling at half of their present prices, the average gains
would be nearly 500% after taxes. How can interest or dividend
income compete with this?

Yet we must also understand that the object of investment of principal is to produce income. If an investment does not produce current income or promise future income, it has no principal value. Let us look at those six stocks. At present prices, they yield less than 1¼% and capitalize earnings some 40 times. But at 1949 prices, present dividends yield about 17% and present earnings are capitalized less than 3 times.

I think a fair analogy is this: principal is to income as virtue is to happiness. If we concentrate on virtue, we can hope for happiness as a by-product. If we concentrate on principal, both its growth and safety, we are choosing a course which will best assure future income. Concentration on principal values is another way of saying concentration on future returns—whether one is thinking of the safe return of principal on a bond or of the growth of earnings and dividends in a stock. This I think is the real secret, concentration on future results as far as one can realistically look ahead.

CHOOSING A STOCK PORTFOLIO

I will try to cover a number of points briefly:

Emphasis on long term prospects brings the best results—short term or long term. At the Trust Company we periodically prepare a list of relatively attractive stocks, usually numbering 30 to 35, out of the considerable larger number that we are willing to buy. This list is prepared informally but carefully for the guidance of our account executives. We find that the less we put our minds on stocks that look temporarily cheap and on short term results, the more we concentrate on the longest period ahead that we can judge, the better do our results become—usually including our short term market results. For example, taking our recent record, we are naturally pleased that our choices of stocks since last October —when we started keeping account of this—have done considerably better than the recognized stock averages. The stocks that have contributed most substantially are those bought for the longest term results: stocks like Eastman Kodak, International Business Machines, Philips Lamp, General Telephone, Vick Chemical, Minnesota Mining, General Foods, American Express, Texas Instruments, Litton Industries, Haloid Xerox, Universal Match, Houston

Lighting, Southern Company and Florida Power and Light. Where we succumbed to high current income as in CIT or Rochester Gas and Electric, our results have been mediocre. If we said: let's pick an automotive stock because 1960 will be a good year—we will sell before the others—our results were particularly poor.

Consider the investor who says: I am retired, I have no family, —no plowback stocks for me—I want my dividends and results now and in the near future. Buy me the income utility or that high income rail. Will he be well served? At any given time he will have his dividends received plus his principal values. But his principal values—with their changes of 10 or 15 or 50 or 100% or more are going to be a lot more important than the difference of 2 or 3% in dividends. Just take those stocks we selected last October. Philips Lamp has advanced the most, over 100%. Goodrich has declined the most, over 20%. This means that the Philips Lamp investor has $250 in market value for every $100 for the Goodrich investor—and continues, I believe, to have better prospects. These are short term results from looking for the superior long term prospects.

Or take the investor who looked over the Dow Jones stocks back in December 1949 and decided that Chrysler's 9% yield was more attractive than Eastman Kodak's 4%. The Chrysler investor has lost over 25% of his market value while the Eastman investor has increased his by 700%. The Eastman investor now has over $1,000 market value for each $100 for the Chrysler investor—as well as having a 12% dividend return on his purchase price versus 1½% for the Chrysler man. It has been the Eastman investor who actually obtained the 9% yield—and more.

But how do we judge the long term prospects? Naturally we are looking for industries with excellent prospects for sales growth, not beset with oversupply or other factors depressing profit margins, and for companies in these industries with excellent management. We find ourselves investing mainly in the attractive industries, such as electrical and electronic equipment, growth utilities, drugs, office equipment, photographic and reproduction, and other labor saving devices; but in the final analysis we are picking companies, especially as many do not fall neatly into an industry pattern. Does General Foods specialize in foods or labor saving? Is it the insurance plus that tips the balance in favor of Sears Roebuck? How do we classify American Express? We did not pick Minnesota Mining as representative of an industry. Why is General American Transportation, generally classified as a railroad equipment, so successful?

An industry or company with attractive prospects is not sufficient. The method of financing—particularly the plowing back of earnings—is usually a decisive factor. Take the electric utilities: the difference between Florida Power and Light's more than 250% growth in earnings per share since 1949 and Southern California Edison's 30% growth results from several factors, but the biggest factor is the Florida company's ability to finance its equity needs largely out of plowed back earnings.

So we must judge future sales prospects, profit margins, management, plowback—and we must estimate from these factors both the potential and the risk. For this there is no real short cut: research must be well equipped and must dig hard; extensive field work and management contacts are required; experienced judgment to use this information is essential.

Can past market action help us? To a limited extent—yes. Experience shows that a stock that has acted well in the past is more likely to act well in the future than one which has been acting poorly. If one looked at the relative market action of International Business Machines and XYZ office equipment and knew nothing else about the companies—and picked IBM on the basis of market action—one would probably be right. Trends—usually being dependent on inherent conditions—have a certain persistence, adverse trends even more than favorable ones.

However, such past market trends we can use only as suggestions. They will not be reliable in forecasting future results. Some trends are soundly based, others not. Conditions—even those that persisted over a long period—can change drastically. The can industry was outstanding for growth before World War II, but well below average since 1950. The steel industry, on the other hand, changed its profit conditions for the better at about the same time. The oil industry, long the giant of successful investment, came to a significant turn in its affairs three years ago. The insurance industry, for so long so outstanding, has come upon more competitive times. The paper industry, pre-war cut throat, postwar steady growth, has for the most part settled down to competitive humdrum conditions. Trends do have a certain persistence, but they are nevertheless dangerously fickle. So we are thrown back on our own hard digging and on our persistence and judgment in visualizing the futures of industries and companies.

Furthermore, we run into the danger of overenthusiasm regarding favorable trends. It is fine to rely heavily on plowed back earnings and growing sales and profits. But in the practical investment world we measure our results to a large extent by market action—by long term market action if we are wise—but still by market action. What if our favorite company has doubled its earnings but multiplied its price by five. What if it is capitalizing the compounded potential of 1965 but taking the inevitable risk element very little into account. We are faced with this problem right now, and the answer is not easy. However, I am confident about where the answer does not lie—it does not lie in buying industries and companies with second and third rate prospects because their stock prices look relatively cheap.

We are looking for future returns and potentials, but with strength and quality of conditions taken into consideration. In our appraisal of future returns, we emphasize both potential and security. The potential of an IBM or Texas Instruments is our first consideration. But we must also judge the degrees of certainty that the potential will be reached and the degree of risk that a drastic change in prospects may occur. While we are not price conscious in the sense of looking for historical cheapness, nevertheless it is obvious that price must bear a satisfactory relationship to potential and to risk. So today we should look hard at the price of a Polaroid. We should give favorable attention to those companies with slower but solid prospects of expanding earnings with a high degree of certainty—selected companies in the food industry, in retailing, and not excluding American Telephone.

And it has seemed to us that substantial attention should be given to the stocks of leading foreign companies in the common market countries and in parts of the British Commonwealth; not only Philips Lamp, but Hoogovens—the low cost Dutch steel company, Broken Hill—the still lower cost Australian steel company—both with well protected and growing markets, the leading West German chemical companies, and many others. These countries are growing more rapidly than we, being earlier on the road we have travelled; their costs are lower; their financial markets and corporate policies are just recently moving toward ours; the stocks are generally cheaper; and internationally speaking we all seem to be in the same boat together. Accurate information has been hard to obtain, but the Dutch have led the way, the Germans are following and we are working hard at our sources of information.

A word is due on diversification of the stock portfolio. We should have some diversification to reduce unnecessary risk, but we should not overdo it. The best results on any long term portfolio at the Trust Company are in that trust received in the 20's entirely in IBM with no power of sale. When we receive a portfolio of stocks, our early reviews are very little concerned with diversification; they are concerned with the investments we consider unattractive or unsuitable. The more we like a stock, the more willing we are to have too much of it. Nevertheless, while we know that we cannot have too much of the right stock, we do normally diversify among a reasonable number of issues. We have a high opinion of quite a few companies. Each field has its peculiar risks. In human terms, a good investment result with security is more important than maximizing profits.

Finally, a word on respectable stocks with mediocre prospects. These are the prime enemy of good results among experienced investors. The experienced investor will not have much trouble with bad stocks. The problem is usually inertia and a portfolio with substantial holdings of respectable tired old blue chips that provide a good current income and may show a substantial capital gain over original cost. These holdings must be attacked with discretion but with energy.

To sum up on choosing a stock portfolio: look to long term results, not short-term; rely on hard research and hard experience; observe trends, but do not rely on them; consider price, but not too much; diversify reasonably; avoid mediocrity.

DETERMINING BOND PROPORTIONS, TYPES AND MATURITIES

How do we determine the proportion of fixed income securities and cash or equivalent?

The first question here is why this proportion should be above that needed for liquid reserves for emergencies. We expect that the economy will continue to grow, that some inflation is more likely than deflation, and that our equity choices will be above average.

Are not well chosen equities always the most productive investments over the long term? Does not this outweigh immediate cash income requirements except in trusts where there is a legal separation of principal and income?

The next question is this. Is not our fixed portion—over and above emergency reserves—primarily a buying reserve for equities? The answer I think is essentially no, except for quite short term reserves desirable as we pursue a buying program, delay to develop our best equity ideas or hold back pending the settling of some acute emergency. A permanent reserve is certainly not a reserve at all, but instead is like the last taxi that could not take an eager fare because of the rule that one taxi had always to stay at the stand—as a reserve.

But what of an intermediate reserve to take advantage of an expected 10 or 20% decline in the stock market? This concept I believe to be of no value whatever. We cannot predict such a decline with any certainty. If we hold stocks with attractive long term prospects, they may well be higher not lower, after the expected decline. And we will not know when to get back in. So our fixed income portion is not best thought of as a reserve.

What, then, are the functions of the fixed income portion?

First, it is insurance: insurance against some drastic upset in the economy or in the state; insurance against the end of an era in which equities have enjoyed satisfactory conditions and the possible coming of an era in which they will not.

Second, it is to help us sleep at nights. In human terms the protection of our basic needs is more important that maximizing investment returns.

Third, it is to produce an investment return with a high element of safety—not ignoring the fact that any inflation will cut sharply into this return. A good bond income does not compete very well against attractive equities. However, as equities become higher priced relative to values, their income potential declines and the risk element increases. A bond's return and safety then become substantially more attractive, particularly a tax exempt return to an individual investor. The rise in equity capitalizations of earnings and dividends and the higher prevailing interest returns have not yet in my opinion swung the balance decisively in favor of bonds; but they have certainly narrowed the margin of equity attractiveness and have made any degree of security that seems desirable in individual portfolios much less costly to obtain. For these reasons, even though we are fairly optimistic on the economic outlook, we believe that bond proportions should be higher in individual portfolios than a few years ago.

As to types of fixed income securities, tax exempts generally have the most to offer in the present market to individuals in a Federal tax bracket above 30%. In our choice of bonds, competent research enables us to buy sound issues which are rated less than AAA. Corporation and government bonds are used in low bracket portfolios. Short Treasuries are frequently used for short term funds, and discount Treasuries are sometimes attractive to individuals. Preferred stocks are used sparingly, if at all, since they are relatively high in price due to their tax advantage to corporate holders. Convertible bonds and preferreds sometimes offer to individuals an attractive combination of a good equity with safety. However, unlike institutional investors, the individual is frequently not interested in the corporation bond or preferred and will generally either buy the equity or avoid the situation. Foreign bonds, International Bank bonds, commercial paper and bankers acceptances offer tax advantages to foreign investors. Obviously, the type of fixed income security depends primarily on the tax situation.

As to selection of maturities, we recommend balanced maturities, particularly in tax exempts, generally on a scale of 1 to 15 or 1 to 20 years. Our objective is to provide greatest safety with reasonable return. When yields were low, we emphasized the shorter maturities. When they are higher, we emphasize the intermediates, i.e., the longer end of our maturity scale. However, even today we try to avoid stretching our maturities too long for two reasons: first, we expect good enough results from our equity holdings to minimize the need, except in trusts requiring full cash income, for reaching for extra bond income; and second, we believe that the demands upon the country's capital resources and the need to protect the dollar are going to keep interest rates in a fairly high range for some years to come.

CONCLUSION

To sum up these comments briefly:

1. When investing for the individual we must take account of taxes, personal needs and personal characteristics.

2. We must concentrate on principal values first, current income only second, in order to best assure both principal and income results.

3. In choosing a stock portfolio, we must concentrate on long term results.

4. In determining fixed income and cash proportions, we must recognize the sacrifice of potential and then seek that amount of insurance and extra security which the human needs and the investment situation suggest.

13. PRICE-LEVEL VARIATIONS AND THE TENETS OF HIGH-GRADE INVESTMENT*

❀ John C. Clendenin

THE TOPIC ASSIGNED TO US for discussion at this meeting clearly implies that there may be price-level variations in this country in the future and that they may be of sufficient moment to require appropriate investment policies. It would therefore be reasonable to debate either the outlook for price levels over the longer term or the nature of conservative investment policies which would best meet the probable situation. However, it has been officially suggested to me that we might focus attention on the suitability of common stocks, especially the variety known as "growth stocks," as high-grade investment vehicles in a period of price-level instability. This is my purpose; and in discussing stocks I shall mean those of competitive industrial and commercial companies only.

Although it is not my intention to involve this meeting in attempts to predict the long-range economic future of the country, it seems idle to discuss investment dispositions without noting the general nature of the situations for which we must be prepared. Obviously, we would not all agree on the details of the economic road ahead, but I suspect that most of us expect a continuation of welfare-minded monetary and public budget interventionism, major

* From *The Journal of Finance,* Vol. XIV, No. 2 (May, 1959), pp. 245–262. Reprinted by permission of *The Journal of Finance.*

emphasis on full-employment objectives, a secondary hope for price stability and a balanced budget, large-scale public expenditures, and extensive research and development efforts by both public and private agencies. Conceding that all quantitative estimates must be liberally sprinkled with plus-and-minus signs, it would appear that a middle-of-the-road investment planner might reasonably visualize the coming decade as follows:

1. General characteristics of high-level and growing output, moderate cycles of buoyancy and recession greatly influenced by monetary and public budget manipulation, long-term money rates swinging widely in and about the 1958 range, and an intermittent price-level inflation averaging about 1 per cent per annum, firmly underwritten by habitual cost-push pressures.

2. Possibility of occasional short booms or depressions which may make sharp temporary impression on the stock market but relatively little permanent impression on either commodity or stock-market price trends.

3. Rapid technological and competitive change, in which products and enterprises are capable of great development or obsolescence in short time.

4. Continuation of heavy taxes.

5. Possibility of war, which would surely distort profit results and dividend rates temporarily and the price level permanently.

The foregoing propositions definitely do not imply that conventional fixed-dollar-amount investments are about to become obsolete or unproductive. On the contrary, they assume that high-grade bond yields of $3\frac{1}{2}$–5 per cent will clearly exceed an inflation-born loss of 1 per cent per year on the principal, even after allowing for the attrition of taxes. The 1 per cent per year inflationary trend is a guess based on evidence of increasing financial sobriety in Washington and relatively greater desire to couple price stability with full employment. If this hopeful projection works out, taxpaying investors may continue to use taxable senior securities and obtain at least a small amount of real net income from them.

Yet the fact remains that inflationary trends impair the real-income productivity of fixed-income investment, while presumably not adversely affecting typically diversified equity positions. Furthermore, public intervention to prevent recession or depression would appear to be a potent insurer of the safety and stability of a diversified equity position. If these things be true, then there may be occasion to indorse the principle of common-stock investment for conservative funds and even to advocate adapting some of our traditional institutions to make better use of common stocks.

At this point we begin to encounter some arguable questions of fact. The first of these is: After a quarter-century of mounting taxes, labor law, and government intervention in business, do the common stocks of leading corporations retain their profitableness and sturdiness and general good prospects?

EVIDENCE ON QUALITY

Since evidence on the trend of stock quality provides only relative data, it is desirable to recall at the outset some of the well-known absolute findings of prior decades. Most famous of these is Edgar L. Smith's *Common Stocks as Long-Term Investments,* which compares the performances of hypothetical good-quality common stock and bond portfolios over 17- to 22-year spans in the period 1866–1922. The results, you will recall, strongly favored the stock portfolios. Many subsequent studies point, on balance, to the same conclusion, especially in periods when the general trend of commodity prices is level or upward.[1] The first concern of the present inquiry is, therefore, to ascertain whether the corporate strength which made these records possible is still with us. Pertinent evidence is afforded in the accompanying Charts I–III.

Chart I reports in line-graph form the net-profit results of leading manufacturing corporations since 1926. The upper line shows profits as a percentage of net worth, the lower one profits as a percentage of sales. These figures are collected by the First National City Bank of New York, mostly by adding figures available in published annual reports. Only large and fairly large concerns are included, and the list of corporations is obviously not uniform through the years, though the large number included—about 1,800

---

[1] E. L. Smith, *Common Stocks as Long Term Investments* (New York: Macmillan Co., 1924); C. C. Bosland, *Common Stock Investment* (New York: Ronald Press Co., 1937); K. S. van Strum, *Investing in Purchasing Power* (New York: Barron's, 1926); D. C. Rose, *A Scientific Approach to Investment Management* (New York: Harper & Bros., 1928); W. J. Eiteman and F. P. Smith, *Common Stock Values and Yields* (Ann Arbor: University of Michigan Press, 1953); W. C. Greenough, *A New Approach to Retirement Income* (T.I.A.A., 1951); P. L. Howell, "Common Stocks and Pension Fund Investing," *Harvard Business Review,* November-December, 1958.

Per Cent

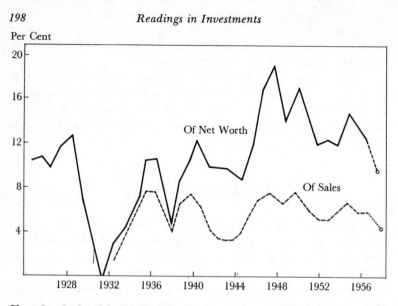

Chart I. *Profits of Large Manufacturing Corporations as Percentages of Net Worth and of Sales. (Source: First National City Bank; 1958 Estimated.)*

in recent years—gives the series impressive validity. The significant facts to be drawn from Chart I are these: First, the percentages earned on net worth in 1953–57 are as good as, or a little better than, those earned in profitable periods in the past—for example, 1940–41, 1936–37, and 1926–29. Labor costs and the corporate income tax have not eroded earning capacity here. Second, there appears to have been a slight decline in the percentage of net profit to the sales of these companies; 1953–57 is a little below 1940–41, and the latter is, in turn, a little below 1936–37. The disparity between the two trends shown on the chart obviously reflects an increase in the ratio of sales to net worth. Economic logic suggests that the earnings rate on net worth has been a dominant criterion in competitive pricing decisions and that the profit percentage on sales has been cut because a lower percentage would still permit a generous return on invested capital.

Chart II presents data drawn from *Statistics of Income,* as compiled by the Internal Revenue Service. The year 1957 is estimated. The bars represent the percentages earned by all manu-facturing corporations in the country on their book net worths and sales, before and after income taxes. The pretax earnings are shown by the total heights of the bars, the posttax net by the solid portions. It will be noted that the net profit margins earned by manufacturing

Per Cent

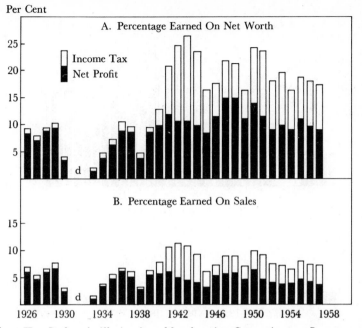

Chart II. *Profits of All American Manufacturing Corporations as Percentages of Net Worth and of Sales. (Source: Statistics of Income; 1957 Estimated.)*

corporations in the aggregate are not nearly so large as those earned by the large corporations canvassed in the First National City series but that the trends over time are similar. The earnings rates on net worth are firmly maintained, while those on sales have declined since the war. However, this chart has two more significant messages. First, it is clear that the heavy corporate income taxes imposed during the last 25 years—as represented on the chart by the unshaded segments at the tops of the bars—have been paid by widening the pretax profit margin, presumably at the expense of the consumer, and not by impairing the stockholders' profit margins on net worth. Second, it appears that the pretax profit margins on sales—as shown by the total height of the sales percentage bars—are actually a little larger in recent years than they were in the 1920's and 1930's. There is thus a little wider margin of safety between normal operations and red-ink deficits than we had before income taxes climbed to their present levels.

Chart III is similar to Chart II, except that it presents the combined record of all American trade corporations instead of

Per Cent

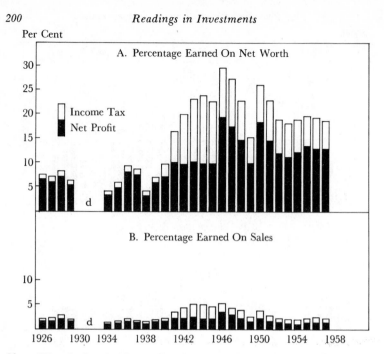

Chart III. *Profits of All American Retail and Wholesale Trade Corporations as Percentages of Net Worth and of Sales. (Source: Statistics of Income; 1957 Estimated.)*

manufacturing concerns. The trends are very similar, though it is apparent that the profit margins of trade corporations are not so high as those of manufacturers. It will also be noted that economic conditions plus inventory and depreciation accounting methods produced almost fantastic profit records for trade corporations in the years 1946–50. These are clearly abnormal and are as little descriptive of earnings trends as are the war years or the years 1931–34.

But reference to depreciation accounting and inventory accounting methods suggest that other accounting devices may be distorting Charts II and III. What of the undervaluation of prewar fixed assets and the consequent understatement of net worth? What of accelerated amortization? Time does not permit an extended review here, but it is possible to cite a study by the Machinery and Allied Products Institute in which a careful attempt is made to measure the ratio of corrected earnings to corrected net worth, the corrections being designed to state both earnings and net worth on an economic replacement-costs basis for each year. The MAPI results indicate that, on a corrected basis, the net profits of all American corporations in 1923–29 and in 1947–56 averaged almost the same percentage on net worth, about 5⅔ per cent.[2] The profit level thus defined is appreciably lower than that shown in Charts I, II, and III; this appears to result both from the revision of profit and net worth figures and from the inclusion of all corporations, especially financial and transportation, in the data—but the absence of any downward trend in the ratio of net earnings to net worth is notable here also.

The data on profit margins thus support the proposition that corporations are retaining their financial strength rather well. Most other aspects of corporate finance corroborate this finding. For example, operating losses seem to be less frequent; in the years 1926–29 corporations operating at a loss had 18 per cent of the gross sales of all corporations in the nation, and their losses amounted to 17 per cent of the pretax earnings of the profitable corporations; but in 1952–56 the losers' sales were less than 10 per cent of the total and their losses less than 6 per cent of the others' profits. Other measures show manufacturers' net worth to be about 65 per cent of total assets in 1956 as compared to 75 per cent in 1928, but the working capital position is about the same and times interest earned coverage and cash flow are substantially improved.

STOCKS AS A PRICE-LEVEL HEDGE

A second issue of fact which must be noted is the matter of the effectiveness of common stocks as price-level hedges or counter-weights. This has been so interminably discussed that one must apologize for raising it—yet this problem is the real reason for the topic we are discussing.

It must be conceded at the outset that public policy, expressed in such media as price controls, excess-profits taxes, credit controls, or public competition with private enterprise, could be the definitive answer to the question at hand. Such public policy has been the answer in certain foreign countries and was partly so in this country during our periods of price controls and excess-profits taxes. However, it seems reasonable to assume that the political hazards to capital in the United States are no greater now than they were in the 1930's. It is therefore pertinent to look at the historical data of the

---

[2] George Terborgh, *Corporate Profit in the Decade 1947–56* (New York: Machinery & Allied Products Institute, 1957).

period 1926–57 for generalized indications of the impact of the price level on common-stock investment performance.

Chart IV presents a 32-year study of the earnings per share and the dividends per share applicable to the Standard and Poor's 50-Stock Industrial Stock Price Index. This index is used because its component stocks are those of large companies, mostly good-quality issues of the type considered for long-term investment. The earnings and dividend figures on the chart have been divided through by the GNP deflator index in order to show the data in terms of the prices which presumably affect them.

Inspection of Chart IV brings out clearly four significant points: (1) Over a span of 32 years the earnings and dividends available on a portfolio of good-grade big-company stocks have risen more than the price level. Their upward trend has averaged between 1¼ and 2 per cent per year, compounded. (2) In periods of price-level gain, the earnings may lag behind the price-level upswings, and the dividends will definitely lag behind the earnings. This observation is not too clear on the chart because of the complications of depression, war, controls, and taxes, but financial common sense adds credence to the rough indications. (3) Depressions, wars, price controls, and excess-profits taxes are contingencies which may depress per share earnings and dividends for considerable periods, at least in terms of purchasing power; and the chart does not show compensating long periods of very large earnings. (4) The data on this chart are of

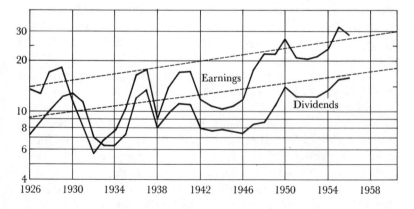

Chart IV. *Growth of Earnings and Dividends Per Share, Standard and Poor's Index of Fifty Industrials. (Real Terms, Adjusted for Price Level.) Indicated Growth Rate 2 Per Cent per Annum.*

dubious quality in certain years, notably 1947–50, when strong earnings data are in part the product of non-economic inventory and depreciation accounting methods.

The major indication of Chart IV is, obviously, the finding that the earnings and dividends on this group of industrials over a generation have outclimbed price-level growth and gained an average of nearly 2 per cent per year in real purchasing power. This, of course, means a substantial capital gain in addition to the mounting tide of dividend income. However, it should be noted that the dividend itself fell by half during the great depression, and, after recovering in part, declined again during the war. It was not until 1947 that the dollar level of dividend payments permanently surpassed the 1927–29 payments. During the interim, the stockholders got less than a fixed-income investment purchased in the 1920's would have brought them and, in addition, had to bear a painful, if temporary, shrinkage in stock prices. This could happen again.

Chart V is in all respects similar to Chart IV, except that it shows only dividend records, not earnings, and compares the performances of a list of 9 growth stocks and 10 non-growth stocks. Data for certain abnormal depression and war years are not shown. This chart has been constructed with the advantage of hindsight; it was prepared in order to compare *ex post facto* the performance of typical high-grade growth stocks with that of high-grade non-growth stocks. The upper line shows the record of the non-growth stocks:

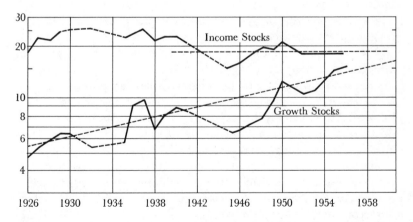

Chart V. *Growth of Dividend Rates in "Real" Terms (Adjusted for Price Level). Indicated Growth Rates 0 and 3.2 Per Cent per Annum.*

their dividends declined less than the price level during the depression years but failed by far to keep pace during the war and early postwar years. By 1948, the buying-power level of the 1920's had been regained, and these stocks have since increased their dividends enough to compensate for further increases in the price level, though they have not made up the deficiencies of 1940–48. They have at no time shown net real-income growth, despite the fact that undistributed profits have been reinvested in the businesses in most years over more than three decades.

The lower line on Chart V shows the record of 9 major growth stocks. Over a 32-year term, these stocks have increased their earnings and dividends in real terms by an average of about 3 per cent per annum. Their depression-time payments declined below the 1920's in dollars but not in purchasing power, but at no time since has a significant shrinkage occurred. Obviously, the capital appreciation on these stocks has been very great. Whether their growth can continue or whether investors seeking to enjoy such growth in the future can select stocks capable of this performance are open questions.

However, one thing is pretty obvious; the average rise of $1\frac{1}{2}$–2 per cent per year in real terms shown by the dividends on the Standard and Poor's 50-stock average must be ascribed to the fact that the average contains an assortment of growth and non-growth stocks. The growth stocks have supplied the vital thrust which makes industrial stocks per se appear to outpace an advancing price level. The ten high-grade non-growth stocks depicted on Chart V have caught up, on the average, but the laggards among them have not; and we all know that there are many lesser stocks and lagging industries which were once vigorous leaders.[3]

Generalizations at this point are perhaps gratuitous, but the facts suggest that a strong and smartly selected industrial stock portfolio might reasonably be expected to advance its dividend production, earnings, and capital values a little faster than the price level advances, even though earnings and dividend production may be somewhat irregular and prone to gaps. Capital appreciation accompanying earnings and dividend growth will in a sense compensate for inadequate earnings during inclement economic periods. However, our economy is subject to political, technological, and economic

[3] Cf. E. S. Mead and Julius Grodinsky, *The Ebb and Flow of Investment Values* (New York: Appleton-Century, 1939).

change. These are forces which can interrupt income and reverse trends, at least so far as individual corporations and industries are concerned. It is therefore reasonable to inquire whether, over a period of diverse economic trends, reasonably competent investment managements have been able to avail themselves in full measure of the opportunities which seem to be available.

Some Performance Records

For a hasty test of the results of actual common-stock portfolios, the records of major open-end investment companies are most readily available. Accordingly, Table 1 presents some investment company performance data, with performance conventionally measured as the percentage excess of this year's closing asset value plus this year's dividend over last year's closing asset value.

For present purposes, the lessons of Table 1 are two in number. First, the common-stock investment companies do not usually surpass the performance of the market averages. True, they bear a measurable handicap in the form of operating expenses, an unproductive cash position, and a compulsion to diversify, but the fact is that their net performance often does not quite equal that of the averages, despite an enviable opportunity. The only reasonable conclusion is that the imponderables in individual stock situations are so great that good work in times like these parallels the averages, assures against falling far below them, but does not far exceed them. The great similarity in the performance of different funds lends credence to this view. The second lesson from Table 1 has to do with investment objectives. Six of the funds in the table announce as objectives the obtaining of income and appreciation. The other four announce that appreciation is their primary objective, with income incidental. The total performance of the two groups is almost identical. Granted that each group is compelled to diversification and that the income-and-appreciation group will seek appreciation avidly when they see a chance to get it, the record still says that stock-market forecasting is an imperfect art and that a competent and conservative analyst will not dependably improve his total score by stressing a search for market gains.

As a further test of the thesis that foresight is a scarce commodity, Table 2 lists the performance records of 22 stocks which constituted

Table 1. *Performance Records of Common-Stock Funds and Certain Indexes*

Performance = (Asset Value End of Year + Dividend during Year) ÷ Asset Value End of Prior Year, Minus 100 Per Cent

	1948	1949	1953	1954	1956	1957	AVERAGE 1948–57	AVERAGE 1940–57
S & P 50 Industrial	6	17	−2	56	7	−11	18	14
S & P 20 Utilities	6	31	8	24	7	6	8	12
S & P 20 Rails	4	8	−12	57	−3	−28	11	13
S & P 90 Stocks	6	18	−1	51	7	−10	17	14
General-Purpose Fund No. 1	0	22	2	31	5	0	12	14
General-Purpose Fund No. 2	−1	17	2	43	9	−4	15	14
General-Purpose Fund No. 3	1	18	0	37	7	−5	13	11
General-Purpose Fund No. 4	2	19	−3	52	13	−14	15	14
General-Purpose Fund No. 5	−2	19	−5	58	12	−22	16	15
General-Purpose Fund No. 6	1	20	0	51	11	−11	16	13
Growth Fund No. 1	−1	16	−1	48	10	−12	13	NA
Growth Fund No. 2	1	18	−3	55	19	−12	17	14
Growth Fund No. 3	4	22	−1	34	8	−12	13	12
Growth Fund No. 4	−3	16	1	63	14	−15	16	NA
Consumer Price Index per cent increase plus 5 per cent	8	3	5	4	7	7	7	10

Table 2. *Performance Records of Leading Stocks Held by Fund Portfolio in 1946–47*

Performance = (Median Price in Stated Year + Dividend of Stated Year) ÷ Median Price of Prior Year, Minus 100 Per Cent

STOCK	1946	1947	1948	AVERAGE 1948–1952	AVERAGE 1953–1957
Allied Chemical	10	9	6	15	8
Atchison T. & S.F.	12	−11	37	26	12
Amerada	17	19	21	40	7
Chrysler	−4	6	13	20	5
du Pont	16	−1	1	21	22
Eastman Kodak	19	2	−6	10	25
General Electric	1	−12	8	17	32
General Motors	−5	0	5	27	24
Gulf Oil	25	4	8	15	31
Int'l Harvester	−2	3	15	11	6
Loew's	11	−27	−18	1	9
Montgomery Ward	33	−18	4	7	9
J. C. Penney	20	−8	7	15	8
Sears, Roebuck	20	−15	19	17	12
Standard Oil, N.J.	17	8	18	28	24
Southern Pacific	15	−14	36	25	4
Texas Company	13	7	4	22	25
20th Century-Fox	43	−30	−25	−2	22
American Telephone	6	5	0	6	7
Commonwealth Edison	8	43	−3	8	12
Swift & Company	8	1	2	6	9
Liggett & Myers	8	2	5	1	6
Consumer Price Index per cent increase + 5 per cent	25	14	8	7	6

the largest stockholdings of one of our major investment companies in 1946 and 1947. These stocks were not all held throughout both years, but most of them were. Unquestionably the poorer performers among these stocks were bought and held in the expectation of good results in each individual case, and beyond doubt a larger quantity of the more successful holdings could have been carried had their success been anticipated. The table looks at first glance as though the selections were made by guess. However, this is a successful fund, whose total performance ranks high and whose management is deemed astute. Table 2 does not record good and bad luck; it records the process by which good results are achieved with reasonable certainty in a very unstable area.

The last two exhibits seem to justify the conclusion that secure and dependable results with common stocks require both selection and diversification. The very high probability of successful workout which characterizes individual good bonds apparently does not exist to the same extent in stocks, and a diversified position which balances fortuitous gains against unforeseeable losses is an indispensable procedure in a conservative stock account.[4]

SOME OBSERVATIONS ON PRICE

The final point of statistical inquiry before us has to do with price. Stocks are non-reproducible goods; they provide a somewhat irregular income and have no maturity date; the eagerness with which the community desires them varies with popular thought and with the political and economic climate; and the demand for them is also affected by the incomes of stock-buying individuals and institutions and the other uses such buyers have for their money. Even in the absence of emergency conditions, stock prices are stubbornly variable; during the middle 1920's stock yields were very close to those of high-grade bonds; in the late 1940's stocks yielded almost twice as much as bonds; and now they yield considerably less than bonds. There is thus no stable and enduring yield basis for stock valuation, yet the absence of maturity places extreme emphasis on capitalization rate in arriving at a value estimate. It is probably inherent in the nature of things that stock prices and price-earnings ratios and yields should move through wide ranges both at short term and over long but irregular cycles.

The quantitative extent of these price cycles is normally not great enough to do unbearable damage to well-diversified common-stock positions which can be held for long periods, particularly if accumulation and liquidation can be advantageously timed or spread over a span of years. This is demonstrated by the studies previously cited. However, we must admit that a wide potential range of stock

[4] For bond performance see W. B. Hickman, *Corporate Bond Quality and Investor Experience* (New York: NBER [National Bureau of Economic Research], 1958).

prices makes an accurate projection of medium-term investment performance almost impossible. Five or even ten years' income plus growth could be heavily impaired by adverse stock-price trends or by adverse liquidating prices. This is not a contingency to be lightly regarded, even in an inflationary era, by any portfolio which must make large distributions or stand ready to do so.[5]

The problem of price may be illustrated by current figures. The immediate dividend yield on the Standard and Poor's 50-stock index, my growth stock index, and my non-growth stock index approximate 3.5 per cent, 2.9 per cent, and 4.5 per cent, respectively. If we make allowance for continued growth and 1 per cent per year of inflation over the next 20 years and assume indefinite retention of holdings, the dividends on each of these groups should over 70 or 80 years amortize today's dollar cost and provide an average income yield of about 5 per cent. But 5 per cent is not an attractive long-term total return by past standards, and principal invested at this level is clearly subject to drastic impairment if the markets revert to a more conservative yield basis.

It is difficult to escape the conclusion that industrial stocks are suitable for conservative investment when the object is the purchase of a very long-term annuity which needs to compensate for price-level changes, but that stocks may be troublesome if the portfolio is subject to market-value solvency tests or liquidation.

TENETS OF INVESTMENT IN STOCKS

This cursory review of fact and fancy has been intended to serve as justification for a statement of "The Tenets of High-Grade Investment" in a period of buoyant price levels. A tenet is a principle or a doctrine and, as such, may state either a fact or a way of life. This review has not covered all phases of investment activity, hence will not attempt to phrase a whole creed of investment, but the following tenets certainly would seem to belong in the creed:

> 1. The corporate institution is as sturdy and vigorous as it was 30 years ago, and a managed cross-section of the better common-stock equities may be regarded as productive and safe for the very long term.

[5] W. A. Berridge, "Economic Facts Bearing on Some Variable Annuity Arguments," *Journal of Insurance,* November, 1957.

2. Diversification is indispensable.

3. Both stable-income and growth industrial company stocks seem to earn and pay more dollars after an inflation takes place, but decadent industries or companies may not do so.

4. Price-level protection in an era in which the cost of living may rise drastically justifies the investment of relatively large amounts in stocks, by individuals and by institutions whose liabilities may have to be discharged in future years in large amounts of depreciated dollars.

5. Common-stock dividends, earnings, and prices may decline or lag during depressions, wars, periods of price control, and periods of rapid inflation.

6. Extensive common-stock fluctuations appear likely in the foreseeable future. This seems to require that accounts subject to continuous dollar-value solvency tests or demand withdrawals use stocks only in modest degree and that those partially obligated make provision for liquid payment-reserve funds, deferred payments, or other ameliorative devices.

7. Finally, it is necessary to admit that we are without any effective capacity to estimate "normal" future prices for stocks or stock groups, even if we believe that we can "guesstimate" their probable future earnings and dividends. We have the price-earnings and yield data of the past, but these are not good benchmarks for judging stock prices in an era when both individuals and institutions fear the value of the dollar and are becoming increasingly uninhibited in their investment policies.

A Concluding Digression

The following are conventional and unsurprising conclusions. They assume mainly a continuation of existing economic trends and no major institutional changes. However, we are not exempt from rather significant institutional changes which may come about as much because of popular beliefs and fears as because of solid economic fact.

There is abroad among us the conviction that the cost of living will continue to trend upward, probably slowly but possibly rapidly. This has seemingly fostered a "flight into stocks" which has already developed stock-price repercussions and stock-price logic reminiscent of the unlamented New Era. Our new New Era has powerful institutional support in the investment company and the pension trust, among trusts and endowments generally, and may soon have the appealing variable annuity on a substantial scale. It is not unlikely that the entire situation may create a more or less permanent shift in the relative prices and immediate yields of stocks and bonds, with equal or lesser immediate yields on the stocks expected to be compensated by increases due to inflation and growth. This kind of stock-bond price relationship, with the stocks yielding less than bonds, already exists in the case of growth stocks.

No real business damage would of necessity result from this stock-bond pricing situation; financial practices could adjust to a case in which bond and mortgage rates remained above high-grade stock yields. Yet it would be unfortunate if, in hedging against an alleged inflationary drift, individuals and institutions were compelled to abandon too completely the security and liquidity of a senior and guaranteed position. It would be safer public policy to induce debtors and creditors to make some of their bond contracts on a purchasing-power basis, with the bond maturity sums and possibly the coupons adjusted up or down in proportion to changes in the price level. In fact, I am confident that several billions of long-term federal purchasing-power bonds could be sold over a few months' time to people and institutions who are now reluctantly turning to stocks, at an interest rate well below the market rate for straight bonds. Quite possibly the savings on interest rate would finance the excess payments required by our slow inflation. In any event, a successful step in this direction might help to solve several pressing economic needs,[6] including that of holding our second New Era stock market somewhere near the bounds of common sense.

---

[6] Nearly a third of the 11 million employees now covered by trusteed pension plans enjoy protective clauses which to some extent adjust pension expectations to final pay rates or similar measures. Many of the others obtain revisions of plan as economic elements change (see New York State Banking Department, *Pension and Other Employee Welfare Plans*, 1955).

14. CHANGING INTEREST RATES

AND THE

INVESTMENT PORTFOLIO*

❀ Harry C. Sauvain

LAST SUMMER THERE WAS some unusual excitement in Wall Street
and in the financial community. The cause of the disturbance was
not the behavior of stock prices, as is usually the case, but rather
the fluctuation of market prices in the ordinarily unexciting bond
market. There were days last July when prices for some Treasury
bonds fluctuated more than prices for some leading common stocks.
In a period of three months, from mid-June to mid-September,
1958, prices for several long-term Treasury issues declined 9–11
points, and the price of the new Treasury bond offered on June 15,
1958, dropped 6 points. These were rather sensational developments
in the market for the highest-grade securities in the country. Some
speculators in government bonds realized heavy losses, and a lot
of people who thought of government bonds as the safest and most
conservative media for investment of money to be found anywhere
in the world were deeply shocked.

One of the important implications of developments in the bond
market during 1958 is that changes in the level of interest rates
prevailing in the market may have serious consequences for bond

* From *The Journal of Finance,* Vol XIV, No. 2 (May, 1959), pp. 230–244. Reprinted by permission of *The Journal of Finance.*

investors and that there is a need for further study and more precise delineation of that hazard that has come to be known as "interest-rate risk."

GREATER IMPORTANCE OF INTEREST-RATE RISK RELATIVE TO FINANCIAL RISK

Two or three decades ago the main concern of the conservative investor, and sometimes his sole concern, was to obtain "safety of principal." I put that term in quotation marks because it had a particular meaning. It meant safety of principal as far as the ability to pay of bond issuers was concerned. It meant little risk that an issuer would fail to make payments of principal and interest in dollars, in full and precisely when due. It also meant little fluctuation in market prices for "safe" securities due to uncertainties about future payment of principal and interest.

Investors have known for a long time that market prices for the better grades of bonds are affected by changes in interest rates. Investments textbooks written in the 1920's sometimes refer to high-grade bonds as "money-rate" bonds and observe that their market prices fluctuate with changes in interest rates. But changes in prices for such securities due to interest-rate changes have not been considered very important even in some fairly recent writings. Graham and Dodd in their excellent book on security analysis, which has been virtually a bible for many of us, say that in the field of high-grade bonds the security analyst does not ordinarily concern himself with price fluctuations. "He knows from experience," they say, "that, while price fluctuations do occur, they are only rarely so wide as to affect the finances or confidence of those holding this type of security."[1]

I submit that in this era of the 1950's security analysts or investment managers must concern themselves with market-price fluctuations even in the field of high-grade bonds because they are often so wide as to affect the finances of investors. When government bonds drop 10 points in a few months and when high-grade corporate bonds lose one-fourth of their market value in the course

---

[1] Benjamin Graham and David L. Dodd, *Security Analysis* (3d ed.; New York: McGraw-Hill Book Co., Inc., 1951), p. 24.

of a few years because of change in interest rates, the finances of those holding such securities are likely to be very much affected. I suggest that investors in high-grade securities should be even more concerned with interest rate than with financial risk. There is, of course, the important problem of classifying securities as to grade; but when a bond qualifies as high-grade, it is protected by such large margins of earnings and assets that the usual fluctuations in the financial condition of issuers accompanying cyclical movements in business have little influence upon market price. On the other hand, the market prices of such securities and the yields at which they may be purchased from time to time are very much affected by cyclical changes in interest rates.

We have always had fluctuations in interest rates and corresponding changes in market prices and rates of yield on high-grade securities, but it seems to me that interest-rate risk has become more important in recent years. For one thing, there has been a great increase in the amount of high-grade and medium-grade bonds in the hands of investors over the past decade or two. The amount of United States government marketable securities outstanding has grown from $42 billion at the end of 1941 to about $172 billion at the end of last October; the amount of corporate long-term debt has increased about two and one-half times since 1946 and currently stands at a figure somewhat in excess of $100 billion. There has been a similar expansion in the total amount of state and municipal obligations to a current figure of more than $50 billion. In addition, there are some foreign dollar bonds and some preferred stocks that qualify as high-grade. The fact is that investors now hold somewhere in the neighborhood of $325 billions of securities mostly of the grade that fluctuates in market price with changes in interest rates.

A second development that makes interest-rate risk more important is an apparent increase in the amplitude of cyclical fluctuation in interest rates. I make this observation rather tentatively because it is difficult to measure a trend in the amplitude of such fluctuations over a long period of years and because the experience of the 1950's may not be indicative of basic change in the stability of long-term interest rates. But if you examine the record of yields on government securities over the last forty years as shown in the *Federal Reserve Chart Book* (Historical Supplement), you must be impressed by the relative steepness of the decline in rates for all maturities in the recession of 1953–54 and again in the recession of 1957–58. Similarly, the rise in rates between about the middle of 1954 and the middle of 1957 was very marked. The Treasury bill rate rose from a fraction of 1 per cent to more than 3½ per cent in that period of about three years, and the average yield on long-term Treasury bonds rose from 2½ to about 3¾ per cent. This is an increase of 50 per cent in the long-term rate. The magnitude of these fluctuations is particularly remarkable because the period of the 1950's has been one of relatively mild cyclical fluctuations. If we except certain periods of great financial crisis, such as 1920–21 and 1931–32, the amplitude of fluctuations in interest rates in the 1950's has been greater than in any similar period of time since World War I.

These developments of recent years support the idea that we need to examine more closely the manner in which changes in interest rates affect market prices and rates of yield for securities and to generalize more accurately the cause-and-effect relationships.

GRADES OF SECURITIES INFLUENCED PARTICULARLY BY INTEREST RATES

We may very well begin the present effort to examine further the influence of interest-rate changes on security investments by consideration of the elementary generalization that prices of high-grade bonds fluctuate inversely with changes in interest rates. This principle is a product of the simple arithmetic of bond-yield computation. When interest rates rise so that bonds must be sold to provide a higher yield than formerly, the increase in yield is accomplished by a downward adjustment of market price. When interest rates in the market change in such a manner that a bond may be sold at a lower yield than formerly, market price is adjusted upward.

But is it sufficient to say that changes in interest rates are important only for high-grade securities? Most of us think of high-grade bonds as comprising governments and corporates and municipals in the first two rating categories. Experience of recent years indicates that this concept is not broad enough. If you compare the average yields on the highest-grade corporate bonds, those rated triple A, and average yields on medium-grade corporate bonds, those rated triple B, over the last ten years, you find that they have fluctuated in much the same pattern. I have worked out the correlation between Standard & Poor's average yields on triple A and triple B bonds, using end-of-month data, for the period from January, 1948, to September, 1958. The coefficient of correlation is 0.957 per cent; R^2 is 91.6 per cent. This is a surprisingly high correlation.

The differential in yield between the two series tends to vary both ways from about 75 yield basis points. In periods of economic improvement when investor confidence is high, the differential declines about 50 basis points. In periods of recession investors seem to have less confidence in triple B bonds, and the differential rises to somewhat more than 100 basis points. In the last ten years the greatest aberration from the pattern of correlation occurred during the sharp decline in business activity from August, 1957, to January, 1958. In these months the yield differential between triple A and triple B bonds increased from about 75 basis points to about 125 basis points. In spite of these variations, the relatively high degree of correlation between the two series over a period of a little more than ten years indicates that changes in interest rates are a major influence upon yields and prices for medium-grade bonds.

It is interesting to observe, too, the close correlation between yields on triple A corporate bonds and yields on a group of high-grade preferred stocks. The coefficient of correlation for these two series as published by Standard & Poor for the period January, 1948, to September, 1958, was 0.931 per cent and R^2 was 86.7 per cent. This, too, is a high coefficient of correlation, and it would be higher but for the long-term shrinkage in the size of the yield differential between triple A corporate bonds and the group of high-grade preferred stocks. Thus inclusion of high-grade preferred stocks and probably some that are not quite so high grade further enlarges the area of security investment in which interest rates appear to be the major influence upon price changes.

The increase in the importance of interest-rate risk relative to financial risk for these classes of fixed-income securities below the top grade is due not only to the greater amplitude of fluctuation in interest rates but also to the lesser amplitude of fluctuation in the business cycle. In the past decade business recessions have caused little impairment generally in the ability of corporate issuers to make payments of interest and preferred dividends and have not been so severe as to shake seriously the confidence of investors in their continued ability to do so. Many economists think that evolutionary changes in our economic system have brought about this stability and that it will continue in the future. Perhaps it is too soon to be sure about this, but I think that a recurrence of conditions such as those of the 1930's, which sent yields on medium-grade bonds soaring to 10 or 11 per cent, is very unlikely.

It is possible to go further with this kind of analysis and to show that prices for lower-grade bonds and preferred stocks and even for common stocks are affected in some degree by changes in the level of interest rates prevailing in the market. However, casual observation of the behavior of the market prices indicates that as the degree of financial risk in securities increases, considerations of financial risk become increasingly important as an influence upon price and that, in the general category of common stocks, changes in earnings and dividends and changes in investors' expectations concerning earnings and dividends far outweigh the effect of changes in interest rates as an influence upon market prices.

Therefore, I am satisfied to stop with the proposition that the area of security investment in which interest-rate changes are of major importance consists of those grades of securities down to and including the grade represented by the triple B rating. I think that this is a significant enlargement of the usual concept of the investment area affected by interest-rate risk and that it has some important implications for investment policy.

INTEREST-RATE RISK AND THE LENGTH OF MATURITY

Moving further into the relationship between market prices for money-rate securities and changes in interest rates, we come to the generalization that the amplitude of fluctuation in prices with changes in interest rates varies with the length of the period to maturity of securities. In other words, the greater the length of maturity, the greater is the fluctuation of price with a given change in interest rates. Developments in the bond markets recently suggest the need for more careful examination of variation in the amplitude of price fluctuations with differences in length of maturity.

The amplitude of price fluctuations for securities of different maturities with fluctuations in interest rates is governed by two variables. One is difference in the length of maturity of securities. The other is variation in the size of fluctuations in interest rates, or market rates of yield, for securities of different maturities. For the present discussion we assume that changes in interest rates are the sole influence upon market prices for money-rate type securities.

Length of maturity as the sole variable. The second variable, difference in the size of fluctuation of rates for different maturities, can be held constant by assuming that change in rates of yield required by the market from one time to another is proportionately the same for all maturities. Then the effect of changes in interest rates upon market prices is solely a function of difference in length of maturities. In order to observe the effect of a change of interest rates of the same proportion for all maturities, I assumed that a number of securities with different maturities from one to fifty years, all bearing 3 per cent coupons, were all selling on a 3 per cent yield basis and thus were priced at par. Then I examined the effect upon market price of shifting all maturities to a 3½ per cent yield basis. Thus the increase in rate of yield was 16⅔ per cent for all maturities.

The effect of this change in interest rates upon prices is shown by the lower curve in Chart I, which is a line drawn through the market prices that would prevail for securities of the different

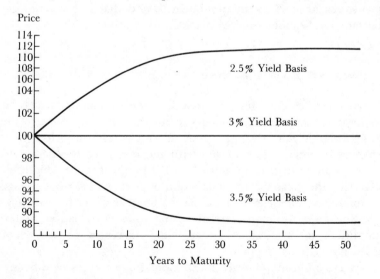

Chart I.   *The Change in Market Prices for Securities of Different Maturities with a Proportionate Change in Interest Rates.*

maturities on a $3\frac{1}{2}$ per cent yield basis. The line forms a curve declining at a decreasing rate from the shorter to the longer maturities. Next I assumed that securities of all maturities in this group were selling on a $2\frac{1}{2}$ per cent yield basis and determined their market prices on this basis. The upper curve in Chart I is a line drawn through the market prices that would prevail for all maturities after such a decline in interest rates. The line forms a curve rising at a decreasing rate from the shorter to the longer maturities.

The important idea that emerges from these observations is that the size of price changes with a uniform change in interest rates for all maturities does not increase in proportions varying directly with increase in length of maturity but that the size of price changes increases in proportions that decrease with each period of time added to length of maturity.

The detail of this change in price at a decreasing rate with increase in length of maturity can be seen clearly in the data from which Chart I was prepared. They show that when an obligation bearing a 3 per cent coupon and due in 5 years is shifted from a 3 to a $3\frac{1}{2}$ per cent basis, there is a price decline of 2.28 per cent. When a similar obligation due in 10 years is priced on a $3\frac{1}{2}$ per cent yield basis, the further decline in price beyond that of the 5-year maturity is 1.95 per cent of the price of the 5-year maturity. When a 3 per cent obligation due in 15 years is priced on a $3\frac{1}{2}$ per cent yield basis, the further decline in price beyond that of the 10-year maturity is 1.61 per cent of the price of the 10-year maturity. This illustration could be continued by 5-year intervals to the point where the price of a 50-year maturity declines only 0.48 per cent more than the price of a 45-year maturity. This is how price declines at a decreasing rate.

The explanation for the increase in size of price change at a decreasing rate with addition of units of time to maturity is to be found in the arithmetic of bond-yield calculations. The annual rate of discount created by a decline in market price below par is the total discount divided by the number of years to maturity. The addition of each year to maturity requires a larger total discount to achieve a given annual rate of discount. However, as years are added to the length of the period to maturity, each year is a smaller proportion of the total number of years to maturity over which the total discount must be spread. Thus the addition of proportionately smaller units of time requires relatively smaller increases in the size of the total discount required to achieve a given increase in rate of yield to maturity.

You may notice that the upper curve in Chart I moves farther away from par than the lower curve. Thus the price of a 3 per cent bond due in 50 years rises 14.23 percentage points above par when it is priced on a 2½ per cent yield basis. But the price of a 50-year, 3 per cent bond priced on a 3½ per cent yield basis declines only 11.77 percentage points below par. This is due to the fact that, as price declines, yield is computed on a smaller cost price; while as price rises, yield is computed on a larger cost price.

Difference in size of rate fluctuation for different maturities. If we stopped here, we would have an unrealistic conclusion about the effect of changes in market rates of interest upon prices for securities of different maturities because even casual observation of the behavior of interest rates in the market shows that short-term interest rates fluctuate much more widely than do long-term rates. To cite an extreme instance, the market rate of yield on 3 months' Treasury bills increased from 0.58 per cent on May 31, 1958, to 2.23 per cent on August 30, 1958. In the same period the average yield on Treasury bonds maturing or callable in 10 years or more increased only from 3.13 to 3.67 per cent. The greater amplitude of fluctuation in short-term rates relative to long-term rates would, except for differences in length of maturity, cause wider fluctuations in prices for the shorter maturities as interest rates changed. In the market this relative instability of short-term rates operates in direct opposition to the stabilizing influence of shortness of maturity. The balance of the two influences determines the amplitude of market-price fluctuations for securities of different maturities.

In order to observe variation in size of change in interest rates for securities of different maturities in a period of rising interest rates, I have prepared a schedule of the yields at which eleven Treasury obligations of different maturities ranging from 8 months to about 37 years were selling on June 13, 1958, and a similar schedule of the yields at which these same issues were selling on September 12, 1958. The time interval between dates is 3 months. Then I expressed the yield for each issue on September 12 as a percentage of its yield on June 13. The result is shown in Chart II.

The increase in yields was very much greater for the short maturities than for the longer issues. For example, the shortest

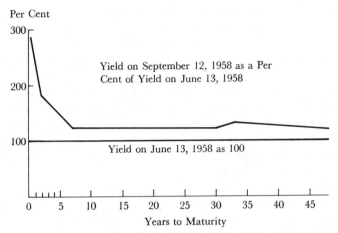

Per Cent

Chart II.   *The Change in Market Rates of Yield on Treasury Securities from June 13, 1958 to September 12, 1958.*

maturity in this schedule is the Treasury 1⅜ per cent note due February 15, 1959. The interval to maturity was approximately 8 months on June 13 and 5 months on September 12, 1958. On June 13 it was selling on a 0.97 per cent yield basis, and on September 12 it was selling on a 2.86 per cent yield basis. The yield on the latter date was 295 per cent of the yield on June 13. By contrast, the longest maturity in the schedule is the Treasury 3 per cent bond due February 15, 1955, with a time interval to maturity on June 13 of 36 years and 8 months. On June 13 it was selling on a 3.12 per cent yield basis, and on September 12 it was priced to yield 3.55 per cent. Its yield on the latter date was about 114 per cent of its yield on June 13. Chart II shows that the relative size of the increase in yield declined sharply as the interval to maturity increased from 8 months to about 3 years, then declined more moderately for maturities from 3 to about 10 years, and that the size of increase was about the same for maturities beyond 10 years. In some other period of rising interest rates, the size of change in yields on securities of varying maturities may be different from that in the period I have examined, but this period is a good test of the effect on market prices of a much steeper rise in short-term than in long-term rates.

Now how did the proportionately much greater rise in short-term rates affect the magnitude of change in market prices for these Treasury securities of widely varying maturities? I have taken the market price on September 12, 1958, for each of the issues included in this study and expressed it as a percentage of its market price on June 13. These percentages measure the relative size of the decline in market prices for the different maturities. Chart III shows clearly that the much greater changes in market rates of yield for the shorter maturities had less effect on market prices than did the much smaller changes in market rates of yield for the longer maturities. In general, the line connecting the September 12 price percentages declined steeply from the shortest maturity to the maturity in about 7 years and then declined more slowly, and with some irregularity, to the longest maturities.

If the irregularities in the curve of Chart III were smoothed out, we would have a curve somewhat like the lower curve in Chart I. This leads me to the conclusion that length of maturity is the dominant influence upon the magnitude of fluctuations in market price as interest rates change, in spite of the much greater fluctuations in short-term than in long-term rates. The conclusion may be generalized by saying that, as interest rates in the market change, the magnitude of fluctuation in market prices for securities of different maturities tends to increase with increase in length of maturity but at a decreasing rate of increase. This generalization has significance for investors who seek relative stability of price in money-rate type obligations. It means that a high degree of price

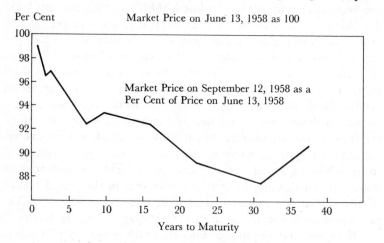

Chart III. *The Change in Market Prices for Treasury Securities from June 13, 1958 to September 12, 1958.*

stability may be obtained only in relatively short maturities, say, maturities of less than 1 year, and that price instability increases markedly as maturities are extended from 1 to about 7 years. It also means that there is no great difference in price instability for maturities longer than 20 or 25 years. Obviously, the pattern of price change would vary in different periods according to the magnitude of the change in shorter-term rates relative to longer-term rates.

INTEREST-RATE RISK AND THE SIZE OF INVESTMENT INCOME

The phenomenon of change in rates of interest prevailing in the market for money-rate type securities affects not only the market prices for these securities but also the size of income obtainable at any particular time and from time to time by investment reinvestment in money-rate type securities.

We have first the general proposition that at any particular time yields on securities of different maturities tend to be higher as the length of maturity increases. Thus, generally, the longer the maturities selected for investment, the larger is the rate of yield. When the structure of yields in the market follows this pattern, it is said to form an upsloping yield curve. The pattern of yields on government obligations of different maturities that prevailed on June 13, 1958, as shown by Chart IV, is an example of a markedly upsloping yield curve for maturities up to about 10 years. This chart is constructed from yield data for the same eleven issues used in the two preceding charts.

However, the pattern of the yield curve changes at times. Sometimes it is much less upsloping and thus flatter. Chart IV also shows the yield curve on September 12, 1958, which was only moderately upsloping. The data are for the same issues. There have, in fact, been times when the yield curve was somewhat downsloping, with yields on the shortest maturities higher than those on longer maturities. The fact that the yield curve does become relatively flat at times, and even assumes odd shapes with a "hump" toward the middle, raises the question of whether there is any basic tendency for the curve to be upsloping. I submit that there is such a tendency.

The tendency for yield curve to be upsloping. We have seen that, as interest rates change, the size of market price fluctuations

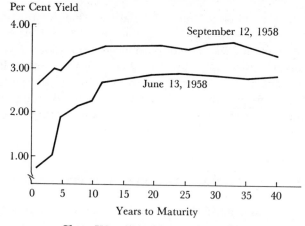

Chart IV.   *Yield Curves on Recent Dates.*

is greater for longer maturities of securities than for short-term obligations. Thus there is more risk of loss of principal inherent in the longer maturities in the event that they have to be liquidated at market prices. Investors in money-rate type securities generally like to minimize this risk, although the intensity of their effort to do so varies considerably among the different types of investors. Thus there is a preference for the shorter-term and less risky issues. Because investors prefer the less risky issues, they are generally willing to buy them at lower rates of yield than the rates at which they are willing to buy the longer-term and more risky issues. This preference for liquidity is the reason why there is a tendency for the yield curve to be upsloping. The upsloping curve is perfectly logical, in that it provides smaller returns to those who demand the more advantageous terms of investment and provides the larger returns to those who are willing and able to assume the risk of greater fluctuations in market price. In brief, it provides a premium for assuming interest-rate risk.

The yield curve is most steeply upsloping when conditions in the money market are "easy," that is, when there is a relative abundance of funds seeking investment in money-rate type securities. At such times a considerable amount of money comes into the market for more or less temporary investment, pending some other use at some other time. Then the competition of investors for investment media with small financial risk and small interest-rate risk results in a bidding-down of yields on the shorter maturities of high-grade obligations relative to yields on longer maturities.

However, there are times when conditions in the money market become "tight." Demand for money increases, and the demand for short-term money increases more than the demand for long-term money. Under these conditions yields on the shorter maturities rise to a much greater extent than yields on longer maturities. This is not because the shorter maturities have become less desirable from the investors' standpoint but because the stronger demand for short-term money relative to supply has caused a bidding-up of money rates. Investors still prefer short maturities to long maturities, but they are not obliged to accept the smaller returns at the short end of the maturity schedule that prevailed when their preferences dominated the structure of interest rates. With users of money offering higher rates, they happily accept the higher rates.

In the last analysis, the question whether an upsloping yield curve is normal, or usually to be expected, depends upon the question whether relatively easy-money market conditions are normal. I think that in the kind of economy we have now, with the federal government committed to responsibility for economic growth and full employment, a condition of relatively easy money is much more often to be expected than a condition of tight money.

The instability of income on short-term investment. Regardless of the shape of the yield curve at any particular time, the fluctuations of interest rates cause changes in the amount of income realized from a given amount of principal invested and reinvested in money-rate type obligations. When principal is invested, a rate of yield is obtained. If securities are held to maturity and the proceeds reinvested, the new rate is the yield prevailing in the market at the time of reinvestment. Except by coincidence, the new rate is different from the old rate. And insofar as it is different, the amount of income from a given amount of principal increases or decreases.

There is fluctuation of income upon reinvestment caused by changes in interest rates for securities of all maturities because rates for all maturities change from time to time. However, the fluctuation is greater for short-term obligations than for those of long maturity. In general, stability of income from funds invested and reinvested varies inversely with length of maturity.

The relative instability of income from short-term obligations is due to two conditions. One is the much greater amplitude of fluctuation in short-term rates. We have observed in Chart II the much greater rise in yields on short maturities than on long-term

issues in the period from June 13 to September 12, 1958. Inspection
of the chart of interest rates in the *Federal Reserve Chart Book*
(Historical Supplement) covering the last forty years shows that
relatively wide swings in short-term rates have been characteristic
• of the money markets. It follows, therefore, that when short-term
obligations mature, the rate obtainable upon reinvestment in
short-term issues may vary widely from the rate obtained on the
original investment. Since long-term rates fluctuate in a narrower
range, the yield obtained upon reinvestment of long-term funds is
likely to vary to a smaller extent from the original rate.

The other condition is simply the length of the period of investment. Funds invested in short maturities and reinvested in similar
obligations come back into the market in a relatively short period
of time. Whatever change has occurred in short-term rates in the
interval is realized in terms of income. Thus, if funds are invested
and reinvested in obligations maturing in one year, there would be
a different rate of yield and a different amount of income each year.
In recent years the income from a given amount of principal invested
and reinvested in one-year maturities of government obligations
would have fluctuated much more than the income from a diversified
group of good common stocks.

By contrast, reinvestment of funds invested in long maturities
occurs only at long intervals, if bonds are held to maturity. Income
is stable during the period to maturity and changes only when
reinvestment occurs after a considerable period of years. Over
a long time there may be secular changes in long-term rates that
cause the difference in yields from one time to another to be greater
than the normally small cyclical fluctuation in long-term rates. This
modifies, but does not invalidate, the general proposition that the
stability of income upon investment and reinvestment in long-term
issues is greater than that obtained by investment and reinvestment
in short maturities.

Thus we have a sort of paradox. Market prices of short-term
issues fluctuate much less than prices of long-term issues with changes
in interest rates. But the stability of income from long-term issues
is much greater than that from short-term issues upon investment
and reinvestment at maturity. Clearly, the manager of a portfolio
of money-rate type securities must decide whether stability of income
or stability of principal is the more important in his particular
circumstances.

15. EFFECT OF DEFAULTS AND CREDIT DETERIORATION ON YIELDS OF CORPORATE BONDS*

❀ Harold G. Fraine
Robert H. Mills

THE AUTHORS WERE FACED WITH the problem of estimating the size of reserve which would have been necessary for absorbing losses on medium-and high-grade corporate bonds during the first half of this century. Upon searching the literature to see what help could be gained from past authorities, we found that there is a gap between the doctrines by theorists as to the kind of experience expectable and the best published statistics of realized yields and loss rates.[1] We are passing along the results of a small effort to plug this gap in the hope that it will help others who are similarly faced with the necessity

* From *The Journal of Finance*, Vol. XVI, No. 3 (September, 1961), pp. 423–434. Reprinted by permission of *The Journal of Finance*.

[1] The best published statistics on the realized yields and loss rates on corporate bonds are in W. Braddock Hickman, *Corporate Bond Quality and Investor Experience* and *Statistical Measures of Corporate Bond Financing* (Princeton: Princeton University Press, 1959 and 1960, respectively). Inasmuch as our purpose is to supplement and build upon the material already published by Mr. Hickman, our debt to him is obvious. We are also deeply indebted to the National Bureau of Economic Research for tabulating individual yields from their punched cards in such a manner as to permit the derivation of our "modified" realized yields and loss rates—particularly to Dr. Geoffrey Moore for his stimulating ideas and to Miss Elizabeth T. Simpson, whose grasp of our problem and knowledge of the basic records were extremely helpful. Grateful acknowledgment is made to Robert Morrison, William Dawn, and Gary L. Swenson, graduate students at the University of Wisconsin, for statistical assistance.

of using the record of the past performance of corporate bonds in connection with problems of evaluation of probable future performance.

Theorists in the field of investments seem generally to offer support for the idea that some reserve is desirable. This is found in such doctrines that, in contrast with common stocks, where either gain or loss may be expected, the nature of the contract in unconvertible corporate bonds severely limits the possibilities of gain but leaves quite open the possibilities of loss up to 100 per cent. Again, there is the doctrine that bond investment is a "negative art," requiring principally the gauging of the chances for loss and the estimating of what premium in yield is appropriate for acceptance of those chances. Many writers have regarded the difference between the prospective yield from market price on a bond and the yield prevailing at the same time on riskless securities of similar term as consisting mainly of premium offered the investor for assuming risk of later loss. This sort of theory reached perhaps its most extreme form in the writings of Kirshman, who implied that, within a diversified portfolio of bonds, sufficiently large for averages to work out, greater losses would later be incurred among the bonds of higher-risk premiums which would reduce their average realized yield below the prospective, probably down to the level of the prospective yields prevailing on only the riskless ones.[2] Thus there is the implication that the interest receipts in excess of those on the safest bonds should not be regarded as income but as an offset to losses expected to be experienced on the portfolio of such bonds later when defaults occur and that, for the institutional investor capable of reserving income, such risk premiums presumably indicate the proper rates of reservation for later losses.

Turning now to the literature on statistics of yields of corporate bonds, most of the published statistics have been, as in the case of Macaulay[3] and Durand,[4] in terms of the prospective yields—looking forward from market prices in anticipation of performance according to the contract. Such yields might also be characterized as "ex ante," "expected," "anticipatory," or "market" yields. There has

[2] J. E. Kirshman, *Principles of Investment* (New York: McGraw-Hill Book Co., Inc., 1933), pp. 109–10.

[3] Frederick A. Macaulay, *Interest Rates, Bond Yields, and Stock Prices* (New York: National Bureau of Economic Research, 1938).

[4] David Durand, "Basic Yields of Corporate Bonds, 1900–1942" (Technical Paper No. 3 [New York: National Bureau of Economic Research, 1942]).

been a growing literature reflecting attempts to contrast such anticipatory yields with yields which measure the departures of actual
from anticipated performance.[5] This latter type of yield is variously
characterized as "actual," "realized," "ex post," or "life-span" yields.
And the deficiencies of the ex post from the ex ante yields—of the
realized from the prospective yields—have been characterized as "loss
rates"—measuring the rates of annual reservations from interest
receipts which would have been necessary in order to offset subsequent losses. Such realized yields and loss rates have been computed
not only for various categories of corporate bonds but also for varying length and calendar terminal points of assumed periods of holding. They have been computed on the basis of holding from issue to
extinguishment of the contract, as well as on the basis of purchase
on certain dates and sale at other dates. For the purpose of measuring default risk, the measures covering holdings during the years of
the depression of the 1930's are most useful because during that
period bonds suffered as much from default and value depreciation
as seems likely ever to be experienced in the future. The period of
the thirties is thus regarded as furnishing a sort of acid test.

All the various realized yields for which statistics have been
published have one characteristic in common. They reflect the effects
on realized yields of money-market changes just as readily as they do
effects of credit impairment or default. The realized yields are increased above the prospective yields by reason of calls for redemption
at prices higher than the maturity value, as well as lowered below
the prospective yield as the result of impairments in the payment
of interest or principal. For bonds outstanding on a date of assumed
market liquidation, as at the end of a period of study, the realized
yields are pushed above the prospective yields if the market rate
of interest at such a time is below the market level at the time of assumed purchase, as well as pushed below the prospective yields by
declines in market values by reason of impairment of the credit standing of the debtor. The published realized-yield statistics which average these diverse effects are found to be very reassuring by some institutional investors, who cite them as evidence that the history of

[5] For some "pre-Hickman" studies involving "realized" yields, see A. S. Dewing,
The Financial Policy of Corporations (New York: Ronald Press Co., 1926), pp.
1194–95; H. G. Fraine, "Superiority of High-Yield Bonds Not Substantiated by
1927–1936 Performance," *Annalist* (New York Times Publishing Co.), October 1,
1937; Leo Spurrier, "Common Stocks and Bonds as Long-Term Investments,"
Journal of Business (January, 1941), XIV, 9.

this period of admittedly acid test indicates that no reserve is necessary.

Those taking this position are fond of citing that the most comprehensive and useful publication of such yields shows that the average realized yield on a representative portfolio of corporate bonds of the four highest agency rating grades during the span of years from early 1900 to early 1944 was actually in excess of, instead of deficient from, the prospective yield, in spite of the facts that in each of those years actual interest payments were less than contracted for[6] and that the proportion of all outstanding straight corporate bonds in default reached as high as about 15 per cent in 1936 and 1940.[7] Had the large issues of the top four rating grades run to maturity with interest and principal payments unimpaired, they would have given the investor a yield of 4.8 per cent.[8] In spite of some bonds defaulting and many others declining in liquidating value because of impairment of credit condition, the average[9] realized yield for the entire group was 5.2 per cent.[8] Some investors are un-duly impressed by the fact that, instead of an expected loss rate, there was an average rate of gain of the realized over the prospective yield of 0.4 per cent per annum (5.2 − 4.8). Such a result is at least superficially contrary to the theoretical doctrines and came about, of course, because the gains in redemption values and final market values of many bonds, due mainly to changes in money-market con-ditions, more than offset the defection of the realized from the prospective yields of other bonds within the portfolio caused by defaults in interest and principal payments and by depreciation in final liquidation value due to deterioration in credit prospects. Hickman says:

> Thus, if all of the bond issues in this study are conceived of as pooled into a single portfolio held from offering to extinguishment or 1944, the portfolio would have suffered no loss in current dollars. This is a truly remarkable finding in view of the fact that the record spans a period of forty-four years that includes a great war and a great depression.[10]

[6] See W. Braddock Hickman, *The Volume of Corporate Bond Financing since 1900* (Princeton: Princeton University Press, 1953), Table A-25, p. 380.
[7] Calculated from Tables A-2 and A-17 of Hickman, *ibid.*, pp. 257 and 340.
[8] Hickman, *Statistical Measures*, p. 394.
[9] Mean of individual percentage annual yields of individual bonds weighted by dollar volume at issuance. For detailed background on the computation and averaging of bond yields, see Hickman, *Bond Quality*, pp. 54–66.
[10] *Ibid.*, p. 73.

For the purpose of estimating the reserve needs of large-scale continuing investors, it was desired to supplement the already published realized yields and loss rates with "modified" realized yields and loss rates which reduce, though do not completely remove, the effect of money-market influences on final liquidation values. To continuing investors the retirement of an issue before maturity at a premium over the maturity payment is usually a disadvantage rather than an advantage, because retirements by call are usually at the option of the issuer rather than the investor and are usually under conditions which are advantageous to the issuer and disadvantageous to the investor—namely, when the market rate of interest for refunding and therefore for reinvestment in the same degree of risk is lower than the contract rate in the security already outstanding. Under such circumstances reinvestment at the same degree of risk usually involves a loss on the reinvestment much greater than the gain on liquidation of the issue which is terminated.[11] For the continuing investor, the call premium is, in effect, inadequate "liquidated damages" for loss to be suffered on reinvestment.

That there was a drastic decline in rates earned on invested funds by life insurance companies during the period of abnormally high calls and refundings of the 1930's and 1940's can be noted from Table 1. The realized yields now available in the literature are affected not only by calls but also by the market prices assumed for purchase or liquidation of bonds outstanding at terminal dates of the study record. Hickman was obviously concerned with the possible distortion of yields caused by unprecedentedly low interest rates, hence by unprecedentedly high bond prices on the date of assumed liquidation in the market of the population of bonds still outstand-

---

[11] The following hypothetical illustration uses interest-rate changes that are within the record of recent experience: Assume an investor purchases at par $1,000,000 of 4¼ per cent bonds due in thirty years at par but callable in ten years at 105. The prospective yield would be 4.5 per cent. Assume that, ten years later, interest rates for that degree of risk decline to 3 per cent and that the bonds are called by the issuer. The investor would then receive $1,050,000. This would appear to represent a capital gain of $50,000.The reinvestment of the $1,050,000 would have to be at the lower interest rates prevailing, namely, 3 per cent for comparable quality securities. Upon reinvestment, there would be a decline in annual interest receipts from $45,000 to $31,500 (3 per cent $\times$ $1,050,000), or an income loss of $13,500 annually. The $270,000 loss (20 $\times$ 13,500) in income over the twenty years foregone of the old contract is substantially greater that the $50,000 premium received on the call of the old bonds. And the new bond, because of its lower coupon rate. would have less chance of eventual liquidation above maturity value.

Table 1. *Net Rates Earned on Invested Life Insurance Company Funds (Per Cent)**

YEAR	RATE	YEAR	RATE	YEAR	RATE
1920	4.83	1930	5.05	1940	3.45
1921	5.02	1931	4.93	1941	3.41
1922	5.12	1932	4.65	1942	3.40
1923	5.18	1933	4.25	1943	3.29
1924	5.17	1934	3.92	1944	3.19
1925	5.11	1935	3.70	1945	3.07
1926	5.09	1936	3.71	1946	2.92
1927	5.05	1937	3.69	1947	2.88
1928	5.05	1938	3.59	1948	2.96
1929	5.05	1939	3.54	1949	3.04

* From *Life Insurance Fact Book, 1952* (New York: Institute of Life Insurance, 1953), p. 49.

ing at the end of the study period. He dealt with the difficulty by breaking up or refining his population in different ways, but without modifying the realized yields. He shows, for example, that when the issues outstanding at the termini of the study are excluded and the population confined to issues which were both issued and extinguished within the span of years of the study, . . . the loss rate rises from −0.1 per cent (inferring capital gains) to 0.1 per cent (inferring capital losses). The implication would seem to be that investors who are unable to take advantage of market appreciation on outstanding issues (but are required by statute to write securities down to market under certain circumstances) would require somewhat higher loss reserves than those needed by investors generally. So far as can be judged from the record before us, a reserve accumulated at the rate of 0.1 per cent on book value would have been adequate to take care of default losses on large issues offered and extinguished within the period studied.[12]

This refinement is at the cost of omitting, from averaging, the yields of the great population of bonds outstanding at the end of the record, some of which were still suffering from credit impairment and from failure to complete reorganization following default. Also, it still leaves in the record the abnormally high gains from calls, which also resulted from the drop in interest rates. Most of the bonds extinguished during this period were extinguished by call.

[12] Hickman, *Bond Quality*, p. 83.

The calls at premiums were allowed to push the realized yields above the prospective yields. Inasmuch as most of such retirements were toward the end of the period, reinvestment would have been made in bonds which were issued at such low interest rates as not so likely in turn to be redeemed at premiums. The abnormality of the volume of redemption at premiums is indicated by the fact that the average proportion of redemptions by call during the latter half of the period studied was about ten times that of the earlier half.[13] The problem is to retain the successful along with the unsuccessful bonds without retaining the gains in realized yields caused by the change in level of interest rates.

In order to retain as much as possible of the effects of defaults and impairment of credit prospects and eliminate as much as possible of the effects of purely money-market influences, the authors have derived "modified" averages of the realized (life-span) yields and loss rates for all large[14] straight corporate bonds outstanding during the period 1900–1944. This was done by the simple device of substituting the contractual yield for the realized yield for those undefaulting bonds for which the realized was in excess of the prospective yield. For such bonds the somewhat dubious gains of the realized over the expected yields—reflecting mainly the effect of the falling level of interest rates on redemption values and final market prices—are eliminated.

This treatment involves the working assumption (some qualifications of which are noted in the next paragraph) that the excesses of realized over prospective yields on undefaulted bonds were due to lower interest rates and not to improved credit prospects. (The unprecedentedly low interest rates during the time of abnormally high call volume and at the end of the experience record were accompanied by stock prices well below half their 1929 high.) In other words, the working assumption is that the bonds which were called at premiums over face would have run to maturity and been redeemed at face value. And that those undefaulted bonds still outstanding at the end which were quoted in the market at liquidating prices such that the realized yields were above the prospective owed the gain to the influence on bond prices of the unprecedentedly low interest rates prevailing at the end of 1943. From these assumptions it would follow that, had there been no change in the level of basic

[13] Computed from Hickman, *Statistical Measures,* Table 165, p. 297.
[14] More than $5,000,000 in size of issue.

interest rate, the realized yields on both groups of bonds mentioned above would have been equal to, instead of in excess of, their prospective yields.[15] Substituting the individual prospective yields on this population of bonds for their actual realized yields, in averaging the realized yields of these plus of those of the population of bonds whose actual realized yields were not in excess of their prospective yields, gives us our "modified" realized-yield average for the combined population without loss of the record of any of the bonds.

The lower realized yields and higher loss rates resulting, however, do not give a complete separation of the effects of default and credit impairment from the effects of changes in the interest-rate level. Some of the premium redemptions and higher liquidating values may have resulted from other causes than a decline in the general level of interest rates, perhaps because of better cash position or improved financial prospects of the issuer. Much of the small volume of calls during the first two decades of the century was probably for such reasons. However, it was during the last decade and a half of the period studied that the volume of bonds outstanding was the largest, that the proportion of calls and refundings was abnormally high, and that the interest-rate level became unprecedentedly low.[16] Inasmuch as the favorable money-market conditions were accompanied by a severe business depression and abnormally high volume of defaults, it seems likely that most of the individual excesses of realized over prospective yields, on the other hand, were due to ease of money rather than to improvement in credit standing of the issuers. It must be recognized also that money-market influences have not been removed from the realized yields and loss rates of those bonds which defaulted or of those bonds whose market values at the close of the experience record were such as to produce a deficiency of realized from expected yield.[17]

---

[15] It might be argued that the uptilting term structure of the interest rate prevailing toward the end of the experience record would alone have caused the bonds to be higher in price because their terms would have become shorter. But the tilt of the term structure could well have resulted from the descent of interest rates to an abnormally low level. See, for example, R. I. Robinson, *The Management of Bank Funds* (New York: McGraw-Hill Book Co., Inc., 1951), p. 328.

[16] See Hickman, *Corporate Bond Financing*, pp. 250, 292, 300, and 129.

[17] Limitations of data on the punched cards did not permit this step. The modified averages of realized yield would presumably have been even lower and the resulting loss rates even higher, had we found it possible to remove the effect of interest-level change on their final market values.

Except, then, for minor impurities, the modified averages of realized yields tend to approach, but not quite reach, what the bonds would have yielded without the fortunate and abnormal gains from interest-rate-level changes. The modified averages of loss rates indicate roughly how much of the interest receipts of the entire portfolio would have had to be reserved in order to compensate for losses on the portion of the portfolio that defaulted and on the portion suffering from decline in market value at the end of the study because of credit deterioration.

The modified loss rate represents the rate which it would have been wise to have reserved under a policy of treating any gains over the prospective yield as purely fortuitous. Such a policy has its points, not only because of the questionableness of such "gains" as income for a continuing investor, but also because of the erratic pattern of calls and the imprudence of counting upon the repetition of the abnormally high proportion of them.

The resulting modified averages of realized yields and loss rates are presented in the last two columns of Table 2.[18] The modified and unmodified average realized yields for the population of most interest to our argument—on all large corporate bonds issued and outstanding between January 1, 1900, and December 1, 1943, and carrying at time of issuance one of the four highest agency rating grades—compare with their average promised yields as shown in the accompanying table.

	WEIGHTED MEAN ANNUAL RATE (PER CENT)		
AGENCY RATING	PROMISED YIELD	REALIZED YIELD UNMODIFIED	MODIFIED
I	4.5	5.1	4.3
II	4.5	5.1	4.3
III	4.9	5.0	4.3
IV	5.4	5.8	4.5
I–III	4.7	5.0	4.3
I–IV	4.8	5.2	4.3

* Median of various agency ratings at time of offering: I comparable to AAA, AI+, etc.; II, to AA, AI, etc.; IV, to BAA, BI+.

[18] The population on which they are based is the $55,181 million of large issues mentioned on p. 35 of Hickman's *Bond Quality*, less $2,743 million of irregular offerings.

Table 2. *Unmodified and Modified Realized Yields and Differences from Prospective Yields of Large Issues of Corporate Bonds by Agency Ratings, 1900–1943**

AGENCY RATING	PAR AMOUNT (IN MILLIONS OF DOLLARS) (1)	PROPORTION DEFAULTED (PER CENT) (2)	PROPORTION CALLED (PER CENT) (3)	PROMISED YIELD (PER CENT) (4)	AV. ANNUAL RATE OF REALIZED YIELD UNMODIFIED (PER CENT) (5)	MODIFIED (PER CENT) (6)	DIFFERENCE: REALIZED FROM PROSPECTIVE YIELD UNMODIFIED (PER CENT) (7)†	MODIFIED (PER CENT) (8)†
Summary (rails, utilities, industrials):								
I	$ 6,398	5.9	40.5	4.5	5.1	4.3	+0.6	−0.1
II	10,048	6.0	40.8	4.5	5.1	4.3	+0.5	−0.3
III	11,701	13.4	52.7	4.9	5.0	4.3	+0.1	−0.6
IV	8,506	19.1	45.7	5.4	5.8	4.5	+0.4	−0.9
V	3,170	41.1	39.3	6.3	4.1	3.5	−2.1	−2.8
VI–IX	555	50.1	21.5	7.6	4.7	3.7	−3.0	−3.9
I–III	28,747	9.0	45.6	4.7	5.0	4.3	+0.4	−0.4
I–IV	37,253	11.3	45.6	4.8	5.2	4.3	+0.4	−0.5
All rated bonds	40,978	14.1	44.8	5.0	5.1	4.3	+0.1	−0.7
Unrated bonds	11,460	28.6	17.0	4.7	4.6	4.3	−0.1	−0.4
All rated and unrated	52,438	17.3	38.7	4.9	5.0	4.3	+0.1	−0.6
Railroads:								
I	2,561	14.5	24.3	4.9	5.4	4.6	+0.4	−0.3
II	3,007	18.6	13.8	4.8	4.2	3.9	−0.6	−0.9
III	2,363	41.0	13.3	4.9	3.3	2.7	−1.5	−2.1
IV	1,276	36.6	25.1	5.1	4.2	4.1	−0.9	−1.1
V	727	70.7	7.9	5.9	2.3	2.2	−3.6	−3.7
VI–IX	149	69.0	0.0	5.7	2.1	2.1	−3.7	−3.7
I–III	7,931	23.9	17.0	4.8	4.3	3.8	−0.5	−1.1
I–IV	9,207	25.7	18.2	4.9	4.3	3.8	−0.6	−1.1
All rated bonds	10,083	29.6	17.1	5.0	4.1	3.7	−0.9	−1.3
Unrated bonds	6,897	25.9	9.8	4.3	4.0	3.9	−0.3	−0.4
All rated and unrated	16,980	28.1	14.1	4.7	4.0	3.8	−0.6	−0.9

Public utilities:

I	$ 2,684	0.0	47.5	4.0	4.8	3.9	+0.8	0.0
II	5,660	0.0	45.9	4.2	5.3	4.2	+1.0	0.0
III	5,955	5.0	58.6	4.9	5.5	4.8	+0.6	−0.1
IV	4,124	14.0	45.9	5.3	6.1	4.5	+0.8	−0.8
V	1,559	32.5	43.6	6.5	4.9	4.0	−1.6	−2.5
VI–IX	256	45.7	20.1	8.1	4.4	3.1	−3.7	−5.0
I–III	14,299	2.2	51.5	4.5	5.3	4.4	+0.8	−0.1
I–IV	18,423	4.9	50.2	4.7	5.4	4.4	+0.8	−0.2
All rated bonds	20,238	7.5	49.3	4.8	5.4	4.4	+0.6	−0.4
Unrated bonds	2,661	34.3	16.0	5.1	4.5	4.5	−0.6	−0.7
All rated and unrated	22,899	10.6	45.5	4.9	5.3	4.4	+0.4	−0.5

Industrials:

I	1,154	0.0	60.0	4.5	5.2	4.5	+0.7	0.0
II	1,981	3.2	67.3	5.1	5.8	5.1	+0.7	0.0
III	3,383	8.8	70.0	5.0	5.3	4.4	+0.3	−0.6
IV	3,106	18.5	53.9	5.5	5.9	4.6	+0.3	−0.9
V	884	31.9	57.6	6.2	4.2	3.5	−1.9	−2.7
VI–IX	150	37.5	45.4	8.7	7.6	6.5	−1.0	−2.1
I–III	6,519	5.6	67.4	4.9	5.5	4.6	+0.5	−0.3
I–IV	9,625	9.8	63.1	5.1	5.6	4.6	+0.5	−0.5
All rated bonds	10,659	12.0	62.4	5.3	5.5	4.6	−0.3	−0.7
Unrated bonds	1,903	30.3	44.9	5.6	7.1	5.7	−0.3	+0.1
All rated and unrated	12,562	14.8	59.7	5.3	5.8	4.7	−0.5	−0.6

* Slight discrepancies between the loss rates and differences in yields are due to rounding of figures to first decimal place.

† The pluses and minuses in these two columns represent, respectively, gains and losses and should not be confused with the opposite use in the quotation from Hickman which appears . . . above.

Source: Data developed from special tabulations supplied by the National Bureau of Economic Research, 1959.

It may be of some interest to note that the modified realized yields give a pattern much closer to the uniformity expected by Kirshman than do the unmodified. The pattern of the mean deficiency (loss rate)[19] of the modified realized from the prospective yields is much more in line with the default frequency and the differentials in risk implied by both the median ratings of the leading rating agencies and the prospective yields (as in the accompanying table). Reservations at the rate of 0.2 per cent of the portfolio per

AGENCY RATING	GAIN (+) OR LOSS (−) OF REALIZED COMPARED WITH PROSPECTIVE YIELD (PER CENT)	
	UNMODIFIED	MODIFIED
I	+0.6	−0.1
II	+0.5	−0.3
III	+0.1	−0.6
IV	+0.4	−0.9
I–III	+0.4	−0.4
I–IV	+0.4	−0.5

annum would have been enough for the real losses from default and credit impairment on a conservative portfolio of the two top agency grades, but almost 1 per cent would have been necessary for a portfolio concentrating in a representative cross-section of fourth-grade corporates. While the modified loss rates indicate that higher reservations out of interest receipts would have been necessary for the riskier issues, the uniformity of modified realized yields compared with the stepping-up of offering yields shows that buyers through their bidding generally anticipated about the correct amount of prospective-yield differential necessary to level the realized yields, in the absence of money-market changes. Reference to the other parts of Table 2 shows that the patterns become more erratic, as might be expected, with fragmentation of the universe.

But such departures among the three parts of the universe—railroads, public utilities, and industrials—from the average of all corporates imply that discrimination in selection would have reduced the rate of loss.

---

[19] Difference between the above arithmetic means of weighted individual prospective and realized yields. Slight discrepancies are due to rounding to first decimal place.

16. VALUE APPROACHES TO INVESTING DECISIONS*

❀ A. Wilfred May

I HAVE THE BASIC CONVICTION and philosophy, confirmed by long practical experience, that one's entire approach in the making of investment decisions should be concentrated on evaluating individual issues instead of trying to time market movements.

Fundamentally, my philosophy is based on the invalidity of picturing the market as a whole, as well as of attempts to time movements of the market or individual issues either by technical tools or by ear. It is premised on disapproval of concentrating on market liquidity and on changes in price as such.

Affirmatively, I maintain exclusive emphasis on value factors instead of attempts to time fluctuations of the market. I assume that market price tends to depart from market value, creating in this spread continuing investment opportunities. Also, I disregard the historical significance of the price level and believe that the general market will take care of itself following the proper evaluation of individual issues; with the overall conclusion, and I want you to remember this please, that any time is a good time to buy a good value, and as a corollary, no time is a good time to buy a bad value—emphasizing the word value instead of price. It is not even enough to say any time is a good time to buy a "good stock," but that any time is the time to buy a good value. You can measure value but you cannot judge timing!

* From *The Commercial and Financial Chronicle*, Vol. 186, No. 5686 (Thursday, October 31, 1957), p. 5. Reprinted by permission of *The Commercial and Financial Chronicle*, 25 Park Place, New York 7, New York.

Of course, I would be the first to admit that the value approach, that is, through appraisals, also contains imponderables and other "bugs." But, from long experience I can tell you that the "bugs," the imponderables and the difficulties concerned with making appraisals are less harsh and destructive than those that are involved in market forecasting—which means trying to time movements of the market rather than the buying of individual stocks.

Incidentally, from the practical side, experience shows that this individual approach often happens secondarily to furnish a good clue to the condition of the general market—the market's general position, to the extent that there could be said to be one, being generally correlated with a number of individual issues which are found to be under- or over-valued. With the market as a whole, as with individual issues, a good investment frequently turns out to be also a good speculation.

THE SHAREHOLDER ESSENTIALLY A PROPERTY-OWNER

Remember that basically, stockholding is really a share in a property, not a quotation on the ticker. Remember that if you are buying a share of stock in a company you are doing the same thing as if you buy part ownership of the corner grocery store, or a piece of real estate in which you would figure the value over a long period, and not concentrate on the price quotation from minute to minute.

More concretely, my method, which satisfies the need for realism concerning the concept of yield and multiplier, rests on the hard-boiled common sense assumption that the money-use and risk-element of one's capital investment should be compensated for in the buying price. For example, your criterion might require that the price should be such that the buyer can foresee the probability of recouping his principal with interest over a reasonable period, plus retaining a continuing equity, that is, interest in the property, as "gravy." In stocks, as there occurs in real estate, our buying price should provide for annual amortization from out of dividend payments sufficient to get back the invested capital within a reasonable time. Such buying value determination should depend on a number of factors classified according to the kind of company being considered. But, in any event, giving practical and definable meaning to the dividend yield and the multiplier, rather than having them conform to tradition or other superficial determination, such as being thought of as some kind of score-keeping game.

Earnings data and balance sheet factors should be scrutinized cold-bloodedly by you the investor as media for the preservation and profitable employment of your capital and not, as I said before, as a score-keeping game.

GIVING MEANING TO MULTIPLIER AND YIELD

Our basic concept will give meaning to composition of the price earnings ratio furnishing rationality to the size of the multiplier making the market price, and you know that the multiplier means the price divided by the dividend or the earnings per share. In other words, if the earnings are $4 and the market price is $40, the multiplier is 10. Now this multiplier, which gives the dividend yield or the earnings yield, should have some reason based on value instead of being just a theoretical or arbitrary figure. Too often yield is merely based on historical precedent or convention, or comparison between one group of securities and another, or, as is most often the case, the product of psychological changes of mind.

VALUATION MUSTS

Now, for a few musts in valuing securities: First, basically there are the earnings, and I want to remind you to consider not those of a year or two years, but to go back over a 10 year period. Such statistics are readily available with most of the important companies, which you can get from their stockholder report, from their statements filed with the SEC, or from the services which were itemized for you in my last lecture. Remember the importance of earnings because they are the source of your dividends, which are in turn the usual way of getting your money back from your investment. In addition to taking the long-view attitude of earnings, I want to give you two other pointers. First, watch for the company's rate of return on the capital invested in the business, and second, and very important, the ratio of the earnings to sales. In other words, particularly in the last few months, as has been publicized, there is what we call "profitless prosperity" or a "profit squeeze" where many companies, like in the chemical industry, have increased their volume, but their earnings have gone down. That's all right over a short period of time, but if it persists over a longer interval in relation to any individual company, it's a danger signal. Also, very important, watch the rate of return and earnings of the company that you are looking at, in relation to other companies in the same industry, as a yardstick. For example, you can't expect the company you're looking at in the textile industry, where the rate of return is traditionally very, very low, to be the same as in the chemical industry where the profit margins are regularly much higher.

On the matter of growth, which is so widely publicized now and possibly overdone, look for growth but don't overrate it, and don't exaggerate it.

Pointers Regarding the Dividend

Here are some pointers on another important item in valuing a security, namely the dividend, which is what you get as the return on the capital that you have invested: (1) Does the dividend paid give you a fair return on the capital invested? (2) Is it a reasonable proportion of the earnings, because you must figure whether the earnings are better being paid out, or, as in some cases, they might earn their keep if they are plowed back, as in the Life Insurance Companies. (3) Look at the continuity of the dividend and go back 10 or 15 years to see whether it has been interrupted or whether it has been maintained steadily, or better yet, with slow and constant growth. (4) In the case of an unusually low-dividend pay-out, this should be a springboard for your careful further exploration. While on the one hand it may be in order, as is so often done, to squawk about a low dividend, on the other hand, if a dividend is low in the face of high earnings and a good balance sheet position, it might indicate grounds for suspicion that the management knows that something is wrong which is not readily discernible.

The Balance Sheet

Along with earnings and dividends, a third important thing to look for in valuing a security is the balance sheet of the company. Among the balance sheet items is book value, which is often referred to and, as you know, is the amount of all the assets less the liabilities, but which is not really of very vital importance because it is full of fixed and unrealizable assets. Much more important is the working capital which is composed of the current assets which are cash, accounts receivable, and inventory—those are the main items. The liabilities, which are the other side of the medal, comprise accounts payable, short-term taxes payable and debts. The current assets less the current liabilities gives you what is called working capital. This is a very important factor, particularly in conjunction with earnings. Of course, if a company has a very high working capital and no earnings, that is not good. The ideal combination is to have liberal working capital with good earnings, with which there are still some companies around. In any event, the working capital is an extra safety valve behind your investment.

Another item to look at on the balance sheet is "debt, long-term and short-term." See whether there is any pressing debt of a short-term nature, scrutinize the size of the long-term debt and how much it is compensated for by the current assets which I have just mentioned. Regarding the debt, see if there are any provisions on the debt agreement which, by the way, you can find on the company report to stockholders, which prohibit or restrict dividend payments. What is extremely important is that a company may have liberal earnings but there may be provisions regarding the debt which prohibit it from paying dividends, which would prevent you from getting anything out of the company, possibly for a number of years.

There are a number of additional miscellaneous items which you should look for such as unfilled orders on the books which are usually given in one of the previous reports to stockholders, and also the proportion of export business, possibly including exchange restrictions. Assets, including plant and machinery, usually mean very little marketwise by themselves when not linked to the earnings. However, the plant item is worth examining, particularly the expenditures on new plant, and in this connection, I would like you to remember that you should examine the percentage of profit ratio that is earned on plant. In other words, it isn't sufficient merely to spend money on plant, but the new additions must be profitable, and you should see whether the new capital expenditures are paying off.

Specific Valuation Techniques

Now for some specific methods for determining the approximate value of a stock, or, at least, an advantageous buying price. Concretely, my method, which satisfies the need for realism concerning the concept of yield and the multiplier which I have just mentioned, rests on the hard-boiled assumption that the money-use and risk elements of one's capital investments should be compensated for in the buying price. In the case of the great majority of companies yielding a continuing annual return the price may be so calculated that the buyer can foresee the probability of recouping his principal along with the interest on his money over a reasonable period of time, plus retaining a continuing equity in the property as "gravy." In stocks, just as there occurs in real estate, your buying price might provide for annual amortizations from dividend payments which are sufficient to recoup for your invested capital within a reasonable time.

Example of Calculation:

1. Estimated future average annual earnings	$7.00
2. Estimated future annual dividend	$4.50
3. Annual rental value of capital investment	$3\frac{1}{2}\%$
4. Annual amortization reserve (25-year life)	$4\ \%$
5. Annual deductions (3) plus (4)	$7\frac{1}{2}\%$
6. Capitalization of (2) at rate of (5) gives advantageous buying price	$60

Thus, in this example which could apply to a strong but not a "growth" company, a price giving an average annual dividend yield of $7\frac{1}{2}\%$ would in 25 years, completely amortize the capital invested after compensating for the use of the money. My estimate of future average earnings, in line (1) is based on a number of varied factors, including the company's past record and its discernible prospects, as well as economic elements including inflation. The annual dividend expectation, item (2), takes into account evidence of management policy as well as the respective company's backlog of financial strength. The annual rental value, item (3), at $3\frac{1}{2}\%$ represents an estimate of the future average interest rate on U. S. Treasury Bond issues and on savings bank deposits. The annual amortization reserve, item (4), is calculated—most liberally— at a rate sufficient to retrieve your complete capital invested over a 25-year period.

The amount, and more particularly, the duration allocated to the amortization deductions, vary. The strength of the balance sheet and other risk elements are important here. Other factors include the nature of the business. For example, in valuing United States Steel common we might set 5% as the annual amortization reserve to be apportioned, with 20 years as the proper "run" of our investment, because of this company's heavy plant investment entailing sizable long-term debt and also the somewhat cyclical nature of the business. In the case of American Telephone, while you likewise have a heavy capitalization, that drawback is counterbalanced by the apparent permanence of a floor under the current dividend because of social implications of the number and kind of its stockholders. Hence a 25-year instead of 20-year amortization, with an annual depreciation of 4% instead of 5%, would seem to be appropriate in calculating a buying price for Telephone.

That is the way an owner—and that should be recognized as your role when buying a share of stock—would calculate when buying real estate or an interest in a business.

THE TAX INCIDENCE

The income tax levy on the stock owner's annual dividend injects a subtraction from the total number of the calculated amortization which is actually usable by him for this purpose. The differing demand of each individual's income-and-tax situation renders impossible a formula with a fixed deduction for tax. But it should be realized that there are two offsets to such diminution of the amortization; namely, the earning power of the annual amounts set aside for amortization, and the taxability to him of the "rental value" (figured at $3\frac{1}{2}\%$) which he would otherwise have received on his capital invested.

INCIDENCE OF FINANCIAL STRENGTH
ON THE AMORTIZATION TOTAL

The company's financial strength as manifested by the balance sheet also in some cases alters the total proportion of your invested capital to be amortized—as distinguished from the time-length of the amortization which I have just discussed. This would apply to situations with high net working capital and liquidating value. Thus, as is demonstrated in our tabulation following, the common stockholder of Montgomery Ward owns liquid assets after deducting all debt, including the preferred stock capitalization, of $47 per share (which is considerably in excess of its market price). Cash-and-equivalent alone, at $15 per share, are almost double total liabilities.

I now give you an example of a company with high net working capital and "liquidating value."

Typified by Montgomery Ward as follows:

	PER SHARE
1. Total liabilities (including preferred stock)	$ 7.00
2. Cash-and-equivalent	$15.00
3. Unsold time accounts (fundable)	$18.00
4. Total current assets	$54.00
5. "Liquidating value" (4th minus 1st item)	$47.00
6. Estimated future annual earnings	$ 3.50
7. Estimated future dividend	$ 2.50
8. Annual deduction for "rental" & amortization	7½%
9. Capitalization of (7) at rate of (8) gives an advantageous buying price of	$33.00
10. Add excess equity unneeded for full amortization	$10.00
11. Final advantageous buying price	$43.00

There are numerous other instances of calculable high liquid value, as in the textile area (Manhattan Shirt has an after-debt liquidating value of $22 per share and earnings ranging around $2, with a market price of $14). Many bank stocks also afford a high net increment of realistically realizable assets backing their dividends, near, and often above the market price of their shares.

The business future of liquid asset-laden companies like Montgomery Ward would seem to lie between these three following alternatives: (1) the company will remain static and the liquid assets retained, perhaps unjustifiably. Or (2), the excess liquid assets will be used for expansion with profitable results. Or (3) the excess assets will be used for expansion and dissipated. Under the subsequent occurrence of probabilities (1) and (2), under which the assets would not be lost, the need for full amortization for the entire recouping of your investment is not required. Hence, in the example pertaining to Montgomery Ward, $10 of our normal full amortization reserve is deducted as unneeded and added to the usual appraisal figure, giving us $43 instead of $33 as an "advantageous buying price."

Here I want to make it clear that my suggested technique of valuation merely results in an advantageous buying price, that is, an approximate advantageous buying price, rather than a pinpointed appraisal furnishing a hard and fast dividing line between continuing buying and selling. It is merely to indicate a value approach to give you an approximate idea or figure which is advantageous.

EVALUATING GROWTH STOCKS

Growth stocks also require special provision regarding money-back amortization. The vitally necessary element being certainty in your knowledge that real long-term growth actually exists, right here I want to give you some additional rules about growth stocks which are so important now in speculative markets. Remember, first, the enchantment that people have, and have conferred on some growth companies, giving them a premium which is not always justified by the statistical background. There are two parts to the selection of stocks for future appreciation on the bases of growth: (1) You must satisfy yourself that the company is likely to continue to grow at above-the-average rate in earning power, and (2) that the price is relatively low enough at the time of purchase so that the increased earning power has a good chance to be reflected in greater value to the holder. In other words, if you are buying a stock at 40 or 50 times earnings on the basis of either real or imagined growth, it will take you 10 or 15 years to catch up with yourself for a decent yield when and if the company expected earnings continue to come through. (3) Be sure that you still have a continuing growth situation, not just a historical, glamorous record from the past, which would be nothing more than hindsight in basing your future expectations on what was. (4) And, most important, remember please that in investing nothing beats the discovery of an undervalued stock based on a variety of quantitative criteria along with the growth factor. Purchasing so-called growth stocks without thorough and realistic investigation leads to the selection of over-valued stocks.

QUANTITATIVE VALUE OPPORTUNITIES

Now, in the area of various other kinds of companies which offer the opportunity for calculating a profitable return on your capital investment, there first comes to mind the liquidating and semi-liquidating issues. Such a clearly discernible situation is exemplified by the numerous public utility holding companies in the 1940's, which were in the process of actual dissolution under the close direction and supervision of the Securities and Exchange Commission following the strict provisions of the Public Utility Holding Company Act. Under such Government regulation, there surely was no doubt or lack of information about their valuation. But these holding companies were for a long time available on the market at prices which assured a realization after dissolution into split units of a total appreciably in excess of the ruling market price of the original whole.

This was in line with Wall Street's chronic perversion of simple arithmetic. Whereas in the flamboyant 1920's, the Street persisted in figuring that three pieces of paper were worth more than the whole, in the more sober 1940's they were figured at less than the whole; and now in the stock-split craze era they are back to arguing that the sum of the parts is worth more than the whole.

There exist now numerous clear-cut discount-from-asset categories of companies, where the time of realization of the profit from the discount may be doubtful, but where the underlying values are clearly calculable and where meanwhile income throw-off is being gained with an equivalent premium. Current examples are Pennroad Corporation, a closed-end investment company, or Transamerica.

In the case of many closed-end investment companies that are selling at a discount from asset value, they may not open-end or liquidate-out in the foreseeable future, but meanwhile you are profiting from a higher dividend yield.

BANK AND INSURANCE STOCKS

In the case of the equity shares, that is, the common stocks of banks, and fire and casualty insurance companies, they can be also considered as giving the opportunity for buying assets at a discount from genuine value, resulting in income expectable at yields that are liberal and well protected. Insurance companies, for example, distribute less than their income from their investments alone. The smaller absorbable company selling at a discount offers an extra bonus in the form of possible lightning to strike from future mergers. And you will find, irrespective of exactly how it works out, that in one way or another value "will out" in the long-run.

VALUES IN THE DEPRESSED AREAS

More complicated in the field of liquidating approach are companies which are retrogressing in a recognizably declining industry. A present example of this is an investment in the "depressed area" anthracite coal industry where favorable investing opportunities, nevertheless, exist through acquisition of equities whose cash flow, plus income tax advantages, provide a reasonably foreseeable payback in excess of the amount invested. If you feel inclined to follow the crowd in blandly classifying stocks as "good" stocks and "bad" stocks and saying you won't buy a "bad" stock, in other words, a stock which is not either romantically or otherwise glowing— remember that every security is worth some price, obviously even if down to an eighth of a dollar, unless it's in bankruptcy. What I'd like you to do with the value approach is to scrutinize so-called "good" stocks, "medium" stocks, and so-called "bad" or depressed stocks, figuring some value for the unpopular issues of the moment, because there's where the real bargains, on a logical basis, exist year in and year out.

STOCKS VS. REAL ESTATE

On our bases of valuation, incidentally, and answering a question that is quite often asked—even after our 1953–1957 bull-market stocks are more reasonably priced than real estate—I've found from my extensive surveys. But I want to remind you again to apply the same amortization approach in buying your stocks as that of a hard-boiled real estate investor in buying real estate. In other words, see some way of getting your money back along with income over a period of time.

17. MAGIC FORMULA?

Dollar Averaging Sometimes

Can Lead to Losses*

✿ Rodger W. Bridwell

I⊤ IS NO SECRET that the prices of most securities today are considerably below the highs of 1957. Many brokers, consequently, are ad-
vising their customers that they now can buy as many as 20% more
shares of a given issue, with the same number of dollars, than they
could have at the top. Dollar averaging, in short, is being touted
more and more as the bear market's answer to an investor's prayers.

Perhaps it is, and perhaps not. For the man in a position to
take full advantage of it, dollar averaging certainly can be a very
useful method of investing. Pursued consistently over the years, in
carefully chosen securities, it can produce handsome results. But
like many another investment technique, it is no magic formula
that automatically will bring rich results to anyone who relies on
it. Its widely-publicized advantages are offset at least in part by
pitfalls that somehow seem to attract less attention.

*　　*　　*

In theory, at any rate, the advantages are impressive. Dollar
averaging, as the name signifies, simply calls for buying equal dollar
amounts of a stock at regular intervals. In this way the investor
gets fewer shares when prices are high, more when prices are low.
As a result, the average cost of the shares purchased is always lower
than the average of the prices paid.

* From *Barron's* (February 3, 1958), p. 9. Reprinted by permission of *Barron's*.

Table 1. *Dollar Averaging—Units of $500 per Quarter*

				NUMBER OF SHARES PURCHASED			
YEAR	CAPITAL INVESTED	D-J INDUSTRIALS	GENERAL MOTORS*	WOOLWORTH	TRI-CONTINENTAL	MUTUAL FUND "A" (2)	MUTUAL FUND "B" (2)
1939(1)	$ 500	3.3	37	13	221	83	23
1940	2,500	15.1	81	63	1155	376	96
1941	4,500	16.6	203	80	1911	451	105
1942	6,500	18.6	210	67	1894	385	99
1943	8,500	14.4	154	56	531	293	87
1944	10,500	13.7	129	48	449	243	80
1945	12,500	11.6	114	38	269	162	68
1946	14,500	10.7	66	43	236	174	69
1947	16,500	11.2	68	43	302	190	73
1948	18,500	11.1	66	44	252	210	75
1949	20,500	11.0	66	41	259	179	69
1950	22,500	9.1	46	45	198	154	63
1951	24,500	7.8	40	47	160	129	60
1952	26,500	7.8	33	44	128	127	58
1953	28,500	7.3	33	46	129	128	59
1954	30,500	5.0	20	38	78	91	49
1955	32,500	4.1	14	42	73	68	43
1956	34,500	4.0	15	46	73	66	42
1957	36,500	4.6	20	55	68	80	46
Value 12-31-57		$81,475	$146,225	$32,400	$230,400	$89,725	$55,050
Appreciation on Total Investment		122.9%	300.6%	—11.2%	531.8%	145.8%	50.8%

(1) Last quarter only. * Calculated before 3-for-1 split. (2) Before stock splits.

Furthermore, it doesn't seem to matter greatly when such a program is started. To illustrate, assume an investor had bought the 30 Dow-Jones Industrials, at quarterly intervals, for ten years starting in 1929. The average price paid would be less than 2% greater than had the first purchase been made in 1932, after stock prices had plunged 85% below their level in 1929. The reason is simple: the high prices paid in 1929 and 1930 would be offset by the low ones paid for a much larger number of shares in 1932 and 1933.

The accompanying table dramatizes the happy results an investor could have achieved by dollar averaging over the years in several issues. In General Motors, for instance, an investment of $36,500—in regular amounts of $500 per quarter since the final three months of 1939—would have resulted by now in a portfolio worth $146,225. Even more spectacular would have been periodic investment over the same period in Tri-Continental Corp., where the original $36,500 would have multiplied to no less than $230,400.

There are, however, other less cheerful lessons in the table. For it illustrates the wide divergence in the results obtained from dollar averaging in different companies over the years. Compare, for example, General Motors and Woolworth. Back in 1939, at least one prominent advisory service rated them equal in investment stature. Yet periodic amounts put into G.M. since then would have yielded a 300% profit, while the same investment in Woolworth would show an actual loss today. Indeed, if decline in purchasing power is taken into account, the real value of a $36,500 investment in Woolworth would be substantially less than the $32,400 shown. Moreover, since 1937 the market has risen 200%, and the percentage gains shown in the table should be evaluated in the light of this steady advance.

A basic drawback to periodic investment plans, then, lies in the necessity of making a shrewd choice of stocks. Numerous tabulations have been published, illustrating how fortunes could have been made by regularly investing small sums in Eastman Kodak, Dow Chemical, du Pont, and other blue chips. Such records may be perfectly correct, but unfortunately they are based on hindsight rather than foresight.

For that matter, regular investment in stocks that once were regarded highly, such as Pennsylvania Railroad (which recently touched a new 15-year low), American T. & T., American Tobacco, United Fruit, Underwood Corp., Texas Gulf Sulphur, Coca-Cola, and many others, would have produced results ranging from mediocre to disastrous. The fact is that no one can be certain that today's favorite growth stocks may not prove equally disappointing investments over the next 10 or 15 years. Dollar averaging, like any sound investment program, requires adequate diversification if it is to succeed with a minimum of risk.

A second point, and one which is no less important, is that successful dollar averaging stands or falls on the investor's ability to continue the program when stock prices are down. Yet this is precisely the time when most people are least able and least inclined to carry through. After all, when the market is scraping bottom, business is generally slow, money is scarce and most people have trouble (which they did not anticipate) even meeting day-to-day expenses. Yet if a program of periodic investment is abandoned when prices are down, paper losses are turned into actual losses, which may represent a real blow to a family's financial well being.

Even those individuals who do have ample purchasing power may become discouraged with a program which has netted them nothing but paper losses for several years. Thus, should the earning power of the company they are investing in decline sharply, they will question the wisdom of throwing "good money after bad." For example, although systematic purchases of Tri-Continental Corp., as noted, produced spectacular results in the end, consider the position of an investor who, because of unforeseen circumstances, was forced to liquidate his position in 1941 or 1942. With Tri selling as low as $\frac{5}{8}$, his loss amounted to 50% or more of his original investment. Furthermore, at the time net asset value was less than nothing, a circumstance which hardly inspired continued confidence in the stock as a vehicle for a conservative averaging program.

The point is that a few individuals can be absolutely certain that they will be able to invest a fixed number of dollars each quarter for the next 10 or 15 years. Incomes fall as well as rise, even prosperous businesses can lose money, and unforeseen circumstances may arise which take all available funds. Unfortunately, these emergencies are likely to occur at the worst possible time for those who dollar average, i.e., when stock prices are down.

*   *   *

Parenthetically, we might note that one of the neglected uses of dollar averaging is when stock prices are historically high. At such a time, the individual with a sizable amount of cash to invest may be reluctant to commit it all at once. Under those conditions, the man with $100,000 to spare, for example, can earmark $2,500 for investment during each quarter for the next 10 years. The remainder he can put in a bank or a savings and loan association until its turn comes. True, the final result may compare unfavorably with an initial investment of $100,000 in a diversified list of stocks. Nevertheless, the built-in advantages of dollar averaging virtually will insure a degree of safety, and results at least as good as those turned in by the market averages—if the stocks chosen prove to be the right ones.

Dollar averaging, in short, can pay off for the man who is selective as well as patient. But as the foregoing makes clear, it has its pitfalls, like any other formula approach to the stock market. The prudent investor will want to be fully aware of them before he launches such a program. For all its allure, dollar averaging is no easy road to riches.

INVESTMENT POLICY
AND THE
INSTITUTIONAL
INVESTOR

IV ✸

INTRODUCTION

OVER A LONG PERIOD of years and within a wide range of economic and political events, new concepts of investment policy have emerged to compensate for the various perils of capital management. Capital managers were once sheltered by general legal and operational rules which stressed only the nominal preservation of principal and income for beneficiaries of the various institutions important in money management. Our changing world and the changing needs of investors have put new responsibilities and pressures on the investment policies of financial institutions. New risks, new techniques of capital management, new patterns of legal and political philosophy have combined to challenge sacred practices of institutional investors. The essays in this section were chosen to emphasize these problems. They suggest possible techniques and philosophies to lessen and deal with, from the viewpoint of manager and beneficiary, the widespread hazards to prudent money management in our turbulent times.

Morton Smith, in the opening essay, points out the rational development of trustee response to the problem of conserving the purchasing power of monies entrusted to their care. This development grew from the changing legal and economic factors of recent years, principally the secular inflation which resulted from World War II and its aftermath.

J. Harry Wood, in his didactic essay on the nature and virtues of common trust funds, combines a primer on common trust fund operation with an appraisal of the contributions these funds make to fiduciary money management. Their importance is a current phenomenon little understood by millions of would-be investors. The extensively-researched article by George E. Rejda shows the role of dollar averaging in the portfolio operations of life insurance companies. The virtues and limitations of this pattern of portfolio management, as utilized by a major form of institutional investor, are appraised in detail. These lessons are applicable to individual portfolio management as well.

This section ends with two well-reasoned articles on the theory and practice of investing pension fund assets. John G. Heimann reviews a wide array of historical, legal, and current economic factors to support his defense of flexible media choice for investment. Paul L. Howell presents a strong case for the almost total use of common stocks for institutional investing, with particular emphasis upon the insistent problem of maintaining pension fund purchasing power for the savings of millions of retired workers.

18. CHANGING CONCEPTS OF TRUST INVESTMENT POLICY*

❁ Morton Smith

THERE IS NO SUCH THING as a safe trust investment. That is to say, there is no way to determine by legislative action or otherwise that what looks like a safe trust investment today will be safe tomorrow, or next year. Massachusetts recognized this 121 years ago when the Supreme Judicial Court in *Harvard College v. Amory*[1] stated, "Do what you will, the capital is at hazard"; but it took the legal list States 100 years to discover it. The realization has led to two important changes in trust investment policies: (1) the widespread adoption of the prudent-man rule; and (2) the realization that during a period of inflation trustees may have a duty to preserve not only the "dollar value" of the funds committed to their care, but also their "real" or "purchasing power value."

This discussion concerns itself with the second of these changes. It will try to answer two questions: (1) Why has it come about? (2) What should corporate trustees do about it?

CONSERVATION OF DOLLAR VALUES
UNDER THE GOLD STANDARD

The answer to the first question is, broadly speaking, contained in the one word inflation, but, as a glance at the chart [below] shows,

---

* *Trust Bulletin*, Vol. 37, No. 1 (September, 1957), pp. 11–17. Reprinted by permission of *Trust Bulletin*.
[1] 9 Pick. 446 (1830).

inflation is nothing new—the inflation of commodity prices preceding and accompanying the First World War was at least as great as that which occurred during the period embracing the Second World War. Not only did commodity prices rise materially from 1897 to 1920, but bond prices declined, while stock prices held fairly steady.[2]

Per Cent

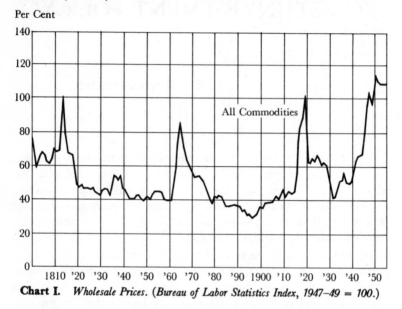

Chart I.   *Wholesale Prices. (Bureau of Labor Statistics Index, 1947–49 = 100.)*

This combination of events, however, appears to have had little or no effect on institutional investment policies, which all during the 1920's continued to concentrate mainly on bonds and real estate mortgages. A book on *Investment Analysis* written in 1921 by Professor Lagerquist of Northwestern University contained no reference at all to common stock investments and Edgar Lawrence Smith in his famous work *Common Stocks As Long Term Investments* written in 1924 stated that "in the minds of most investors bonds hold an unassailable position, common stocks are rarely even mentioned." At the Eleventh Mid-Winter Trust Con-

[2]

	12/31/1902	Low — 1920
Atchison, Topeka & Sante Fe. Gen. Mtge. 4%, 1995	103	69
Dow-Jones Industrial Average	64.29	66.75

ference in February 1930, six out of seven speakers stated that they never bought common stocks in trust accounts unless they were directed to do so in the instrument. The only exception was, as might be expected, a gentleman from a Boston bank who admitted that his institution bought common stocks as a matter of considered policy. In 1934 Professor Riddle of Ohio State University in his book *The Investment Policies of Trust Institutions* traced the investments of 196 separate trusts administered by institutions in leading financial centers from Boston to St. Louis during the years from 1919 to 1932. He found that during this period the book value of the bond portfolios increased from 23 per cent to 34 per cent, real estate mortgages from 16 per cent to 24 per cent, while the book value of common stocks decreased from 35 per cent to 32 per cent.

The failure of trustees and other conservative investors to think in terms of common stocks and conservation of purchasing power following the inflation of 1897 to 1920 may be explained as follows:

1. During the '20's the country was firmly on the gold standard and most bonds and mortgages were payable in gold coin of the then existing weight and fineness.

2. As reference to the chart will disclose, commodity prices after reaching a peak in 1920 declined precipitately and within a year had lost about 50 per cent of the wartime rise. Thereafter until 1929 commodity prices fluctuated within a narrow range at about the new level and no one was much concerned over the possibility of any further increase.

3. The government pursued orthodox fiscal policies and retirement of the public debt was steady and substantial.

4. Adequate yields were available on bonds and taxes were lower.

5. Equities had a predominantly speculative background, as is illustrated by the fact that the total number of shares traded on the New York Stock Exchange in 1901 was more than three times the number of shares listed. In 1919 the ratio was still one and one-half times, while in 1956 all the stock transactions on the New York Stock Exchange were equivalent to only 13 per cent of the total number of shares listed.[3] In other words, during the first 20 years of this century common stocks were used primarily as a medium for making short-term trading profits, while more recently they have been purchased for yield and long-term gains.

While bonds remained the most widely accepted medium for investing trust funds, common stocks were acquiring a degree of respectability they had never previously enjoyed. Edgar Lawrence Smith's book, a milestone in investment analysis, compared the

[3] *New York Stock Exchange Fact Book,* 1957.

results which could have been achieved by investing in selected lists of stocks and bonds, objectively chosen without benefit of hindsight, during the period from 1866 to 1922. In the great majority of cases the stock lists outperformed the bonds by a substantial margin, due, in Mr. Smith's opinion, to the compounding effect of plowed back earnings.

In 1928 Dwight Rose, a partner of Scudder, Stevens, and Clark, in his book entitled *A Scientific Approach to Investment Management* compared the investment results achieved by the principal fire insurance companies from 1903 to 1926. The company with the best investment performance had an average of 38 per cent in common stocks whereas the company with the poorest investment performance had an average of only 11 per cent invested in equities.

Both Smith and Rose advocated a balanced investment policy as between stocks and bonds and both pointed out the danger of buying stocks regardless of price, but Smith's book, in particular, was used as an argument for doing just that. As a consequence, when the market collapsed, Smith's reputation collapsed with it at precisely the time when application of his theory would have paid off handsomely.

Conservation of "Real" Values and Managed Money

1. *Depression—Recovery—Recession* (1929–1940). From 1929 to 1932 the high-grade bond market gave an excellent account of itself relative to other forms of investment. True, Atchison General 4s sold down from 95 to 75, but there was no interruption of income. In the meantime wholesale commodity prices had declined from 62 to 42 so that the income beneficiary was actually better off in 1932 than he had been in 1929. Stocks, on the other hand, performed very poorly. The Dow-Jones Industrial Average declined from 381 to 41, and dividends on that average declined from $12.75 to $4.62. However, at precisely the time when truly high-grade bonds had proved their value, two factors came into play to undermine investor confidence in fixed-income securities and the theory of conservation of dollar value:

> a. Widespread defaults in two areas which had hitherto been regarded as the safest repositories for conservative funds—railroad bonds and real estate mortgages.

b. Departure of the United States from the gold standard in April, 1933—not because of a shortage of gold but for the deliberate purpose of inflating the price level. This action touched off spectacular advances in common stock prices which in the words of the *Commercial and Financial Chronicle,* were "paralleled only by the wild speculation of 1928–1929." Two years later, in 1935, the United States Supreme Court in the so-called "Gold Cases" [4] held that Congress had the right, in pursuance of its authority to control the currency, to abrogate clauses in private contracts calling for payment in gold.

These events were a severe shock to investor confidence. Together with government-fostered "pump priming" and low interest rates they provided the background for the inflationary psychology which has been such an important market factor ever since. In the middle 1930's the courts began to adopt a more liberal attitude toward trust investments. In Pennsylvania, for example, a lower court decided in 1937 that a common stock was a "security." Said Judge Bok of the Philadelphia Orphans Court, "The modern stock market offers opportunities for investment substantially as safe as mortgage bonds." [5] The movement to liberalize the investment statutes of legal list states got under way at about this time, and corporate trustees started to buy common stocks as a matter of policy—my own bank, for example, set up its first "approved list" of common stocks in 1935. It should be noted, however, that all of these trends were actuated more by the desire to maintain the income of the life beneficiary during a period of declining interest rates than by fear of a depreciating dollar.

However, the move into equities in the 1930's did not go very far. In a country whose productive capacity was far in excess of effective demand, an increase in money supply brought about by revaluing gold and by deficit spending was not enough to insure for long either rising prices or general prosperity. Business confidence remained at a low ebb and in 1937 there was a severe collapse. Once again high-grade bonds returned to favor. Atchison General 4s declined from 116 in 1937 to 98 in 1938, while the Dow-Jones Average declined from 194 to 98, and the dividends on the Dow-Jones stocks declined from $8.78 to $4.98. In the meantime high-grade bonds coupons continued to be paid in full.

[4] Norman v. Baltimore & Ohio Railroad Co., 294 U. S. 240; Nortz v. United States, 294 U. S. 317.
[5] Carwithen's Estate, 28 D & C 66.

Another negative factor was apparent in the pre-World War II period. The 1930's were occupied with the "mature economy" theory. The United States had reached the last frontier, population growth was slowing down and would soon stop entirely, and capital was accumulating faster than outlets for its productive employment could be developed. Consequently, it seemed to many intelligent people that the only way to keep things going was for the government to take over the responsibility for making capital investment and maintaining employment.

In sum, the pre-World War II policies of the government were highly inflationary, but they were carried out in an atmosphere which was unfriendly to business and pessimistic as to the future of the country's economy. As a result wholesale commodity prices recovered only about 60 per cent of the 1929–1932 decline, and by the time World War II broke out trustee inclination to hedge against a depreciating dollar had increased very little since the initial shocks to the dollar conservation theory in 1933–35.

2. *War and Postwar Inflation (1941–1957)*. During the war the development of normal investment policies was obscured by the necessities of the time. Although war is inflationary and theoretically favorable to stocks, investors do not, as a rule, regard it as a good background against which to buy equities—at least, until war's end appears to be in sight. For a number of reasons, including the scarcity of corporate bonds, U. S. Governments and particularly Series "G" bonds were a favorite medium for investors' funds from 1941 to 1945.

It was not until the end of World War II that the inflationary policies of the previous twelve years began to have their greatest effect on the investment practices of corporate trustees. Although the inflation of commodity prices had been approximately the same at the end of both World Wars, the effect on investment sentiment was wholly different for the following reasons:

a. In contrast to World War I, interest rates had been pegged and trustees found themselves with large funds invested at $2\frac{1}{4}$ per cent at a time when commodity prices had doubled and beneficiaries were clamoring for "real" grocery store income. Common stocks yielding 5–6 per cent or more were a natural, indeed the only practical, answer to this problem. But other factors besides the need for income emphasized the importance of conserving "real" (as distinct from dollar) values.

b. The United States was deeply shocked by the Russian invasion of Iran in 1946 and the subsequent activities of the Communists. We were faced with the fact that the war had not ended in 1945, but had, in effect, started all over again with a more dangerous enemy than the ones we had just defeated. There is little doubt that the Cold War and the Korean War had a lot to do with preventing the postwar deflation of commodity prices which had always previously taken place when farms and factories were converted from producing goods to be wasted to producing goods for which markets had to be found among willing buyers who could use them and had the money to pay for them. (Reference to the Commodity Price Chart shows that when the periods embracing the War of 1812, the Civil War, the First World War, the Second World War, and the Cold War are eliminated, there is little evidence of long-term inflation of wholesale commodity prices in the United States.) United States Government expenditures, which had dropped from a war-time high of $95-billion to $36-billion in 1948, climbed back again to $75-billion in 1953 after the Korean War, and commodity prices, far from collapsing, exceeded their wartime highs.

As a consequence, trustees again started to buy stocks not only for immediate income but because they believed they provided a long-term hedge against a declining dollar. The Cold War might go on for a generation, or it might end suddenly in a holocaust of atom bombs. In either event, oil or coal or ownership of productive enterprises looked like better means of conserving "real" values than promises to pay paper money. It should be noted, however, that there is another possibility which, although slight, seems worthy of some consideration, although at the moment it appears to be receiving none. That is that the United States and Russia will work out some sort of *modus vivendi,* which will materially reduce the threat of a suicidal atomic war and restore the international temperature to a commercially comfortable level. Any such development could have considerable impact on the theory of inevitable inflation.

c. Added to the risk of continuing armament inflation has been the threat of long-term peacetime inflation implicit in the Full Employment Act of 1946. If budgetary deficits and deliberate inflation of the money supply are to be the answers to any future depression, this does not furnish a good argument for buying bonds.

d. The steady inflation of costs and wages forced on industry by the power of the labor unions, operating on an inadequate labor supply, has provided further impetus to the preference for common stocks, on the theory (which may be dubious) that industry will be able to pass along the increased costs to the consumer and maintain reasonable profit margins.

e. To these, on the whole, negative reasons for buying stocks, there has been added a positive one. The "mature economy" theory of the tired 1930's had been replaced by the "growing economy" theory of the dynamic 1950's. This attractive proposition has 150 years of United States history to back it up. It provides the final and perhaps the most convincing reason for preferring stocks to bonds. It should be noted, however, that while the reasons for it change, the theory itself is not new. Note, also, that it has few, if any, adherents during periods of low economic visibility. Accepted as gospel in 1929, rejected as nonsense in the 1930's, it is embraced once again as gospel in 1957.

In describing the reasons which have led trustees, consciously or unconsciously, to seek conservation of purchasing power as well as dollar values, one question remains unanswered. What will be the attitude of the courts towards a trustee who makes no attempt to conserve "real" values, on the one hand, or on the other hand, a trustee who makes one attempt and fails? A Michigan Court in the Dodge[6] case last year refused to surcharge a trustee in the first of these situations, and indeed it is difficult to see how a standard could be set up to measure the damages arising out of a trustee's failure to conserve "real" values, assuming that he had the power to do so. Stocks per se are not the answer to conservation of "real" values. It has been entirely possible to buy high-grade stocks which have not maintained "dollar" values, let alone "real" values. Forty per cent of all the stocks listed on the New York Stock Exchange sold at lower prices in 1956 than the highs of 1946, including such high-grade issues as American Telephone & Telegraph, Abbott Laboratories, and Woolworth.

But, surcharge or not, it is the duty of a trustee to act as a reasonable man. To what extent he has a duty to hedge against inflation is perhaps a matter of degree. To put an extreme case, if the United States ever experienced a German-type inflation where a million dollars wouldn't buy a postage stamp, no one would say that a trustee deserved the confidence of the public, if, under a broad investment power, he had invested only in bonds.

FUNCTION OF DIVERSIFICATION UNDER TODAY'S CONDITIONS

1. *Bonds.*   In the light of what has been said, is a policy of diversification between bonds and common stocks desirable? Assuming long-term inflation is inevitable, would not beneficiaries be better off if trustees bought nothing but high-grade common shares? The common practice of keeping a balanced position of perhaps 50 per cent in bonds and 50 per cent in commons gives a trustee the feeling that

[6] Horace E. Dodge Estate, Probate Court, Wayne County, Michigan, October 6, 1955.

no matter what happens he cannot be criticized, but, aside from this, does diversification by type of security have any positive advantages? I think it does for the following reasons:

a. Conservation of dollar values is still the duty of a trustee, and the public and the courts are not likely to settle for anything less. If the commodity price level should, by any chance, drop by 50 per cent, a trustee who had lost half the principal of a trust in the stock market would not receive a very sympathetic reaction either from his beneficiaries or from the courts by pointing out that he had done a very good job of conserving "real" values even though dollar values had been cut in half. While inflation is a long-term risk against which a trustee should seek protection, experience shows that deflation can be a serious short-term risk against which bonds form a useful hedge. This is particularly true of short-term trusts set up during periods of high stock prices.

b. Bonds are also useful for the purpose of providing reserve buying power for stocks. Most trusts do not have a continuous flow of funds of a type which makes "dollar averaging" practicable, and, as a consequence, a trust which is placed wholly in common stocks at a given time is not in a flexible position to take advantage of changes in business conditions and market sentiment.

c. The function of tax-exempt bonds in preserving real values in high-tax bracket accounts under today's conditions should not be over-looked. With good grade tax-exempts selling to yield about $3\frac{1}{2}$ per cent, the yield to a beneficiary in a 50 per cent or higher tax bracket is roughly three times the present income on many growth stocks. The beneficiary can obtain now a rate of return for which he will have to wait from five to ten years in the leading growth stocks, assuming continuance of present tax rates and the same rate of dividend increase as has occurred during the last ten years of unprecedented boom. In addition to this many tax-exempt bonds are selling at substantial discounts to afford a virtually certain prospect of substantial capital appreciation if held to maturity.

2. *Preferred Stocks.*   Preferred stocks have not been popular as trust investments aside from states like Pennsylvania where they enjoy a considerable advantage over most bonds because of the exemption of a wide list of high-grade preferred stocks from the personal property tax. Preferred stocks have frequently been dismissed from consideration as trust investments on the grounds that "they are neither fish, flesh, nor fowl," having none of the advantages of a common stock and none of the protection of a bond. However, a comparison of the price record of truly high-grade preferred stocks over a 30-year period with high-grade long-term bonds will show that issues such as National Biscuit 7% Preferred, du Pont $4\frac{1}{2}$% Preferred, and Consolidated Edison 5% Preferred have fluctuated little

more than the bonds from the highs to the lows of the price cycle, and in the meantime they have yielded an average of about 1 per cent more over a long period of years.

Two risks, however, are present in preferred stocks which are not present in bonds. The first is that the price is completely at the mercy of interest rates (unless the issue has a sinking fund), having no maturity which will insure the holder a particular price at a fixed date. The second is, that, when a company or an industry loses investor acceptance to any degree, the price of a preferred stock may be permanently affected even if there is no interruption of dividends or even any risk thereof. A good rule to follow in buying preferred stocks is to buy them only when money rates are high, and then to purchase the issues of those companies whose common stocks enjoy widespread investment acceptance and are likely to continue to do so.

3. *Common Stocks.* Although common stocks are widely regarded as the best and only practicable hedge against inflation, it has already been pointed out that a large number of good stocks have made no progress in the past ten years despite inflation and unprecedented prosperity. However, it is still true that almost any well diversified list of common stocks purchased in 1946, which would doubtless have included such issues as du Pont, Standard Oil of New Jersey, and General Electric, would, on the average, have performed very well even though it included some of the poorer acting stocks previously mentioned. A well diversified list of common stocks has, in fact, been a good inflation hedge, even though many individual stocks have not, because diversification applied to equities tends to be a positive factor insuring profits whereas in the case of bonds its only purpose is to insure against loss. A rise of 200 per cent in du Pont, for example, will more than offset a 50 per cent decline in two or three other stocks.

There is a tendency on the part of trustees to think of equities either as "growth" stocks or as "defensive" stocks, but growth stocks which have no defensive characteristics and defensive stocks with no growth characteristics are equally suspect as trust investments. For most investors a growth stock is one which goes up and a defensive stock is one which does not go down. From the standpoint of results, and that is what we are interested in, these definitions are satisfactory, but they do not help in the selection of the investment to begin with.

. A good definition of a growth company is one where (a) sales are growing at a faster rate than the economy as a whole, (b) a substantial proportion of the earnings are being plowed back into the business, and (c) the business is earning a better than normal rate of return on its invested capital. (It is the plow back and the rate of return on it which Edgar Lawrence Smith recognized in 1924 as being the principal reason why common stocks have outperformed bonds over the years.) However, such a company must have sufficiently stable earnings to be able to pay some dividend when times are bad.

By contrast, a defensive stock may be described as one whose earnings and dividends will fluctuate less than the average during poor business conditions, and which can be depended upon to pay a reasonable rate of return on the purchase price even when times are bad. Such a stock, however, is not likely to be a good inflation hedge unless the company has some prospect of increasing the stockholders' equity, as a business never stands still for long, and if it does not grow at all, it will decline.

PRICE RISK IN BUYING COMMON STOCKS

Although at the top of any market the only price risk which gives people much concern is the risk that if they don't buy a stock it will be higher next week, the experience of the past 25 years shows that the downside risk in purchasing almost any stock is very real when purchases are made after a long rise. However, the characteristics of the market have changed greatly during this period. There was a time when virtually all stocks went up and down together; but just as the economy has been marked by "rolling readjustments" in one industry after another, so the stock market has been characterized by over-valuation in some shares and under-valuation in others in terms of price times earnings ratios and yields. "Formulas" for determining under-valuation and over-valuation have proved to be of doubtful value, and as a consequence a tendency has grown up on the part of trustees to buy "good" stocks, particularly "good growth stocks," almost regardless of price on the theory that investment judgment has done all that it can when it has selected a good company in a good industry with good growth prospects and that the price that is paid for such a company's stock is a matter of opinion and does not lend itself to analysis. It is suggested, however, (i) that not much investment judgment is required to arrive at the conclusion that

I.B.M., Minneapolis Honeywell, Minnesota Mining, and General Electric are high-grade companies with good growth prospects, and (ii) that there is a limit to what should be paid for growth. Air Reduction was widely regarded as a growth company in 1937 when its earnings reached an all-time high. In that year the company earned $2.85 a share and the price of its stock ranged between 45 and 80. In 1950 the company earned $3.15 a share but it had lost its growth "halo" and the shares ranged from 21 to 29. Even though earnings per share had increased by about 10 per cent, the return on capital had declined from 20 per cent to 10.4 per cent and the dividend had been cut from $3.00 to $1.00. In 1957 the stock has sold as high as 66 on the basis of 1956 earnings of $4.20 per share and it is again being recommended as a growth stock. This performance has been very disheartening to anyone who purchased Air Reduction in 1937 on the theory that it was a good growth stock and that price didn't matter. On the other hand those who bought the shares in 1950 when they were out of favor and selling at a reasonable price in relation to earning have done very well.

The point is that while a trustee is required to observe what prudent men are doing in the way of investing their funds, he isn't required to follow the crowd. He should take into account the actions of others, but if, based on his own investigations, he arrives at a conclusion which differs from the majority, he is acting prudently if he follows his own judgment. It needs no argument to show that if all prudent men constantly buy and sell the same stocks at the same times, the results will not bring credit on the prudent-man rule.

The theory that any price is a good price to pay for a good stock is extremely dangerous. But the fact that no one can say what is a prudent price to pay for a stock does not mean that trustees should not make the attempt. A given price may be prudent in a long-term trust where current income is of no importance and imprudent in a short-term trust where income is essential. Discrimination between what is a good value and what is not, as applied to particular trust accounts, is essential. Informed independent judgment plus common sense can be relied upon to produce reasonably good results.

In conclusion, there is a sound basis for the emphasis trustees have placed on conserving real values through the purchase of common stocks. But the duty to conserve dollar values as well still remains. The perpetual inflation argument may not be flawless—at least inflation in this country has not been a continuous process, and there have been long periods when there was none at all. Consequently, bonds and preferred stocks continue to have an important place in trust portfolios, particularly where they yield significantly more than equities. As to common shares, diversification, is, as a general rule, the key to good investment performance. Every reader of this article can cite instances from his own experience of spectacular results which have been achieved by breaking this rule, but absent special circumstances, the rule is still a good one. Finally, in a free society diversity of opinion among prudent men is healthy and desirable. The prudent trustee should not seek the false sense of security which comes from doing what everybody else is doing. If he has made a careful analysis of a security and has taken the opinion of others into account, it is his duty to be guided by his own judgment even though it is contrary to that of the majority.

19. COMMON TRUST FUNDS*

❀ J. Harry Wood

INTRODUCTION

IT IS TRUE, TRADITIONALLY SPEAKING, that the very name "common trust fund" makes use of contradictory terms; historically the idea may be old, but in its modern dress and practical application it is very new; its development and expansion has been rapid, but its importance is such that the growth to-date should be considered only as a mere beginning.

The long established legal principle is that the funds of one trust must not be commingled with those of another. For the funds of different trusts to be commingled in a common fund, and administered as one, seemed a contradiction in terms to many people in both legal and trust work.

The first modern common trust funds were not established until 1937, and the law which made them practicable was not enacted until 1936. Historically, however, common trust funds may be said to date from the early 1820's when The Farmers Fire Insurance and Loan Company and the Massachusetts Hospital Life Insurance Company were chartered to act in fiduciary capacities, and solicited trust business. The corpus of each trust received was commingled in a common fund.

The trusts accepted, however, were not trusts in any proper sense of the word, being scarcely more than time deposits. The creator of

* From *The Journal of The American Society of Chartered Life Underwriters*, Vol. IX, No. 4 (Fall, 1955), pp. 364–380. Reprinted by permission of *The Journal of The American Society of Chartered Life Underwriters*.

the "trust" deposited his funds with the company under an agreement, and the company paid the beneficiaries, not the income from that particular fund, but their share of the income from all the funds of the company . . . the words "trust company" and "trusts" had very different connotations in the early 1800's than they do today.[1]

It is possible to say that these first common investment funds established back in the early 1820's were the forerunners not only of common trust funds, but also of the present day open-end investment companies or so-called mutual funds.[2] The reader should not confuse in his own mind these two quite different institutions, even though the operation of the investment portfolios may be very much alike in principle.

Little or no further interest was shown in common or commingled trust funds until the 1920's when a few banks and trust companies inaugurated such plans. This development was stopped almost before it had started, however, when a federal court held that these funds were themselves taxable entities for income tax purposes. Thus the income of the funds were taxed twice: once as income of the fund itself, and once as income to the beneficiaries of the participating trusts.[3]

The growing need for common trust funds was becoming ever more obvious, but it required time and irrefutable logic to convince legislatures, courts and supervisory authorities, not only that they were needed but that they could be properly set up and properly administered. When Congress became convinced that a common trust fund was not a separate financial business but merely a mechanism to improve trust service, they provided that the income from such funds would not be taxable to the fund, provided it was operated by a bank (or trust company) for the exclusive use of its own "bona fide" trusts,[4] according to rules and regulations to be prescribed for national banks by the Board of Governors of the Federal Reserve System.[5]

---

[1] Gilbert T. Stephenson, "Ye Beginnings of Trust Companies," *Trusts and Estates*, Vol. 93 (March '54), p. 312.
[2] Gilbert T. Stephenson, *op. cit.*, p. 313.
[3] Gilbert T. Stephenson, "The Use and Purpose of Trusts," *The C.L.U. Journal*, Vol. 7 (June '53), p. 277.
[4] Common trust funds are available to executors and guardians as well as trustees so far as Regulation F goes, but some states have limited this by statute.
[5] George C. Barclay, "Common Trust Funds," *Trusts and Estates*, Vol. 93 (Nov. '54), p. 1000.

The creation of common trust funds by trust companies and by banks having trust departments has now been authorized by state law in all except Rhode Island and Iowa, and in the case of national banks by the Federal Reserve Board in Section 17 of Regulation F. This Regulation refers to the requirements of the Internal Revenue Code (Section 584) which permits exemption from taxation if the fund qualifies by being:

1. Exclusively for the collective investment and reinvestment of moneys contributed thereto by the bank in its capacity as a trustee, executor, administrator or guardian, and,
2. In conformity with the rules and regulations prevailing from time to time of the Board of Governors of the Federal Reserve System pertaining to the collective investment of trust funds by national banks.

The City Bank Farmers Trust Company, of New York (1929), and the Equitable Trust Company, of Wilmington (1930), created the prototype of the present day common trust funds in their commingled funds: as soon as Section 17 of Regulation F had been adopted by the Board of Governors of the Federal Reserve System, some of these commingled funds, such as "Fund B" of the Equitable Trust Company, were converted into the new or modern, and of course, tax exempt common trust funds. Other banks and trust companies started from scratch. There are now 160 banks and trust companies operating a total of more than 200 common trust funds in 32 states, District of Columbia and the Territory of Hawaii. The total assets of these funds exceeds $1¼ billion in 66,000 separate participating accounts.

This is an amazing growth. The available evidence, on a limited basis, indicates that the number of separate trust accounts invested in common trust funds increased by 8% during the past 12 months.[6] This is a fast growth, but only a forerunner for the development which surely lies ahead. The assets of all "personal" living and testamentary trusts is between $25–30 billion, but the average individual trust consists of less than $25,000 in assets, providing an annual income of less than $750.[7] An increasing number of small and medium size trusts created in the future should and will make use of the

[6] "Common Funds Increase Equities," *Trusts and Estates,* Vol. 94 (June '55), p. 506.
[7] Gilbert T. Stephenson, *op. cit.,* p. 271.

common trust fund. (Funds held in various capacities in trust departments for individuals approximate $100 billion.)

A trust is a property arrangement whereby one person (individual or corporation) owns (i.e., holds title to) property but holds and, in most cases, manages it for the use of someone else.[8]

The instrument creating the trust may be a Will, a trust agreement, or a declaration of trust.

One part of the instrument will usually refer to the kind of property or investment which may, or shall, be held by the trustee. It may be a particular piece of real estate, or certain company stocks, or United States Government bonds; it is more likely to be broad categories, such as mortgages, bonds, real estate, or common stocks; the trustee may be given little or no discretion as to investments, or he may be given unlimited discretion as to the investments to be made with the assets of the trust.

The Common Trust Fund—Described

The common trust fund is merely the, or one of the, investments held by a particular trust. It is not the trust instrument; it is not the trust.

It is a commingled fund or investment portfolio created from the assets of the many separate participating trust accounts. The common trust fund at any given time has "x" dollars of assets, divided for convenience into "y" number of units. The value of the unit will fluctuate with the market prices of the securities in the fund. As new participating trust accounts are admitted, the number of units outstanding is increased; conversely, as participating trust accounts are withdrawn, in whole or in part, the number of outstanding units is decreased.

The "common trust fund" is not the only name which is used: some banks use other titles such as "combined or general trust fund," "composite," "diversified," or "uniform collective" investment fund.[9] Some of these other titles are used because to many people "common trust fund" implies investment in common stocks, only, but of course this inference is unwarranted.

[8] Gilbert T. Stephenson, *op. cit.*, 271.
[9] Christian C. Luhnow, "Common Trust Fund Publicity," *Trusts and Estates,* Vol. 93 (Dec. '54), p. 1126.

Authority: laws and regulations. These funds are operated in accordance with:

a. The provision of written plans which have been approved by the board of directors of the bank or trust company, which include among other things, the conditions and dates for admission and withdrawals, the investment policy (balanced fund, common stock fund, etc.) to be followed, and so on;

b. The laws of the state in which the institution is domiciled. Every state has permissive and restrictive laws concerning trusteeship, hence state law must be followed too; for example, some states permit trustees to follow the prudent man rule for investments while others require that the legal list procedure be followed unless the power of discretion has been specifically bestowed by the creator of the trust; and

c. The regulations of the Board of Governors of the Federal Reserve System, known as Regulation F, governing the operation and management of common trust funds.

Purpose. The primary objective in the establishment of a common trust fund is to bring together assets of many participating trust accounts into one common fund for investment, and thereby obtain for these accounts greater stability of income and safety of principal as a result of a much broader diversification of investments, a better balance of investments between bonds and stocks, and a better and more continuous supervision than is generally possible for accounts of moderate size when invested independently. Furthermore, the establishment of a common trust fund both encourages and enables the bank or trust company to broaden its area of active interest in the trust field by welcoming more small trusts than it might otherwise feel could be handled, either economically or physically.

Management. Under the terms of the plans referred to above, the bank or trust company is sole trustee, custodian, and manager of the securities.

Starting a common trust fund. One requirement for the bank or trust company may be of interest to participants, present and prospective, namely that no one participating trust account may own more than 10% of the total assets of any common trust fund. To the participating accounts this requirement insures from the very beginning of the fund the advantages of this type of investment. To the bank or trust company it means in effect that a common trust fund cannot be started without 20 to 25 participating accounts from the very first day of operation, because it would be impossible to start with an even 10 accounts all of the exact same size. The fact that the assets of old trust accounts may often be invested in a common trust fund makes the starting of one a much easier and simpler process than it would otherwise be.

Participating trust accounts. The federal regulations permit the use of the common trust fund in any case where the bank is a fiduciary, which includes besides trustee the capacity of guardian, conservator, executor or administrator. Some states do not permit the use in all of these capacities; for example, Massachusetts permits the use in only the first three.

Thus the institutions are bound to restrict, under present regulations, the use of common trust funds to trusts created for bona fide fiduciary purposes; they may not be used as media for investment management accounts such as would be implied when no individual remaindermen or successor life tenants are named. In other words, the bank or trust company will not permit the investment of funds by a trust in the common trust fund unless it believes that the trust is an essential part of the settlor's estate plan.

Regulation F reads in part: "the term 'Common Trust Fund' means a fund maintained . . . for the investment of funds for true fiduciary purposes; and the operation of such common trust funds for other than strictly fiduciary purposes is hereby prohibited. . . ."

No question of participation, on this score, would arise in the case of either a testamentary or irrevocable *inter vivos* or living trust; questions would only arise in the case of revocable *inter vivos* trusts where the facts at the time of setting up the trust seemed to indicate that the settlor was attempting to make use of the common trust fund as a temporary medium for saving and investing, with no intention to use it as an essential part of his estate plan.

If the settlor has no intention of using a trust as an essential part of his estate plan, he would be well advised to make use of a trust with its own separate investment account, or to make use of publicly available and readily marketable investment company shares.

The use of the common trust fund is of course not limited to trusts set up by or for individuals; employee pension trusts, cemetery associations, and so on, may and do make use of them.

How to provide for participation. The trustee, either in the Will, or in the trust agreement, or declaration of trust, can be advised to consider the investment or can be instructed to make the investment of some or all of the assets of the trust, up to the maximum permitted by law, in a common trust fund. If there is no such advice or instruction, but the trustee is permitted the use of discretion, he may make use of the common trust fund for the investment of some or all of the assets of the trust.

It is possible in states which follow the prudent man rule, and even in the "legal" list states where the trustee has been given discretion, to make use of the common trust fund under the terms of many existing trusts. Consequently, many of the 65,000 participating trust accounts now invested in common trust funds were invested in them long after the original creation of the trust. This is as it should be, because it usually gave marked advantages to such "old" trusts.

Limitation in participation. Federal Reserve regulations limit the maximum amount of any one trust which may be invested in a common trust fund to $100,000.[10] (Originally the maximum was set at $25,000, later it was raised to $50,000, and finally on February 5, 1951 to the present amount.) At present six states also set a maximum of $100,000, Georgia will permit $150,000, while the other jurisdictions have no established limit.[11]

There is a real question whether any maximum amount should be set because the settlor should be the one to decide at what, if any, point in size he would prefer a separate investment account for the trust he is creating. A maximum limitation creates problems, for example: A testamentary trust is drawn up; assets are estimated at $75,000, and it is desired that they be invested in a common trust fund; at the time of death, the net assets finally available to the trustee for investment amount to $115,000. The trustee now has the alternative of investing $100,000 in the common trust fund setting up a separate investment fund for the remaining $15,000, or of setting up a separate investment fund for the entire $115,000. In either event the probability is that some of the desired advantages are lost to the trust. If limitation there must be, then it should be higher because in terms of income a $100,000 trust is a small one.

Under the regulations, however, one person may create several trusts each of which may invest in one or more common trust funds. A father with five children, for example, could set up a trust for each of them, with investments in the same common trust fund up to $100,000 each.

---

[10] There is no minimum amount for participation by any jurisdiction except in Massachusetts, where it is $4,000.

[11] Bascom H. Torrance, "50 Years of Trust Investment," *Trusts and Estates*, Vol. 93 (March '54), p. 253.

Admissions and withdrawals; periodic valuation. Regulation F requires that the value of the fund shall be determined not less frequently than once during each period of three months. This is done for a very practical reason: to establish the price or value of units for admission and withdrawals by participating accounts, and as a matter of both equity and convenience such admissions or withdrawals may be made only within a day or two (depending upon the rules of the particular fund) of the valuation dates.

Units of value. At the beginning each fund is divided into units of equal value, for example, $10 or $100. The unit value will then increase, decrease, or remain the same on each successive valuation date, depending upon the market value of the securities held at that time.

Example. A new common trust fund is started with $1,000,000 of assets divided among a number of accounts. Each unit is assigned a value of $10, so the million dollars divided by the assigned original value of the unit, $10, results in a total of 100,000 units.

At the next valuation date the market prices of the assets have increased to $1,050,000. There have been no admissions or withdrawals, so the number of units, 100,000, remain the same, resulting in an increase of the value of the unit to $10.50.

A new trust account is coming in as of this date with $10,500 to be invested. This amount, $10,500, serves to purchase an even 1,000 units.

The common trust fund invests the $10,500 at the immediate market prices. The total assets of the common trust fund now amounts to $1,060,500, and the number of units outstanding are now 101,000.

The value of the units owned by the "old" accounts has not been changed by this admission of a new account. In short, the admission of new accounts (or new money by old accounts), or withdrawal of some account, in whole or in part, is done without any effect whatever on the value of the units.

Investment of Funds. There have been four great revolutionary changes in trust development during the past 150 years. One of them has been in the investment media and this has occurred for the most part in the course of this generation.[12]

---

[12] The second and third were . . . the acceptance of the corporation as a suitable fiduciary, and to its right of compensation. "From Kings to Corporations," Louis S. Headley, *Trusts and Estates*, Vol. 93 (March '54), p. 231. The fourth revolutionary development is the subject of this article, namely, the emergence and development of the common trust fund idea.

Without exception, during the early and middle 1800's, conservative funds, including trust funds, were placed in mortgages or real estate. Then came railroad mortgage bonds, as well as obligations of the United States Government and the various states and municipalities. The view of common stocks at that time is suggested by this quotation from an opinion by the New York Court of Appeals in 1869:

> "The moment the fund is invested in stock, it has left the control of the trustees; its safety or risk of loss is no longer dependent upon their skill, care, or discretion; and the terms of the investment do not contemplate that it ever be returned to the trustees."

Today it is a rarity if any [discretionary trusts] do not use common stocks to some degree. Legal requirements have been relaxed over the years; and other barriers removed. Public opinion, both amateur and professional, has accepted this liberalization and is now committed to the granting of broad investment powers. I do not believe that inflation accounts for the whole movement, despite the fact that majority opinion would probably give it as the principal reason. I am sure that no one claims the wisdom to eliminate, or substantially reduce, equities from his trust accounts before the next deflationary period comes.

Common stocks are now a necessary part of our conservative investment fabric; and they will stay so, in good times and bad, war and peace, inflation and deflation. We will therefore have to take the inevitable hazards involved; and by careful selection and timing, we must keep these risks to a minimum.[13]

In 1904 we find trust investments in most jurisdictions limited to fixed income securities . . . generally . . . mortgages, United States Government obligations and those of states and political subdivisions . . . and in some states certain designated classes of corporate bonds . . . only Massachusetts, Maine, Maryland, Rhode Island and Vermont were following the prudent man rule, and all of these under court decision, not statute law.[14]

There are now 39 States, District of Columbia and Hawaii in which the full or partial prudent man rule of trust investment may be followed. This leaves only eleven states, some of which do not

[13] Benjamin Strong, "The Big Change in Trust Investment," *Trusts and Estates*, Vol. 93 (Nov. '54), p. 1023.
[14] Bascom H. Torrance, *op. cit.*, p. 252.

have clear investment statutes, while the remainder require the legal list procedure in the investment of trust funds where specific discretionary authority has not been granted to the trustee. The prudent man rule may be stated as follows:

In acquiring, investing, reinvesting, exchanging, retaining, selling, and managing property for another, a fiduciary shall exercise the judgment and care, under the circumstances then prevailing, which men of prudence, discretion, and intelligence exercise in the management of their own affairs not in regard to speculation but in regard to the permanent disposition of their funds, considering the probable income as well as the probable safety of their capital.

The function of trusteeship is to conserve, not to create, wealth. But since preservation of purchasing power as well as dollar value is a desirable objective, a balanced investment between fixed-income securities and equities has become recognized as prudent and protective[15] in most discretionary trust funds where needs and obligations are not attainable with fixed dollars.

Certainly almost all of the common trust funds operate on the basis of a balanced, diversified investment portfolio, although there are a few whose investments are limited to bonds, to mortgages, or to common stocks, only.

Where both are used the proportion as between bonds and common stocks in a balanced common trust fund can be changed to a degree, in accordance with prudent judgment: when stock prices are too high a larger percentage of the total assets may be invested in bonds, and conversely, when stock prices are believed to be low a larger percentage could be invested in common equities. No great shifts would be contemplated by most funds, but common sense, and a wide acceptance of the formula plan idea in investment policy, would at times compel some change.[16]

The equity, or common stock, portion of common trust fund portfolios, as of their various 1954 annual report dates, represented more than 45% of the total billion and a half dollar investments of

[15] Christian C. Luhnow, *op. cit.*, p. 1074.
[16] Some authorities believe that instead of a bank having one, or several common trust funds of similar balance, it should have two or more funds of vastly different balance, because the human requirements of various trusts differ widely in indicating the needed proportion of investment between equities and dollar obligations, length of the term of investment, et cetera. Thus the individual participating accounts could be placed in the fund with a balance approximating what would be done if they were invested separately on an ideal basis.

these funds . . . of the . . . 199 common trust funds 137 are "discretionary," 45 are "legal," seven are exclusively common stock funds, the
rest are fixed-income or bond funds . . . in the 137 different discretionary funds the percentage of common stocks held varied from 27%
to 99.9%. Only a few common trust funds held more than 60% or
less than 30% in common stocks. One-fifth of the common trust funds
held between 41–50%, and another one-fifth between 51–60% in
common stocks.

The 137 discretionary and the seven exclusively common stock
funds had an aggregate portfolio (at the end of their various 1954
annual report dates) as follows:[17]

U. S. Obligations	$231,912,256	19%
Other Gov't issues	17,840,669	1
Corporate bonds	186,275,311	16
Preferred stocks	138,944,895	12
Common stocks	593,051,391	50
Other	22,608,110	2
Total		100%

The "legal" and restricted common trust funds, by their very
nature, hold a larger percentage of bonds to stocks; even so, in the
aggregate, common stocks composed 25% of their portfolios with
14% more in preferred stocks.

It should be realized, however, that the percentage of common
stocks in all types of common trust funds is as high as it is currently
because of the market appreciation of the stocks they already owned,
rather than the result of large commitments of new monies during
the past year or so.

The individual creating a trust may have an investment policy
in mind, so specific and inflexible, that it could be carried out only
by the trustee setting up a separate investment account. Except in
such unusual instances, however, one of the common trust funds is
almost certain to fit the requirements of most settlors.

The important Regulation F restrictions as to investments
should be mentioned, inasmuch as they are in the nature of "safeguards":

1. No investment (other than U. S. Government obligations) shall
be made in the securities of any corporation exceeding 10% of the value
of the fund;

[17] "Broadening Horizon for Equities in Common Funds," *Trusts and Estates*, Vol.
94 (March '55), pp. 204 and 207.

2. No investment shall be made in any class of shares or stock in any corporation exceeding 5% of the total shares outstanding. If more than one common trust fund is administered (by the same bank or trust company) the aggregate investment may not exceed 5%.

3. At least 40% of the fund must at all times be in cash and readily marketable securities. If the liquid assets fall below 40% as of the valuation date, no admissions to or withdrawals from the fund are permitted except that ratable distribution upon participations is not prohibited.

4. No investment may be made in securities owned or issued by any affiliate of the bank nor securities of any corporation engaged in the underwriting and distribution of securities.

It has been mentioned that various states may have laws and regulations to be followed by trustees within their jurisdiction. Massachusetts, for example, limits the investments of common trust funds entirely to readily marketable securities.

Yields. The yield is given in dollars and cents per unit. This is because different participating accounts over the years will have paid more or less per unit than the others. Suppose, in the foregoing example, the income on the total fund during a year had been $40,400 or 40¢ per unit. To those participating accounts whose units had been purchased at $10 the return could be said to be 4%, but to the participating account which had paid $10.50 per unit, the return would be less than 4%.

Yields between different common trust funds are not comparable because of the difference in starting dates, in the rate of growth as market prices of securities were changing, and a difference in the proportions held of bonds and of stocks. Any comparison of "results" between such funds would not only be meaningless, but actually misleading.

Income Payments. All income collected on securities held in a fund is generally distributed quarterly among all the participating trusts. Income payments are then made to the beneficiaries in accordance with the requirements of each individual trust.

Gains and losses on sales or exchange of securities can be apportioned between principal and income as the bank shall deem proper; the usual practice is to follow reasonable trust accounting practices by recording gains or losses in the principal account. The administrators may distribute all or part of realized capital gains as of any quarterly valuation date, but generally speaking, distributions of gains are seldom made, both because of the small amount per participating account, and because in effect it would constitute continuous distribution of principal.

Tax status.　It has already been brought out that common trust funds which meet the legal requirements do not pay corporate taxes.

Each trust which has investments in the common trust fund will, of course, be subject to taxes on the income paid to it. The participating trusts or estates are entitled for tax purposes to the benefit of partially or wholly tax exempt income received by the common trust fund.

Each participating trust must include in income, however, its proportionate share of the gains and losses of the common trust fund, resulting from sales or exchanges of capital assets, classified according to short term or long term (Section 584 of the Internal Revenue Code of 1954). Naturally, this detailed information has to be furnished by the common trust fund to each trust participating.

The requirement that taxes of the participating trusts or estates be determined on the tax basis of the individual investments held by the common trust fund rather than on the participation in the common trust fund has resulted in an unusual situation. Undoubtedly with the substantial rise in equity security prices over the past year or two, common trust funds have experienced unrealized appreciation in their holdings. This means that a trust or estate wishing to enter an established common trust fund may in the future be subject to tax on substantial gains upon disposition of securities acquired before its entry. This has probably caused many trusts or estates to defer participation in the established funds.[18]

This is the only disadvantage for participation in a common trust fund and it will be or can be avoided in one or more of several ways, except possibly in one contingency. This one exception is where a trustee is directed to invest in a specifically named common trust fund, at a specific time, say the death of the testator, which might happen to coincide with the time when that common trust fund had large unrealized gains, and even then tax liability would not occur until and unless the gains were actually realized.

This is a risk which does not have to be taken; there are several ways of avoiding it. For one, the Will or trust agreement may be drawn to give permission, not specific direction; this will enable the trustee to wait for a propitious time for such investment.

Second, even when the trustee is given discretion, a specific common trust fund should not be named, such as "Common Trust

[18] Weston, Rankin, "Accounting for Common Trust Funds," *Trusts and Estates,* Vol. 94 (June '55), pp. 541–42.

Fund B" but rather "any common trust fund managed by the . . . bank or trust company." Some banks already have more than one common trust fund; for example, several have a balanced fund, and an all common stock fund, and a few have a mortgage fund. Even more important in this respect, however, is that some banks have already and others are no doubt contemplating the establishment of new common trust funds to overcome this tax disadvantage. There is no reason why a bank or trust company should not have several common trust funds of the same kind, with securities in approximately the same proportions, set up at different times, for the sole purpose of protecting new accounts from the unfair, and usually to the settlor entirely unknown, tax danger. For a bank or trust company to have several similar common trust funds would be a little inconvenient, and is not to be desired for its own sake, but it is a practical, and not an expensive solution to this tax danger to new accounts. Such a large percentage of common trust funds have been created since the war, and the big rise in security prices has been so recent that the problem is just now becoming real.

The third solution, of course, is through a change in the tax law.

Compensation. The regulations of the Federal Reserve Board, and the terms of the individual plans, do not permit the bank or trust company to charge any fee, commission or compensation for its services in operating the funds.

All trusts of such banks and trust companies pay trustees fees regardless of how the assets of such trusts are invested . . . but no additional fee or compensation is charged by reason of the fact that the assets of a trust may be invested in the common trust fund.

On the other hand, some corporate trustees provide for a lower charge on trusts whose assets are invested in one of their common trust funds on the assumption that economies warrant it. Merely to cite an example: The St. Louis Union Trust Company provides that their usual trustee's fees for trusts separately invested shall be reduced by 20% in respect to funds invested in one of their common trust funds.

The schedule of charges for personal trust services may vary by territory, by the composition of the trust, by size and other factors such as whether there is an initial charge, a distribution charge (on distributions of principal), and the amount of the minimum annual charge. In practically all cases the annual compensation schedule is determined largely as the result of two factors, the amount of the principal in the trust, and the amount of income earned on the principal.

If one had to wrap all of these variables together and make a rule-of-thumb estimate of trustees' fees for trusts of $25,000 to $100,-000, country-wide, and for ease in figuring, to measure the total charges against income only, a figure of 10% of the income of the trust would not be far from the mark.

The reasonableness of these charges for discharging the many duties of a trustee including that of managing the investment portfolio may be realized when one considers that the investor in investment company or so-called mutual fund shares on the average receives about 86% of the gross income, the 14% going for management and investment expenses; in addition, most open-end investment companies have a first year "set-up charge" that will probably average $7\frac{1}{2}$% in the aggregate. This is not to say that the investor pays too much for the privilege of owning investment company shares; he does not.[19] The comparison is made to show the very reasonableness of trust charges in general. The charge is so low that far more people in the future will avail themselves of the service if it can be brought effectively to their attention.

It should be mentioned again, that there is, and can be, no competition between common trust funds and investment company shares. The former is for bona fide trust use; the latter is for anyone who wants to make use of it for whatever reason he may have.

Common Trust Fund Report.   The federal regulations require reports to made annually to principals, beneficiaries and co-fiduciaries. The objective is a full disclosure of all pertinent information, including yield and principal value. The trustee is able to account not only on a uniform but a more informative basis than is usually possible for separate accounts.

Some banks have published very effective graphic as well as textual material covering function, investment policy, trust management, tax-status, audits, compensation, admission and withdrawal and other aspects, as well as portfolio lists and breakdowns, yields and unit values, average size of account participation and statement of condition.[20]

Safeguards and supervision.   Regulation F provides that a common trust fund shall be audited at least once during each period of

[19] See J. Harry Wood, "Investment Companies," *The C.L.U. Journal,* Vol. VIII (Summer '54), pp. 277–290.
[20] Christian C. Luhnow, *op. cit.,* pp. 1117–18.

12 months by auditors responsible only to the board of directors of the bank. The report of the audit is to include a list of investments showing valuations, a statement of purchases, sales, and other investment changes, income and disbursements and comments as to any investments in default. The expense of such audit is, with one possible exception, the only charge made against such funds.

The funds are also examined periodically by the Federal Reserve Bank of their district.

In addition, many of the states have their own supervision. For example in Massachusetts the funds are examined periodically by the Massachusetts Commissioner of Banks. Further, a Massachusetts bank or trust company managing a common trust fund must present its account annually to the Probate Court for its allowance. Where the courts make a charge, it is payable by the fund, and is the exception referred to above.

The investments of each common trust fund must be kept separate for other property belonging to, or in the custody of, the bank or trust company.

A common stock which was not paying dividends would not be eligible for investment by a common trust fund. What happens upon a valuation date if a stock is in the portfolio which has passed its dividend?

If a common trust fund holds any security in which funds of such trust might not lawfully be invested, new trusts may be allowed to enter until the offending security is segregated or sold. Withdrawals may be permitted if the so-called unlawful investment is sold, distributed in kind, or segregated. The only practical solution, generally, is to sell the security, even though about the worst time to sell any stock is right after it has passed its dividend. The net result is probably to make common trust funds more than a little careful to buy only seasoned dividend payers. However, the names of the different common stocks owned by common trust funds number about 580; even 531 different preferred stocks are owned.

Advantages in the Use of Common Trust Funds

There are several very important advantages to be achieved through the use of a common trust fund in the investments of trust funds. Any one of these advantages might be sufficient in a given case to determine such investment; all of them together make a convincing case even for some of the assets of large trusts to be so invested. The main advantages will be treated in this section, but there are others which could be listed.

1. Increased investment protection through wide diversification. This advantage is of particular importance to small trusts, especially those which may have to use principal from time to time. Not only is the trustee virtually compelled to use practically riskless investments in many small trusts, which are low in yield, but because of the interest rate risk he may feel compelled to use short maturities with an even lower return, which in effect forces the use of more principal. Moreover the trustee could not afford to diversify effectively a small trust account. The investment of the assets of a small trust in a common trust fund gives a degree of diversification that only the very largest of trusts could hope to attain.

2. Increased income as a result of commingling and diversification. Mention has been made above of the extreme conservatism which a trustee often feels must be followed in the separate investment of small trusts. Most trustees would have more confidence in investing the funds of a small trust in a common trust fund than in one gilt-edge long term bond, because the risk is less. Important to the beneficiary is the fact that the income will most likely to be considerably higher.

3. Increased purchasing power protection. To the extent that one believes that purchasing power protection is needed, and to the extent he believes that it may be approached by way of the balanced fund idea, then certain it is that the "balanced" common trust fund provides the means to this end for small and moderate size trusts, and even for fairly large ones.

4. More complete employment of the funds with resulting benefit from the income standpoint. It has already been mentioned that in many small trusts the income is insufficient for the beneficiaries, making it necessary to supplement the income by either regular or infrequent payments from principal. This requires the sales of securities in order to provide cash from the principal and results in loss of income because the trust assets are not fully invested. Although payments from principal may be only a few dollars a month, the time comes when a thousand dollar bond has to be sold. The cash balance does not earn income. If the investment is in a common trust fund, withdrawals of principal may be made periodically in units of small value, usually $10 to $20 each, and this is the only part of the assets which cease to earn interest.

5. Better supervision of investments. Common sense compels the conclusion that the common trust fund, growing, comprised of many separate accounts, with a certain amount of glamour attached to it, is going to receive better and more continuous investment supervision than the small separately invested trust. There is the positive motivation which comes because of the knowledge that the results are to be seen by examining officials of the Federal Reserve Bank, the state banking department, by the board of directors of the bank or trust company, sometimes

the court, and periodically by the interested parties of the various participating accounts. It would be a very indifferent investment officer who wasn't driven to do his best under such circumstances.

6. Lower investment expense; other economies. Purchases and sales of stocks are made in large blocks, rather than in odd lots, and this results in substantial savings in brokers' commissions. Accounting records, investment decisions and actions, and other items require little more time for the large common trust fund than for the separately invested trust. The "savings" are substantial, and they are of importance to the participating trust because in many instances, as has been mentioned, fees are smaller, or the minimum fee is less, as a result.

WHY COMMON TRUST FUNDS HAVE NOT GROWN FASTER

In the beginning of this article attention was called to the rapid growth of common trust funds. In the light of all their many advantages, however, the growth to date is not so great as it should have been. Why?

In the first place there are too many people who do not know enough about trusts to realize that setting up of one, either testamentary or *inter vivos*, would provide the most practical solution to their particular problem.

And a trust must be created before a common trust fund is used.

There are many other who realize, vaguely or clearly, that a trust arrangement with its flexibility and management would help to solve their estate problems, but imagine that it costs too much, or that the trust company wouldn't be interested in their size of estate.

There is the belief on the part of some that a trust company usually takes the easy riskless road in investments, so why pay a trustee to make investments in United States Government bonds, which anyone can make.

All of the above comes under the heading of lack of information. This is evident not only among the "public" but there is even a lack of professional understanding.

Regulation F, or perhaps the interpretation of it by many banks and trust companies, has done nothing to spread enlightenment. Wide understanding of common trust funds would be, in effect, education about trusts. That part of Regulation F to which reference is made reads as follows:

A bank administering a common trust fund shall not, in soliciting business or otherwise, publish or make representations which are inconsistent with this paragraph (which refers to the fact that common trust funds are to be used only for true fiduciary purposes) or the other provisions of this regulation and, subject to the applicable requirements of the laws of any state, shall not advertise or publicize the earnings realized on any common trust fund or the value of the assets thereof.

The reports to the interested parties, previously referred to, must be so protected that publicity will not seep out as to yields or unit values. This is a good rule, but in order to be certain that the regulations are not violated, too many banks in the past have leaned over so far backwards that the impression given even to bona fide prospective settlors has seemed sometimes to be one of evasiveness. Undoubtedly this is fast being corrected but it has been a factor.

The Future for Common Trust Funds

The future is bound to be good because the value of trusts as well as the advantages of the common trust funds for the investment of trusts will become better known.

Estate planning is growing, and it frequently if not usually results in the establishment of a trust.

Many professional advisers who have an interest in estate analysis have or will develop an interest in the workings of common trust funds that they may better serve the interests of their clients; not only estate attorneys, but life insurance underwriters, investment counsellors, accountants and others.

There is a great latent demand for the revocable *inter vivos* or living trust as an essential part of the settlor's estate plan, and hence such trusts would be legally eligible to make use of the common trust fund. This development has not been as widely or effectively promoted as it might have been, perhaps because of the small original size that so many of the trusts would be; perhaps the promotion would have been greater except for the realization that the only economical way for the bank, and the only appealing way to the prospective trustor, was to make use of the common trust fund, and there was fear of running afoul of the regulations.

The use of trusts and of common trust funds will grow as trust companies provide and promote a systematic plan for accumulation from a modest base. Manufacturers Trust Company in New York, for example, is inviting special trust accounts from $5,000 up at proportionately small charges . . . perhaps too small for some banks. Starting with a trust fund of $5,000 for an annual charge of only $25 the bank makes available the facilities and diversification usually associated with large estates. Interesting it is to note their emphasis on the facility "to place additional sums in your special trust account from time to time, so that your account can be a steadily growing trust fund." The investments of these small trusts are in one of the bank's common trust funds. This type of activity should encourage the setting up of bona fide living trusts.

All of us could list many friends and acquaintances who would be well advised to set up an *inter vivos* trust now, turning over to it the management of their present investment savings, and any future funds which became available for the same purpose. Not only would the investment results be as good or better, not only would the individuals be free from having to "keep up" on investments, or rely on "tips and hunches," but they would achieve the other advantages of a living trust: it would not have to be administered in the Probate Court; there would be no court costs, no executors' fees, no administrative expenses, and the trust agreement being a private document would not be open to public inspection as is a Will when probated at the death of the testator.

Some banks may find it impossible to set up common trust funds because of the limitations of their clientele. There may be whole towns and areas where this condition may prevail.[21]

With this in mind, and feeling that the idea of the joint investment of trust funds is sound and if unavailable for small banks through the common trust fund ought nevertheless to be available to them in some manner, a bill was drafted and passed by the New York legislature making joint investment possible. Fundamentally, the mechanism consists of an open-end investment company or mutual fund, so designed to enjoy the tax advantages available under the Investment Company Act of 1940. Only banks having trust departments in New York state and not already maintaining a common trust fund may participate. The mechanics of operating the fund will be exactly the same as those required to operate a common trust fund but the practical difference is that the fund will be taxable by the federal government as a regulated investment company, which

[21] However, a trust company in Proctor, Vermont (population 1813), has for several years operated a common trust fund. It has about 60 participating trust accounts.

means if capital gains are realized, either the fund will have to pay a capital gains tax, or more likely, the fund will pay out capital gains dividends to participants. Since by hypothesis the participants will be relatively small trusts, it is unlikely that such capital gains dividends will result in any appreciable tax to the participants, especially in view of the increased exemption of $300 and, of course, the net amount of such dividends can immediately be reinvested in additional units of the fund.[22]

The number of other states which may follow this example is unknown, but it is one more bit of evidence of the high regard and the need for common trust funds, and the fact that many circumstances and developments will promote their growth.

[22] George C. Barclay, *op. cit.*, p. 1001.

20. THE ROLE OF DOLLAR AVERAGING IN THE COMMON STOCK INVESTMENT OPERATIONS OF LIFE INSURANCE COMPANIES*

❀ George E. Rejda

T HIS PAPER IS AN EMPIRICAL ANALYSIS of the role of dollar averaging in the investment operations of life insurance companies. The data for this study were derived from interviews with investment officers of life insurance companies and from a questionnaire which was sent to fifty-seven life insurance companies and four variable annuity companies. Of this total, forty-seven companies are domestic life insurance companies which own 88 per cent of the assets and 86 per cent of all the common and preferred stock in the life insurance industry in this country. Major emphasis is placed upon these forty-seven companies in order to determine the extent of use of dollar averaging in their common stock investment operations.

CRITERIA FOR DOLLAR AVERAGING

Dollar averaging is defined as the investment of a constant number of dollars in a stock or group of stocks at regular intervals of time,

* From *The Journal of Insurance*, Vol. XXIX, No. 4 (Dec., 1962), pp. 533–545. Reprinted by permission of *The Journal of Insurance*.

with the objective of attaining an average cost per share which is less than the average market price.

For example, assume that $1000 is invested in a stock on three separate dates, and that the price of the stock on each of the three dates is respectively $20, $40, and $50. On the first date fifty shares are purchased; on the second date twenty-five shares are purchased, and on the third date twenty share are purchased. Thus, the average market price is $37, while the average cost per share is $32.

This effect takes place because the investment of a constant number of dollars results in the purchase of a relatively larger number of shares when market prices are lower. Thus, over an extended period of time, in both rising and falling markets, an average cost per share which is less than the average market price should be attained.[1]

The success of any dollar averaging plan, however, is dependent upon certain criteria which must be fulfilled. They are: (1) regularity of funds to invest, (2) continuation of stock purchases in market declines, and (3) willingness to purchase stocks over a long period of time, usually five to ten years.[2]

REGULARITY OF FUNDS TO INVEST

In periods of business downturns when stock prices are depressed, funds must be available to continue the necessary stock purchases in order to offset the purchases which are made at higher market levels. If purchases are not made at lower market levels, a favorable average or unit cost per share will not be attained, and the dollar averaging plan will fail.

The life insurance industry is characterized by a regularity of cash funds which are available for investment purposes. Cash income

---

[1] The advantage of attaining an average cost which is less that the average market price appears to be over-emphasized by many financial writers. When stocks are valued or sold, they are not valued or sold at the average market price, but at the current market price, which may be above or below the average market price. One might argue that the objective of dollar averaging is the attainment of an average cost per share which is less than the current market price.

[2] A fourth requirement is that the stocks which are dollar averaged must be of the proper type. A dollar averaging plan will fail if the stocks do not meet the usual tests of a sound investment. However, dollar averaging is concerned with the timing of stock purchases and not stock selectivity. Stock selectivity is a separate and distinct problem, entirely separate from the timing problem and is beyond the scope of this paper.

usually exceeds cash disbursements which means that all death claims and expenses can be met out of the current year's income, precluding the possibility of liquidating some ledger asset in order to raise cash funds to pay these items. This excess of cash income over cash disbursements is explained by the fact that policyholders are paying redundant premiums during the early years of their policies, and these excess premiums are invested and accumulated, as offsets to the reserve liabilities, in order to pay death claims at the advanced ages of life. From the viewpoint of a dollar averaging plan, this is significant since cash funds are available for common stock purchases during all phases of a market price cycle.

OTHER FACTORS STABILIZING CASH FLOW

There are other factors which contribute to the regularity of cash funds, and the ability to continue a dollar averaging plan is enhanced by the influence of these elements.

One such factor is that renewal premiums constitute the largest source of premium income for life insurance companies.[3] This is significant because it illustrates the point that the life insurance industry is not primarily dependent on new business as a source of cash income. New premium income is strongly influenced by the business cycle. When business conditions are poor and unemployment is rampant, many individuals are reluctant to aggravate their current financial condition by purchasing new insurance. However, renewal income is not subject to the business cycle in the same degree that first year premium income is; individuals will usually try to continue their premium payments during periods of unemployment and will let the policy lapse or surrender the policy only as a measure of last resort. Thus, stability of renewal premiums is an important element which enables a life insurance company to continue a dollar averaging plan, because funds are available for common stock purchases during periods of recessions or depressions when stock prices are depressed.

Another element which tends to strengthen a dollar averaging plan is mortgage amortizations. Although technically the repayment

---

[3] For example, the total premium income in 1958 for life insurance companies which did business in the state of New York was $5.0 billion. Of this total approximately $4.4 billion or 88 per cent was accounted for by renewal premiums. See *New York Insurance Reports*, Vol. I, pp. 279a–282a.

of the principal is not a source of new cash, cash does become available for investment as the principal is repaid over the lifetime of the mortgage, and the periodic payment of principal and interest increases the ability of a life insurance company to continue a dollar averaging plan.

Still another element which contributes to the stability of cash flow by which a dollar averaging plan can be continued is the trend towards direct placement of bond investments.

Many investment officers were confronted with the problem of bond maturities and refunding, with the subsequent problem of reinvestment of large amounts of cash. This became particularly acute during periods of low interest rates when substantial refunding of bonds and mortgages took place. However, this problem is not so acute currently because of the trend towards direct placement of bonds, since investment officers usually insert restrictive convenants in the bonds, such as abnormally high call prices, noncall provisions, or nonrefundability provisions.

This trend is beneficial to a dollar averaging plan because direct placements smooth out the cash flows of insurance companies; bond maturities can be better spaced, and the regular flow of cash funds is enhanced.

Finally, there is little or no seasonality in the cash flows of life insurance companies. Unlike the cash flows of property and casualty companies which are distinctly seasonal,[4] the funds of life insurance companies are available for investment during all periods of the year. From a dollar averaging viewpoint, this is advantageous because companies do not have to be concerned as to the time for making their dollar averaging investment.

FACTORS DECREASING CASH FLOWS

Several factors tend to decrease the cash flow of life insurance companies, and dollar averaging may be affected by these elements.

---

[4] Several investment officers of property insurance companies who were also interviewed in this study stated that the most common seasonal pattern is that funds are restricted during the first quarter of the year. This is attributed to increased fire losses during the winter months, windstorm losses during the early spring months, and taxes which become payable during the first quarter. Many of the companies experienced negative cash flows during this period, and their investment funds were restricted.

One factor which tends to decrease the cash funds available for investment is policy loans. During periods of business recession when stock prices are at favorable levels, policy loans usually increase, and the cash funds for investment purposes may be reduced during such a period.

It would appear, however, that the effect of policy loans upon a dollar averaging plan is small. Although there are cash withdrawals in a business recession, the available industry data indicate that there has not been any tendency for policy loans to increase substantially during periods of recent economic down-turns. During the economic recessions of 1949, 1953, and 1958, policy loans were respectively 3.7 per cent, 3.7 per cent, and 3.9 per cent of assets.[5] Thus, the data indicate that although cash withdrawals in the form of policy loans may be expected, the effect on the total cash flow of a company would be small, and a dollar averaging plan would not be significantly affected by the lack of cash funds to continue common stock investments. Only one company in this study stated that its funds for common stock investments were seriously interrupted by heavy disbursements of cash for policy loans.

Another element which may affect a dollar averaging plan is the trend towards group, term, and credit life insurance. Many investment officers expressed concern because their cash flows did not increase as rapidly as they desired because of this trend towards the nonpermanent types of insurance. This can be illustrated by Table 1, which indicates that the excess of cash income over cash disburse-

Table 1. *Comparison of the Relative Decline in Cash Income Over Cash Disbursements with the Relative Increase of Group and Credit Life Insurance.*

YEAR	EXCESS OF CASH INCOME OVER CASH DISBURSE- MENTS AS A PER CENT OF CASH INCOME	GROUP AND CREDIT LIFE INSURANCE AS A PER CENT OF TOTAL LIFE INSURANCE IN FORCE
1945	45%	15%
1950	37	22
1955	32	32
1958	26	35

Source: Computed from *The Historical Statistics of Life Insurance*: Institute of Life Insurance, March, 1960.

[5] *Life Insurance Fact Book*, 1960 ed., p. 88.

ments has been in a downward trend since 1945, while group, term, and credit life insurance have become relatively more important in terms of total insurance in force.

Table 1 indicates that the excess of cash income over cash disbursements was 45 per cent of cash income in 1945, while group and credit life insurance constituted 15 per cent of the total insurance in force. However, by 1958 the excess of cash income over cash disbursements declined to 26 per cent of total cash income, while group and credit life insurance increased to 35 per cent of the total insurance in force. Thus, the large margin between cash income and cash disbursements has been declining steadily. As mentioned earlier, this large excess of cash income over cash disbursements is attributed to the excess premiums which are collected during the early years of a policyholder's life; but with the trend towards group, term, and credit life insurance, this is no longer true. Most group insurance is written on a yearly renewable term basis, and the premiums which are collected are the premiums necessary to pay the death claims for such groups at the various attained ages. Therefore, there is very little excess which can be invested, and a company could not expect its cash flow to increase rapidly because smaller premiums are being collected. The decline in the excess of cash income over cash disbursements can be attributed largely to the trend towards group, term, and credit life insurance.

If this trend should continue, the excess of cash income over cash disbursements could approach zero. If such an event should occur, the life insurance companies would revaluate their entire investment philosophies, and a dollar averaging program and the probability of continuing such a plan would be carefully revaluated. Under such conditions it is not unreasonable to assume that dollar averaging for some companies would be discontinued. Since, for purposes of this study, the assumption is made that regularity of funds implies new cash available for investment from current operations, it is difficult to visualize a dollar averaging plan being continued when there is little or no new cash available for common stock purchases.

In conclusion, the life insurance industry has demonstrated that there is a regularity of cash funds which are made available for investment during periods of economic downturns when stock prices are depressed. The data present strong evidence that dollar averaging could be continued during such periods; but this may not be true in the future if the trend towards the nonpermanent types of insurance should continue.

CONTINUATION OF STOCK PURCHASES IN MARKET DECLINES

For a dollar averaging plan to function properly, it is necessary that stock purchases be continued during periods of market declines; it is important, therefore, to determine if the life insurance industry exhibits a willingness to purchase common stocks in market declines.

The available data, although very limited, present some evidence that life insurance companies continue to purchase common stocks during market declines.

Table 2. *Common Stock Purchases of United States Life Insurance Companies, Selected Time Periods 1957–1960*
($000,000 Omitted)

PERIOD	TYPE OF MARKET	NO. OF MONTHS	COMMON STOCK PURCHASES
July–Dec. 1957	Falling	6	$147
Jan.–July 1958	Rising	6	114
Mar.–Dec. 1959	Rising	10	287
Jan.–Oct. 1960	Falling	10	325

Source: Computed from the *Tally of Life Insurance Statistics,* 1957–1960.

This is illustrated by Table 2 which indicates the common stock purchases by the life insurance industry during two market declines.

The first period under study was the period between July 1957 and December 1957, a period of declining stock prices.[6] During this period the life insurance industry purchased $147 million of common stocks. However, between January 1958 and July 1958, a period of rising stock prices, only $114 million of common stocks were acquired.

[6] Standard & Poor's Composite Stock Index declined from 47.43 to 39.99, or a decline of 16 per cent.

The second period under study was the sharp market decline of 1960. From March 1959 to December 1959, a period of rising stock prices, the life insurance industry purchased $287 million of common stocks. However, between January 1960 and September 1960, a period of declining stock prices,[7] the life insurance industry acquired $325 million of common stocks, or an increase of 13 per cent in the rate of acquisition.

Although the data are very limited, it is not unreasonable to assume that the life insurance industry can fulfill this requirement for a successful dollar averaging plan.

ABILITY TO PURCHASE STOCKS OVER A LONG PERIOD

Dollar averaging is not a system for quick profits but is primarily a method for long term capital gains. A period of five to ten years is usually required in order for the dollar averaging technique to function properly. Since insurance companies are long term investors, it would appear that this requirement can be fulfilled by life insurance companies which desire to dollar average.

EMPIRICAL RESULTS OF THE STUDY

NUMBER OF COMPANIES

Table 3 indicates the number of life insurance companies which utilize the dollar averaging technique. The data indicate that 31

Table 3.　*Results of Questionnaire Sent to 61 Life Insurance Companies*

	NO. OF COMPANIES	PER CENT
Questionnaire Was Sent To	61	100%
No. of Companies Responding	61	100
No. of Companies Dollar Averaging	19	31
No. of Companies Which Discontinued Dollar Averaging Plan	6	10

Note: The total for life insurance companies includes four variable annuity companies.
Source: Questionnaires.

[7] Standard & Poor's Composite Stock Index declinded from 59.89 to 53.39, or a decline of 11 per cent.

per cent of the reporting life insurance companies utilize the dollar averaging technique. Table 3 also indicates that several companies have discontinued dollar averaging plans.

DATE OF INITIATION

Dollar averaging for most life insurance companies is a relatively recent phenomenon. This is indicated by Table 4 which shows that thirteen of the nineteen companies initiated their dollar averaging plans after 1955.

Table 4. *Period of Initiation of Dollar Averaging Plans*

PERIOD OF INITIATION OF DOLLAR AVERAGING PLANS	NUMBER OF LIFE COMPANIES
1955–1959	13
1950–1954	6
1945–1949	0

Source: Questionnaires.

The recent introduction of dollar averaging may be explained, in part, by the fact that life insurance companies domiciled in New York were forbidden to invest in common stocks before 1951, and this technique could not be used by these companies prior to that time. After the legislation forbidding common stock investments was changed, the life insurance industry did not immediately react with increased common stock purchases. Because of historically high stock prices after 1955, the dollar averaging technique was employed as a defensive measure for entering the stock market at high levels.

Table 5 illustrates in greater detail the primary reasons for adoption of a dollar averaging plan. The most common reason given was that common stocks provided an inflation hedge, and since common stocks were to be purchased continually to achieve this inflation hedge, dollar averaging was employed to reduce the timing error.

Table 5. *Reasons Given for Initiation of a Dollar Averaging Plan*
by 13 Life Insurance Companies

REASONS FOR INITIATION	NUMBER OF COMPANIES
Inflation hedge and capital appreciation; dollar averaging was the most efficient technique for constant accumulation	7
Wanted to increase stock holdings and dollar averaging was the most efficient method	1
Dollar averaging is simple for a financial committee to understand	1
Competition forced the company into common stocks; dollar averaging was the best method to enter the stock market at historically high levels	1
Increased yield on portfolio; dollar averaging was the most efficient method of achieving this objective	1
Wanted to formalize stock purchases	1
Company entered the variable annuity field and dollar averaging was the technique utilized for common stock acquisitions	1

Source: Questionnaires.

REASONS FOR TERMINATION

Table 6 indicates some of the reasons for abandonment of dollar averaging by some companies. One company discontinued dollar averaging because alternative investments (bonds) were more attractive. One company discontinued dollar averaging because the stock

Table 6. *Reasons for Termination of a Dollar Averaging Plan*

COMPANY	PERIOD USED	REASONS FOR TERMINATION
A	Jan. 1958–1959	Bond yields were more attractive.
B	1954–1957	Stock market was overpriced.
C	1956–1957	Mandatory Security Valuation Reserve was inadequate to absorb a market decline.

Source: Questionnaires and interviews.

market was considered to be overpriced. Finally, one company abandoned dollar averaging because of an inadequate Mandatory Security Valuation Reserve.[8] The dollar averaging technique requires continued purchases of stocks during market declines. This means that dollar averaging during such a period will result in the constant accumulation of capital losses which must be charged against this reserve. If this reserve is inadequate to absorb all capital losses, the remainder of such losses must be charged against surplus. Company C did not wish to have any capital losses reflected in its surplus position, and the dollar averaging technique was abandoned.

TYPES OF DOLLAR AVERAGING PLANS

The most noticeable fact about the types of dollar averaging plans employed currently is the almost complete absence of the conventional theory of dollar averaging, which assumes the investment of a constant sum in a stock or group of stocks at fixed intervals of time. Most of the companies employ some type of modified dollar averaging plan. This is illustrated by Table 7.

Table 7. *Types of Dollar Averaging Plans Utilized by 15 Life Insurance Companies*

	NO. OF COMPANIES
Dollar Averaging Currently:	
Conventional Dollar Averaging	2
Modified Dollar Averaging	11
Terminated Dollar Averaging:	
Conventional Dollar Averaging	0
Modified Dollar Averaging	2

Source: Questionnaires and interviews.

The most common modification of the conventional theory is to invest an aggregate fixed amount at regular intervals of time. However, the allocation of this fixed aggregate amount among the various

[8] In 1951 the National Association of Insurance Commissioners required all life insurance companies to set up a reserve liability against fluctuations in the market value of securities. The purpose of this reserve was to prevent future capital losses from falling with their full weight upon the narrow unassigned surpluses of the life insurance companies.

stocks on the approved list is not in constant amounts as the conventional theory assumes, but may be in varying amounts. For example, assume that fifty stocks are dollar averaged monthly, and the aggregate amount invested is $500,000. For sake of simplicity assume that $10,000 is invested in each of the fifty stocks. According to the conventional theory of dollar averaging, this fixed sum of $10,000 would be invested in each stock during all phases of a market cycle. Thus, the fixed $10,000 would be invested at both high and low points in a market cycle. However, under the modified plans employed by most companies, $20,000 might be invested in a stock one month, $30,000 the next month, and so forth. Although the aggregate monthly amount is fixed (i.e. $500,000), the allocation of this total among the individual stocks may vary each month.

Many investment officers who were interviewed stated that conventional dollar averaging was too rigid and mechanical, and a modified plan which provided flexibility was desirable because such a plan could be adapted very easily to changing economic conditions.

One advantage of a modified plan is the flexibility which is provided in allocating the aggregate dollar amounts among the various stocks on the approved list. Many investment officers desire to invest more of their funds in stocks which are relatively underpriced when compared to the other stocks in their portfolios. If the conventional theory is practiced, however, the sums which are invested in each of the stocks would be in constant amounts, and the advantage of investing relatively more of the funds in the stocks which are underpriced relative to the other stocks on the approved list would be lost. Also, if the conventional theory is practiced, a stock may be purchased when it is over-priced since it is purchased at fixed intervals of time, regardless of the level of the stock market. To avoid purchasing a stock when it is overpriced, many investment officers employ some type of modified dollar averaging plan.

Another advantage of modified dollar averaging is that odd-lot purchases are avoided. If stocks are purchased in constant dollar amounts, as the conventional theory assumes, some odd-lot purchases would be made. The price per share would be greater because of the odd-lot price differential which must be paid. An extra $\frac{1}{8}$ point per share must be paid when the price of the stock is over $40, and an extra $\frac{1}{4}$ point per share must be paid when the price of the stock is under $40. Insurance companies purchase thousands of shares during a period of a year, and this small price differential should not be ignored. Most investment officers purchase stocks in round lots to avoid these odd-lot expenses.

INVESTMENT EXPERIENCE OF THE COMPANIES

Sources of Data. The common stock records of the various companies were employed as primary sources; they were supplemented by Schedule D in the annual convention statement, which lists the common stock purchases and sales of a company, the amount of common stock owned, and cash dividends received during the year.

Computation of Capital Gains and Dividend Returns. The following method was employed for computing capital gains.[9] Each year was treated separately, and the market value was computed from one year to the next. However, part of the increase in market value may have been attributable to new stock purchases. Transactions, therefore, which represented new purchases were subtracted from the gross market change from one year to the next. On the other hand, capital gains may have been realized because of common stock sales, and failure to consider these sales would understate the capital gain return. Thus, the proceeds from common stock sales were added to the change in market value from one year to the next. This procedure can be illustrated better by Table 8, which indicates the actual investment experience of one life insurance company for the year 1959.

The above method was based on market value rather than cost because cost data would introduce a bias in the study and make comparisons among the several companies impossible. If cost alone were considered, a company which initiated its common stock program earlier than the other companies would show a larger capital gain or dividend return. This bias is eliminated by treating each year separately and considering only the market value at the beginning of the year. The market value at the beginning of the year becomes a common base by which the performance of each company during the year can be measured.

---

[9] The author is indebted to Dr. G. Wright Hoffman, Wharton School of Finance, University of Pennsylvania, for his suggestion as to the method of computing capital gains and dividend returns.

Table 8. *Method of Computation of Capital Gains and Dividends*

($000,000 Omitted)

YEAR	YEAR END MARKET	MEAN MARKET VALUE	EXCESS OF PURCHASES OVER SALES[a]	MARKET GAIN[b]	APPREC. (%)[c]	CASH DIVIDENDS RECEIVED	YIELD (%)[d]
1958	$34.4						
1959	38.6	$36.5	$1.3	2.9	7.93%	$1.3	3.47%

[a] Total cost of stocks acquired during the year minus the total consideration received on common stock sales.
[b] Total advance of the year-end market value over the previous year-end market value minus the excess of purchases over sales.
[c] Market gain divided by the mean market value.
[d] Actual cash dividends received divided by the mean market value.
Source: Schedule D of the annual convention statement.

Dollar Averaging Companies. Table 9 illustrates the capital gains and dividend returns for twelve life insurance companies for the period between 1957 and 1959. The year 1957 was a year of declining stock prices, and all reporting companies experienced capital losses, both realized and unrealized, for the year. The year 1958 was a year of rising stock prices, and all companies experienced fine capital gains for the year. The year 1959 was a year of slightly rising stock prices, and all companies experienced moderate capital gains for the year.

Judgment Technique Versus Dollar Averaging. Many investment officers who did not dollar average stated that judgment, with respect to the timing of common stock purchases, was clearly superior to a dollar averaging plan, and that companies which employed dollar averaging would not do as well with respect to capital gains and dividend returns as the companies which did not employ dollar averaging. It was necessary, therefore, to compare empirically the investment results of the dollar averaging and non-dollar averaging groups to determine if important differences existed between them.

In comparing the investment results of the two groups, it was necessary to separate the initial universe of sixty-one companies into two distinct groups—companies which acquired stocks by dollar averaging and companies which acquired stocks by some other technique. Companies which employed dollar averaging were eliminated from the non-dollar averaging group. Ten Canadian life insurance companies were also eliminated because of the more liberal investment regulations in Canada, and more importantly, because the Canadian companies purchased their stocks in world-wide markets. Thus, there would be a problem of exchange rates and refinement of data in order to use the investment experience of these companies. They were, therefore, eliminated because of the possible bias which might have been introduced into the study by including them. Finally, many companies invested only in bonds, and they were also eliminated.

After eliminating companies for the reasons described above, eighteen remained. These eighteen companies accounted for a large percentage of the common stock purchases in the life insurance industry but did not employ the dollar averaging technique. From this group of eighteen companies, a random sample of ten companies was drawn. The data for the sample companies were gathered from Schedule D of the annual convention statement. While not con-

Table 9. *Capital Gains and Dividend Returns for 12 Life Insurance Companies 1957–1959*
(per cent)

COMPANY	CAPITAL GAINS			DIVIDEND RETURNS		
	1957	1958	1959	1957	1958	1959
D	−9.83%	30.11%	4.22%	4.53%	4.04%	3.56%
E	−8.19	31.62	10.66	3.28	2.88	2.47
F	−6.82	23.50	7.93	4.23	3.86	3.47
G	−0.43	31.34	7.43	4.46	3.85	3.48
H	−18.47	38.31	13.24	2.91	2.60	2.23
I	−3.40	33.85	6.37	4.29	3.56	3.23
J*	−16.57	30.08	5.36	5.05	4.44	3.86
K	−9.81	33.11	7.65	4.57	4.21	3.87
L	−11.78	32.17	11.78	3.99	3.51	2.99
M	—	29.45	5.96	—	na	na
N	—	—	7.03	—	—	3.49
O	—	—	5.00	—	—	3.13
Unweighted Average	−9.48%	31.35%	7.72%	4.15%	3.66%	3.25%
Weighted Average	−9.78%	30.57%	7.87%	4.16%	3.66%	3.17%

* This is a pension fund of a property insurance company.
Source: Common stock records of the various companies and Schedule D of the annual convention statement.

clusive, the data indicated that some companies tended to buy common stocks in large blocks, in contrast to the dollar averaging companies which purchased stocks in smaller amounts over a period of time. Thus, there was some indication that the judgment technique was being exercised.

There were only nine companies which comprised the dollar averaging group. Although thirteen companies in this study indicated they were dollar averaging, only nine of them were dollar averaging during the three year period between 1957 and 1959.

Table 10 compares the capital gains and dividend returns for both groups during the three year period between 1957 and 1959. It should be noted that the differences between capital gains and dividend returns for both groups are very slight for all of the three years which were tested. With respect to capital gains, the difference between the two groups for each of the three years is approximately one percentage point. With respect to dividend returns, the difference between the two groups for each of the three years is less than one-fourth of one per cent. Although the non-dollar averaging group has slightly superior returns, it is erroneous to conclude that the judgment technique is superior to the dollar averaging technique. The differences between the two groups are not large enough to justify such a statement. Although the investment officers who do not dollar average state that the judgment technique is clearly superior to the dollar averaging technique, the limited statistical evidence does not support such an hypothesis.

Limitations of the Test. Greater validity could have been attributed to the findings if the time periods were longer. Only three years were used in the study. There were few companies dollar averaging before 1957 and to have used a longer time period would have severely restricted the number of companies which could be used.

A second limitation is that the element of judgment is injected into the modified forms of dollar averaging. Since the element of judgment is utilized by both groups, the findings are not as significant as they would be if all companies followed the conventional theory of dollar averaging, where little judgment is employed with respect to the timing of stock purchases.

The final limitation, and perhaps the most serious, is that a level of significance test could not be applied validly to the data in order to test for a significant difference between the two groups. The

Table 10. *Capital Gains and Dividend Returns for Life Insurance Companies Which Dollar Average and Life Insurance Companies Which Do Not Dollar Average 1957–1959*

DOLLAR AVERAGE COMPANIES	CAPITAL GAINS			DIVIDEND RETURNS		
	1957	1958	1959	1957	1958	1959
Arithmetic mean, Dollar Average Companies	−9.48%	31.57%	8.29%	4.15%	3.66%	3.24%
Arithmetic mean, Non-Dollar Average Companies	−8.32	30.03	9.37	4.38	3.89	3.35
Standard Deviation, Dollar Average Companies	4.93	3.70	2.84	.63	.57	.55
Standard Deviation, Non-Dollar Average Companies	3.66	2.15	4.26	.42	.47	.44

Source: Computed from the common stock records of the various companies and Schedule D of the annual convention statement.

mathematical assumptions underlying a level of significance test were not fully met in the study, and the results of such tests could not be accepted with complete validity.[10]

AMOUNT OF COMMON STOCK DOLLAR AVERAGED

Table 11 illustrates the amount of common stock purchases by the life insurance companies which dollar average, and it illustrates the relative importance of these acquisitions to the total industry acquisitions.

The data indicate that dollar averaging is becoming relatively more important as a timing device for the acquisition of common stocks. Approximately 14 per cent of the total industry common stock acquisitions were purchased by the dollar averaging technique in 1955, while 27 per cent of the total industry acquisitions were accounted for by the dollar averaging companies in 1960.

It is important to note that common stock purchases are concentrated heavily in a few companies. Of some 1400 life insurance companies domiciled in the United States, the eight companies illustrated in Table 11 accounted for 27 per cent of the total industry purchases of common stock in 1960. Three of the eight companies accounted for 22 per cent of the entire industry purchases of common stock in 1960. One of these companies entered the common stock field in 1959, and it dollar averages $750,00 weekly or $39 million a year. Thus, one company accounts for a large portion of the entire industry purchases of common stock.

---

[10] The author did conduct a series of null hypothesis tests to discover if the differences between the two groups were attributable to chance or to the technique for acquiring stocks. The results of these tests indicated that the null hypothesis could not be rejected, that is, there was no significant difference with respect to capital gains and dividend returns between the two groups. However, the results of these tests could not be accepted with validity because one of the mathematical assumptions, random sampling, was not fulfilled. The data for the non-dollar averaging group were computed from a random sample. The data for the dollar averaging group were not computed from a random sample. Because of the small number of dollar averaging companies, a complete count of the dollar averaging universe was attempted, but the data for some companies were not available. Thus, it was impossible to compare validly a universe mean and a sample mean when the true universe mean was not known.

Table 11. *Common Stock Purchases by Life Insurance Companies Which Dollar Average Compared to the Total Industry Purchases of Common Stock 1955–1960*

($000,000 Omitted)

YEAR	TOTAL COMMON STOCK PURCHASES OF THE LIFE INSURANCE INDUSTRY	COMMON STOCK PURCHASES OF DOLLAR AVERAGE COMPANIES	NUMBER OF DOLLAR AVERAGE COMPANIES	PER CENT OF INDUSTRY PURCHASES BY DOLLAR AVERAGE COMPANIES
1955	$226	$31	3	13.72%
1956	216	32	4	14.81
1957	257	30	7	11.67
1958	277	33	8	11.91
1959	354	71	11	20.06
1960[a]	296	79	8[b]	26.69

[a] The data for 1960 are only to September 30.
[b] The data for four other life insurance companies which dollar average are not available.
Source: Columns 1 and 2 were computed from the *Tally of Life Insurance Statistics,* Institute of Life Insurance, 1955–1960; columns 2, 3, and 4 were computed from data supplied by the dollar averaging companies.

312

EVALUATION OF DOLLAR AVERAGING PLANS
FOR LIFE INSURANCE COMPANIES

ADVANTAGES OF DOLLAR AVERAGING

One advantage of dollar averaging is that the cash flow of a company is better utilized. As stated earlier, most companies have a cash inflow of funds which is very large relative to their cash disbursements. When dollar averaging is employed, price fluctuations can be ignored, and as funds become available for common stock investments, they can be invested immediately with little concern as to the current level of the stock market. However, when the judgment technique is employed, these funds cannot be invested immediately, and the investment officer must wait until the appropriate market level is reached before the common stock investment is made. In the interim period an outlet must be found for these funds which subsequently will be invested in common stocks. The investment officer who is dollar averaging is not concerned with the finding of an outlet to absorb these funds since common stock investments can be made immediately.

Dollar averaging is also desirable when investment experience is limited. Many companies have only recently initiated a common stock program, and their experience with common stocks is limited. Under such circumstances dollar averaging is desirable because the problem of timing is eliminated, and the investment officers are in a much better position to concentrate entirely on stock selection. Also, with limited stock experience, the exercise of judgment as to the proper time to make common stock investments may lead to large amounts being invested at the wrong time. Use of the dollar averaging technique will preclude this possibility.

Finally, dollar averaging is desirable when the stock market is at historically high levels. Many companies initiated their common stock programs at a time of historically high prices, and under such conditions, it would be imprudent to commit all funds at such high levels of the market. Dollar averaging was specifically chosen by many companies because such a technique permitted them to enter the common stock field during a period of high prices, and the risk of purchasing stocks at the wrong time was reduced.

LIMITATIONS OF DOLLAR AVERAGING

Many of the suggested limitations of dollar averaging represent replies received from a second questionnaire which was sent to investment officers who did not utilize dollar averaging in their investment operations. It should be noted that many of the replies represent an erroneous understanding of dollar averaging and are not limitations of the dollar averaging technique, per se.

Stocks Are Purchased When Over-priced. Many investment officers stated that dollar averaging was not employed because a stock may be purchased when it is overpriced—overpriced expressed in terms of a high price-earnings ratio. This argument is erroneous. Under the modified plans which most companies employ, stocks which have high price-earnings ratios relative to the other stocks on the approved list need not be purchased, and the funds can be invested in stocks with lower price-earnings ratios. A company utilizing a modified plan still achieves the primary objective of dollar averaging—elimination of the timing problem—and yet is not committed to the purchase of a stock when it is overpriced.

Common Stocks Receive Little Supervision. Many investment officers stated that common stocks would get little supervision when dollar averaging is employed, and that if the investment outlook for a stock deteriorates, the company is committed to the purchase of a stock under a dollar averaging plan. Therefore, only stocks of inferior quality would be owned. This argument is dubious. Most companies which dollar average have a policy on the switching of stocks, and if the financial condition of a stock deteriorates, the funds are switched to another stock whose financial outlook is more favorable. Examination of the portfolios of many companies indicates that most of the stocks dollar averaged are of the "blue chip" growth variety. Such stocks can hardly be called stocks of inferior quality.

Valuation Factors Are Not Considered. Another argument is that dollar averaging does not consider cyclical factors, fashion and fad, secular trends, or industry outlook. This argument again is erroneous. There is confusion between stock selection and the timing of the purchase of a stock. Dollar averaging does not consider these factors because it is a timing technique and not a device for stock selection. The factors mentioned above belong in the area of stock selection. Whether a company dollar averages or not, it must still select suitable stocks, and there is no justification in assuming that these factors would not be considered by investment officers who dollar average.

Stocks May Be Sold Too Soon or Purchased Too Late. This argument is that dollar averaging will force one to sell stocks too quickly and purchase stocks too late. This argument is completely erroneous. First, dollar averaging is a technique for purchasing a stock and not for selling a stock. The decision to sell a stock is a separate and distinct problem from its purchase. Second, dollar averaging requires the purchase of stocks in a declining market. It is hardly justifiable to state that a company will purchase stocks too late when stocks are purchased during periods of depressed stock prices under the dollar averaging technique.

Alternative Investment Opportunities Are Lost. Some companies believe that alternative investment opportunities must be forsaken when a dollar averaging plan is employed. The argument is that when stock prices are advancing, with a subsequent reduction in yield, the funds which are invested under a dollar averaging plan could be invested in bonds because bonds will usually be declining in price, and bond yields will be more favorable.

There is considerable weight to this argument. In some periods the disparity in yields between stocks and bonds has become very wide. This is illustrated by Table 12 which shows the range of yields between corporation bonds and growth stocks. This disparity between bond yields and stock yields has been an important factor in the termination of a dollar averaging plan by one company. Bond yields were more attractive than stock yields, and the funds which

Table 12. *Comparison of Bond Yields with the Yields from Growth Stocks 1958–1961*

(per cent)

PERIOD	RANGE OF YIELDS AAA AND BAA BONDS	RANGE OF YIELDS FOR MOODY'S TWENTY GROWTH STOCKS
1960–61	4.92%–4.52%	2.34%–1.99%
1959	4.91 –4.40	2.22 –1.91
1958	4.44 –3.96	3.13 –2.18

Source: Computed from Moody's Stock Survey, *passim.*

were invested in stocks under its dollar averaging plan did not permit a maximum yield on the portfolio to be realized, and the plan was discontinued.

This reduction in yield may be partially overcome by dollar averaging income stocks. It should also be noted that if stock yields are declining relative to bond yields, the stock market will be steadily advancing. If this is the case, the current yield which is sacrificed by investing in growth stocks may be recovered in the form of capital appreciation.

CONCLUSION

It would appear that dollar averaging is a suitable technique for common stock purchases in the life insurance industry. The regularity of cash flow, the long term stability of the industry, and the elimination of the timing problem all weigh heavily in the direction of dollar averaging. Most of the arguments advanced against dollar averaging have little or no validity, with the exception, of course, that some alternative investment opportunities must be forsaken at times. Many of the arguments advanced for dollar averaging are cogent, and the characteristics of the industry are of such a nature that a dollar averaging plan can be adapted very easily to the investment operations of life insurance companies.

21. WHAT IS THE PRUDENT POLICY TODAY IN INVESTING PENSION FUND ASSETS?*

❈ John G. Heimann

DURING THE PAST 15 YEARS, a multitude of theories have been argued regarding the investment of pension fund assets. These discussions have ranged far and wide across the investment horizon and have included the extremes of the total fixed fund (insured) to the completely variable fund (100% in common stocks). No two investment theories could conceivably be any more opposite, yet both have been realistically and well defended. The result has been something of a compromise. The trustees of a great majority of pension funds have adopted some of the thinking of both sides, resulting in the practices of the "balanced fund" which includes both fixed and variable types of investment in differing proportions. Let us explore this question of prudence in logical fashion: (1) What is prudence? (2) What is prudent for the trustees of a pension fund? (3) Did the popularly accepted investment policies of the past answer this concept? and (4) What investment policies should be followed at the present time?

The answer begins with *Harvard College v. Amory*[1] where the court stated: "He (the trustee) is to observe how men of prudence, discretion and intelligence manage their own affairs, not in regard

---

* From *The Commercial and Financial Chronicle*, Vol. 194, No. 6098 (Thursday, October 12, 1961), p. 1. Reprinted by permission of *The Commercial and Financial Chronicle*, 25 Park Place, New York 7, New York.
[1] 9 Pick 446, 461 (Mass. 1830).

to speculation, but in regard to the permanent disposition of their funds, considering the probable income as well as the safety of the capital to be invested." This was modified in *Marshall v. Frazier*[2] in which the court recognized some of the realities of human nature by concluding that even prudent men take risks for themselves which should not be assumed for another.

From these earliest decisions, the body of law regarding the actions of a prudent man has been slowly built by court interpretation. An interesting recent study on the prudent man theory and what it means to a trustee can be found in an article by Harold B. Elsom in the *Financial Analyst's Journal*[3] in which he concludes that ". . . the concern for safety of capital dollars is . . . logically, chronologically and technically correct. The sequence . . . shows the idea of safety to be associated with wealth . . . not funds. . . . We have then a reasonable interpretation of court opinion suggesting that wealth protective measures are in order. . . . If safety of wealth rather than a sum certain were ever in question, doubt has been removed." Or, in non-legal language, the courts have strongly suggested that they consider it prudent for a trustee to invest in securities which protect wealth (purchasing power) in addition to or in replacement of those securities which only protect dollar capital.

These factors not withstanding, it is important to realize that the courts have consistently concerned themselves with the problem of "preservation" but nowhere have the courts stated or even intimated that it is the duty of a prudent man to create dollar capital other than that necessary to preserve the purchasing power of those dollars.

However, as far as I know, there has been no court ruling on factors pertaining to what would be considered prudent for the trustee of a pension fund. Therefore, our next step is to examine the requirements of a special type of trust fund—the pension fund—in order to apply our knowledge of prudence to this specific problem.

WHAT IS A PENSION FUND?

The typical pension fund is a trust which has been established to provide a certain schedule of retirement benefits. These benefits are

[2] 80 P. 2nd 42, 55 (Oregon 1938); see also in re Cook's Estate, 171 Atl. 730 (Delaware 1934).
[3] Volume XVI, No. 4, July-August 1960, p. 27.

obtainable by those individuals who are covered by the particular trust and who meet a detailed schedule of requirements. If the covered individual satisfies the requirement, then he is entitled to the benefit which most often is expressed in dollar amounts.

We are all aware of the facts of life in a collectively-bargained industrial society in which the dollar benefit is subject to periodic renegotiation and change. But the trustees' task, at any given moment, is to make certain that the fund is sufficiently sound to meet the existing dollar payment when it comes due. All other considerations are less important.

There are many types of plans available to the trustees and a variety of investment theories from which he can choose. Be this as it may, his primary responsibility does not change regardless of the route finally chosen. His first thought and responsibility is still the preservation of that dollar capital and, if possible, the preservation of the purchasing power of that capital. This is the basic task with which he has been charged.

For many years the theory of dollar capital preservation was paramount with the trustees of pension funds. For this reason, most funds turned to insurance companies, who, for a scheduled premium payment, guaranteed the fixed-dollar benefit. In the 1930's, the insurance companies held the bulk of pension fund reserves. This, however, has changed dramatically during the past 15 years. During the late 1940's, the trustees of many funds became aware that the self-insured method of funding was considerably more attractive than that of purchasing annuities in one form or another. The reasons for this shift were manifold. For one thing, the acceptance by the courts of the theory of preservation of wealth (purchasing power) opened the doors to new types of investment. This factor, combined with the continuation of inflation and the rise in the market values of common stocks, gave impetus to the acceptance of equity investment. Other reasons that contributed to the change included the fact that life insurance companies were taxed on their earnings; whereas the pension fund was a tax-free institution; non-insured funds had greater flexibility concerning contributions and the like; and, in many cases it could be proved that the self-insured fund was less expensive than the insured fund.

The end result of these trends has been an explosive growth in the assets of the self-insured funds. By the end of 1960, 62.0% of total pension fund assets was self-insured compared to 38.0% administered by the insurance companies.

There is little question in my mind that this change in philosophy was "prudent" when it was undertaken in the late 1940's and 1950's. We shall discuss this at greater length later. However, it is worth repeating that this change was a direct result of the acceptance of the theory that "prudence" consisted not only of the preservation of dollar capital but also the preservation of the purchasing power of that capital. The switch to investment in common stocks was a partial recognition of this theory and has, for the most part, proven successful to date.

THE INVESTMENT PROBLEM FOR THE PRUDENT TRUSTEE

Few investment professionals would question the theory that an investment policy must be flexible. A specific approach is valid until (1) either the outlook for the economy or the condition of the securities markets change in such a way as to modify the original investment policy or (2) the specific needs of the fund change sufficiently to require a different policy.

The primary task for the trustee of a pension fund is to undertake an investment program which will preserve both capital and purchasing power. The trustee or his professional advisor is charged with the problem of choosing the investment route which will satisfy these needs most satisfactorily. The solution must be based upon current considerations, in light of historical patterns.

All investors should recognize any investment entails the acceptance of some degree of risk. There is no such thing as a riskless investment, including the retention of cash (the ownership of cash during the past 20 years certainly did not preserve purchasing power even though it preserved capital). For this reason, all investment programs entail the measurement and balance of risk exposure. The more capital is exposed to risk, the greater should be the rewards to the investor. There is nothing new in this theory. It only makes financial sense to expect a higher rate of return from an investment which exposes the investor to a greater degree of risk than from some other type of investment, available at the same time, but whose exposure to risk is less. For this reason, common stocks historically yielded more than corporate bonds and corporate bonds have yielded more than government bonds.

Therefore, in order to answer our question, "What is a prudent investment for a pension fund?" and simultaneously, give recognition to the ever-changing climate of investment markets, I think that it would be fair to divide our question as follows:

1. What can be considered a prudent investment for a pension fund on a long-term basis?

2. What can be considered a prudent investment for a pension fund at the present time?

Since we are now concerned with investment in light of that which we have discovered can be considered prudent, there are additional characteristics of a pension fund that bear importantly upon investment matters. Specifically, a pension fund is tax-exempt; it has a long period of accumulation and distribution of funds; inflow of money may exceed outflow for many years to come; it is not subject to substantial hazard; and, there are no legislative investment restrictions governing the selection of securities other than those that might have been voluntarily included in the trust instrument.

THE EARNINGS FACTOR

In addition, all pension funds have calculated into their basic structure an earnings factor, typically called the actuarial assumption on interest earnings. This figure is arrived at by the fund's actuary when he calculates the cost of the fund. It usually represents a conservative estimate of long-term return and is a minimum earnings objective for the fund. However, if the earnings experience exceeds the actuarial assumption, the benefit to the fund can be considerable. Suppose that the actuarial assumption required for a particular fund is 3%. If, over a period of time, the over-all yield on that fund is 4%, 1% in excess of the actuarial assumption, then in 25 years the fund will have earned sufficient excess funds to provide either a 25% increase in benefits or a 20% savings in costs or some combination of the two.

Before attempting to answer the questions posed previously, we should recognize that any discussion such as this must be essentially general regarding the peculiar requirements of an individual fund. No two funds are exactly alike. Each fund deserves individual attention to its problems so that suitable investment policy can be formed. Our task today is to discuss the general investment problems of this type of fund and to attempt to arrive at an investment philosophy which most closely satisfies the question of prudence. What we discover can be applied to a specific fund and its particular investment portfolio.

The Long-Term Solution

The self-insured fund has available two types of investment; fixed-income securities such as bonds and mortgages and variable-income securities such as common stocks and real estate. Studies based upon statistics collected and collated from 1879 through the present show that the average yield on representative fixed-income securities has been 4.32% per year. For the same perid of time, a broad cross-section of common stocks has shown an annual return of 8.12%, including both dividend earnings and appreciation in the price of the stock. Of this, 4.91% came from dividend income and 3.21% from appreciation.

In recognition of these long-term trends, the investment solution has been the substantial increase in the ownership of common stocks by pension funds. In addition, to the long-term advantage in return over other types of investment which was mentioned previously, the process of investing in common stock was supported by studies which led to the conclusion that, over a long period of time, this type of investment tended to compensate for the steady depreciation in the purchasing power of the dollar. Inflation has accounted for an approximate 2% per year depreciation in the purchasing power of the dollar since the turn of the century, whereas, common stocks have appreciated 3.21% per annum for the same period of time. It is important to recognize that neither inflation nor the rise in the prices of common stocks proceed at the same rate in any given period of time. These patterns are only valuable if viewed as an extremely long-term measurement. There have been periods in our history when there was no inflation and the prices of stocks rose and vice versa.

EQUITY HOLDINGS INCREASED

Because of all these various factors, the percentage of common stocks owned by the funds increased rapidly. This was due not only to a greater allotment of the annual contributions invested in stocks but also due to the rise in common stock prices. During the late 1940's and early 1950's when the common stock philosophy first came to the fore, Moody's Corporate bonds were yielding approximately 3%-3½%, whereas at the same time Moody's 125 Industrial common stocks were yielding between 4% and 7%. Obviously, the attraction of high-grade commons plus the potential capital appreciation possibilities made this type of investment a logical vehicle for the trustees of a self-insured fund.

The end result has been that by 1960 all corporate pension funds showed 43.6% invested in common stocks at market value, compared with 33.1% at book or cost, the 10.2 point differential resulting from the appreciation in prices. Numerous examples of the acceptance of this long-term philosophy can be mentioned. In general, though, it should be sufficient to note that in 1951 only 21.6% of pension fund receipts was invested in common stocks. This rose to approximately 50% by the end of 1960.

This increased reliance upon common stock investment has proven quite successful to date. Even now, any truly long-term extrapolation of historical statistics would continue to favor stock investment for a pension fund. Therefore, in answer to our first question, "What can be considered prudent pension investment for the long-term?", the answer remains in favor of a substantial commitment in common stocks.

However, we must not allow ourselves to be so blinded by history that we stumble over the immediate future. No investment policy can be pursued successfully if it does not consider tomorrow even if its eye is upon the future. A man looking through a pair of binoculars may be able to view a distant object clearly, but if he should take a step while looking at that object and not look down, he could break his neck. A pension fund has much the same problem. Money must be invested continuously, each investment another immediate step. So, perhaps, the time has come for us to look at the ground directly beneath us.

Present Investment Conditions

Most investment professionals will agree, I believe, that the long-term future for our economy is bright barring the incidence of a major catastrophe. It is upon this forecast that a long-term investment in common stock is predicated. Personally, I do not take issue with these predictions, though I must confess that I am not as optimistic as many others. What I would like to investigate, however, is the current relative value of the different types of securities usually purchased by pension funds. This investigation would be pursued in light of past performance, future potentials, and securities which conform most closely to the dictates of prudence within this framework.

This is not to be an essay in market timing, nor will I attempt to guess the future short-term course of market prices. Rather, this is an evaluation of the present opportunities in investment with some judgment as to which type or types of securities are now most attractive for a pension fund.

The stock market reached an all-time high a few weeks ago. Likewise, the evaluation of earnings in relationship to the price of the stock (price times earnings ratio) has approached historical highs. Conversely, as prices have gone up, current yields have dropped so that at the present time they average less than 3% on a broad cross-section of common stocks.

Only four times in the last 80 years have common stock yields been so low (in 1899, in 1933, in 1936, and in July and August 1959). More significant, perhaps, is the fact that since 1880 common stock yields have averaged 3.2% only 13 times. In each instance, stock prices have turned downward not more than 13 months later. The decrease in prices ranged from 16% to 90%; there were 25% to 50% declines in nine of the 13 instances. This relationship between stock price peaks and unusually low dividend yields has appeared regardless of the business cycle or of circumstances such as war, peace, speculative enthusiasm, monetary stringency or ease, etc., and regardless of the trend of dividend payments.

3% Versus 4.91%

This current yield of less than 3% must be considered in light of the long-term yield on common stocks of 4.91%. Our acceptance of this yield indicates that we are willing to pay a premium for our common stocks of 38.9% above the historical values.

Representative bonds, on the other hand, are currently priced to provide a yield somewhat in excess of the 4.32% average on a long-term basis. Presently, Moody's AAA Industrials yield to maturity 4.30% and newly issued corporate bonds provide yields of 4.55% to 5.00% depending upon maturity, quality, and the like. Furthermore, it should be recognized that even though the long-term average yield for bonds is 4.32%, there have been periods in our history for as long as 20 years when bond yields never climbed above 4.00%.

MORTGAGES ATTRACTIVE

Up to this point, we have not discussed mortgages as a form of investment for pension funds, since at the present time they only account for a very small percentage of total pension fund assets. However, interest in mortgage investment is growing rapidly and, in my opinion, rightly so. An investment in mortgages makes a great deal of financial sense for the typical pension fund if they are purchased in proper relationship to the other securities in the fund's portfolio. Skipping the factors of social usefulness and other non-investment considerations, mortgages currently provide an attractive rate of return. For example, a government-insured mortgage, net after servicing charges, is priced to provide a yield to maturity of approximately 5% or better, depending upon location of the underlying property and the like.

This review of current conditions certainly indicates that, on a basis of history, bonds now provide a rate of return somewhat better than the long-term averages, whereas common stocks are so priced as to provide a current rate of return substantially below the long-term average. Plain common sense dictates that we look a lot closer at our common stock investments, since this warning cannot be ignored. Furthermore, any trustee charged with prudence must consider the factor of relative risk. Since his investment choices include securities of varying degrees of risk, he should view with a cold eye those whose purchase involves more risk than those in which his dollar capital is relatively safe.

As pointed out previously, the long-term rate of return for common stocks has averaged 8.12% per year. This is the result of both dividends and price appreciation to which a pension fund draws no distinction because of its tax-exemption. Since our current yield on stocks is approximately 3%, this would indicate that we are looking for an additional 5.12% per annum, either from increased dividends or price appreciation, to remain abreast of the long-term average. Where will this come from, if it is at all available?

EARNINGS CRUCIAL FACTOR

Equity investment is based upon the theory that as a company prospers, so will its stockholders. This will be the result of both increased dividends paid to the stockholder plus appreciation in the price of the stock. For this reason, one of the most important methods of evaluating a particular company's past record is a study of growth or lack of growth in earnings per share. Furthermore, earnings per share are of utmost importance to the stockholder since it is out of earnings that dividends are paid and it is partially out of earnings that a company will finance its future expansion.

We all realize that there are other factors which affect the price of a stock, such as public psychology. But, in the long run, either a company prospers and earns more money for its stockholders or it does not. Since the typical pension fund is a long-term investor and should be concerned with long-term value, this investigation of earnings is of great importance.

If we buy a stock today which yields but 3% and our reason for the purchase of any common stock is predicated upon the long-term efficacy of this form of investment, then we would need an additional 5.12% to keep us even with the average. Since this 5% plus will be a direct result, over the years, of earnings per share, does the specific investment being considered show this type of annual increase for a representative period of time? If it does not and there are no extenuating circumstances, why should it be purchased at all? Let's look at some typical pension fund stock investments and see how they compare with this yardstick.

LOOKING BACKWARD

In 1954 the New York State Banking Department compiled a study of pension funds managed by the major New York City banks on a discretionary basis. At that time, a list was provided of the 10 stocks which were then the favorites of the pension trust departments. I realize, of course, that some of these companies may no longer be in favor with the pension trust departments of those banks and that others may have been added. However, of these 10 stocks seven appeared in the Fall, 1961 edition of "The Favorite 50" indicating that these stocks are still very much in favor with certain segments of the investment community. Each one of these 10 companies has been measured in a way to provide:

> 1. The compound annual rate of increase or decrease in earnings per share.
> 2. The compound annual rate of increase or decrease in market price per share.

Since the end of World War II, no period of time has been what we could fairly title as "typical." Certainly, our present semi-peace, semi-war economy is not typical. Therefore, I have selected two postwar periods of time for this study, 1951-60 and 1957-61 inclusive, (earnings for 1961 are estimated). This dual view should present a fair or at least representative picture of the earnings trends of these companies.

Record Is Illuminating

The accompanying table provides some illuminating facts. For example, during the 10-year period, 1951-60, The Standard & Poor's Composite Index showed an annual rate of increase in earnings per share of 1.5% and an annual rate of increase in the market value of the index of 11.8%. During the latter five-year period, 1957-1961, earnings remained unchanged, whereas market prices went up 6.3%. The figures speak for themselves and are hardly conducive to comfort regarding current market values. Another way of looking at what has happened to the prices of stocks is that they have risen 45% since 1955 when their profits reached an all-time high, a point to which we have not as yet returned. Will corporate earnings justify the faith of the investing public? Perhaps, they will. The point is that the current market is discounting a good portion of the immediate future. They do not represent outstanding values in anyone's book.

Table 1. *Compound Annual Rate of Increase or Decrease in Earnings Per Share and Mean Market Price*

	1951–1960 COMPOUND ANNUAL RATE OF INCREASE OR DECREASE		1957–1961 (a) COMPOUND ANNUAL RATE OF INCREASE OR DECREASE		CURRENT YIELD	ANNUAL INCREASE IN EPS REQUIRED TO EQUAL HIST. AVERAGE
	EARNINGS PER SHARE %	MEAN MARKET PRICE %	EARNINGS PER SHARE %	MEAN MARKET PRICE %	%	%
American Tel. & Tel.*	3.0	6.3	6.5	14.7	3.0	5.12
General Electric*	1.0	18.7	0.3	2.8	2.9	5.22
General Motors	0.7	12.5	(1.5)	0.1	4.4	3.72
IBM*	15.9	27.2	20.2	39.9	0.5	7.62
International Paper*	(3.4)	10.8	(6.3)	(3.8)	2.9	5.22
J. C. Penney	0.0	7.0	1.1	7.9	3.1	5.02
Socony Mobil	1.6	8.7	(5.7)	(5.4)	4.5	3.62
Standard Oil, N.J.*	3.5	12.9	(4.3)	(4.2)	5.1	3.02
Texaco*	8.9	15.8	4.6	10.7	2.9	5.22
Westinghouse	(1.9)	13.0	(b)	9.0	2.8	5.32
Dow Jones Industrials	0.5	11.2	(1.1)	6.3	2.8	5.32
Standard & Poor's Comp. 500	1.5	11.8	0.0	6.3	2.9	5.22

(a) Estimated 1961 earnings.
(b) Earnings for 1956 (base year) distorted due to strike; reported $0.05 per share.
* One of Vicker's Favorite 50 for Investment Companies, Fall 1961.

The table also lists the current return on these 10 companies plus an indication of the rate of growth necessary in earnings per share to justify investment on a historical basis. What we have calculated is the direct result of subtracting current yield from our long-term objective and arriving at a figure which represents the necessary minimum growth in earnings per share in order for that investment to come up to par with the average. Suppose we purchase General Electric with a current yield of 2.9%. This means that we would need an additional 5.22% per annum to achieve the historical standard. Does GE make it on the basis of earnings experience for the past 10 years? Earnings per share grew at a compounded rate of 1.0% and for the latter five-year period at a rate of 0.3%. This does not mean that GE cannot improve its earnings in the future, but past facts indicate the necessity for closely scrutinizing the future prospects of the company.

On the five year basis, only two of these 10 companies would satisfy this requirement—IBM and American Telephone. On the basis of 10 years, three companies make the mark: IBM, Standard Oil of New Jersey, and Texaco. Note, however, that two of the three are international oil companies whose future prospects have dimmed somewhat in recent years. Since the results of this study speak for themselves, I do not wish to belabor that which can be reviewed at leisure. Certainly, it is reasonable to conclude that the prospects of most of these 10 companies are something less than inspiring.

SELECTIVITY VS. AVERAGES

Of necessity, our discussions have concerned themselves thus far with averages. This makes no allowance for better-than-average selectivity of individual investment commitments. There is no substitute for selection, since it should be apparent that all individual investments either are better or worse than the arithmetical average. Investment is not now nor ever has been an absolute science based upon some mathematic formula. Many intangibles come to play in the selection of a security, such as an evaluation of the capabilities of management. Therefore, this factor of selectivity is of major importance. Whether a fund's investment performance will better the averages will depend directly upon the sagacity of the investment policies and investment selection of that fund. This is not predictable.

Therefore, we must concern ourselves with the guideposts of the averages. For this reason, the recommendations which follow must be viewed as a flexible framework within which specific judgments are to be made. There is no one answer which will satisfactorily answer the needs and problems of all pension funds. If there were, it would have been discovered long ago.

An Investment Policy for Today

If an investment policy is to be successful over a long period of time, it must dodge the rigidity of a fixed formula which is applied regardless of current conditions. That which was applicable in the past, may no longer be valid or justified. That which is applicable today, may be discarded in the future not because of a lack of success but because of a fundamental change in those conditions governing the investment policies of a fund. What we must do is evaluate the present in terms of the fund and weigh the alternative investment routes in order to ascertain that which is justifiable for a prudent trustee. The past is a guide, the future is unpredictable. But we are able to evaluate the present.

As mentioned at some length previously, it is the responsibility of a trustee to select his investments in order to protect the dollar capital of the fund and, hopefully, preserve its purchasing power with a minimum of risk. His choice of investments is as broad today as it was in years past. Only the relative positions and values of these securities have changed with the years. Under present conditions, bonds provide a higher yield. Simultaneously, we are all in accord with the idea that, as far as safety of principal is concerned, bonds are a better protection than common stocks. What is prudent today? I think that it is clear that greater emphasis should be given to bond and mortgage investment than in the recent past. If the yield relationships should return to their normal pattern, then the prices of bonds will go up or stock prices will fall or some combination of the two. If on the other hand, history does not repeat itself and the future portends a continuance of higher than common stock yields for bonds, the typical pension fund with its cash flow can easily return to the purchase of common stocks.

THE CASE FOR BONDS

Since I do not believe that it is the province of a trustee to take unwarranted risk, then increasing the emphasis on bond investment in light of all the historical data available would appear to me to be exercising prudent judgment. Obviously, if there is a substantial justification of relative yields between bonds and stocks and we return to a more normal relationship, then another change in policy should be seriously considered.

A further refinement of this thinking would be that applied to the selection of individual stock investments. The best way to approach this problem is to consider for a moment something about the type of stock a fund should not purchase. Since the rationalization of stock ownership for a pension fund is based upon long-term performance, it only makes sense that no commitment should be made in any security which does not equal the average. Certainly, there will be exceptions to the rule. In general, however, this long-term performance is as good a guide as any available and can be applied without too much difficulty.

I do not wish to lay down any hard and fast rule regarding what percentage should be invested in bonds and mortgages versus the percentage in common stocks, at the present time. This can only be judged on a fund by fund basis and depends directly upon its specific requirements. What is the current percentage diversification of assets between these types of securities? How long has it been investing its money? Whatever the specific answers happen to be, and assuming they had been well conceived prior to this time, then I think that a more conservative attitude is warranted in light of present market conditions.

How prudent are your pension investments? The answer is twofold and predicated upon the recognition that prudence is primarily concerned with preservation—the preservation of dollar capital and the preservation of the purchasing power of that dollar capital. Furthermore, this preservation must be accomplished with a minimum acceptance of risk by the prudent trustee.

On a long-term basis, a substantial reliance upon common stocks apparently satisfies the definition of prudence as well as taking advantage of undeniable long-term trends. As far as current policies are concerned, I believe that prudence would dictate some deviation from the long-term solution, namely, more reliance upon bonds and mortgages.

I have attempted to place the investment problem within the framework of current conditions. Surely changes can and will take place in the future, and when they happen our investment programs will change in order to take full advantage of the new conditions. The point to remember is that security markets are hardly static and it is both prudent and sage to seize attractive opportunities when they exist. Any unquestioning reliance upon a fixed formula can lead to disaster.

Prudent investment can be achieved if the trustees are willing to consider objectively the investment alternatives, selecting that medium which will provide the necessary preservation with the least amount of risk under current market conditions. This measurement is not necessarily difficult. It only needs to be done.

22. COMMON STOCKS AND PENSION FUND INVESTING*

❁ Paul L. Howell

Management must develop a dynamic portfolio to keep up with the dynamic economy.

Rising wages, higher living costs, and lower bond yields demand a more dynamic and productive investment policy for the huge pension reserves which are now being accumulated for the protection of the aged. With the development of collective bargaining for "fringe benefits," the responsibility for supplying a major portion of this old-age security is being transferred from the individual to the enterprise that employed him during his working life. Consider these facts and problems of the existing pension fund situation:

Inflation has already doubled and may soon triple the expense of providing this deferred wage benefit for the retired worker. The impact on pension costs of the rising price level is only beginning to be felt by industry as the demand mounts for increased benefits based on higher future terminal wages, together with fuller funding, earlier vesting, and earlier retirement. This impact on costs is forcefully illustrated by the fact that even at the present time one-third of the current pension contributions of the Bell Telephone System are required to make up the inadequacies of past contributions caused

* From *Harvard Business Review*, Vol. 36, No. 6, Nov.-Dec., 1958, pp. 92–106. Reprinted by permission of *Harvard Business Review*.

by subsequently rising wage levels and liberalization of benefits which could not have been forecast when the original accrual rates were established. The pension expense now constitutes over 6% of the Bell payroll, exclusive of OASI taxes.

The percentage of the wage bill attributable to pensions will increase. Walter Reuther, in the pattern-setting negotiations with the Big Three in the automobile industry, has already demanded a "cost of living" adjustment in pensions for auto workers. Moreover, further inflation seems indicated, what with increased defense spending, the Federal Reserve's easy-money policy, Treasury deficits, and recession spending for schools, roads, and so forth. Forward-looking actuaries are suggesting the inclusion of a factor in their cost estimates for secular inflation.

In the implementation of these retirement programs, pension funds have become a new financial giant. These funds are growing at a rate of $4.3 billion a year and currently aggregate $14 billion and $19 billion for insured and corporate-trusteed plans, respectively. The public interest in these industrial pension funds centers around their earning power, since this is fundamental in minimizing the cost of the increased retirement benefits. Current easy-credit policies and the resulting lower interest rates are of special significance, for they reduce the earning power of these funds at a most crucial time.

Of similar importance are the amounts and quality of the fund assets "guaranteeing" the ability of the employer corporation to perform its promise of a deferred wage payment. These accumulating funds may be considered as collateral or a pledge for the specific performance of the employer's promise to pay pension benefits years or even several decades later. Currently, 11 million workers, plus a substantial number of dependents, rely on private noninsured retirement plans as a major portion of their old-age security. To them, the employers' contributions are, in effect, a form of involuntary savings.

With situations such as these in existence, it is appropriate now, after 15 years of mushroom growth, to review the principles and accomplishments of pension fund management. It is the purpose of this article to question the validity of certain customarily accepted institutional thinking and the resultant "orthodox" practices. In essence, one might call this article a study of the more efficient use of a major business resource.

Proposed Approach

Careful analysis of retirement programs brings to light the following factors that are of significance in the current formulation of fund investment policy:

There is an extremely long period of accumulation and distribution of funds. In fact, although employees come and go, there is no prospect that accumulating pension funds will ever be liquidated.

Inflow of money (contributions and earnings) will exceed outgo by a substantial margin for the foreseeable future. Sustained growth of pension funds is to be expected for the next generation.

A qualified pension fund is completely exempt from income and capital gains taxation as a "charitable" trust.

Retirement plans are not subject to catastrophic hazards; retirements and payouts can be forecast years in advance.

There are virtually no legislative investment restrictions.

There is no need to distinguish between principal and income in recording capital appreciation and cash receipts as is required for life tenant or remainderman interests.

Investment-portfolio managers are generally concerned with a few basic specifications. Safety of principal and liquidity are major items of interest. Others include: certainty and adequacy of return, capital appreciation, marketability, collateral value and maturity, and, finally, the tax aspects of the portfolio. The attainment of some of these objectives necessarily conflicts with or limits the achievement of other objectives.

In the light of the framework outlined above, I submit that these five criteria should govern the formulation and execution of pension fund investment policy:

1. In the management of pension funds, their productivity (dividend yield and capital appreciation) should be the primary objective, completely overshadowing all others.

2. As a corollary of this, inflation should not play a part in determining pension fund investment policy. Investment management should get as large a return as is feasible, regardless of stable or rising prices. The only situation in which inflation becomes a factor is the selection of industries and companies which will be benefited or impeded by changing price levels.

3. There is almost complete absence of any need for liquidity.

4. Pension funds should be invested as received, i.e., full investment all the time. This amounts to "dollar-cost averaging."

5. Because of full investment, growth, the absence of catastrophic hazards, and dollar-cost averaging (instead of formula programing), there is little need to take a defensive position with the resultant lowering of over-all portfolio yield.

INCREASING THE RETURN

Most retirement plans are set up on an actuarial expectation of earning 2.5% to 3.0%. Because of the long period of accumulation and subsequent distribution, the rate of return on invested funds is the dominant factor in determining pension costs to employers or benefits to retired workers.

An increase of pension fund yield of 1% (e.g., from 2.5% to 3.5%) will increase benefits approximately 25% or decrease costs about 20%. Needless to say, an increase of benefits to retired employees is of no small significance, whether there are stable prices or inflationary losses of purchasing power, for in many cases industrial pensions are not far above the subsistence level for most workers.

Because of the time period over which compound interest has an opportunity to work its miracle, an increase in the effective return from 2.5% to 6% will increase the accumulations so that benefits can be nearly doubled or costs correspondingly reduced. Is the achievement of a 6% return so difficult or revolutionary? Or is it reasonably attainable in actual conservative practice? I believe that it is attainable, and that a systematic program of periodic purchases of diversified, professionally selected common stocks is the soundest way to achieve the lowest cost or the greatest retirement benefits.

I recognize that a program of 100% investment in common stock is quite contrary to orthodox institutional investment thinking. At the same time, I want to emphasize that my quarrel is not with accepted pension fund objectives—who can dispute the soundness of such goals as liquidity and safety of the principal? Rather, I challenge the appropriateness, under modern conditions, of conventional assumptions as to how these objectives can best be attained. It is time to break out of the strait jacket of past thinking, which, in my opinion, is most inept and extremely costly.

RECORD OVER TIME

What does the record reveal? The monumental investigation of the performance of common stocks by the Cowles Commission[1] shows that the achievement of a 6% return over a sustained period is not impossible. On the contrary, the mediocre results of the market averages do better than 6%. In fact, when the Cowles Commission made its intensive analysis of the market and income results of a broad list of industrial, rail, and utility common stocks, covering the period from just after the Civil War to the middle of the 1930's depression, it found that these stocks averaged a net return (dividends and market appreciation) over this 68-year period of nearly 7%. In detail:

	DIVIDENDS	GAINS	TOTAL
Industrials	5.3%	2.8%	8.1%
Rails	4.8	0.0	4.8
Utilities	5.5	0.6	6.1
Composite	5.0%	1.8%	6.8%

If this study were extended through 1957 it would be found that the average return (dividends and appreciation) would exceed 7.5%.[2]

Similarly, The Dow-Jones industrial average of market prices has increased nearly 3% per year during the past 50 years, with an annual dividend yield exceeding 5% and an earnings payout of less than 60%. As Edgar Lawrence Smith pointed out many years ago, the compound effect of retained earnings upon market performance is enormous.[3] If $100 had been invested in the Dow-Jones industrial average securities each year beginning with 1929, results at the end of 1957 would be as follows:

Total investment	$2,900
Market value (at 1957 average prices)	$8,551
Compound annual increase in market value	6.60%
Total dividends received (29 years); not reinvested	3,903
Average dividend yield on cumulative investment	7.20%
Over-all effective rate of increase	13.80%

[1] Alfred Cowles et al., *Common-Stock Indexes, 1871–1937*, Cowles Commission for Research in Economics, Monograph No. 3 (Bloomington, Principia Press, 1938); see also R. Minturn Sedgwick, "A New Pension Plan," HBR, January-February 1953, p. 70.
[2] See performance of *Standard & Poor's Common Stock Index* during the past two decades.
[3] *Common Stocks as Long Term Investments* (New York, The Macmillan Company, 1924).

That the attainment of a 6% yield is a reasonable pension fund objective is corroborated by the actual accomplishment by conservatively minded life insurance companies during 1929-1955, a period which included one of the most disastrous depressions in our economic history.

While life insurance investment has been predominantly in bonds, there has been sufficient common stock investment to provide a reliable guide to what these institutions have been able to earn in the crucible of actual performance. Combined common stock holdings of 18 representative life insurance companies have grown from $57 million in 1929 to over $700 million today. For the 27-year period, 1929-1955, the over-all rate of total return was 6.49%; this exceeded the bond return by 100%. The earnings experience of these life insurance companies is summarized in Exhibit I. (Many other studies have been made which also confirm this long-run productivity of common stocks.[4])

Exhibit I. *Comparison of Rates of Return Secured on Bonds and on Preferred and Common Stocks by 18 Life Insurance Companies, 1929–1955*

	OVER-ALL RATE OF RETURN*	RATE OF INTEREST OR DIVIDEND RETURN†
Bonds	3.26%	3.15%
Preferred	4.71	4.52
Common	6.49	5.55

* Includes interest earnings (dividend earnings) plus net profits or losses on the disposal of securities.
† Includes interest earnings (dividend earnings) only.
Note: Base is the average cost of the portfolios as of beginning and end of year. The bond portfolios include accrued interest.
Source: James J. O'Leary, 1957 *Record of Life Insurance Investments* (New York, Life Insurance Association of America, December 1957), Table 7, p. 22.

[4] See, for instance, Chelcie C. Bosland, *The Common Stock Theory of Investment* (New York, The Ronald Press Company, 1937); Wilford J. Eiteman, "Yield on Common Stock Investment," *The Analysts Journal*, February 1957, p. 13; Wilford J. Eiteman and Frank P. Smith, "Common Stock Values and Yields," Michigan Business Studies (Ann Arbor, University of Michigan Press, June 1953); Benjamin Graham, "Long Term Outlook for Equities," *The Commercial and Financial Chronicle*, November 27, 1952, p. 4; August Ihlefeld, *Equity Investing by Mutual Savings Banks* (New York, Savings Bank Trust Company, 1953); *A Report in Support of the Proposed Amendments to Article 5, Section 81 of the New York Insurance Law* (New York, Life Insurance Association of America, January 30, 1951); Dwight C. Rose, *A Scientific Approach to Investment Management* (New

It is indeed true that if an entire fund had been invested in 1928 or 1929, history would show that it would take nearly 15 years to recoup itself. But pension funds do not invest huge amounts en masse at the top of a bull market. Regular periodic investment or dollar averaging, during the subsequent depression, would have more than compensated for the losses sustained on the small proportion of funds invested at the height of the stock market boom.

PROFESSIONAL COUNSELING

Who should oversee the handling of pension fund investment policy? Investment management is a complex technical job which requires experienced managerial skill supported by extensive staff research. Such specialized management should show earnings results substantially above the unsupervised averages. A professionally managed common stock fund should earn at least 25% more than does the average unmanaged stock fund. Thus, a professionally managed pension fund should earn, over an extended period, a net return, including allowances for capital losses, in excess of 7.5%.

If such returns are to be realized, the pension fund should have the services of an investment counselor upon whose competence, personal attention, research staff, and continuity of advice the fund can depend. Too often lawyers or accountants are asked to advise when they do not have either the specialized training, a research staff, or the time to devote to this activity. Trust officers, through long adherence to fiduciary principles of protecting the principal of the estate, may not have the proper mental attitude for equity investment.

The professional investment analyst, with his training and staff, can provide the type of direction a fund must have to earn its fullest potential. Moreover, such counseling should be retained on a fee basis (as opposed to the way stockbrokers are compensated) to avoid conflicts of interest where a commission is at stake.

NEED FOR BALANCE?

It is frequently urged that portfolios should contain a "proper" balance. Although this is of the utmost importance in certain types of

---

York, Harper & Brothers, 1928); Winthrop B. Walker, *A Re-examination of Common Stocks as Long Term Investments* (Portland, Maine, Anthoesen Press, 1954); and James J. Jehring, *The Investment and Administration of Profit Sharing Trust Funds* (Evanston, Profit Sharing Research Foundation, 1957).

portfolios, a pension fund has the characteristics of being large, diversified, dollar-averaged, fully invested, long-term, and growing— with almost no need for liquidity. For such a fund there is virtually no need for a bond defense.

There may be times—as in the summer of 1957, when interest rates were high, stock yields low, and stock prices beginning to soften —when it would seem appropriate for an alert management to switch to bonds. This, however, would probably be a short-run operation which might obscure or even defeat the long-run dollar-averaging objective. As a matter of fact, most of such switch investors remained in bonds too long and thus missed out on the market rise in early 1958. Consequently, their over-all investment performance was inferior to those who consistently dollar-averaged in equities. Fixed-dollar obligations, since they are no protection against inflation, may be just as speculative as common stocks. It should be remembered that investment in bonds is not all a bed of roses. Bonds can default, too!

The memory of 1929 and 1932 is still strong. Actually, the stock market fall from 1929 to 1932 offset the previous unwarranted rise. A person who was in equities before 1928 would have found his book losses of 1932–1933 soon converted back into profits. Persons who practiced dollar-cost averaging by systematic stock purchases month by month through this period came out much better than those who kept their funds in fixed-income obligations.

In speaking of balance, it should be recalled that balance refers to the over-all situation. Most pension recipients will be receiving Social Security which, of course, is backed up by government bonds. Also, many will have savings accounts and insurance programs, with perhaps an interest in real estate. These all help provide "balance." Cash reserves in the pension fund do not do the retired worker any good.

HIGHER STANDARDS

Great institutional changes have taken place which make common stock investment increasingly appropriate. And substantial progress has been made in developing financial responsibility and adherence to high fiduciary standards since the Armstrong Insurance Investigation of 1906. Moreover, improved accounting and auditing standards, together with full disclosure and Securities and Exchange Commission (SEC) supervision, have made company reports a sturdy foundation on which to analyze common stock earnings prospects.

Administrative controls of common stock trading, by the stock exchanges and the SEC, likewise provide a much steadier foundation for common stock purchases and subsequent valuations. In addition, current controls by the Federal Reserve Board on margins, credit, and interest rates are far more effective.

Recent legislative events point to a liberalizing of investment thinking. In 1950–1957 New York State amended its laws to allow up to 35% investment in common stocks for nondiscretionary trusts, and for insurance companies, up to 50% of surplus or 5% of assets, whichever is smaller. Commercial banks' commingled trust funds, developed pursuant to Regulation F of the Federal Reserve Board, now hold substantial amounts of common stock.

In brief, the country has matured substantially. Cannot we expect a diversified list of common stocks, professionally selected, to provide, over a long period of time and on a reliable basis, substantially greater net results than a bond fund?

SOME ACCOMPLISHMENTS

In evaluating investment management it is of utmost importance to look at the record and see what has been accomplished. There are, however, several difficulties in comparing the performance of various pension funds:

Many pension funds, for real or fancied reasons, have different managerial objectives. These may be influenced by what is considered to be the best interests of prospective pensioners, by the financial or tax status of the employer, and by the financial status of the pension fund. These varying influences affect management policy and trust-indenture instructions. In fact, it may not be appropriate to compare the operating results of two funds managed by the same trustee. Furthermore, short-term comparisons may be quite inappropriate where one fund is investing for income and another for long-pull capital gains. Nevertheless, market averages do provide a rough standard for measurement of performance.

A serious shortcoming in evaluating management performance is the lack of adequate and reliable data on fund earnings. Despite the public interest in pension funds and the fact that they do not belong to the employer corporation, there is at present only a grudging release of fragmentary data with respect to the composition and earnings of funds. The recent passage during the closing days of the 85th Congress of the Welfare and Pension Plans Act of 1958 should go far in providing these desirable data.

Comparison of actual management performance is currently difficult because of lack of homogeneity of the data. For instance, are comparisons being made on a cost, accrual, or market basis? Are realized capital gains taken into account? What considerations should be weighed in evaluating management performance with respect to unrealized appreciation? Does not the decision to sell or hold assets with capital gains change the resulting yield without changing the actual performance?

Exhibit II. *Distribution by Types of Assets of Corporate Pension Funds, as of December 31, 1957*

(In millions of dollars)

TYPE OF ASSET	AMOUNT — VALUE			PER CENT OF EXCESS MARKET OVER BOOK
	BOOK	PER CENT	MARKET	
Cash and deposits	$ 368	2.9%	$ 368	—
U.S. Government securities	2,032	10.5	1,987	−2.3%
Corporate Bonds	10,392	53.8	9,784	−5.9
Own company	641	—	*	—
Other companies	9,751	—	*	—
Preferred stock	611	3.1	550	−10.0
Common stock	4,770	24.7	6,024	26.2
Own company	584	—	860	47.3
Other companies	4,186	—	5,164	23.2
Mortgages	313	1.6	313	—
Other assets	833	4.3	833	—
Total assets	$19,319	100.0%	$19,859	2.7%

* Data not available.
Source: Securities and Exchange Commission, Statistical Release No. 1533 (June 8, 1958), pp. 3–4.

PORTFOLIO STRUCTURE

Exhibit II shows the fixed-income component of corporate-trusteed pension funds to be 70%. Common stock holdings on a book value basis amount to 25%, while on a market value basis they represent 30% of the combined funds. The distribution of common stock holdings is shown in Exhibit III (derived from the Mooney Report[5]). Common stock holdings of trusteed pension funds are concentrated in the industrial field to the extent of 72%, while bond holdings are concentrated in the utility field. A list of the 20 most popular stocks with pension trustees is set forth in Exhibit IV. On a cost basis, net purchases of common stock aggregating $970 million were made in 1957. This is as much as 37% of net receipts of trusteed funds.

Exhibit III. *Distribution by Industry of Common Stock Holdings of Pension Funds Trusteed with New York Banks, as of September 30, 1954*
(In millions of dollars)

INDUSTRY	AMOUNT	PER CENT
Railroads	$ 11.7	0.9%
Public utilities	181.3	13.4
Industrials	981.0	72.4
Banks & insurance companies	139.6	10.3
Investment companies	26.0	1.9
Finance companies	7.1	0.5
Miscellaneous	8.0	0.6
Total	$1,354.7	100.0%

Source: Mooney Report, Table 3.

Two other points worthy of note are (a) the small amount of preferred stock holdings and (b) the almost insignificant holdings of real estate mortgages and related assets. It is alleged that administrative details deter entrance into this latter field. Insurance companies, however, have overcome these servicing difficulties, and mortgages are the backbone of their earnings assets. Recent proposals

[5] George A. Mooney, *Pension and Other Employee Welfare Plans: A Survey of Funds Held by State and National Banks in New York State* (New York, New York State Banking Department, December 30, 1955).

Exhibit IV. *List of 20 Most Popular Common Stocks Held by Pension Funds Trusteed with New York Banks, as of December 31, 1954*

(In millions of dollars)

COMPANY	NUMBER OF BANKS	MARKET VALUE
Socony Mobil Oil Co.	30	$50.3
J. C. Penney & Co.	17	49.4
General Electric Co.	24	39.4
International Business Machines	15	38.3
Standard Oil Co. (New Jersey)	37	35.6
Texas Co.	21	35.3
American Tel. & Tel.	45	33.4
Westinghouse Electric Co.	29	29.0
General Motors Corp.	29	27.6
International Paper Co.	15	25.6
Union Carbide & Carbon	13	23.0
E. I. Du Pont de Nemours	36	21.9
Gulf Oil Corp.	25	17.3
Standard Oil Co. of California	16	16.5
B. F. Goodrich Co.	9	16.0
Christiana Securities Co.	8	15.5
National Lead Co.	15	15.3
Dow Chemical Co.	21	15.0
Sears, Roebuck & Co.	17	13.9
American Can Co.	17	13.3

Source: Mooney Report, Table 4.

Exhibit V. *Corporate Pension Funds Classified by Industry of Employer*

(In millions of dollars)

INDUSTRY	AMOUNT*	PER CENT	YIELD†
Manufacturing	$12,224	63%	3.83%
Electric, gas, & water	928	5	3.94
Transportation	873	5	4.03
Communication	2,769	14	3.24
Trade	1,528	8	4.57
Financial & real estate	734	4	4.41
Other‡	263	1	3.86
All industries	$19,319	100%	3.84%

* Assets listed at book value.
† Income from dividends, interest, and rent divided by average of assets at book value at beginning and end of year, less one-half investment income; no allowance made for realized or unrealized capital gains.
‡ Extractive, construction, and services.
Source: Securities and Exchange Commission, *op. cit.*, Tables 2 and 4.

have been made for central servicing and should go far to improve the marketability and attractiveness of such an outlet for funds.

The distribution shown in Exhibit II is, of course, not typical of any particular portfolio. There are great individual variations, with some funds invested almost entirely in government bonds while other funds have a substantial proportion of their assets invested in common stock of the employer corporation. Distribution of pension funds according to industrial groups accumulating them and their relative earnings is set forth in Exhibit V.

KINDS OF EARNINGS

Exhibit VI tabulates the reported investment return for 541 pension funds in the fiscal year 1953. From this exhibit it is easily seen that there is substantial variation in the earnings rate of different pension funds. Earnings average about a quarter of a per cent lower when net capital gains are excluded. What is surprising is the number of funds earning less than 3%. (Of course, true comparisons of performance should take into consideration unrealized capital gains, which would make the figures of Exhibit VI higher. Though not an

Exhibit VI. *Distribution of Pension Funds According to the Approximate Rate of Investment Return Earned for Fiscal 1953*

REPORTED RATES OF RETURN (INCLUDING PROFITS AND LOSSES)	NUMBER OF FUNDS	PER CENT OF TOTAL	CUMULATIVE PER CENT OF TOTAL
0.01%–1.99%	15	2.8%	2.8%
2.00 –2.24	7	1.3	4.1
2.25 –2.49	26	4.8	8.9
2.50 –2.74	41	7.6	16.5
2.75 –2.99	87	16.1	32.6
3.00 –3.24	116	21.4	54.0
3.25 –3.49	97	17.9	71.9
3.50 –3.74	70	12.9	84.8
3.75 –3.99	38	7.0	91.8
4.00 –4.49	23	4.3	96.1
4.50 –4.99	10	1.9	98.0
5.00 and over	11	2.0	100.0
Total number of funds	541	100.0%	

Source: Mooney Report, Table 33.

advocate of "counting chickens before they are hatched," I think that capital gains—or losses—are an important aspect of investment proficiency.)

Analysis of the SEC data shows that, except for very small ones, the size of the fund does not seem to be correlated with the rate of return. Small funds, reported as earning much less than other funds, may be new and may not have had a chance to "hit their stride," or they may be funds of small corporations "conservatively" managed with a large holding of governments.

Exhibit VII classifies pension funds managed by New York bank trustees according to whether the trust indenture restricted trustees to "legals" for New York life insurance companies or whether the trustees were permitted general investment discretion. This exhibit shows that discretionary funds earned 56 basis points (i.e., hundredths of 1%) or 19% more than the restricted accounts. Although the restricted accounts include 126 funds, the dollar amount is dominated by the conservative Bell Telephone pension fund.

This differential, of course, does not represent or express the true differential between bonds and common stocks as investments. A number of the so-called discretionary funds are still heavily weighted with fixed-income assets.

IMPORTANCE OF CAPITAL GAINS

Exhibit VIII shows net income from interest and dividends and realized net profits from capital transactions (principally net capital gains) for each of the last three years.

Security and Exchange Commission figures, presented in Exhibit IX, show that the over-all rate of earnings, exclusive of capital gains, was 3.58%, 3.68%, and 3.84% for the past three years. Capital gains would, when added, increase the yield rate to 4.22%, 3.92%, and 3.90%, respectively. When compounded over a number of years, such an increment in yield is an important supplement in fund accumulation.

Net capital gains were not large in 1957, according to Exhibit VIII, because the gross gains realized were greatly reduced by losses, primarily in the bond account. For example, the net earnings rate on the all-bond portfolio of the New York Telephone Company was reduced from 3.23% to 3.02% by the losses sustained on liquidation of governments.

Exhibit VII. *Average Rate of Investment Return Earned on Pension Funds Trusted with New York Banks*

(In millions of dollars)

TYPE OF PORTFOLIO	NUMBER OF FUNDS	AMOUNT	PER CENT	RATE OF RETURN*
Only in "legals" for New York life insurance companies	126	$1,954†	39.9%	2.93%
No general investment restrictions	627	2,051	41.9	3.49
Others	271	890	18.2	—
Total	1,024	$4,895	100.0%	3.18%

* Covers last available year prior to September 30, 1954. Excluded from "earnings" are all profits or losses on sale or redemption of investments. The common stock funds might well have a "real" return of a much larger amount.
† Mostly Bell Telephone System.
Source: Mooney Report, Table 27.

Exhibit VIII. *Analysis of Receipts of Pension Funds, 1955–1957*

(In millions of dollars)

SOURCE	AMOUNT			PER CENT		
	1955	1956	1957	1955	1956	1957
Employer contributions	$1,802	$2,052	$2,303	69.8%	69.7%	69.3%
Employee contributions	222	267	316	8.6	9.1	9.5
Income (interest & dividends)	463	558	677	17.9	18.8	20.3
Net profits realized from capital transactions	84	49	11	3.3	1.7	0.4
Miscellaneous	12	19	15	0.4	0.7	0.5
Total	$2,583	$2,945	$3,322	100.0%	100.0%	100.0%

Source: Securities and Exchange Commission, *op. cit.*, Table 3.

Exhibit IX. *Rate of Return Earned on Corporate Pension Funds Compared with Earnings of Insurance Companies, 1951–1957*

| | | INSURANCE COMPANIES | |
YEAR	PENSION FUNDS*	BEFORE FEDERAL INCOME TAX	AFTER FEDERAL INCOME TAX
1951	3.05%	3.18%	2.98%
1952	3.21	3.28	3.07
1953	3.34	3.36	3.15
1954	3.65	3.46	3.24
1955	3.58	3.51	3.23
1956	3.68	3.63	3.33
1957	3.84	3.75	3.44

* No adjustment for capital gains or losses sustained.

Note: For 1951-1954, return computed as follows: income from dividends, interest, and rent divided by average of assets at book value at beginning and end of year for universe data. For 1955-1957, return computed as follows: averages of assets at book value at beginning and end of year, less one-half of investment income.

Source: Vito Natrella, *Implications of Pension Fund Accumulations*, Proceedings of the Business and Economic Statistics Section of the American Statistical Association (Washington, 1957), pp. 140 ff; Securities and Exchange Commission, *Survey of Corporate Pension Funds*, 1951-1954 (Washington, 1956), Table 8, p. 32; Securities and Exchange Commission, Statistical Release No. 1533 (June 8, 1958), Table 4; and Institute of Life Insurance, *Life Insurance Fact Book* (New York, 1957), p. 55.

The importance, however, of common stocks and capital gains for pension funds is greatly understated even in these figures, because:

In the first place, the common stock component of pension funds is still relatively small as a per cent of the total fund. Thus, realized capital gains represent a very substantial addition to the dividend income of common stocks.

A large amount of the capital gains realized on common stocks was used to offset losses on the bond account, such as liquidation of governments.

Another factor that does not show in the realized-gains figures is the fact that most of the common stock held by pension funds has been of recent acquisition and that it takes time for capital to appreciate.

Another factor, and one of great importance, is that a large amount of capital gains is below the surface—unrealized and only occasionally recognized. The fact that these gains are unrealized does not make them any less important in achieving the long-run fund objectives. There is not much point in simply selling stocks to record the capital gain. The fact that these gains exist is of extreme significance in helping to fund liabilities and to pay future benefits.

It is a conventional, and probably sound, accounting practice in most business situations not to record unrealized capital appreciation—sometimes referred to as "paper profits." Nevertheless, it is absolutely necessary to consider such gains in making valid or appropriate comparisons of fund policy and performance. To leave such gains out of consideration would be to omit an essential element.

APPRECIATION GIVES PROTECTION

Although an increase in earnings of 10% (or 35 basis points) resulting from realized capital gains is not to be dismissed lightly, the magnitude of unrealized capital appreciation is even larger and should become still more important as larger proportions of common stock are held, and held for longer periods of time. For example, Exhibit II contrasts the book cost and market values of pension assets as of the end of 1957, after interest rates and stock prices had reached a peak. Government and corporate bonds showed unrealized capital losses of 2.3% and 5.9%, respectively, and fixed-dividend preferred stock showed a decline of 10.0%; but common stock, which probably had an average holding of less than four years, showed an appreciation of 26%.

Thus, the common stock component provided a net over-all portfolio appreciation of 2.7% on funds reporting to the SEC. Instead of bonds being a defensive protection, common stock appreciation provided the protective reserve against fluctuations in the interest rate. The sometimes maligned common stock came to the rescue of the "conservative bonds." Of course, for pension funds these short-term fluctuations are largely irrelevant; my thesis is that only the earnings—current receipts and appreciation over the long run—are important.

Although the dividend yield on current market price may be quite modest, when the dividend income is related to invested capital the return is often surprisingly high. A 6% return on a stock which has doubled in market value means a 12% return on book cost. For example, Consolidated Edison Company of New York, Inc., which is not considered a dynamic growth utility, sold for an average price of about $25 in 1949, with a dividend of $1.60 to yield 6.40%. As of the middle of 1958, the stock was paying $2.80 to yield 5.10% on its market price of $55. In terms of 1949 investment cost of $25, the actual dividend yield experienced is 11.40% with a market appreciation of 100% lurking in the background in case of sale at some future date.

The unrealized capital appreciation can also act as a "hidden reserve." Because of market swings and actuaries' desire for continuity and stability, it is appropriate—in fact, almost imperative—that a reserve be set up. Treasury regulations, however, prevent employer corporations from setting up any portfolio reserves out of deductible contributions or even out of realized capital gains on the contention that the pension liabilities would be overfunded. In lieu of such formal reserves, market appreciation can be used as a "hidden reserve."

A CONSERVATIVE CASE

An illustration of a conservatively managed pension portfolio is that of the Bell Telephone System. This is a noncontributory plan which now covers almost a million employees and pensioners in the 33 corporations that make up the Bell System. Pension fund reserves for each corporate entity are kept separate. Founded in 1913, the fund is by far the largest private industrial fund in the country, with its aggregate investment of $2.6 billion. It is growing at the rate of nearly $1 million every working day.

In 1938 the Bell System management completely reversed itself from its previous policy of investing 100% in telephone properties and went to a policy of 100% investment in a diversified bond portfolio with no member company holding its own bonds. In that year the pension fund trustee (Bankers Trust Company of New York) was instructed by the company's board of directors to invest the pension fund assets solely in "legals" for New York insurance companies. Furthermore, investments were restricted to governments, municipals, and obligations of domestic corporations of the highest quality. This has been construed to mean bonds rated "A" or better, and to exclude railroad equipment certificates, sale and leaseback properties, and real estate mortgages.

The wisdom of limiting investments only to high-grade bonds conflicts with the findings of the monumental bond survey undertaken by the National Bureau of Economic Research. This study reveals that, despite their greater loss ratio, the net investment return from lower-grade bonds exceeds that of top-rated bonds because of the importance of yield differential.[6] Thus, while there is danger to small funds in low-quality bonds, with diversification there is safety and greater yield. Since 1945, the New York Telephone Company pension fund (which is slightly more than 10% of the Bell System) has earned an average of 2.77%. This is 24 basis points less than the average cost of its "Aaa"-rated mortgage bonds.

COMPARATIVE EARNINGS

It is interesting to note (see Exhibit X) that during the postwar period gains and losses on the sale of securities have made a considerable difference in earnings in particular years, but have been a small factor over the entire period. As with all big funds, the Bell System earnings rate has a substantial inertia from past commitments. On funds invested during 1957 the Bell companies achieved a return in the neighborhood of 3.96%. In 1957 the American Telephone & Telegraph Company's pension fund earned approximately 3.19%, excluding gains or losses on sales of securities, and earned 3.06%, including capital transactions. As of December 31, 1957, the market value of its portfolio was about 7% below the amortized book cost.

Exhibit X also presents a comparison of the Bell pension fund earnings with those of leading life insurance companies, most of which are qualified to do business in New York State. The earnings of Metropolitan Life Insurance are also shown separately. It is important to note in comparing investment results that pension funds pay no federal income taxes, while insurance companies do.

It is also instructive to contrast Bell pension fund earnings with those achieved in alternative investment opportunities. As Exhibit XI shows, the dividend yield on AT&T common stock (which is not noted for its growth characteristics) is 5.53% for the 12 postwar years. If allowance were made for the value of rights received during this period, the yield would have been over 6.50%. AT&T's dividend yield has averaged approximately 6% since the retirement program was installed in 1913. The returns on Moody's utilities and on life insurance company investments, by class of security, are also set forth in Exhibit XI.

[6] W. Braddock Hickman, *Corporate Bond Quality and Investor Experience* (New York, National Bureau of Economic Research, 1958).

Exhibit X. *New York Telephone Company Pension Fund Earnings Rate Compared with Earnings Rate of United States Life Insurance Companies*

	N. Y. TELEPHONE PENSION FUND			N. Y. TELEPHONE DEBT COST	LIFE INSURANCE COMPANIES' EARNINGS		METROPOLITAN LIFE'S EARNINGS BEFORE FEDERAL INCOME TAX‡
YEAR	AVERAGE BALANCE (MILLIONS OF DOLLARS)	NET RATE EARNED*	EARNINGS†		BEFORE FEDERAL INCOME TAX	AFTER FEDERAL INCOME TAX	
1946	$ 79.8	2.64%	2.53%	3.21%	2.99%	2.89%	3.01%
1947	91.5	2.51	2.53	3.08	2.88	2.88	2.94
1948	105.3	2.58	2.58	2.87	2.96	2.96	3.03
1949	121.0	2.66	2.65	2.85	3.06	2.98	3.07
1950	138.6	2.77	2.67	2.95	3.13	3.00	3.07
1951	157.6	2.65	2.71	2.86	3.18	2.98	3.07
1952	178.2	2.67	2.83	2.90	3.28	3.07	3.21
1953	201.3	2.96	2.93	3.03	3.26	3.15	3.31
1954	226.2	3.05	2.99	3.31	3.46	3.24	3.41
1955	250.8	2.99	2.99	2.95	3.51	3.23	3.48
1956	274.8	2.74	3.06	2.87	3.63	3.23	3.65
1957	299.3	3.02	3.23	3.15	3.75	3.44	3.75
Average		2.77%	2.81%	3.01%	3.25%	3.08%	3.25%

* Determined by dividing the net amount realized for each year, including profit or loss on sale or redemption of fund assets, by the average of beginning and end-of-year balances in the fund, less one-half of the net amount realized. Trustee's fee (ranging from 2 to 4 basis points of yield) deducted to compute the net earnings rate.

† Before adjustment for realized capital gains and losses.

‡ After all investment expenses and charges, such as real estate taxes, depreciation, acquisition and servicing fees, mortgage loans, operating cost of housing, and proportionate amount of company overhead at head office (salaries, etc. of investment department).

Sources: Institute of Life Insurance, *Life Insurance Fact Book* (New York, 1957); Metropolitan Life Insurance Company, *Annual Reports* (New York, 1946-1957); and American Telephone & Telegraph Company, Treasury Office.

Exhibit XI. *Earnings Achieved in Alternative Investment Opportunities, 1946–1957*

| YEAR | AT&T DIVIDEND YIELD* | MOODY'S UTILITIES | | 18 LIFE INSURANCE COMPANIES† | | |
| | | YIELD "AA" | 24 PUBLIC UTILITY STOCKS | EXPERIENCED RATE OF RETURN | | |
				BONDS	PREFERRED	COMMON
1946	4.85%	2.58%	4.23%	3.09%	4.71%	5.17%
1947	5.58	2.67	5.32	2.78	4.46	4.82
1948	5.91	2.92	5.85	2.84	4.57	5.35
1949	6.22	2.76	5.86	2.96	4.16	5.28
1950	5.91	2.66	5.66	3.07	4.47	6.22
1951	5.77	2.95	5.77	2.94	4.50	8.63
1952	5.81	3.05	5.39	3.05	4.41	7.65
1953	5.77	3.32	5.33	3.11	4.36	7.38
1954	5.35	3.00	4.81	3.35	5.06	8.32
1955	4.98	3.13	4.50	3.29	4.94	10.02
1956	5.03	3.43	4.68	‡	‡	‡
1957	5.19	4.03	4.92	‡	‡	‡
Average	5.53%	3.04%	5.20%	3.04%	4.56%	6.88%

* If the $9 dividend were augmented by the average market value of the rights received for the postwar period, the experienced yield on AT&T common stock would be over 6.50%.

† James J. O'Leary, *op. cit.* (Exhibit I); includes realized gains and losses.

‡ Data not available.

From these data, it is seen that the earnings on the Bell System pension fund are substantially less than the yield on its own common stock and less than the average net earnings for life insurance companies, which have to pay taxes.

The Bell pension fund investment policy was drafted in the light of the depressed economic conditions that existed during the early 1930's. Twenty years have passed since the last major change in investment policy. Is not a more dynamic, aggressive, and enterprising investment policy needed—at least, for the typical fund today? Many other funds do earn substantially more with safety— and even at that their averages are mediocre (3.84% in 1957, according to SEC figures). It is time to undertake a review of portfolio policy, considering the comparative record of bonds and stocks from the point of view of stability, capital appreciation, earnings, and purchasing power.[7]

A Dynamic Portfolio

By way of contrast, let us now look at the pension fund of the General Electric Company. Starting in 1912, GE pioneered a liberal retirement program on a "pay as you go" basis. As experience accumulated, the wisdom of voluntary funding became apparent. In 1927 a separate trust fund was set up and administered by the company. GE, unlike most industrials, has had a long investment experience. In fact, Electric Bond & Share Company, formerly a subsidiary, was formed by GE in 1904 to help buyers finance costly electrical equipment.

The investment management of these accumulating funds falls into distinct periods:

When funding was begun in 1927, the assets of the pension trust were invested in notes of the Electrical Securities Corporation, whose common stock was owned by GE. In turn, the Electrical Securities Corporation invested in a diversified portfolio.

---

[7] In line with the author's recommendation the American Telephone & Telegraph Company announced on September 11, 1958, a basic change in the investment policy for its pension fund. The trustee is now authorized to purchase listed common stocks in amounts not to exceed 10% of the total fund. No limitation, other than the listing requirement, was placed on the trustee's discretion as to individual selections. It is expected that the common stock component will not reach this modest percentage for several years and will include shares of AT&T. Preferred stocks and mortgages remain in the excluded category. — The Editors

Nearly 20 years later, in 1946, Electrical Securities Corporation was dissolved and the pension fund assets invested entirely in government bonds.

In 1947—in response to changing times—a more flexible approach was adopted for these funds, which had by then accumulated to $150 million. Policy was altered to permit investments in "legals" for New York life insurance companies, which at that time included corporate bonds, mortgages, preferred stock—but no common stock.

With further postwar economic changes taking place, management remained flexible and continued to shift its position. In 1950 a decision to go into equities was made after careful consideration and was executed according to a detailed plan worked out in advance. This permitted the purchase of common stocks on a dollar-averaging basis with provision for accelerated purchases on market declines.

The reasons stated for following a stock purchase program were: (a) to secure a higher yield, and (b) to set up a hedge against inflation. A higher yield offered the advantage, of course, of reducing the funding cost of the plan. Prior to 1950 it had sometimes been difficult to obtain a $2\frac{1}{2}\%$ rate to meet the actuarial requirements. The investment managers of the fund felt that if bond quality were to be sacrificed in order to secure a higher yield, there would be few, if any, capital gains to offset the inevitable losses of principal on the lower-grade obligations. Consequently, a partial solution to the problem was the inclusion of a limited amount of carefully selected equities in the portfolio. However, preferred stocks have been left out of the program in favor of common stocks because it was felt that the yield on preferred stocks was not sufficiently above that obtainable on bonds to justify the purchase. Bonds also have the maturity and cash flowback features that preferred stocks lack.

Thus, GE feels that securities which represent ownership can reasonably be expected to grow in both value and income return as the economy grows. Careful consideration has been given to the effect of decreased dividends during a period of recession. With 30% of the fund in common stocks, dividends can be reduced about 40% below the average 5% rate before the fund as a whole will earn less than 3%.

STRUCTURE & SIZE

Exhibit XII sets forth in detail the changing structure of the GE pension fund during the postwar period. The decline in government bonds and the increase in diversified common stock holding are noteworthy. GE's thinking on the common stock component is not fixed. Currently management is inching above its earlier limit of 30%. In addition, the fund trustees have raised their investment horizon and have included commitments in industrial mortgages, sales and leasebacks, and oil-production participations (an equity-type security).

The GE pension fund has nearly quintupled in the last decade. Currently the fund is increasing at the rate of $88 million a year. This yearly increment, plus maturities and switches to more attractive investments, requires new investment commitments approaching $500,000 each working day. A fund which is growing so rapidly is, of course, constantly faced with broad questions of investment policy, with a tremendous need for flexibility of administration.

RELATIVE EARNINGS

The earnings of the GE fund should be analyzed in relation to the structure of the fund, as set forth in Exhibit XII. With changing interest rates one cannot make too dogmatic a deduction, but it does seem fair to conclude that the increasing common stock proportion has had a definite influence in increasing the over-all yield. This exhibit also sets forth the "going rate of return," as of the year end, on amortized book value. Note that realized capital gains are not included.

A forceful illustration of the extent to which common stocks can provide not only an increase in earning capacity but also re-

Exhibit XII. *Structure and Earnings of the General Electric Company Pension Fund Portfolio*

YEAR END	U.S. GOVERNMENT BONDS	OTHER FIXED INCOME	MISCELLA-NEOUS	COMMON STOCKS	GOING RATE OF RETURN
1947	98%	2%	—	—	2.20%
1950	33	63	—	4%	2.74
1952	17	73	—	10	3.15
1954	13	70	2%	15	3.40
1957	7	53	9	31	3.80

Source: General Electric Company, Pension Investment Department.

Exhibit XIII. *Analysis of Market Values and Capital Gains of the Electric Company Pension Fund, December 31, 1957*
(In millions of dollars)

HOLDINGS	BOOK VALUE	MARKET VALUE	DIFFERENCE AMOUNT	DIFFERENCE PER CENT
Cash & Receivables	$ 21.4	$ 21.4	—	—
U.S. Government bonds	52.8	49.9	—$ 2.9	—5.5%
Corporation bonds	412.9	380.9	— 32.0	—7.8
Common stocks	242.2	283.7	41.5	17.1
Miscellaneous	74.1	74.1	—	—
Total	$803.4	$810.0	$ 6.6	0.8%

Source: General Electric Company, Pension Investment Department.

serve for market fluctuations is set forth in Exhibit XIII, which compares the amortized book and market values as of the end of 1957. The $41 million of common stock market appreciation is indeed an important "hidden reserve" or an important adjunct to the formally reported earnings. This appreciation more than offsets the market depreciation in the larger defensive portion.

The importance of the capital appreciation should be related to the average life of the common stock portion of the fund, which, at the end of 1957, was about three years. A $41 million unrealized appreciation in seven years on the common stock component, which has averaged less than $90 million (from zero at the beginning of 1950 to $242 million book value at the end of 1957—see Exhibits XII and XIII) is very substantial indeed. It would be most interesting if the GE pension fund accountants segregated the equity earnings from the fixed-income earnings return and compared the two yields, both before and after capital gain.

STOCK SELECTION

Although the portfolio is under continuous study and is in a perpetual state of flux, a basic diversification pattern for stocks has been followed. In early 1958, about one-half of the common stock fund was in oils, chemicals, and utilities. Around one-quarter of the common stock portion of the portfolio was in retail trade, foods, automobiles and accessories, and building. The balance was spread over other groups of industries.

No more than 4% of the stock component is put into any one company, and no more than 1% of a corporation's outstanding stock is ever held. Depending on the relative attractiveness of current yields, the trustees may go all the way from putting all of the new money in common stock to committing themselves for months in advance for private placements. Though self-administered, the GE treasury department retains outside investment counsel.

While the principle of dollar averaging has been followed in buying common stocks, purchases are not made straight across the board. Furthermore, purchases are not made every day, open orders are not given at the market, and there is no individual stock purchased at regular intervals. Rather, purchases of common stocks are made selectively from an approved list of about 85 stocks on the basis of whichever selected issues seem to be the most attractive. The stock purchase policy also calls for accelerated purchases with a falling market, with emphasis on stocks which have been the hardest hit.

Although the past is no sure guide for the future, the experience of the GE fund to date has been most favorable. A conservatively enterprising investment policy has been followed. A modest portion of common stock has assisted in increasing the net yield and has augmented its value with substantial capital gains. The important thing is that the management has adopted a dynamic and adaptable investment policy for our changing world.

CREF—Variable Annuity

Postwar declining purchasing power has resulted in an intense interest in variable annuity retirement plans.[8] Unlike the Bell pension, which has been wholly in bonds, or the GE pension, only partly in equities, these funds are invested wholly in equities. The recent court holding that variable annuity contracts could be sold by insurance companies without registration with the SEC has provided further advancement for this new development.[9]

[8] See William C. Greenough, *A New Approach to Retirement Income* (New York, Teachers Insurance and Annuity Association, 1951); and Leonard E. Morrissey, "Dispute Over the Variable Annuity," HBR, January-February 1957, p. 75.
[9] *SEC v. Variable Annuity Life Insurance Co. et al.*, May 22, 1958, Docket No. 14253, U. S. Court of Appeals for the District of Columbia.

Variable annuity retirement plans have now been adopted by over 30 employer organizations. Among these are the air transport industry, the Wisconsin State Employees Retirement Fund, the Tennessee Valley Authority, and Atlas Corporation.

INVESTMENT LESSON

College Retirement Equities Fund (CREF), set up by the Teachers Insurance and Annuity Association in 1952, led the way. From the start, CREF funds have been invested in a diversified list of quality common stocks which had a market value, as of the end of the fiscal year March 31, 1958, of $55 million. Already $8 million of unrealized appreciation has been accumulated during its short existence.

The investment performance of the fund is compartively easy to measure. Monthly joint teacher-university contributions buy "accumulation units," much as periodic purchases might buy shares in an open-end investment company. Dividends received on the fund's holdings are credited to participants in the form of additional accumulation units. Thus, the value of each unit is an exact measure of price changes in the fund's stocks and is directly comparable with stock averages like Dow-Jones and the others. As shown in Exhibit XIV, the accumulation unit has grown from $10.00 to $18.45, an

Exhibit XIV. *College Retirement Equities Fund Earnings and Capital Gains*

FISCAL YEAR ENDING MARCH 31	TOTAL MARKET VALUE (MILLIONS OF DOLLARS)	ACCUMULA- TION UNIT VALUE*	PER CENT OF APPRECIATION	CREF DIVIDEND RATE†	TIAA YIELD‡
1953	$ 1.8	$10.00	–	4.43%	3.33
1954	7.6	11.46	14.6%	4.04	3.48
1955	17.9	15.17	32.4	3.34	3.51
1956	33.0	19.84	30.8	2.84	3.58
1957	41.2	18.37	−7.4	3.23	3.70
1958	55.8	18.45	0.4	3.36	3.78

* Accumulation unit values stated at market price; the most recent figure (September 30, 1958) is $21.76.
† Yield on market value at end of period.
‡ Yields computed on the usual life insurance formula and for calendar years; i.e., they should be set back three months.

increase of 84.5% in five fiscal years. On a compound interest basis, this rate of growth exceeds 13% annually. Supplemented by the reinvestment of the cash dividends in additional units, a participation purchased early in 1953 has more than doubled in total worth five years later. And as of July 31, 1958, the accumulation unit alone has further increased from $18.45 to $20.71.

Although five years is too short a period to make sweeping, long-run investment generalizations, the contrast between CREF and any fixed-income fund, including the Teachers Insurance Annuity Association, is disconcertingly sharp. It should be emphasized that this is an actual and not a theoretical performance. Whatever the future may bring, there has already been created a substantial amount of capital appreciation to cushion any future market declines and still to maintain a substantial earnings differential over bond fund performance. The investment lesson of the competitive advantage of common stock is most evident.

Union Funds

The investment policies of the GE fund and certain other corporate-trusteed funds contrast sharply with the policies of funds administered by unions for the benefit of their members. The latter are noteworthy for their extreme conservatism and poor investment performance. For example:

The Amalgamated Clothing Workers union has a sizable retirement fund invested, as of the end of 1957, as follows:

U.S. Government bonds	$44,500,000
Cash	8,400,000
Other assets	400,000
Total	$53,300,000

There is almost a complete absence of any investment management, and there is no diversification. The fund also shows a lack of alert management in that 15% of it is in idle cash. In 1957 earnings of $1,200,000 provided a return of only 2.35% on the average fund, and there still appears to be little attempt to obtain better yields. In fact, at the end of 1957, the market value of the portfolio had declined as much as $1,800,000 below purchase price.

Again, International Ladies' Garment Workers' Union has a pension fund which was invested as follows at the end of 1957:

Cash accounts	$ 3,000,000
Savings	3,600,000
U.S. Government bonds	93,400,000
East River Housing bonds	4,700,000
VA and FHA mortgages	6,000,000
Other	800,000
Total resources	$111,500,000

Like the Amalgamated Clothing Workers fund, the Garment Workers fund is heavily committed to government securities. However, it has broadened its investment horizon. A controller with financial experience has been appointed to administer the fund. Recently, it was announced by David Dubinsky that the fund was going into the corporate-bond market. This is a slight improvement, but at this rate it will take years to reconstitute the fund on a more economic basis.

The high-minded officials who set up the Amalgamated Clothing Workers and Garment Workers pension funds in the pioneer days leaned over backwards to prevent any possible mismanagement. These funds were surrounded with safeguards for the prevention of "loss" either through individual crookedness or managerial incompetence, and were put into cash, savings accounts, and government securities because they represented the most conservative type of investments.[10]

Unions still are reluctant to invest in corporate securities, not only because of their unfamiliarity with investment finance, but also because of the belief that such a commitment of funds would constitute an unholy alliance with the employer group, with whom they like to deal at arm's length. Here a basic and, as yet, unresolved conflict arises. If the union wants a high return on its investment, must it support management in its effort to make more profits and thus to keep costs, including wages, low? Should picket lines be observed or products boycotted when that means a lower return on the union fund?

---

[10] Paul L. Howell, "Investment Management of Union Pension Funds," *The Commercial and Financial Chronicle*, August 1, 1957, p. 11.

AN EXCEPTIONAL CASE

In striking contrast, the enterprising policies adopted by the Amalgamated Lithographers of America are an exception to the union rule. The First National City Bank of New York has been appointed investment advisory agent and custodian for the Lithographers pension fund. The bank has been directed to exercise its discretion in making investments for the fund as long as it does not put more than 15% of the portfolio in preferred stocks and not more than 10% in common stocks. The balance of the portfolio handled by the bank must consist of government and corporate bonds. The results, as of March 31, 1957, are shown in Exhibit XV.

Exhibit XV.   *The Portfolio of Amalgamated Lithographers of America Pension Fund*

TYPE OF SECURITY	BOOK VALUE	RATIO	YIELD ON BOOK VALUE
U.S. Government bonds	$ 4,300,000	27%	2.53%
Public utility bonds	5,300,000	34	3.22
Industrial bonds	2,000,000	12	3.42
Railroad bonds	400,000	2	3.58
Preferred stocks	1,900,000	12	4.16
Common stocks	1,400,000	9	3.89
First mortgages	600,000	4	4.18
	$15,900,000	100%	3.27%

A shortcoming of the Amalgamated Lithographers setup is that union members must pay income taxes on all contributions to the fund since the employers make no direct contribution. To avoid Taft-Hartley Act surveillance, when the fund was set up in 1947 an increase in wages and dues was negotiated instead of pension fringe benefits. Furthermore, although currently segregated from other treasury funds, the fund does not appear to be irrevocably dedicated to pensions, but is subject, under certain conditions, to reversion into the general union treasury. The rights of the union members in these funds are only vaguely defined by the general wording of the union constitution. Funding and vesting appear to be insecure.

CONCLUSIONS

To sum up, I believe that six conclusions are justified by a careful examination of past experience in pension fund investment and of developing trends in the economy.

1. Pension costs will continue to rise because of: the demand for more adequate benefits in relation to a given level of wages, rising wage levels that make past contributions inadequate, and the trend toward earlier vesting to give greater coverage and mobility to labor.

2. Pension funds, although not a formal asset of the employer corporation, are nevertheless an important industrial resource which can be utilized to reduce wage costs. Better earnings (yield and appreciation) are the only effective method of holding pension costs to a minimum. Therefore, every effort should be made to invest pension funds so that they will earn the greatest return possible over the long run.

3. Investment is a complex, technical job requiring the highest skill and adherence to fiduciary responsibilities. Corporate management, just as in many other fields, needs expert, independent, professional investment counsel, without conflicts of interest. Good advice is worth many times its cost.

4. Earnings and appreciation are jointly of the utmost importance in providing retirement benefits because of the duration of the investment period and the absence of the need for liquidity. History demonstrates that a well-diversified list of professionally selected common stocks will, over the long run—and taking into consideration cash dividends and capital appreciation—earn a substantial differential over fixed-income obligations.

5. Insured pension plans which must operate under severe investment limitations and pay taxes are at a distinct disadvantage compared with nonrestricted trusteed funds that can participate in the growth of the economy through holdings of good common stocks.

6. There is imperative need for a more aggressive and enterprising investment policy in the management of pension funds. Retirement benefits that are based on low earning power of bonds become an expensive luxury for stockholders and consumers and a source of hardship to the aged. In the long run, pensions will be no sounder than the industrial economy to which they are tied. Everybody concerned—employers, employees, and the financial institutions—should move away from the concept that a pension plan can provide iron-clad financial guarantees into a recognition that it is essentially a cooperative effort to accumulate an old-age savings reserve.

The end result may well be a dynamic investment policy which will lie somewhere between the ultraconservatism of many trustees and insurance companies, on the one hand, and the very liberal policies of some of the investment trusts, on the other hand.

PORTFOLIO MANAGEMENT AND TECHNICAL MARKET FACTORS

V ❀

INTRODUCTION

TECHNICAL MARKET ANALYSIS is both fact and fetish, and the prudent securities manager must respect the many approaches to security market actions which are combined under the term "technical analysis." There is a rising interest in technical analysis among professional money managers. There is also a militant response by critics of technical techniques who, while not using the various mechanical forecasting devices, nevertheless cannot completely ignore them. Many investors and money managers may reduce the frustrations of investment management by using some mechanical aids to analyze market patterns. Many believe the security markets themselves hold, in their history, the secret of future price movements of the securities traded within these markets.

The first essay by Professor Harry V. Roberts examines the rationale of using historical market patterns to predict the future behavior of security prices. He emphasizes the possibility that stock market behavior may be the simplest of all economic time series by exploring the chance model and its application to security prices movements. A seasoned writer on investment management, A. Wilfred May, attempts to refute the mechanistic emphasis on stock market forecasting. He presents a balanced argument of theory and practice, and highlights the perils and pitfalls which surround devotees of technical analysis.

George K. Freeman's article focuses on an automatic market system, the so-called "10% rule" which is argued to have been particularly effective during the security actions of recent years. Simplicity, resistance to emotionalism, and acceptance of fundamental trend momentum underlie the arguments of this mechanical program. Devoid of any serious requirement for precise prediction, it is defended as an objective formula for even the most sophisticated investor.

For those who, despite the burden of all the essays preceding this final one, are faced with a large capital loss, the technical tips by James Dines would seem invaluable as a practical implement to portfolio management. Stop-Loss orders, their theory and practice, may not be an investor's epitaph, but rather show a respect for reality. This is the hard reality of the many complicated variables which must be uncovered, measured, and acted upon for eventual investment success.

23. STOCK MARKET "PATTERNS" AND FINANCIAL ANALYSIS: METHODOLOGICAL SUGGESTIONS*

❉ Harry V. Roberts**

INTRODUCTION

OF ALL ECONOMIC TIME SERIES, the history of security prices, both individual and aggregate, has probably been most widely and intensively studied. While financial analysts agree that underlying economic facts and relationships are important, many also believe that the history of the market itself contains "patterns" that give clues to the future, if only these patterns can be properly understood. The Dow theory and its many offspring are evidence of this conviction. In extreme form such theories maintain that only the patterns of the past need be studied, since the effect of everything else is reflected "on the tape."

A common and convenient name for analysis of stock-market patterns is "technical analysis." Perhaps no one in the financial world completely ignores technical analysis—indeed, its terminology

* From *The Journal of Finance,* Vol. XIV, No. 1 (March, 1959), pp. 1–10. Reprinted by permission of *The Journal of Finance.*
** I am indebted to Lawrence West and Arnold Moore for help in the preparation of this paper.

is ingrained in market reporting—and some rely intensively on it. Technical analysis includes many different approaches, most requiring a good deal of subjective judgment in application. In part these approaches are purely empirical; in part they are based on analogy with physical processes, such as tides and waves.

In light of this intense interest in patterns and of the publicity given to statistics in recent years, it seems curious that there has not been widespread recognition among financial analysts that the patterns of technical analysis may be little, if anything, more than a statistical artifact. At least, it is safe to say that the close resemblance between market behavior over relatively long time periods and that of simple chance devices has escaped general attention, though the role of chance variation in very short time periods has often been recognized. One possible explanation is that the usual method of graphing stock prices gives a picture of successive levels rather than of changes, and levels can give an artificial appearance of "patterns" that invite spurious interpretations.

More evidence for this assertion about stock market behavior is still needed, but almost all the fragmentary evidence known to me is consistent with it. The major published evidence from recent years is a paper about British stock indexes (and American commodity prices) by the British statistician, M. G. Kendall, which appeared in 1953.[1] I have done similar, though less comprehensive, work with recent American data, for both indexes and individual companies, which has been entirely consistant with Kendall's findings. If, for example, weekly changes of the Dow Jones Index are examined statistically, it is apparent that these changes behave very much as if they had been generated by an extremely simple chance model. The history of market levels behaves very much as if levels had been generated by a cumulation of results given by the chance model.

These general conclusions have been reached, probably repeatedly, long before Kendall's study. Thus Holbrook Working, writing in 1934, said:

> It has several times been noted that time series commonly possess in many respects the characteristics of series of cumulated random numbers. The separate items in such time series are by no means random in character, but the changes between successive items tend to be largely random. This characteristic has been noted conspicuously in

[1] Maurice G. Kendall, "The Analysis of Economic Time Series. I," *Journal of the Royal Statistical Society* (Ser. A), CXVI (1953), 11–25.

sensitive commodity prices. . . . King has concluded that stock prices resemble cumulations of purely random changes even more strongly than do commodity prices.[2]

Indeed, the main reason for this paper is to call to the attention of financial analysts empirical results that seem to have been ignored in the past, for whatever reason, and to point out some methodological implications of these results for the study of securities.

From the point of view of the scholar, much more research is needed to establish more precisely the limits to which these generalizations can be carried. For example, do they apply to changes for periods other than weekly? (In my own explorations they have worked fairly well for both longer and shorter periods.) How well do they apply to individual securities? (Most work has been done on indexes.) What slight departures from the chance model are detectable? Perhaps the traditional academic suspicion about the stock market as an object of scholarly research will be overcome, and this work will be done.[3] This paper, however, is concerned with the methodological problems of the financial analyst who cannot afford to ignore evidence that is easily obtainable from the most casual empirical analysis. From his point of view there should be great interest in the possibility that, to a first approximation, stock-market behavior may be statistically the simplest, by far, of all economic time series.

This paper will describe the chance model more precisely, discuss briefly the common-sense interpretation of the model, and outline a number of methodological suggestions for financial analysts.

THE CHANCE MODEL

Kendall found that changes in security prices behaved nearly as if they had been generated by a suitably designed roulette wheel for which each outcome was statistically independent of past history and for which relative frequencies were reasonably stable through time. This means that, once a person accumulates enough evidence to make good estimates of the relative frequencies (probabilities) of different outcomes of the wheel, he would base his predictions only

[2] Holbrook Working, "A Random-Difference Series for Use in the Analysis of Time Series," *Journal of the American Statistical Association*, XXIX (1934), 11.
[3] Holbrook Working has worked for many years on the behavior of commodities markets, and full publication of his findings is still forthcoming.

on these relative frequencies and pay no attention to the pattern of recent spins. Recent spins are relevant to prediction only insofar as they contribute to more precise estimates of relative frequencies. In a gambling expression, this roulette wheel "has no memory."

The chance model just described insists on independence but makes no commitment about the relative frequencies, or probabilities, of different outcomes except that these must be stable over time. A frequency distribution of past changes is a good basis for estimating these probabilities, so long as the independence assumption holds. For concreteness in demonstration, we shall assume that weekly changes of a particular index behave as if they were independent observations on a normal distribution, with mean +0.5 and standard deviation 5.0. The details of constructing such a roulette wheel need not concern us here. We shall, in fact, employ for our purpose a published table of random numbers that can be modified easily to conform to the specifications stated above.[4] Assuming that the series starts at 450, we obtain a hypothetical year's experience graphed in Figures 1 and 2.

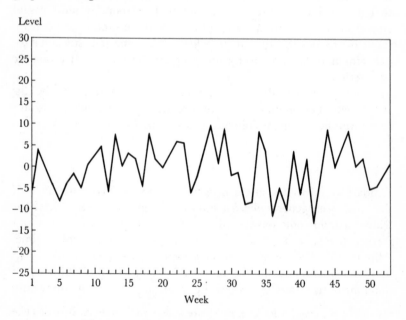

Figure 1. *Simulated Market Changes for 52 Weeks.*

[4] The RAND Corporation, *A Million Random Digits with 100,000 Normal Deviates* (Glencoe, Ill.: Free Press, 1955).

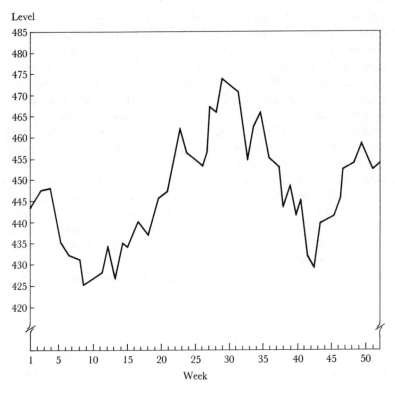

Figure 2. *Simulated Market Levels for 52 Weeks.*

To even a casual observer of the stock market, Figure 2 is hauntingly realistic, even to the "head and shoulders" top. Probably all the classical patterns of technical analysis can be generated artificially by a suitable roulette wheel or random-number table. Figure 1 gives much less evidence of patterns, although intensive and imaginative scrutiny would undoubtedly suggest some. The only persistent patterns of Figure 1 (and its continuation beyond 52 weeks) are (1) the relative frequency of different outcomes and (2) the clustering tendency for similar outcomes. The clustering phenomenon runs contrary to intuitive feelings about chance and raises temporary hopes about predictability. These hopes, however, can be crushed by theoretical analysis that shows clustering to give no information beyond that contained in the relative frequencies.

Figures 3 and 4 give the corresponding diagrams for the Dow Jones Industrial Index for 1956. The general resemblance between

Figures 3-4 and Figures 1-2 is unmistakable, although no pains were taken to devise a "roulette" wheel that would simulate closely the actual history of 1956. The major difference in detail between Figures 1 and 3 is that Figure 3 shows greater dispersion. We probably could have imitated Figure 3 more closely by using a somewhat larger standard deviation than 5 in constructing the artificial series. It is well, however, to avoid giving the wrong impression by showing too striking a parallel in all details. Two artificial series constructed by precisely the same method typically differ from each other just as would two brothers or two years of market history. To put it differently, the chance model cannot duplicate history in any sense other than that in which one evening in a gambling casino duplicates another. For relatively short periods of history like 52 weeks, there can be substantial differences. In fact, however, the dispersion of Figure 3 is almost surely greater than that of Figure 1 by more than we would expect from the same chance mechanism. We subsequently obtained a better simulation by using a standard deviation of 7 rather than 5.

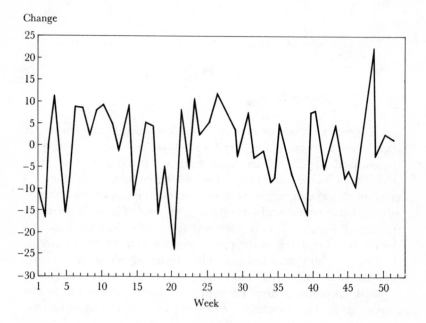

Figure 3. *Changes from Friday to Friday (closing) January 6, 1956—December 28, 1956. Dow Jones Industrial Index.*

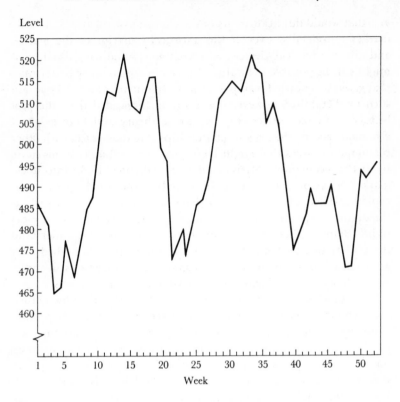

Figure 4. *Friday Closing Levels, December 30, 1955—December 28, 1956. Dow Jones Industrial Index.*

MEANING OF THE CHANCE MODEL

There are two common reactions to this chance model: (1) while "chance" may be important in extemely short-run stock-market movements, it is inconceivable that the longer-term movement should be a cumulation of short-term "chance" development; (2) once one reflects on the situation, it is obvious that a simple chance model must hold. We shall discuss each reaction briefly.

The first reaction stems partly from a misunderstanding of the term "chance." The chance model of the previous section was meant to illustrate the possibility of constructing a simple mechanical device that would duplicate many of the characteristic features of stock-market movements. Even if the statistical behavior of the market and the mechanical device were completely indistinguishable, it might still be possible to attain a degree of predictability better than that given by knowledge of past relative frequencies alone. To attain such predictability, however, more would be needed than the past history of market prices: e.g., economic theory and knowledge of economic facts might suggest relationships of market prices with other economic variables that might be of predictive value. It seems more likely that economic analysis could give predictive insight into stock-market behavior than that physical analysis could help with a real roulette wheel. Even completely deterministic phenomena, such as the decimal expansions of irrational numbers (e.g., e and π), appear to be "chance" phenomena to an observer who does not understand the underlying mechanism. Phenomena that can be described only as "chance" today, such as the emission of alpha particles in radio-active decay, may ultimately be understood in a deeper sense.

In another sense the reaction against "chance" is sound. Much more empirical work is needed, and it seems likely that departure from simple chance models will be found—if not for stock-market averages, then for individual stocks; if not for weekly periods, then for some other period; if not from the independence assumption, then from the assumption of a stable underlying distribution; etc. Indeed, the analytical proposals of this paper are based on the assumption that such departures will occasionally be found. Holbrook Working has discovered such departures in his commodity market research.[5]

As to the second reaction, that the chance model is obvious, there is a plausible rationale. "If the stock market behaved like a mechanically imperfect roulette wheel, people would notice the imperfections and by acting on them, remove them." This rationale is appealing, if for no other reason than its value as counterweight to the popular view of stock market "irrationality," but it is obviously incomplete. For example, why should not observation of market imperfection lead to greater imperfection rather than less? All we can do is to suggest the importance of the study of such questions.

[5] Holbrook Working, "New Ideas and Methods for Price Research," *Journal of Farm Economics*, XXXVIII (1956), pp. 1427–36.

Suggestions For Financial Analysis

This section is devoted to statistical suggestions to financial analysts and others who make their living by the study of the market. The fundamental suggestion, of course, is to analyze price changes as well as price levels. Initially, the weekly change seems worth using, but other time periods may also be useful. This suggestion seems trivial, but it is not. If the simple chance hypothesis is correct, then the statistical behavior of changes, which are independent, is much simpler than that of levels, which are not. There already exists, for example, a body of statistical techniques for analysis of independent data: in fact, modern statistical theory has been largely built up on the assumption of independence. Much of it also assumes, as we did for convenience in the artificial example, that the underlying distribution is a normal distribution in the technical sense of that term. The assumption of normality usually seems far less crucial to the applicability of statistical methods than does that of independence, and some statistical techniques, called "non-parametric," do not make the normality assumption.

If one graphs weekly changes without any formal statistical analysis, he will have taken the most important single step. So long as the stock or stock index behaves like a reasonably good roulette wheel, the visual impression will be similar to that of Figures 1 and 3. If there is a really fundamental shift in the underlying situation, it can be detected visually more readily by an analysis of changes than of levels. Conversely, if there has been no fundamental shift, a graph of changes will be much less likely to give the impression that there has been a shift.

There are formal statistical techniques to supplement visual analysis (though never to replace it entirely, since graphical study is always partial insurance against misapplication of statistical analysis). The most popular field of applied statistics—industrial quality control—draws on these techniques extensively. Though there would undoubtedly be many differences in detail, a financial analyst should find much of interest and relevance in methods of quality control.[6]

[6] W. Allen Wallis and Harry V. Roberts, *Statistics: A New Approach* (Glencoe, Ill.: Free Press, 1956), chaps. 16, 18; A. Hald, *Statistical Theory with Engineering Applications* (New York: John Wiley & Sons, Inc., 1952), chap. 13; Eugene L. Grant, *Statistical Quality Control* (rev. ed; New York: McGraw-Hill Book Co., Inc., 1952).

We shall illustrate briefly how these ideas might be applied in financial analysis. For concreteness, we begin with the data given graphically in Figure 3.

1. The first question is that of independence: Can we regard these weekly changes as independent? Purely to illustrate one test of independence, we shall apply a test based on runs above and below zero. If we denote a positive change by "+" and a negative change by "−", Figure 3 yields the following sequence of +'s and −'s.

− − + + − + + + + + + − + − − + + − − − − + − + + + + + +
− + − − − − + − − − + + − − + − − − + + − + +

A "run" is a consecutive sequence of the same symbol: e.g., − −, + +, −, and + + + + + + are the first four runs. We count 24 runs, which does not differ significantly from the expected number of 26.41.[7]

There are many tests for independence, and experience will show the most useful ones for this kind of application. I would guess that the mean-square successive difference[8] would prove useful. This has the virtue of providing a descriptive measure of the degree of independence or dependence, as well as a test that gives simply an all-or-none verdict or a significance level. A slight degree of dependence may not invalidate subsequent analysis of the kind proposed here, while substantial dependence may open the way for forecasts that exploit the observed pattern, just as one might do by careful study of a defective roulette wheel.

The idea of "rational subgroups" commonly used in industrial practice may be useful,[9] particularly in relating changes for different intervals of time, such as days and weeks.

2. If substantial dependence is found, it may be directly useful for forecasting, using the well-known methods of autoregression. Dependence may also suggest useful avenues for investigation. A sharp jump in the level of price changes for a particular stock, for example, might be found to coincide with a change in management. The company's history since that change would then be the object of an analysis like that described in the preceding paragraph.

3. If a close approximation to independence is found for any moderately large number of weeks (say at least 52, as a rule of thumb), set up "control limits" to aid visual analysis in the future. These limits can be calculated in many ways.[10] If a point falls outside the control limits, this gives a signal for the analyst to search for an explanation beyond the series itself: e.g., company developments, economic changes, governmental actions. So long as points stay within the limits, there is no need

[7] For mechanical details see Wallis and Roberts, *op. cit.*
[8] *Ibid.*
[9] Grant, *op. cit.*
[10] Wallis and Roberts, *op. cit.*; Hald, *op. cit.*; and Grant, *op. cit.*

for special attention, although there may also be supplemental warning signals based on gradual shifts that cause trends but do not immediately throw points outside control limits. There will be risks of failing to search when a search is warranted and of searching when nothing is to be found. These risks can be evaluated and the control limits determined accordingly. The aim of the procedure is to economize the time of the financial analyst, who cannot possibly be simultaneously in close contact with the many individual companies that he must be familiar with. It should tend to avoid the numerous false signals that are so strongly suggested by examination of levels rather than changes.

This outline of statistical procedure is meant only to be suggestive. The general nature of the statistical attack is obvious, but the details will be supplied with practical experience guided by sound statistical theory. It may be found, for example, that it is wiser to analyze changes of logarithms or square roots of levels than absolute changes, especially when long periods of time are examined. But much is to be gained simply by viewing a familiar problem from a new vantage point, and minor statistical refinements or blemishes may not be crucial.

These statistical suggestions are only a preliminary to the real work of the financial analyst, which extends far beyond the tape itself and draws on knowledge and skills, including statistical knowledge and skills, that are not discussed here. There is every reason to believe, however, that this method of looking at the tape will facilitate all that takes place afterward. Further statistical analysis, such as multiple regression, will be sounder if based on independent changes rather than dependent levels. Judgment and intuition will proceed more soundly if not hindered by an unnecessary grappling with market "patterns."

24. ON MARKET FORECASTING AND TIMING*

A. Wilfred May

IN DISCUSSING STOCK MARKET FORECASTABILITY, let us first consider the proper place of forecasting in the investing process. Second, the reasons for the continuous boom in the public's forecasting proclivities. Third, weighing of the results in actual practice which have been actually achieved by various categories of experts in their attempts to time market movements. Fourth, the reasons making the negative results inevitable. Fifth, the fundamental fallacy of the concept of The Market as a single entity, and the concept of a trend, and, sixth, the alternative of a sound investing approach.

It is, of course, true that some amount of forecasting is present in all our activities. In conducting a commercial business some risky participation is engaged in, or at least implied, as in the automobile manufacturer's dependence on annual style acceptance of his new models; and as is often inherent in financing arrangements. And in farming, the outlook for the weather is a key to the likely supply and demand situation. But it must be remembered that in productive business and farming, forecasting is engaged in as an unavoidable necessity, as incidental to the major productive effort, and is usually minimized as much as possible. In investing operations, on the other hand, while some assumption about the future of course must be

* From *The Commercial and Financial Chronicle,* Vol. 186, No. 5690 (Thursday, November 14, 1957), p. 5. Reprinted by permission of *The Commercial and Financial Chronicle,* 25 Park Place, New York 7, New York.

made, the investment community stresses the forecasting elements far beyond the incidental and the unavoidable.

Furthermore, an important standard in determining whether one is acting as an investor, speculator, or gambler is the relative emphasis placed on prediction. The closer one approaches a genuine investment attitude, the more will forecasting, along with other risks, be minimized. Conversely, the speculator-gambler dealing in risks concentrates on forecasting.

That Prophets Boom

Let us now talk about the remarkable growth of the Prophets Boom. In direct contrast to the depression which Wall Street as an investment business has had off and on ever since the halcyon 1920's, its "forecasting division" assuredly has been enjoying a boom which is continuing and unceasing.

The attempt to forecast changes in security prices as such, in lieu of concentrating attention on value factors (as outlined in my last lecture) is generally based on market analysis as distinguished from security analysis. Such market analysis is of two kinds: first, that considering all kinds of economic, business and political factors; second, that which, via the so-called "technical" approach, finds the data for its predictions exclusively in the past performance of the market itself (as through charts plotting the action of individual stocks or the averages)—and based on the major premise that the market is its own best forecaster.

Typically, the remarkable growth in the popularity of this category of prediction is evident in the literature now being broadcast by the services, and in the voluminous costly advertising of their wares in our newspapers and financial journals; with the degree of public acceptance of the advisory services seemingly being directly proportioned to the embodiment of the crystal ball—the public loves it!

Reasons for Popularity

Now, for its motivation. There seem to be a variety of reasons, mostly psychological, for such popularity of the prophecy system, particularly of the so-called "technical" methods of gauging the action of the market as a whole. First, an ordered system, particularly when supported by charting, supplies a welcome emotional escape from the difficulties involved in the alternative approaches, such as the ability and rigorous self-discipline required for the business-like analysis and the valuation of individual securities which we are detailing in this course. The popularity of forecasting via market systems also stems from disillusionment over the well-publicized short-comings of past business and general economic predictions. The mental gymnastics involved in contemplating a pictorialized market trend, particularly as projected into the future, is tempting for its seeming simplification as well as for pure enjoyment as an indoor sport. The illusion that it is easy to beat the game, to follow Baron Rothschild's advice to buy sheep and sell deer by catching the swings with tours de hindsight in lieu of tours de forcesight. This normal ambition seems to be irresistibly fostered by one's easy reflection with day dreaming over past-performance charts that depict sharp, but completely irregular up and down swings like the racing form dopesters' technique. "How easy to have caught the up-and-down swings," is the easy thought in rationalizing hindsight as foresight!

THE GAME APPEAL

Then there is the game appeal. Forecasting of all varieties, and certainly in the stock market, seems to afford a liberal measure of appeal as a game as such—playing the market as in indulging in a contest of trying to outguess the crowd. Stock-market playing, as an extension of market forecasting, may be likened to the game of musical chairs in which someone is certain to lose, but in which each of the players—hoping it will not be he—meanwhile has a good time. (As I inserted here when I compiled these notes last July), I'm assuming that you're not always going to have a bull-market or the benefit of a five-year movement in one direction. Another major stimulus to forecasting activities stems from the present and prevailing over-emphasis on, and misconception about, liquidity. So-called market liquidity is a prevalent concept which is completely dangerous and invalid in identifying market price with value, and in concentrating investors' efforts on attempts to discern price trends in lieu of value factors.

In their complete misconception of the basic nature of the common stock, the market timing technicians blithely overlook the fact that, essentially, as I pointed out in my last lecture, a share in a business listed on an exchange is not different from a share in a business not listed; and cause the business value elements of the listed share to be dwarfed in importance by their rapidly changing attitudes toward the market as a whole. In their false concept of market liquidity, the forecasters make of a security a kind of counter in the ebb and flow of market movements. Without realizing it, no doubt, they are dealing in prices instead of dealing in value, attempting to anticipate the extent to which their fellow public will subsequently cause the price level to diverge from value; trying to outwit the market's other buyers and sellers; trying to outforecast their fellow forecasters. In this process of style forecasting and Blue Chip-itis (which term I have coined), also, the investment community has become engaged in a kind of strategic game—like Machiavelli's practicing of the second degree lie—all in contrast to value analysis.

Fourth Degree Beauty Contest Technique

The investor's inordinate attention concentrated style-wise on guessing what his fellow investors are going to think and do, on both sides of the Atlantic, has been aptly described by that ubiquitous economist, Lord Keynes, as follows:

> "Professional investment may be likened to those newspaper competitions in which the competitors have to pick out the six prettiest faces from 100 photographs. The prize being awarded to the competitor whose choice most nearly corresponds to the average preferences of the competitors as a whole. So, each competitor has to pick, not those faces which he, himself, finds prettiest but those which he thinks likeliest to catch the fancy of the other competitors, all of whom are looking at the problem from the same point of view. It is not a case of picking those who, to the best of one's judgement, are really the prettiest, or those which average opinion generally thinks the prettiest; we have reached the third degree where we devote our intelligence to anticipating what average opinion expects the average opinion to be. And there are some, I believe, who are practicing the fourth, fifth and higher degrees."

And there I give you the key to the prevalent neglect of logical value factors—epitomized in the Blue Chip-itis which has been so overdone.

The Actual Results

Now let's take a look at the results actually achieved in practice. So that we are not just engaging in an academic discussion, let us weigh what has actually happened in market performance and assay the results that have been achieved in the market place by various categories of forecasters. Fortunately, there are available findings along this line which are disinterested and reliable. The Cowles Commission for Research and Economics, which you have all heard of, in two major studies found that the forecasting efforts of financial publications, services, and of Dow Theory practitioners have been generally fruitless. In fact, these experts' forecasts were found to be correct less than 50% of the time—in other words, coin-tossing would have yielded better results. Similar negative results in predicting and interpreting movements of the market as a whole, in contrast to their fine work in analyzing individual issues, were arrived at in brokerage house's opinion, as found in an extensive survey made by two students at Columbia, E. F. Underwood and M. C. Nelson, under the direction of Benjamin Graham at the Columbia School of Business.

Further indications of the experts' trend-forecasting difficulties is furnished by the performance of those investment companies which center their efforts in timing the market movements of the standard issues. The long-term record, substantiated by a recent exhaustive study, shows that instead of swing catching, better results were gained through long-continued holding in the same issues, as the Blue Chips in the Dow-Jones average.

"Coppering" the Professionals Advisable

Further evidence of the market forecasting shortcomings by the Street's professional element is offered by the varying size of the short interest as published monthly by the New York Stock Exchange. These data, usually showing a reduction of the bears commitments at market peaks and their enlargement at market bottoms show how the highest echelons of the professionals fail to anticipate market swings. In other words, the professionals are usually bullish at the top and bearish at the bottom. Likewise abortive in forecasting general market movements are the efforts of the economists, statisticians and analysts, who are so able in forming conclusions about individual securities. In fact, Wall Street sophisticates, including these experts themselves, are prone to use "bucketing"—that is, acting contrary to their own experts' majority forecasts, as a guide to the market's future. At their forecasting bull sessions, the surest bet is to "copper" the majority opinion; and the greater the majority, the more confidence is there in the "bucketing." These economists and analysts, along with the services, are highly successful in evaluating individual issues on quantitative criteria, in contrast to their ineffectiveness in general forecasting.

REASONS FOR FAILURE

Within my time limitations, I can only outline a few of the reasons why attempts to time market movements must fail. First, let us consider predictions based on external factors: political, economic and financial. Such incidents have ranged all the way from the President's heart attack to Sputnik Number One. A more constant imponderable is the steadily rising government interventionism, including defense spending which continuingly confronts the short-term market forecaster with the necessity of foretelling and interpreting the highly relevant Washington moves. The tax outlook, always politically governed, also typically illustrates another important imponderable as far as investor effects are concerned. Take the uncertainty of the tax legislation which will be passed in the next session of the Congress—particularly if we should be in a depression.

Currently popularized to the house tops, the inflation threat confronts the short-term forecaster with another dilemma. Will whole-hog dollar depreciation result from armament needs, from wage-price spiralling; or perhaps from anti-depression measures by the government; or, on the other hand will these inflationary elements be counter-balanced by the nation's enormous productive capacity, credit restriction and general controls? Remember midst the prevalent emphasis on inflation—and the assumption that inflation is a one-way street—that after the First World War from 1921 and the price level existing at that time, prices declined and remained lower for 25 years and didn't get back up to their 1921 level until

1946 following another World War. So, even though you may have an inflation over a hundred year cycle, there can be intervening counter movements going on unpredictably for periods of from three months to 25 years. And this has similarly occurred in other countries, as I will show in next week's lecture.

MUST WIN A PARLAY

Now, I would like to talk a moment about what I call the parlayed forecasts—to borrow a race track term. The forecaster must win a double "bet." First he must be correct in foretelling not only the external events; but also, equally important and even more difficult, the effect of these events in terms of the stock market's performance—which is an entirely different thing. Like the difficult feat in horse racing of winning a parlayed bet, he must make a correct double prediction; the second of which, namely the market effect, is enormously difficult to anticipate since psychological forces so largely govern the market participants' reactions to the external events.

THE PSYCHOLOGICAL IMPONDERABLES

Identical events often have successively opposite market effects. For example, in the period following World War II, there was the minority view business forecaster who turned out to be correct in his expectations of high economic activity instead of a demobilization depression such as had occurred after all previous wars. But, even though he was right in his economics and business forecast, he was nevertheless wrong regarding the market; for the market dropped 22% in 1946 and continued its bearish behavior until late 1949—running completely counter to the business boom. Outbreak of war furnishes another example of the difficulty of drawing the correct market conclusion from the correctly predicted outside economic or political event. Throughout the first eight months of 1939, those expecting the outbreak of a World War sold stocks, but the actual occurrence of the event was followed by an immediate market rise, averaging 20%. On the other hand, the Korean outbreak in 1950 was greeted by a market drop of 15%.

Uncertain Inflation Impact

Now, a word about inflation's uncertain market impact. The inflation factor also manifests the difficulty of making short-term market assumptions from a correct long-term economic prediction, particularly when stocks are out of line from value criteria. There are many instances of severe market falls in the midst of an inflationary environment. During the war-time inflation of 1917 stocks nevertheless broke 50% in a seven month period. There was also a "halving" of stock market prices in the midst of the 1937–38 period of monetary expansion. Similarly in the post-OPA price decontrolling period of 1946–48 after the end of the Second World War when inflation really took hold on the economy and commodity prices rose by 40% and the cost of living by 30%—stock price average, nevertheless, fell by 10% net. Likewise, over the longer term from 1929 to 1950 when there was a 52% rise in commodity prices, nevertheless, these was a net decline of 40% during that period in the price of stocks.

Even overall corporate profits constitute another example where correct prediction of short-term changes in even a quantitative element—a difficult enough achievement in itself—do not necessarily supply the key to the future action of the market as a whole. From 1946 to 1947 the per-share earnings comprising the issues on the Dow-Jones Industrial Average rose by 40%, yet the mean of their market price range at the same time fell by 7%.

The "How High Is High?" Obsolete

Then there is the process where a cause-and-effect relationship between outside factors and market performance does exist, but leaves the time of such effect in terms of market performance indeterminable. In other words, the "how high is really high?" problem. Thus several of the expert witnesses at the Fulbright Committee's Stock Market Inquiry back in March, 1955, cited factors both qualitative and quantitative, to show that the market was too high. But, although the demonstration of these excesses was valid, the market subsequently went up an additional 35% during the 17 months from March, 1955, to its peak initially registered in August 1956.

In the market's current collapse the unfavorable dividend yield of stocks compared to bonds has been cited as an important contributing cause—and correctly so. But this highlights the constant impossibility of determining the time when such factors will become effective in terms of market performance. For significantly dangerous narrowing of the stock-bond yield differential went on, but was disregarded or explained away by the avid bull market stock buyers, for years preceding the current market decline. This ration (based on the average yield of Standard & Poor's fifty industrial stocks related to the yield on its high-grade industrial bond index) after years of stability began, starting in December, 1950, a change from 2.92 to a riskier relationship, gradually declining all the way down to 0.94 last July.

Surely, at least at any time after October, 1954, when the ratio descended below the historically significant 1.60 mark, it could have been regarded as an important danger signal. In fact the yield factor was cited before the Fulbright Committee in warning of the "high" market—when the Dow-Jones Average was down in the 380's; after which it registered its further big rise to 523. 380 may have been high. But 523 was much higher—and after 17 months of discomfort, if not embarrassment, to the would-be market timers.

Small wonder then, that in the output of the economic and statistical services there is a sharp contrast between on the one hand the constructive usefulness of the factual data and on the other, the abortive results in their forecasting phases—but the public loves the forecasting.

On Internal Market Analysis

Now, time limitation also prevents me from making more than a brief reference to some of the fundamental fallacies embodied in the current mass effort to anticipate stock price movements by means of so-called internal market analysis—but this being such a very popular activity, we should spend a little time on it. The basic fallacy common to the great mass of so-called "technical" methods used in stock market forecasting is the implied major premise that the future price course can be determined from its past behavior, disregarding the hard and fast line between the past and the future. This error of the technicians applies not only to the chartists of Dow theory, of Ratio systems, Action Reaction signals, Explosion points, Tone-ometers, Island Reversals, sun spot cycle theory; as well to the highly respectable formula-timing practitioners.

THE DOW THEORY

Now, for the basic definition and technique of one of these technical systems—the leading one and becoming ever more popular; the Dow Theory.

At this point let me remind you of the basic definition of the Dow Theory. It holds that at any time the stock market is the composite resultant of these three trends, to be charted and studied:

1. The minor trend; or day-to-day fluctuations, forming lines in either direction.
2. The secondary trend; lasting for several weeks or months; made up of a succession of higher or lower minor movements.
3. The major trend; lasting over a period of years, and made up of a succession of higher or lower major thrusts and secondary movements.

The latter major trend, whose identification is the primary objective of the Dow Theorists, is determined by successive highs and lows of the averages. Successive higher highs and higher lows constitute a bull market trend; and—conversely—successively lower highs and lower lows define a bear market trend. As long as each successive advance of the stock average used carries to a higher peak than the one before it, and each successive secondary reaction stops at a higher bottom than the last, the primary trend is assumed to be up; and the condition is defined as a bull market. Conversely, when each successive downsurge of the market carries to a new low, and each temporary rally ends at a point under the previous one, the primary trend is down and the condition is called a bear market. The final premise is that the performance of the industrial and rail averages (the latter presumably still not an anachronism) must confirm each other.

Now, as a description of the past and present this is useful, but as prediction it signifies absolutely nothing. It functions merely like a weather vane that shows which way the wind has been and is blowing, whether up or down the hill. Actually it does not thereby give any clue as to how long the wind will continue to blow that way. Not even whether it will continue to blow for another day, that is, for another up-tick on the stock exchange ticker. Remember, the weather vane does not insure continuation of the wind. Similarly, recording of a past-price "trend" in stocks should not imply its continuation. Stripped of its surrounding copious jargon, the Dow principle is a logical absurdity.

In effect, I am convinced that essentially the market technicians' assumptions about trend behavior commit the error in the mathematical principle of the maturity of the chances which Professor Steinmetz called the most mischievous of gambling superstitions. This principle embraces the psychological fiction of which Dow thinking is a variation. Namely, that when there has been a repeated run in a series, the mere reoccurrence of that repetition by itself alters the mathematically correct odds concerning the probable outcome of the next event. This is the foible which leads boys who gamble on coin tossing to vary their bets in the belief that a series of successive heads is more than 50% probable to be followed by a tail. The same misconception exists in most systems for out-witting the inexorable mathematical facts of dice, or of black and red turns on the roulette wheel. The roulette player often thus becomes bankrupted by an extraordinary run of the same color against him. Now if you will stop to think you will see that the Dow theory is based on the same fallacy, regarding the projection of a so-called trend from past behavior. Essentially the Dow theory along with other systems, follows the principle that the chances of a succession of identical results are other than even, thereby assuming either extension or reversal of a trend whose course over the next ticker quote or day, or week, or month, is evident from its past direction.

Incidentally, when a system for beating the stock market or a game of chance goes awry, its practitioner is quick to blame himself for his own faulty interpretation and excuse the Sacrosanct system— a masochistic somersault i.e., self-abuse as a device for maintaining one's emotional security through unshattered confidence in the system.

THE MARKET'S DIVERGENCE DIFFICULTY

Now, here's another major category of obstacle to forecasting the so-called market as-a-whole. Those trying to time movements of the stock market considered as a unit, or at least as containing a so-called trend, overlook the very, very fundamental obstacle resulting from the constant divergences within that overall tent termed "the market," (and I say that term "the market" with mental quotation marks around it). First let me give you an example showing this divergence within the market over the long term. The record shows that between 1901 and 1936 the market, as measured by the Dow-Jones Average of industrial stocks, almost tripled in price from $64 to $184. Nevertheless, at the same time during the same years, the 20 most popular dividend paying issues suffered an overall decline of 39%. Although 13 of the most popular issues were railroads, nevertheless the industrial as well as the rail components contributed to the record, and a full one-half of all the issues shrank by 50% or more. In other words, while the so-called market as a whole was going up, half the issues went down, and by over 50%.

And take the record of the market as a whole over last year—1956. Standard & Poor's Index of 480 stocks showed a rise of 4%, with the industrial section gaining 6%. But the rails concurrently lost 8% and the utilities declined 1½%. And there was complete disparity within industry groups: American Cyanamid rising 18% while Allied Chemical was falling 15%, Continental Can up 20%, American Can down 12%, and so on all through the list.

This year—from Jan. 1 through Oct. 25, while the market as a whole, composed of the 1,000 important issues, was declining by 13%—the drug, cigaret, and office equipment groups were rising by as much as 13%; while, on the other hand, aircrafts, airlines, aluminums, and coppers fell by 30 to 40%.

Again, even midst last month's period of severe market breaks, was there striking market divergence between the net changes. For during October, six stocks actually gained more than 10%, seven issues rose by 7%, 133 stocks registered advances up to 6%; 32 ended unchanged—while 368 issues lost up to 6%; 222 declined from 6 to 10%, and 306 fell by more than 10%.

So, showing all these divergences and contrary movements going in several directions at once certainly proves how impossible it is to predict "the market" (again in quotation marks) as a whole. Again referring to a parlayed bet, we see that those trying to forecast the market, once more must win two bets—first, on being right on the market as a whole and second, on being right on some particular stocks within the market.

CONCLUSION

Actually, valid signals are provided neither by economic indices nor by technical factors adduced by the internal market analysts. While offering the appeal of order out of uncertainty through past-performance pictorialization, the latter essentially substitute hindsight for foresight. Relying on resistance points, explosion points, secondary reversals, and other "patterns," they commit the basic fallacy of disregarding the hard and fast line between the past and the future. The popular Dow Theory, the leading example, is useful for definition of the market's past and present action (as a bull or bear market), but concerning the future it signifies absolutely nothing. Just as the weather vane gives no indication of the future direction of the wind, charting of the past course of the market bears no relevance to its future direction.

Fortunately there is available a way of avoiding the difficulties involved in timing market fluctuations that is fruitful as well as logical. Let the investor stockholder discharge his true functions as part owner of a business. In lieu of dealing in changes in market quotations, let him concentrate on evaluating individual issues as a stake in a property, with the purpose of securing preservation of his capital along with adequate income yield. Let him further operate on the premise that continuing disparities of their price from value offer recurring opportunities for advantageous purchases and sales.

He will thus conform to the true and constructive investment principle that ANY time is a good time to buy a good VALUE; with no time being a good time to hold a bad value.

25. THE 10% RULE: It Furnishes a Simple Formula for Catching Broad Market Swings*

☀ George K. Freeman

THE GREAT SURGE OF EQUITY PRICES over the past year has brought into sharp focus the investor's eternal dilemma—how to realize the market's full potential, yet avoid exceptional risks. At today's peak levels, of course, the hazards loom larger than ever. Still, the specter of inflation and the powerful recovery in business and corporate earnings hold out the prospect that stocks will push up to still loftier heights. One resolution for all but the most speculative minds is the "10% rule."

Of the numerous "automatic" market systems, the 10% rule adjusts perhaps most quickly and accurately to swift and unforeseen changes. Thus, as the accompanying table illustrates, the technique has demonstrated its effectiveness quite handsomely in the shifting markets of the 'fifties. Clearly, any investment approach which has withstood the tests posed by the market vagaries of recent years deserves a careful look.

Although mechanical in application, the 10% rule is not strictly a formula plan. What it does essentially is formalize a basic technical principle: that stock prices, having moved a certain distance in one direction, very likely will continue to move in that direction. Most experienced investors will accept this premise. The problem is to

* From *Barron's,* (March 16, 1959), p. 9. Reprinted by permission of *Barron's.*

393

Table 1.   *The 10% Rule in Operation.   Model Portfolio,*
5 Leading Industrial Stocks (1) Value of Account (2)

Jan. 1946 Account established, also monthly high	$100,000	
Sep. 1946 Down 10%: Sell	81,300	
May 1947 Monthly low	76,300*	
Jul. 1947 Up 10%: Buy	81,300	
Jun. 1948 Monthly high	95,300	
Nov. 1948 Down 10%: Sell	85,800	
Jun. 1949 Monthly low	72,400*	
Sep. 1949 Up 10%: Buy	85,800	
Jan. 1953 Monthly high	182,100	
Sep. 1953 Down 10%: Sell; also, monthly low	163,000	
Dec. 1953 Up 10%: Buy	163,000	
Feb. 1955 Monthly high	277,700	
Mar. 1955 Fulbright reaction	262,400†	
Sep. 1955 Monthly high	348,000	
Oct. 1955 Eisenhower reaction	336,400†	
Apr. 1956 Monthly high	398,300	
May 1956 Reaction low	384,000†	
Aug. 1956 Monthly high	413,000	
Mar. 1957 Down 10%: Sell	368,000	
Dec. 1957 Monthly low	312,300*	
Jun. 1958 Up 10%: Buy	368,000	
Jan. 1959 New monthly high	442,100	12%/year

Dow-Jones 30 Industrials	Value of account (2)	
Jan. 1946 Account established	$100,000	
Jun. 1946 Monthly high	104,000	
Sep. 1946 Down 10%: Sell	90,100	
May 1947 Monthly low	86,900*	
May 1948 Up 10%: Buy	90,100	
Jun. 1948 Monthly high	91,600	
Jun. 1949 Down 10%: Sell; also, monthly low	80,900	
Oct. 1949 Up 10%: Buy	80,900	
Jul. 1957 Monthly high	223,600	
Oct. 1957 Down 10%: Sell	191,700	
Dec. 1957 Monthly low	189,000*	
Jul. 1958 Up 10%: Buy	191,700	
Feb. 1959 New monthly high	233,300	6.5%/year

(1) U. S. Steel, General Motors, Standard Oil (New Jersey), International Paper, United Aircraft. (2) Monthly average of weekly closing prices. * Assuming account still fully invested. † 10% selling signal not registered.

recognize which moves are worth following and which represent only ripples in the major trend. The 10% rule assumes the burden of decision. At the cost of being slightly late, it promises to identify the really significant changes in the course of equity prices.

* * *

Not the least of its attributes is that the technique is simple to apply. Unlike some of the true formulas, the 10% rule involves no value judgments or complicated calculations. Instead, the stockholder need only calculate the value of his account at each week's closing prices—something he might very well do in any case.

At the end of each month, the weekly figures are averaged and recorded. So long as the monthly average continues to rise or holds relatively steady, a fully invested position is maintained. However, when the average falls 10% below a previous high, all holdings promptly are sold. No new buying is undertaken until the 30-day average for the former holdings rises 10% above a monthly lowpoint. At that time, the account is fully invested once more.

At first glance, the practice of going all-out for every market move of this size may seem reckless. Indeed, it might appear better suited to a trader than a long-term investor. In fact, however, a leeway of 10% proves amply conservative, particularly since monthly averages, rather than absolute highs and lows, are used as standards. What must be borne in mind is that the objective of the plan is to ascertain only the major moves of the market and to distinguish these from the minor fluctuations.

Herein lies the chief strength of the 10% rule: It places the investor on the right side of the market for the really big swings. As every tapewatcher knows, stock prices usually maintain their direction longer than is reasonable by most yardsticks. In gearing itself to this tendency, the 10% rule has a marked advantage over the buy-and-hold approach as well as over the standard formula plans.

At present, to be sure, the theory of buying "good" stocks and holding them indefinitely has a large and vocal following. The longer prices continue to rise, the more prudent an imperturbable long-term policy appears to be. However, unless it is assumed that the market henceforth will be a one-way street, such "a buy-and-forget" approach is open to grave doubts.

The well-known formula plans also contain a flaw, which ultimately may impair their effectiveness nearly as much as a bear market could set back a buy-hold investor. Invariably, adherents of these techniques act too soon, rather than too late, in both buying and selling stocks. Notwithstanding J. P. Morgan's dictum to the effect that the way he grew rich in the stock market was by selling too soon, premature action can prove highly unrewarding. During extended market moves, only a trend method, with its slightly laggard confirmation signals, can cope with the unexpected or unprecedented.

This is not to say that dollar averaging and other formula plans do not have definite merits. One of their purposes is to cushion the effect of a market break, and, in this regard, they are more or less successful. For novice investors and managers of very large funds, such techniques are extremely useful, possibly even essential. But for the investor who can afford a more aggressive approach, the 10% rule may offer as much safety, with less sacrifice of capital appreciation.

By itself, of course, a trend system can not assure good market results. Like any investment policy, the 10% rule places a premium on stock selection. To illustrate, the 10% rule applied to five of the strongest Dow Industrial stocks would have produced far better returns since 1946 than applied to the Industrial Average as a whole. Thus, a $100,000 portfolio of U. S. Steel, General Motors, Jersey Standard, International Paper and United Aircraft, between January, 1946 and October, 1958, would have grown to $432,800, or at a rate of 12.09% per year. An account made up of all 30 Industrials, on the other hand, would have increased only 6.05% annually, to $212,600.

Moreover, timing signals will vary considerably, depending on the component stocks. The "Average" account rode fully invested through the 1953 decline, while the selected five-stock portfolio was out of the market from September to December, 1953. Similarly, the reversal of the 1953–57 uptrend was signaled in March, 1957, for the five stocks, but not until October of that year for the Average. The latest reinvestment signal came in June, 1958, for the model portfolio, a month earlier than for the full 30-stock list.

Although it makes allowances for individual decision, the 10% rule also has attractive automatic features. For example, it correctly assessed the short-run emotional reactions of 1955–56. The shocks which accompanied the Fulbright investigation, the President's heart

attack, his subsequent relapses, and the Mid-East crises, scarcely
showed up in the monthly average figures.

Obviously, one of the prime virtues of any formula plan is the
restraining hand it places on its user in times of emotional stress.
In the case of the 10% rule, the monthly calculation feature forces
one to wait. By that time, temporary fears and enthusiasms quite
often have been dispelled, and the outlook can be appraised more
realistically.

Unfortunately, no market formula can lay claim to infallibility,
each has its weakness. The prime defect of the 10% rule is its pro-
clivity to produce whipsaws in a tightly restricted market. In the
1946-49 period, when the Industrial Average fluctuated within a 53-
point range, the 10% slack was too great for such a narrow market.
For that reason, the unpropitious 1946 starting time was used in the
above computations. It provides the stiffest conceivable test for the
10% rule, and it did produce some whipsaws. Happily, such markets
are rare; in fact, no other market in this country's history compares
to it, except possibly that of 1911-14.

Another fault of the 10% rule is the uneven tax burden it im-
poses on its user. In part, this drawback can be overcome by regular
changes in the portfolio, with appropriate adjustments in the base
monthly average for each change (new additions of capital require
the same adjustment). However, in any case, the technique is flexible enough so that tax considerations need not intrude on basic investment considerations.

In sum, for the investor who hopes to follow the market's major
uptrends to their conclusion, and yet avoid the serious downtrends,
the 10% rule appears to offer some real advantages. Obviously, any
method works best when supplemented with sound investment judgment. Particularly today, however, a rigid, objective formula can
prove an invaluable aid for even the keenest investor.

26.   STOP-LOSS ORDERS.

A Technician Gives Some Tips

on How to Use Them*

❀ James Dines

AT ONE TIME OR ANOTHER, nearly everybody, in the stock market, whether short or long, is faced by a large loss, at least on paper. When this happens to an investor it often converts him into a trader; when it happens to a trader, it often turns him into a nervous wreck. Yet, one need not suffer the agony of watching a stock drop from say 74 to 19, since there is a safe way to prevent it: the stop technique. Some people manage to bungle this procedure because they do not know how to use it correctly. The key to correct usage is to grasp the method not only intellectually but also emotionally, surely the hardest part.

Accordingly, let us lay down some emotional guide lines. First, it is necessary to reach the stage where one is unafraid to take a small loss. Refusing to take a loss implies an expected profit on every trade, in other words, perfection. To those who still have this complex, we wish good luck. But most hard-nosed businessmen know that not every transaction works out, and that the first loss is usually the best loss.

VIRTUES OF GROPING

Second, it should be clear that the best way to achieve a sizable gain is to buy a stock before a major advance, and then not to sell prema-

* From *Barron's*, (December 17, 1962), p. 9. Reprinted by permission of *Barron's*.

turely. Both steps are more difficult than they sound, and involve considerable groping, Groping, in turn, involves many small profits equaled by many small losses, a few big winners and absolutely no big losses. This approach rules out people who take a few points profit whenever possible, and who do not comprehend that one big loss frequently will wipe out all the small gains. Nor is it for people who are obsessed with tax considerations or dividends. Never let Uncle Sam decide your buying or selling; dividends are miniscule compared with capital gains.

Third, we rule out people who are unwilling to put in some hard work. Those who view the stock market as a glorified casino, to be handled mainly by guesswork and hunches, are bound to be disillusioned. One can guess, and even be lucky, but this is no real substitute for hard work and strict observance of percentages. The crack trader should buy graph paper and chart every investment daily.

Fourth, the stop-loss is not intended to be triggered. When you buy fire insurance for your house you do not want a fire. But if fire occurs, protection prevents a major loss. If you ever used a proper stop and thereby took small losses, but then ceased using it, you did not wait for the law of averages to bail you out.

Fifth, you must no longer try to buy-low-sell-high. Understand why a stock can be a buy at say 50, and a sale at 45. Buy-low-sell-high presupposes a long level trading range, whereas we are interested in long sustained uptrends. Our rule is to buy-high-sell-higher.

Let us turn now to the mechanics of the stop technique. Starting from basics, a stop order is nothing more than an order to be executed automatically if a certain price is reached. For example, you buy a stock at 50 and place the order to "sell at 48 stop." If and when the stock declines to 48, the order will be automatically executed as a market order. Or, if a stock sells at 50 and you want to buy only if and when it rises to 53, you order "buy at 53 stop." Your order to buy automatically becomes a market order only should the stock sell at 53. (If the "limit" is added to the above two orders it means that instead of a market order being placed, it will be limited to the price you specify.)

As for the short sale side, stops can be used in exactly the same way, only inverted. In other words, if a stock is shorted at 50, place the order "cover at 53 stop." Only on an advance to 53 will you be stopped out, making the maximum loss around 3 points. It is especially important to use the stop technique on shorts, for uncontrolled short sales can develop into real catastrophes. So much for the emotional and practical basics.

Yet even those who grasp all of the above often fall down on the next and most important step: where to place the stop order. In determining the proper place for a stop order, beginners frequently try the clumsy approach of using a fixed number of points, or an absolute percentage, apparently on the theory that they are unable to afford a larger loss than that. In other words, stops are placed one, two or even more points (or percent) below the purchase price. The market, of course, is utterly unconcerned with what you can or cannot afford. Even worse, the approach does not distinguish in every case between meaningless variations and the true trend reversal. It is too rigid and dogmatic, for each stock requires a separate decision; only the lazy will use the fixed stop technique, because it is easier. There is but one place for a proper stop depending on whether you use the breakout or trendline method, and both involve toil. Making money on Wall Street is just as hard as making money anywhere else.

BASIC CHART THEORY

All stops are dependent on basic chart theory, which should be reviewed at this point (see *Barron's* June 18, 1962). Briefly, stocks are either in unfolding trends, or locked within limited neutral trading ranges. When concentrating on trading ranges, remember that a move of one point above a trading range shifts percentages from neutrality to favoring a near-term uptrend.

There are three types of stops: buy, long sales and short sales. In Example 1, the proper place for a breakout buy-stop is just one point above the trading range (A) AT 60, developing from either a prior uptrend or downtrend.

There is another type of buy stop. A practical example would be to buy the theoretical stock of Example 1 as close to the bottom of the trading range (B) as possible. The moment the order is executed, a long-sale stop should be placed just below (B), at say 49. This process is called a bottom-guessing buy stop. If there is no downside breakout, purchase will have been made at rock bottom, and if it does not work out, the loss is minimal. Note that placement of the stop is the same whether the stock was bought at 51 or 59, illustrating the inherent weakness in using predetermined numbers of points for stops. Assuming fundamentals and other factors point upward, the trading risks are highly acceptable. The main weakness here is that stocks often spend tediously long periods of time in trading ranges. While not objectionable to investors, traders prefer more speed.

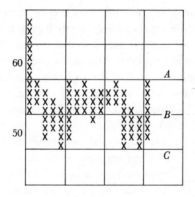

Example 1.

Traders should use the breakout-buy stop. Place the order to "buy at 60 stop, good until cancelled," and forget it. Eventually, if there is an upside breakout, your buy order will be placed automatically. The main weakness here is that the stop loss still must be placed no higher than (C) and the potential loss is larger, although still limited. The trader thus sacrifices safety for speed, although the stop is not intended to be triggered and is only a protective device.

LONG-SALE STOP

The long-sale is simple. For stocks already held, place the stop just below (B), in (C), at say "sell 49 stop, good until cancelled." Or, sell at the top of the trading range, and repurchase only if there is an upside breakout (or use the breakout-buy stop).

The short-sale stop is meant mainly for traders, and reverses all of the above rules. The stock should be shorted as high in trading range (B) as possible, and the stop loss cover placed just above the trading range in (A) at 60. This process is called a top-guessing short. Or, traders may place the order to "sell short at 49, good until cancelled," but the stop loss must still be placed in (A). While this breakout-short stop is more likely to drop, the potential loss is higher, because the nearest cover is quite high. Again, a sacrifice of safety for speed.

With these properly placed stops, true trend reversals are guarded against, while minor unimportant fluctuations are correctly ignored. One important refinement would be to vary the depth in (A) and (C) for the stop orders. So long as they are in (A) and (C), they are correctly placed, and while aggressive traders may use $\frac{1}{8}$ of a point, the cautious often use two points as increased protection against an occasional false breakout. We use a one point variation because it normally works out well.

Before we go on, an important exception to the use of stops should be pointed out. When intrinsic value is so great, or a stock is already so deeply depressed that it is well below intrinsic value, stop losses should not be used. Or, when fundamentals are so overpowering that technical patterns are virtually ignored in a decision to buy or hold, then fundamental methodology is also used in the sale.

Stop loss orders are mainly for stocks that are moving up, or at such high levels that the risk of a major down-trend is present. Here, pure chartists often fail: they fail to blend fundamentals into technical thinking. The essence of our approach is using the two as crosschecks. The exception to blending is close trading, because a slight variation in the price-earnings ratio alone can account for a minor move, making fundamentals virtually worthless in gauging short-term trading timing. This is where technical techniques are unquestionably superior. As a declining stock becomes really cheap on fundamentals, pay less and less attention to charts and move to fundamentals. As a stock gets higher and higher, pay less and less attention to fundamentals and more to charts. Be more and more aggressive with stops as an advance extends to the point where a stock is outrageously high on fundamentals.

Now let us assume that the stock in our example has been bought at the bottom of either (A) or (B) and has not dipped into (C), and thus still is held long. It then has a move to 66 followed by a normal breakout pullback to 62, as in Example 2.

Selling Too Soon

Percentages have shifted to the upside, and the next problem is not selling too soon. This involves raising the stop loss, but still placing it properly. In Example 2, the stop is still properly placed at 49. The next rule is: when the pullback is at least three points, followed by

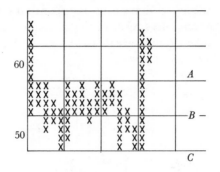

Example 2.

another rise of at least three points, raise the stop to just below the low ebb of the pullback. In Example 3, the stop is thus properly raised to 61. The stop is similarly raised on each leg of the advance. So long as there is an uptrend (rising lows), the stock will not be sold. But when the trend reverses, the stock will be sold automatically to protect accrued profits. On the short side, the whole procedure is

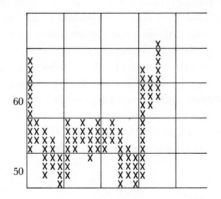

Example 3.

reversed, with stop covers placed just above the previous rally high in a series of descending highs.

The trendline stop is a highly sensitive technique, and so complex that it is advised only for full-time professionals. For those who have mastered the fine art of drawing trendlines, it is largely a matter of placing the stop so that only a broken trend could trigger it (Example 4). The "X's" show where stops are progressively placed just below the uptrendline as the stock advances, until it is finally stopped out (E) when the trend does reverse. The advantage of the trendline stop is that a broken trend reveals itself sooner than for breakout stops, and some points are saved.

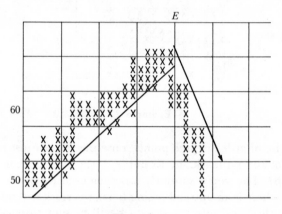

Example 4.

To follow these techniques, it is necessary to have up-to-the-minute charts available. Several services sell them. Or, to economize, buy some K&E 358-16 graph paper and do it yourself. Each box in the graph paper is divided into eight squares vertically (8 eighths to the point) and five squares laterally (for the five trading days).

Those few tape-watchers endowed with iron-nerved discipline can dispense with actually placing the stop order. The advantage is that a slightly higher price normally ensues when a cluster of stops is triggered. However, the first time you fail to sell on the ensuing rally, revert to actually placing the stop orders.

List of Contributors

ROBERT ANDERSON—Investment Adviser, Piedmont Financial Co., New York City.

PETER L. BERNSTEIN—Bernstein-Macauley, Inc., New York City.

RODGER W. BRIDWELL—Founder of Investors Research Co. and *The Insider Report,* and contributor to financial magazines.

O. K. BURRELL—Late Professor of Finance, University of Oregon.

GEOFFREY P. CLARKSON—Assistant Professor, School of Industrial Management, Massachusetts Institute of Technology.

JOHN C. CLENDENIN—Professor of Finance, University of California at Los Angeles.

JAMES DINES—Analyst and author of *The Dines Letter.*

DAVID DURAND—Professor, School of Industrial Management, Massachusetts Institute of Technology.

HAROLD G. FRAINE—Professor of Finance, University of Wisconsin.

GEORGE K. FREEMAN—Analyst and Investment Adviser, New York City.

FREDERICK N. GOODRICH—Vice-President, U.S. Trust Company, New York City.

BENJAMIN GRAHAM—Resident Professor of Finance, University of California at Los Angeles.

JOHN G. HEIMANN—Vice-President, Smith, Barney and Co., New York City.

PAUL L. HOWELL—Investment Adviser and partner, Paul Howell Associates.

A. WILFRED MAY—Editorial staff and columnist, *The Commercial and Financial Chronicle.*

ALLAN H. MELTZER—Associate Professor, Graduate School of Industrial Administration, Carnegie Institute of Technology.

NORMAN O. MILLER—Assistant Professor of Finance, University of Texas.

ROBERT H. MILLS—University of Michigan.

FREDERICK W. PAGE—Vice-President, Tri-Continental Corporation, New York City.

GEORGE E. REJDA—Assistant Professor of Economics, University of Nebraska.

HARRY V. ROBERTS—Professor of Statistics, Graduate School of Business, University of Chicago.

HARRY C. SAUVAIN—Professor of Finance, Graduate School of Business, Indiana University.

MORTON SMITH—Vice-President, Girard Trust Corn Exchange Bank, Philadelphia, Pennsylvania.

JAMES E. WALTER—Professor of Finance, University of Pennsylvania.

J. HARRY WOOD—Former Editor, *Journal of the American Society of Chartered Life Underwriters.*

Cross-Index of Readings to Investments Textbooks

A. BADGER, RALPH E., HAROLD W. TORGERSON, and HARRY G. GUTHMANN, *Investment Principles and Practices*. Englewood Cliffs, N.J.: Prentice-Hall, Inc., 1961.

B. BELLEMORE, DOUGLAS H., *Investments*. New York: Simmons-Boardman Books, 1960.

C. CLENDENIN, JOHN C., *Introduction to Investments*. New York: McGraw-Hill Book Co., 1960.

D. DOWRIE, GEORGE W., DOUGLAS R. FULLER, and FRANCIS J. CALKINS, *Investments*. New York: John Wiley & Sons, Inc., 1961.

E. GRAHAM, BENJAMIN, DAVID L. DODD, and SIDNEY COTTLE, *Security Analysis*. New York: McGraw-Hill Book Co., 1962.

F. HAYES, DOUGLAS A., *Investments: Analysis and Management*. New York: Macmillan Co., 1961.

G. LEFFLER, GEORGE L. and LORING C. FARWELL, *The Stock Market*. New York: Ronald Press Co., 1963.

H. PLUM, LESTER V., JOSEPH H. HUMPHREY, and JOHN W. BOWYER, JR., *Investment Analysis and Management*. Homewood, Ill.: Richard D. Irwin, Inc., 1961.

I. SAUVAIN, HARRY C., *Investment Management*. Englewood Cliffs, N.J.: Prentice-Hall, Inc., 1961.

Cross-Index: Chapter in Investments Textbooks

READING NUMBER	A	B	C	D	E	F	G	H	I
1	8	6	4	5	31,32	3,24	31	18	18,19
2	8	6	4,13	5,14	31,32,39	3,24	31	9,18	18,19
3	8	6	4	5,14	39,53	24	31	9	18,19
4	8	6	4,10	5,14	31,34,35,37	24,25	31	18	18,19
5	9,11,12	14		7		25	30	17,18	20
6	24	6,35	1,28	7,8,14	30,31	8,14	2,30	17	17,20
7	6	5	3	14	35,36,37,38	14		10	14
8	6	5	13,17	14	35,36,37,38	14	2,30	10	14
9	6	5	13,17	14	37,38	14	2,30	12	14
10	10,11	31	16	20	20,21,42,43	15			
11	24,25,26	35	28			25,26,27	31,32,33,34		17,19,20
12	24	35	28	5,13	5	25,27	31,33	5,18	17,18,20
13	23	14	2	6,15	22,23,24	2,11	30	2,13	17
14	23	14	2	9	4,25	3,24	30,31		11
15		8	7	7	22,25	11,12			
16	8	6,20		14,15	1,2,5,7,8	13,14		10	

Cross-Index: continued

17	23	14	10	7,13	5	25		17	19
18	26		24	12	5				24
19	26	35	24	12	5				24
20	25	35	23	11	5				22
21	26	35		12	5		5		24
22	26	14		12	5				24
23	4	14	10		4,5,53	4	32,33,34	8,17	20
24	4	11	10		53	4	34	17	20
25	4	11	9		53	4	32,33,35	7	
26	4		9		53	4	9,13	7	

Index